P9-APU-216

America Transformed

Sixty Years of Revolutionary Change, 1941–2001

Born in the Age of Enlightenment, the American nation was committed to what the contemporary French philosopher Marquis de Condorcet called the Idea of Progress. From the beginning, Americans regarded change as both natural and desirable. In some eras it occurred with great speed and was truly transforming, such as during the Industrial Revolution of the last third of the nineteenth century. During the 35 years after America's entry into the Second World War, the country experienced another remarkably rapid and dramatic transformation. Indeed, the manifold changes in areas of American life – ranging from the country's international role and its business structure to Americans' racial and gender relations, their sexual practices, and their regard for privacy – were nothing less than revolutionary. Abrams has drawn on a wealth of mostly published sources on such diverse subjects to offer a fresh, thematically arranged, and often controversial account of that transformation and of the conservative backlash that followed.

Richard M. Abrams is a professor of history and associate dean of International and Area Studies at the University of California at Berkeley, where he has been teaching since 1961. He received his Ph.D. from Columbia University in 1962. He was a Fulbright Professor at the University of London (1968/69) and Moscow State University (1989), and he has held lectureships in many countries in Europe and Asia. Professor Abrams is the author of several books, including *Conservatism in a Progressive Era* and *The Burdens of Progress,* and of numerous scholarly articles in journals such as *Stanford Law Review, Reviews in American History, American Historical Review, The American Bar Research Journal,* and *Business History Review.*

America Transformed

Sixty Years of Revolutionary Change, 1941–2001

RICHARD M. ABRAMS

University of California, Berkeley

CAMBRIDGE
UNIVERSITY PRESS

E
741
.A22
2006

CAMBRIDGE UNIVERSITY PRESS
Cambridge, New York, Melbourne, Madrid, Cape Town, Singapore, São Paulo

Cambridge University Press
40 West 20th Street, New York, NY 10011-4211, USA

www.cambridge.org
Information on this title: www.cambridge.org/9780521862462

© Richard M. Abrams 2006

This publication is in copyright. Subject to statutory exception
and to the provisions of relevant collective licensing agreements,
no reproduction of any part may take place without
the written permission of Cambridge University Press.

First published 2006

Printed in the United States of America

A catalog record for this publication is available from the British Library.

Library of Congress Cataloging in Publication data
Abrams, Richard M.
America transformed : sixty years of revolutionary change, 1941–2001 /
Richard M. Abrams.
p.   cm.
Includes index.
ISBN 0-521-86246-9 (hardback)
1. United States – History – 1945–   2. United States – Social
conditions – 1945–   3. Social change – United States – History – 20th century.
4. United States – Politics and government – 1945–1989.   I. Title.

E741.A22   2006
973.92 – dc22   2006005049

ISBN-13   978-0-521-86246-2 hardback
ISBN-10   0-521-86246-9 hardback

Cambridge University Press has no responsibility for
the persistence or accuracy of URLs for external or
third-party Internet Web sites referred to in this publication
and does not guarantee that any content on such
Web sites is, or will remain, accurate or appropriate.

604208230

I dedicate this book to my wife, to my children, and to my grandchildren.
May their wonderful capacity for love shield them against troubles.

Contents

Preface

"Revolution" is a strong word, often overused. It implies an overturning of a previous condition or order; a dramatic reversal; a 180-degree turn, or something nearly like it. Yet it is no misuse of the word to describe as revolutionary many changes in American life that occurred during the first quarter-century or so after the United States entered World War II. Most of the changes waxed and endured through the rest of the century, sometimes in the face of strong counterrevolutionary forces. By the end of the century, American society would be transformed at almost every level, from the deeply personal to the far reaches of international engagement.

Nearly all of the revolutions of our half-century owed largely, in some cases mainly, not to great groundswells of grassroots activism but rather to the work of relatively small groups of leaders. "Elites" would not be too pointed a word. They did their work from within some of the least democratic institutions of the country: its universities, its research centers, its corporate boards, its independent regulatory agencies, and its Supreme Court. Most often those leaders challenged the inclinations, and often the opposition, of the nation's democratic or majoritarian forces. That fact would contribute to the counterrevolutionary trends of the last quarter of the century, a central part of the story that this book has to tell.

At the very outset of "our period," precipitously and enduringly the country abandoned its longstanding aloof, unilateral nationalism, its traditional refusal to engage in formal partnership with other nations for joint international purposes. Within a couple of years, America went from isolationism (as its pre–World War II posture is commonly described) to a virtual hegemonic position in international affairs. The aggressive expansion of the fascist powers in Europe and Asia, culminating in Japan's attack on Pearl Harbor and Germany's declaration of war on the United States in December 1941, forced Americans to abandon their aloofness. The challenge of the Soviet Union's postwar ambitions, along with the growing international interests of American business, compelled further U.S. engagement across the globe with implications that affected the entire society, including the robust growth of the American economy.

Indeed, in many respects the most important revolution, the change that had the most profound and widespread effect, was the unprecedentedly swift rise of Americans to affluence. The United States had long been a relatively affluent society; Old World travelers had consistently remarked on it even in the nineteenth century. But the rapidity and dimensions of the *increase* in affluence, beginning with the onset of the Second World War and continuing for the next quarter of a century, constituted something strikingly new, a truly radical change, a revolution in itself that underlay many of the other remarkable changes of the period.

Affluence would contribute significantly to at least three other developments of profound social significance: the transformation of racial relations, the breaching of historic boundaries between male and female roles, and the breaking of virtually all traditional limits on sexual behavior. Each of these changes depended substantially on a sense that its costs were small in an environment of abundance. This was particularly important for the abatement of adverse discrimination against racial minorities. Abundance encouraged a non–zero-sum outlook, so that probably most Americans, at least at the outset, did not view minority gains as impinging on or limiting their own fortunes.

Related to these developments, though perhaps only indirectly, Americans witnessed and experienced a radical erosion of privacy and, more striking, a loss of a *sense* of privacy. That was ironic because, while this was happening, the U.S. Supreme Court for the first time moved to include personal privacy in the constitutional protections afforded by the Bill of Rights. Americans had never been the most private of people. But their much-touted individualism customarily made them cautious about exposure of personal affairs, especially financial and sexual. They were equally cautious about exposing matters concerned with personal health, perhaps from the same squeamishness with which Americans typically approached sex. One spoke of "cancer," for example, only in hushed tones if the word was uttered at all. Money and health, along with sex, were subjects that Americans customarily declined to discuss even with their own children; much less were they subjects for public attention.

For the most part, the custodians of the traditionalist culture insisted that sex was solely for procreation – a sacred, hush-hush procedure even within marriage – and never for recreation. The attitude was reflected in the laws of many states, including of course bans on the sale or purchase of contraceptives. But by the end of the sixties, sex for most Americans became an unquestioned form of recreation with or without marriage or even romance.[1] Indeed, personal exploits became a popular topic for public discussion, description, and revelation as well as a favorite subject of films and prime-time television programs. As it happened, the sexual revolution helped to dissolve most squeamishness about personal health. By the seventies, Betty Ford, the country's First Lady, and Shirley Temple, Hollywood's onetime icon of adorable innocence, could publicly discuss their mastectomies without embarrassment. Meanwhile, revelations about concealed health problems and conflicts of financial interests among government leaders, including presidents, threw open windows for scrutiny of personal lives across broad sectors of the society. It also helped break through long-accepted media restraints on revealing the personal sexual lives of public figures.

Privacy was further battered by technological innovations that expedited a penetrating surveillance of personal life by both governmental and private agencies. At the same time, television shock shows, along with the Internet, which invited the use of personal computer Web sites, seem to have inspired a craving among Jane and John Does for moments of celebrity. As early as the seventies, most Americans seemed to have surrendered a *desire* for privacy, while shame also faded as a constraining force in public behavior.

The country's radical transformation from unilateral aloofness to global interventionism necessarily forced a sharp break with the nation's traditional rejection of a large, standing military establishment. By the seventies, Americans went so far as to move toward a professional military, discarding conscription and the tradition of a "citizen army" in times of danger in favor of volunteer recruits. Meanwhile, the country's new global role contributed to the radical reconstruction of the American business system, facilitating and stimulating the conglomerate merger and multinational corporate phenomena.

The latter especially followed inexorably from major technological changes that affected the entire world and that accelerated life in many areas. Jet propulsion enabled supersonic passenger travel as well as airborne weaponry and space exploration. The development of computer technology, along with the growing perfection of telephonic and telegraphic communications – including the use of satellites orbiting in space as relay points for the transmission of voice and images

---

[1] The attitude of American Roman Catholics may be instructive. A Gallup Poll taken in 1965 showed that more than 60 percent expected the pope to approve the Pill for contraceptive purposes. Despite vigorous lobbying by Dr. John Rock, a Catholic and one of the developers of the Pill, Pope Paul VI – in his Encyclical Letter, *Humanae Vitae,* of July 1968 – said No, insisting that the Pill (like abortion, sterilization, condoms, and other forms of contraception) separated the act of sex from procreation, thereby opening the door to mortal sin. Evidently, the pope notwithstanding, most churchgoing Catholics preferred to separate sex from procreation: a poll taken after the Encyclical showed that only 26 percent of American Catholics accepted the pope's view.

almost seamlessly around the globe – dramatically reduced the costs of transfer-
ring information, goods, and services. These developments completely changed
perceptions of time and space. They forced the globalization of business strategies as they also necessitated a globalization of national security strategies.

The Transformation of Science and Medicine

Medical science and technology underwent spectacular progress during this period. The invention of penicillin just before World War II, soon followed by other
antibiotics, provided for the first time an effective and often swift remedy for a
wide variety of lethal infections. During the war, death followed from disease and
from wounds with only a fraction of the frequency that it did in previous wars.
Dangerous streptococcus and other bacterial infections – including scarlet fever,
some venereal diseases, and even tuberculosis and leprosy, long terrible scourges
of humankind – all but surrendered to the might of modern antibiotics. Preven-
tive immunizations made great progress against other scourges such as bubonic
plague, tetanus, cholera, malaria, measles, diphtheria, typhoid fever, and, most
stunningly, poliomyelitis, commonly known by the descriptive and dreaded
phrase, "infantile paralysis." Smallpox all but disappeared from the world.

The postwar world also witnessed the transforming effect of chemical contraceptives. Along with, shall we say, the "assurance" against most venereal
diseases that penicillin provided, the advent of the Pill (approved in 1960 by the
U.S. Federal Drug Administration) contributed to the revolution in sexual behavior. Access to chemical contraceptives also offered the possibility of controlling
unwanted pregnancies worldwide that threatened ecological as well as personal
disasters – a possibility that, partly for religious and political reasons, enjoyed
little realization outside the industrial regions of the world. Other advances in
medical techniques and surgery made possible once-unthinkable feats regarding
both the conception of life and the conception of sexual identity. By the 1970s,
Americans and peoples all over the world would become familiar with transsexual transformations as well as with test-tube babies and surrogate mothers.

The development of anesthetics made possible further phenomenal revolutions in surgical techniques. They permitted organ transplants, implantation
of prosthetics, and a wide variety of microsurgical techniques on eyes, nerves,
hearts, arteries, and the like that were literally unimaginable before mid-century.
Many of these techniques would not have been possible without new technology that went far beyond X-rays for peering at the body beneath the skin and
permitting precise, even three-dimensional imaging of soft tissue.

Mind-altering narcotics such as heroin, cocaine, and marijuana had had
an ancient history, usually outside the law, but in the last half of the twentieth century pharmaceutical companies reaped megaprofits by inventing various

chemical compounds – many of them similarly addictive – that Americans legally and eagerly consumed for the purpose of altering not merely their mind but even their whole personality. Painkillers, tranquilizers, stimulants, somnolents, hormonal compounds, analgesics, and steroids eased, calmed, energized, empowered, and regulated behavior virtually on demand. They also brought under control often fatal metabolic diseases, such as diabetes and lupus, and did the same for numerous allergies that had produced prolonged misery – and sometimes death – to millions. Death and taxes would still be inevitable, but over the last half of the twentieth century the rates of both, at least in the United States, dramatically declined.

In addition to all this, the discovery of the chemical and physical structure of genes, the fundamental elements of life, opened up the possibility of overcoming "rogue" genetic traits that made individuals susceptible to crippling diseases and offered promise for curing diseases by genetic modification. Indeed, before the end of the century, human beings began to acquire the ability to reshape all life forms and invent new organisms – potentially, to reinvent even themselves.

Such knowledge readily joined with the revolution in computer technology. The invention of the semiconductor and microchips, along with vast progress in electronics and computer technology, gave rise to "biotech" and "genetic engineering." As one expert remarked in 1998, "The marriage of computers and genetic science, in just the last ten years, is one of the seminal events of our age and is likely to change our world more radically than any other technological revolution in history."[2]

Revolutionary as the achievements in medicine, surgery, and biotechnology were, they followed mostly from the internal progress, one might even say the imperatives, of science and technology. In a culture that encouraged curiosity and offered prospects of personal profit, every new discovery and invention impelled further inquiry and development. They deserve full treatment in another book.

The revolutions that I have chosen to focus on in this book entailed changes in policy, attitudes, and behavior. Of course, scientific and technological developments had profound impacts on policy, attitudes, and behavior. As already noted, the availability of penicillin and birth-control pills surely influenced changes in sexual behavior, with implications for gender relations as well. Medical and surgical advances increased longevity, which influenced retirement plans, aged the available workforce, and put strains on pension programs. Computer technology accelerated life. A "slow" personal computer became one that failed to respond reliably to a command in less than two seconds. "Instant gratification" took on

---

[2] Jeremy Rifkin, *The Biotech Century: Harnessing the Gene and Remaking the World* (Tarcher/Putnam, 1998), p. xvi.

new meaning as digital clocks measured time in tenths of a second. Before the end of the century, the use of hormones, antibiotics, and gene manipulation accelerated wool growing, tree growing, vegetable growing, milk producing, and hog, poultry, and cattle raising – with profound effects on farming as a way of life, on the marketing of agricultural goods worldwide, and on the politics of world trade. The residue of hormones in milk from treated cattle feed may also have speeded the onset of puberty, especially among young girls. These are some of the effects of science and technology that bear upon the subjects in this book.

Even the most beneficent of changes produce some unwanted effects. Science and technology helped bring about unprecedented prosperity for Americans but also some problems. The problems included a gap in mentality, in social outlook, between the generation that was born after 1945 and their parents, a schism that induced for many a deep alienation, something of a mutual incomprehension. The problems also included the revolution in expectations among peoples previously out of touch with the possibilities for improved lives that global electronic communications introduced them to but that remained enragingly elusive. The medical advances also helped produce a dramatic reduction in infant mortality and an increase in longevity, but with the consequence of unprecedented population increases in regions that were politically and economically incapable of supporting them. That would be one ingredient in the rise of resentful frustration among millions of people worldwide. By the end of the century, the United States would become a target for such resentment because of its inability, and also its unwillingness, to fulfill the hopes that its own progress had inspired. There were, to be sure, other reasons.

As the century drew to a close, these were global problems about which most Americans generally knew little and – if their political behavior indicated their prevailing attitude – cared less. For a brief period in the middle of the half-century, many Americans confronted and acted to deal with some of the downsides of the progress they were experiencing. But the Sixties[3] proved to be an exceptional era, not typical of the whole. For most Americans who experienced the sixty years of revolutionary change from World War II to the end of the century, life became easier, richer, healthier, and longer. But the pace of economic growth and the spread of affluence through the social strata slowed nearly to a halt by the mid-seventies. So, too, did Americans' attention to social problems abroad and at home. Throughout the last quarter of the century, American politics reflected a cranky resentment of the attention given in the Sixties to those for whom life too nearly remained, as Thomas Hobbes had described it in the seventeenth century, "solitary, poor, nasty, brutish, and short."

---

[3] I use "the sixties" to denote the decade 1960–1969 but use "the Sixties" to describe the era (and ethos) of the period from 1963 to 1973.

One important clue to the turnabout may involve the peculiar force behind the revolutions. That is, most of them primarily resulted not from an upheaval of democratic activism but from the leadership of relatively small groups of liberal men and women who commanded strategic positions in business, education, and government. Although much of the agitation for reform arose with chants of "power to the people," in fact if "the people" – that is, the majority of Americans – had had their way, little would have happened toward enlarging civil rights, civil liberties, sexual freedom, women's rights, the quality of life for the poor, the monitoring of business practices on behalf of consumer interests and the environment, or perhaps even the global expansion of American business. The same could be said, of course, about the medical miracles that owed to the work of a relatively small number of brilliant and hardworking scientists, mathematicians, engineers, and technicians.

By the last quarter of the century, as the economy slowed, as American international leadership underwent challenges from old and new industrial powers, as American government lost respect at home following the Watergate scandals and the fiasco of U.S. intervention in Indochina, and as the dramatic changes in social practices and perceptions began to sink in, a backlash arose among Americans that produced a full-blown counterrevolution. That was in turn led by a militantly conservative intellectual and business elite that mobilized the latent democratic passions while making its way into the Republican Party, in much the same way that liberals had shaped Democratic Party politics earlier.

But I do not wish to engage the sprawling literature about "ruling classes," "power elites," and the like. I acknowledge that in some ways my approach resembles that of John Burnham's *The Managerial Revolution* (1941), C. Wright Mills's *The Power Elite* (1956), and John Kenneth Galbraith's *The New Industrial State* (1967). Each author in his own way makes the argument that policy making follows vectors determined by specialists, top political and business leaders, and bureaucrats, and that economic class analysis is of lesser use in understanding the direction of change. But I do not intend to contribute to a literature that implies some more or less permanent "ruling class" that overrides democratic processes for the purpose of oppressing "the rest of us." Some thoughtful recent essays that attempt to revive the importance of such analysis may be found in Steve Fraser and Gary Gerstel (eds.), *Ruling America: A History of Wealth and Power in a Democracy* (2005).[4] There is on the other hand a growing interest in the opposition of democratic forces to liberalism (a consideration that

---

[4] John Burnham, *The Managerial Revolution* (John Day, 1941); C. Wright Mills, *The Power Elite* (Oxford University Press, 1956); John Kenneth Galbraith, *The New Industrial State* (Houghton-Mifflin, 1967); Steve Fraser & Gary Gerstel, eds., *Ruling America: A History of Wealth and Power in a Democracy* (Harvard University Press, 2005). See also Kevin Phillips, *Wealth and Democracy: A Political History of the American Rich* (Broadway, 2002).

may be traced back to Tocqueville). Fareed Zakaria's *The Future of Freedom: Illiberal Democracy at Home and Abroad* (2003), for example, has much to say about how democratic forces alive in the world today are anything but liberal. Zakaria notes well how democratic forces abroad, especially popular religious forces, make for poor prospects for the liberalization of autocracies around the globe. As for the United States, he highlights the extraordinary rise of politically oriented Protestant evangelicalism and its profoundly negative impact on liberal politics and sensibilities.

In an important way, the surge of modern, political evangelicalism comes from the same generational schism to which I have already alluded. "The fundamentalist involvement in politics," Zakaria observes, "is best understood as a response to [the] weakening of its religious authority and base." In response to popular disinterest in the "don'ts" that were the core of traditional fundamentalism, the new evangelicals exploited the access to mass followings afforded by television, borrowed commercial techniques for attracting followers, and emphasized a "do your own thing" brand of religion. "The key feature of all successful and growing mass Christian sects today," Zakaria writes, "is an emphasis on individual choice and democratic structures." In short: "All it takes to be a fundamentalist these days is to watch the TV shows, go to the theme parks, buy Christian rock, and vote Republican."[5] Co-opted by the militantly conservative business and political elite, these democratic forces contributed in a major way to the ascendancy of the Republican Party during the last quarter of the twentieth century.

Effects of the Revolutions

The sweeping rapidity of change that a mere two generations of Americans experienced produced a society deeply divided, even fragmented. When the American economy shifted in the 1970s from high to low growth and from virtually full employment and rising real median income to substantial percentages of unemployment and underemployment, the elites whose energies and ideas inspired most of the change could not hold the center together. They could not defend politically against the resentments that built up in the democracy over the perceived costs of the changes. By the last quarter of the century, the nation experienced a major breakdown of any consensus on standards or even on a definition of virtue. Nor, it appeared, was there a common vision of a model of "the Good Society." Most of the moral anchors that had held the society together during the comparably transforming decades of a century earlier had pulled loose, leaving large sections of the American polity to drift apart and leaving government to founder amid doubts as to its legitimacy.

[5] Fareed Zakaria, *The Future of Freedom* (Norton, 2003), pp. 214–15.

The collapse of a consensus, a long time coming since even the First World War, underlay some paradoxical historical developments during "our period." One such paradox is how America's "war on poverty" that the country's policy makers launched in the sixties amidst one of the most prosperous eras in U.S. history turned into what many called "a war against the poor" in the mostly prosperous last quarter of the century. After the Watergate scandal and the ignominious demise of a conservative Republican presidency, one might have expected a rejuvenation of the progressive politics that underlay the achievements of the Sixties. Instead, Americans seemed beset by a mood of failure. In the face of remarkable achievements in reducing the miseries of poverty, of a spectacular broad-based rise in Americans' standard of living, of unprecedented progress in equitable gender and racial relations, of international ascendancy and the successful containment of Soviet expansion, of the containment of the damages that industrialization inflicted on the environment and human health – in the face of such remarkable successes, a widespread *failure syndrome* developed that expressed denial of all that had been gained. The defeat of the liberal internationalists' effort to thwart a communist takeover of Indochina had much to do with it, but the collapse of the political coalition that had achieved so much requires more comprehensive attention (and is treated in Part III).

✻   ✻   ✻

In writing this book, I have relied mostly on secondary sources: the rich, voluminous, and ever-growing work of scholars who have done primary-source research on a broad range of specialized subjects. In planning the book, I knew there was no way I could gain fundamental expertise of my own in more than one or two of the areas that needed attention. There were, meanwhile, hundreds of excellent works available on the multitude of particular subjects relevant to my inquiries and upon which I could safely rely for hard information. I have, however, also depended greatly on my own careful reading of scores of contemporary popular and scholarly journals and of daily newspapers over a fifty-year period, as well as on some "primary" investigations of my own. I have attempted to support with footnotes all data, statements, quotations, and the like that are cited in the book, but I have deliberately kept the footnotes to a minimum. I have chosen not to pad the footnotes with every source that could support the same point made in the text, but the notes do provide guidance for any reader who wishes to refer to a source or to an alternative interpretation of materials.

The book represents more than a half-century of reflections on the human condition with particular reference to the history of the United States during that period. It is organized thematically rather than chronologically. Each chapter, as it focuses on a particular subject, follows a chronology of its own, but the book as a whole does not present a chronological narrative. What I have to say about the years of the presidencies of Jimmy Carter and Ronald Reagan through those of the first George Bush and Bill Clinton is well signaled in the previous sections, although because of its pivotal importance I have included a more focused section on "the Reagan revolution." The Epilogue concludes with some reflections on the remarkable postmillennium developments.

The book is designed for any reader – a high-school or college student, or simply any history buff – who possesses a bit more than a bare survey knowledge of the last half of twentieth-century U.S. history. It offers a particular approach to understanding the stunningly rapid and complex transformations of American life in that brief period of time.

I am aware that the subject matter I discuss remains a source of considerable controversy. Indeed, one part of the book's story is the increasing polarization of views among Americans on many vital social and economic issues. I have not attempted to conceal my own preferences, and I confess that those preferences are decidedly of the liberal sort. I take my cues from the eighteenth-century Enlightenment, when a few thinkers – mostly in Western Europe and North America – introduced an argument (barely acknowledged at the time) for a universalist conception of human beings and suggested that the proper function of government is to serve the enhancement of individual freedom and human welfare regardless of nationality, race, religious affinity, or sexual identity. But I am no political partisan. I owe allegiance to no political party or movement. I have attempted to present a balanced account of the diverse forces that have competed for advantage and for input into policy, recognizing that in most cases there were more than two sides to every controversy. I do not expect that every, or any, reader will find my take on the many controversies of the last half-century to be entirely agreeable, but I do hope that readers will find my presentation to be clear, reasonable, nontendentious, and informative.

Acknowledgments

Much of the information in this book was gleaned from hundreds of mono-graphs. I owe a great debt to the innumerable scholars whose careful research informed my work. I am indebted also to the many thousands of students who inspired me with questions and challenges during nearly a half-century of teach-ing in New York, in Berkeley, and in many cities abroad. Many friends and family members have read all or parts of the work in progress, and their com-ments have led to several versions of the book over the years including this final, hopefully more perfect, version. I want to thank especially friends and colleagues David Brody, Robin Einhorn, Edwin Epstein, Patrick Lloyd Hatcher, and Alan Holder, who read all or parts of the manuscript at different stages. I owe a debt also to the anonymous reviewer for Cambridge University Press who read the manuscript with a critical eye and took the time to make dozens of valu-able suggestions and some corrections. Carl Degler and James H. Jones revealed themselves to me as confidential reviewers, kindly offering me their advice for improving the manuscript that they endorsed for publication. My wife, Marcia, and my children, Laura, Robby, and Jennifer read all or parts of many versions of the book with keen eyes and helpful comments. Finally, I have valued the encouragement and advice of senior editor Lew Bateman at Cambridge and of copy-editor Matt Darnell, who scrutinized the manuscript with extraordinary attention for stylistic correctness, clarity, and consistency. Since I did not always accept their suggestions, none of the individuals mentioned here deserves any blame for whatever errors or misstatements appear.

PART ONE

RETROSPECT

I

"The American Century"

The twentieth century did not turn out to be quite what Henry Luce (head of Time, Inc.) had in mind when, at the start of 1941, he declared it "The American Century." "We have," Luce claimed, "that indefinable, unmistakable sign of leadership: prestige," which, he elaborated, "is faith in the good intentions as well as in the ultimate intelligence and ultimate strength of the whole American people." The United States, he noted, was "already a world power in all the trivial ways," including the influence of Hollywood movies, jazz, American slang, and its control of major patented products. It had also already made its mark in science, literature, and the graphic and performing arts. He regretted, however, that in its self-satisfied isolationist absorption during the first forty years of the century, America's failure to use its power responsibly had cost it some prestige. "But most of it is still there," he concluded. He looked forward to the United States taking on its responsibilities as a nation of great resources by accepting the burdens of leadership.[1]

After 1941, the United States would indeed take on a leadership role as one of the world's "superpowers," with dramatic effect on global politics and economy. Its military power would help turn the tide against fascism in Europe and Asia and then hold the line against the expansion of Soviet communism. Its political and economic systems would in many respects become models for many countries of the world where, at least before 1940, liberal democratic institutions had had little apparent attraction. By the last decade of the century, even the powerful Soviet Union would collapse, at least partly because its leaders as well as its people could no longer withstand the appeal of precisely those American-promoted institutions that had made the United States, Western Europe, and Japan amazingly prosperous. These would be among the revolutionary

[1] Henry R. Luce, *The American Century* (Farrar & Rinehart, 1941), pp. 32–4.

3

changes that Americans would experience during the last half of the twentieth century.

The rest of the world would also experience revolutionary changes, many of them for the better. But for most of the peoples of the world, the century did not shape up in the mellow, American-style, God-blessed democratic image Luce had in mind. When in the final months of the war most Americans and Europeans were forced at last to face up to the horrors of the Holocaust, when it became clear that at least 11 million European civilians – men, women, and children – had been murdered in cold blood, including 6 million Jews who were targeted solely because they were Jews, the postwar cry went up: "Never again!" But within 25 years and for the rest of the century, genocide and "ethnic cleansing" would become almost commonplace: Rwanda, Cambodia, Bosnia, Kosovo, Sierra Leone, Nigeria, and Iraq were only some of the places where sustained, massive atrocities occurred. There were also the millions of victims of "The Great Leap Forward" and the "Cultural Revolution" in Mao Zedong's China and of the attempted violent extermination of the Baha'i in post-1979 revolutionary Iran.

In testimony to America's powerful standing in the world, many people at home and abroad blamed the U.S. government for not preventing or doing enough to avert the horrific tragedies. Unhappily, too often the blame was not misplaced. Things got off to a bad start when, despite President Harry Truman's urgings, Congress in 1948 rejected ratification of the Genocide Convention that the United Nations General Assembly had passed. Elected officials of the most powerful democracy in the world expressed fear that their constituents would punish them if they endorsed a commitment to join with the UN to intervene against genocide in some foreign land. Isolationist sentiment – or unilateral nationalism – still prevailed at the time, especially among Republicans who controlled the Congress then. They were powerfully represented by Senate majority leader Robert Taft of Ohio, who, as his most authoritative biographer put it, "was too budget-conscious and too nationalistic to listen to new ideas."[2] It took outrage against President Ronald Reagan's obliviously respectful visit to the graves of German SS officers at Bitberg cemetery in 1986 before another U.S. president felt compelled to endorse the Genocide Convention. Congress finally ratified it in 1988, making the United States the ninety-eighth nation to do so. The ratification, however, did not prevent abstinent or dilatory American responses when prompt action could have stayed at least some of the appalling massacres that the world would witness in the concluding years of the century.[3]

---

[2] James T. Patterson, *Mr. Republican: A Biography of Robert A. Taft* (Houghton-Mifflin, 1972), p. 295.

[3] See Samantha Power, *"A Problem from Hell": America and the Age of Genocide* (Basic Books, 2002).

American power and influence would grow to near dominating levels during the last half of the twentieth century, but the same could not be said of its moral stature. For one thing, the behavior abroad of powerful, profit-fixated American corporations often contradicted the democratic and humanistic ideals that Americans generally liked to profess. Valuing stability and influence with host-country rulers over principle, as most businessmen do, those who ran multinational corporations often found military dictators to be agreeable partners, from Anastasio Somoza of Nicaragua and Castillo Armas of Guatemala in the forties, fifties, and sixties to Saddam Hussein of Iraq in the eighties and Augusto Pinochet of Chile in the seventies through the nineties. Corporations frequently abetted and even subsidized corrupt and barbaric regimes in the impoverished countries they operated in. Meanwhile, the preoccupation of U.S. policy makers with the Cold War against the Soviet Union too often meant assisting tyrannical and corrupt governments whose presumed value to the United States was simply that they were not Communist. Nor did the thrust of U.S. military power abroad increasingly after 1963, in Vietnam and elsewhere, do much for the country's posture as a benevolent democracy. Indeed, as the twentieth century waned, American influence and power sometimes evoked venomous hostility in some impoverished parts of the globe, while people in "Old Europe" smirked at a long-standing belief, held by many of their cousins across the Atlantic, in a benign "American exceptionalism."

It must be said that, when all the goods and bads are toted up for a century's work, the United States probably did significantly more good than harm in the world. But by the turn of the new millennium, the once hallowed image of America – the great hope and model that it had been when the century started – had become badly faded.

2

Before the Revolutions

Probably most Americans looking back fifty years from the end of the century would perceive much that seemed entirely familiar. Clothing, language, architecture, and in general the overall aspect of the country would seem much the same. City high-rises, suburban tract homes, telephones, air travel, radio, and even television were all in place by mid-century. Old movies would show rather less urban traffic, and the autos and airplanes would betray their vintage; perhaps strangest to the modern eye would be how easily automobile drivers found curbside parking spaces. In fact, although it would not be readily evident, America was a far less crowded society back then. The nation's population in 1940, 132 million, was slightly less than half what it became by the end of the century.

On the whole, most modern Americans would comfortably recognize the United States of the 1940s as "their own" country. Only the absence of personal computers and push-button cellular telephones would seem clearly to separate the America of the forties and fifties from the nation in the last decade of the century. Yet the sense of familiarity would be misleading. Quite apart from the fantastic achievements of science and technology, a closer look at the America of the forties and fifties would reveal a society that was virtually an alien country.

Contemplate an America in which tens of thousands of U.S. citizens of Japanese background were interned for years in detention camps and were forced to dispose of their property at a great loss, without trial, without charges of any kind, without compensation, and without serious protest from other Americans; in which the very army that defeated fascism in Europe and the very navy that defeated the Japanese in Asia were racially segregated; in which nonwhite persons could not enter most motels or hotels anywhere in the country except as menial laborers. In at least a dozen states of the Union, even military men were barred from most restaurants, rest rooms, drinking fountains, hospitals, swimming pools, or beaches if they were not white.

How strange must seem an America in which, until almost mid-century, not a single black person was permitted to compete in any major-league team sport; in which female athletes were regarded with skepticism and amusement; and in which most major medical, law, engineering, and business schools formally barred women. Even more enduringly, in most states a man could legally appropriate his wife's income and inheritance, could force his wife to move with him to another city or state against her will, and in most cases could physically brutalize her with impunity. America in the forties and fifties was also a country in which a man and his wife could be pulled from bed in the early morning hours by police who would jail them for violating a state law forbidding interracial marriage; in which more than a dozen states barred nonwhites from serving on juries and from testifying against a white person; in which a poor person accused of a major felony would be tried in court without access to a defense attorney; in which all-white juries in many states routinely acquitted white thugs who had openly kidnapped, tortured, and lynched young black men and teenage boys. Kidnapping had been a federal crime since the notorious Lindbergh case in the 1930s, but it was never applied to lynching because the doctrine of "states' rights" still served to defeat even the most modest proposals to guarantee American citizens equal protection of the law regardless of race, gender, or state of residence.

Not all the contrasts between the America of mid-century and that of the century's end point to progress in civil behavior and humane sensibilities. As late as 1965, an urban homeowner might have difficulty locating the keys to the front door, so common in many cities was the practice of safely leaving doors unlocked. Shops did not require steel shutters after closing. Bicycles could be secured safely to a lamp post or railing with a simple combination lock rather than with special steel-hardened chains. Car alarms and home burglary alarms were virtually unknown. Police still walked their beats singly in most urban neighborhoods, without radio contact with headquarters and without the likelihood of being attacked. No place in America required special scrutiny or devices to prevent children from bringing weapons into a school or to prevent library books from being stolen. Automobile traffic did not yet prevent children from playing games in most urban streets. Public libraries typically were open evenings and on weekends. Most major cities outside parts of the Old South offered tuition-free college education. Smog was not yet an urban commonplace; most rural streams still ran free and unpolluted. Divorce was not yet the rule rather than the exception in urban family relationships. Nor was single teenage motherhood a widespread problem.

Personal integrity – a term that had not yet lost a commonly understood meaning – still implied a strong sense of personal privacy. It was beyond decency, as the word was commonly understood, to publicly boast of one's own extramarital escapades or other familial betrayals, as became the fashion a quarter century later for numerous celebrities whose autobiographies made best-seller lists. Nor would it have been viewed as anything but repugnant for celebrity-craving exhibitionists to air on television their own, their spouses', their parents', and their children's sexual and other intimate activities, as became a daily phenomenon by the seventies. Before 1970, embarrassment and shame still exerted a powerful influence on personal behavior.

There were other, more subtle signs that America in the forties and fifties was not quite the familiar country that a young American at the end of the century might imagine. Of course the language would be familiar, although nouns like "interface," "impact," and "access" were not yet common as verbs while "incentivize" was not a recognizable word at all. People would "sleep *late*" rather than "sleep *in*," and they would say "how *much* fun" something was, not "how fun." More significantly, "Ms." was 25 years away from being invented to take its place beside "Mr." as a maritally neutral term of address for women. "Black" was a not altogether friendly way of describing an Afro-American owing to its historical association with slavery and linguistic association with evil. "Negro" and "colored" were the preferred, polite terms. But after 1968, especially young black people made clear that they viewed "colored" as condescending, "Negro" as reminiscent of a subservient "Uncle Tom," but "black" as defiant, proud, and assertive. The new terminology stuck, signifying the revolutionary change in attitude that marked the late 1960s.

Because language is an important clue for understanding the deeper sensitivities of a people, it must signify how different was the world of the forties that Americans then watched movies and read books completely lacking in the provocative "four-letter words" that, by the 1970s, regularly punctuated dialog in popularly distributed movies and proliferated in best-selling novels. In fact, by the seventies it seemed that some people would have become completely inarticulate without them. Not that those words didn't exist in the forties: everyone knew them and probably most used them, at least sometimes. But official America felt a strong need to repress them. A person could be jailed for using such words in a public address, a song, or a comic routine on stage, as occurred even in the Sixties to the notoriously popular comedian, Lenny Bruce. Publishers ludicrously forced Norman Mailer to fudge the real, colorful language of combat troops in his prize-winning *The Naked and the Dead,* probably the best World War II novel ever written. Major literary works went without publishers, were kept from library shelves, or – like Henry Miller's *Tropic of Cancer,* James Joyce's *Ulysses,* D. H. Lawrence's *Lady Chatterly's Lover,* and Edmund Wilson's *Memoirs of Hecate County* – were banned entirely from the country. These books contained in dialog one or more of the forbidden words that anyone could hear in a crowd and could read on the walls of every public rest room and train station. As J. D. Salinger's troubled teenager, Holden Caulfield, would complain in *The Catcher in the Rye*: "It's hopeless, anyway. If you had a million years to do it in, you couldn't rub out even *half* the 'Fuck you' signs in the world. It's impossible."

Published in 1951, *Catcher* became a runaway best-seller. Custodians of village culture throughout America worked fiercely to keep it out of schools and libraries, with spotty success. They were right: the scatological breakthrough was at hand, and village culture went reeling. For better but also for worse, other standards of traditional decorum and civility would soon be falling.

The way people present themselves also tells a story. Most properly dressed adults in the forties wore hats outdoors, even in summer. The fedora, a high-crowned and wide-brimmed felt hat, was favored among males, while the once elaborate women's chapeaus had dwindled to virtual skullcaps with ribbons, feathers, and/or decorative veils. A white or light-colored shirt with necktie was the public uniform for proper males aged 5 to 85. Women of every age remained tied to their skirts; slacks or jeans might be worn in the house, on the job in a factory, or on a country holiday, but they would result in rejection at the door of "better" restaurants, clubs, and hotels, and even at college mess halls and libraries. No socially sensitive male under 60 sported any kind of beard unless to make a religious statement or to affect an Old World allure. (The mustachioed Republican Thomas E. Dewey was the last man to seek the presidency on a major ticket with any kind of facial hair; he lost to FDR in 1944 and lost to Truman in 1948.) Men's haircuts uniformly left ears outstanding and neck conspicuously bare. Straight hair was "in" for males and females, and for blacks as well as for whites. Although most Negroes could not or would not spend the money to use them, pharmaceutical companies made fortunes selling hair straighteners to the thousands who did. Until the "Afro" became a symbol of racial pride in the late 1960s, most black males were content to keep their hair cropped close to the skull. (By the 1990s, bald would become the macho, "in your face" fashion for young males and for some females, too.)

These are just some of the evidences of a society that was self-conscious about propriety, concerned with rules, deferential to standards of decorum, "individualistic" by most historical measures and yet – certainly by comparison with American society as it evolved over the next two decades – strikingly bound by limits prescribed by custom and authority. Of course many people chafed against the constraints of custom and authority, especially those members of minority groups whose sometimes maliciously enforced exclusion inspired rebelliousness or bitterness. Even so, the pressures for conformity were usually greater. The canons of "good taste," indeed of "goodness," generally were not yet seriously challenged. The sense of belonging to a large, encompassing community that transcended racial, religious, ethnic, class, or expatriate loyalties may not have been universal, but it ran strong. Patriotism was not yet a word of scorn among social critics; it came naturally to both progressive reformers and militant conservatives, reinforced by the felt exigencies of the war effort and perhaps also by the camaraderie fostered by people's common struggle with the privations of the Depression. The challenges of major wars and economic need tended to make life relatively simple.

This touches on more subtle differences, differences in mentality, outlook, attitude, and mindset. The adult population of the forties and fifties had endured hardships in life rarely experienced by most Americans born after 1940. Most adults would have lived through the traumas of both World Wars and the decade-long Great Depression that came between the wars. They had intimate knowledge of material want and personal anguish. For them, life had always seemed difficult, fearsome, unpredictable, even treacherous. Their experience engendered in them cautious, order- and security-coveting attitudes as well as frugal habits that would outlast the postwar affluence to which most of them rapidly ascended.

The generations born after 1940 had starkly contrasting experiences. Over the course of fewer than two decades after the Second World War, Americans (and people of the other industrial countries) would experience a greater increase in material wealth than any people in the history of the world. A rapid, sustained, and widespread increase in affluence would become the most conspicuous feature of the postwar era. Most of the young during the third quarter of the twentieth century would have difficulty comprehending their parents' "hang-ups." Charles Reich, author of the popular book, *The Greening of America,* remarked in 1970: "Older people are inclined to think of work, injustice and war, and of the bitter frustrations of life, as the human condition."[1] Not so their children, many of whom believed they knew how to end war and injustice once and for all, thought work to be greatly overrated, and refused to abide frustration.

The increase in real disposable income for Americans in the 1940–1970 period was one of the revolutionary developments of the times, as it would approach the increase for the entire 75 years since the close of the Civil War. This prosperity would have the most transforming effect on a multitude of features of American society. In emancipating the great mass of Americans from the anguish or even the threat of poverty, it would contribute to major changes in racial and gender relations as well as in American foreign policy and the structure of the business system. It would inspire a rampant individualism, though for a while it would

---

[1] Charles Reich, *The Greening of America* (Random House, 1970), p. 6.

also contribute to a broad-based, good-spirited social consciousness. Americans in general during the quarter century following the Second World War would have much to celebrate, most particularly their growing personal prosperity.

And yet ....

3

The Challenge of Power

The unparalleled ascendancy to wealth that most Americans enjoyed in the first quarter-century following World War II did not mean that even that lucky majority enjoyed unalloyed happiness or serenity. Everyone did not live happily ever after. As the burdens of poverty lightened and the oppression of racism and other forms of bigotry began to lift, awareness of what evils remained and what progress could yet be made cultivated its own discontents. It was a phenomenon that the French commentator on American life, Alexis de Tocqueville, had noted a century earlier:

It happens most frequently that a people, which had supported the most crushing laws without complaint, and apparently as if they were unfelt, throws them off with violence as soon as the burthen begins to be diminished .... The evils which were endured patiently so long as they were inevitable seem intolerable as soon as a hope can be entertained of escaping from them. The abuses which are removed seem to lay bare those which remain, and to render the sense of them more acute; the evil has decreased, it is true, but the perception of the evil is more keen.[1]

"Empowerment," an expression that gained much currency in the 1960s as something to be desired, raised difficulties of its own. Emancipation from traditionalist roles, especially for women, permitted open-ended lifestyle options that would produce new anxieties. Largely successful challenges to constrictive traditions discomfited many who craved stability and who identified tradition not simply with custom but with morality. Modern technology in industry, medicine, transportation, and communications created new jobs and economic opportunities and made life easier, healthier, wealthier, and wiser, but it also

---

[1] Alexis de Tocqueville, *On the State of Society in France before the Revolution of 1789*, trans. Henry Reeve (John Murray, 1856), pp. 323–4.

eliminated millions of long-standing jobs while empowering the state and a variety of private agencies to intervene more insidiously in Americans' private lives.

Perhaps most of all, the country's new international position as a "world power" posed a daunting array of perilous choices. Confronting the perceived threat to liberal values of Soviet imperialist ambitions, the United States risked devastating warfare. The advent of nuclear weapons raised the stakes of warfare. It kept Americans, and much of the world, on edge.

In short, the generation that was lifted out of the Great Depression by the Second World War and ascended further on the great swell of prosperity that followed would find its attention to the newly achieved Good Life continually diverted by the storm clouds of a major war hovering on the horizon – and sometimes even closer.

Superimposed over the postwar landscape lay the macabre images of a two-headed incubus – the Holocaust and the Bomb. While the prospects of a rich life beckoned in plain view, the spectre of death shrouded the scene. It was not merely the threat of death, which after all is a condition of life in any age. For thousands of years, most people had lived with the prospect of early personal mortality if not impending apocalypse. It was rather the unprecedented scale of the massacres of innocents and the prospect of meaninglessness that appalled. At Auschwitz and Hiroshima, Maidenek and Nagasaki, the angel of annihilation declined to select with discriminating finger among the armed and unarmed, nor among the robust and the frail, the prudent, the heedless, the young, the aged, the willful, the whatever. It didn't matter, because they all were chosen to suffocate in the gas and be reduced to ashes in the furnaces or were scorched and irradiated when only moments before they stood looking at a peaceful sky or lay asleep in their beds.

These facts of modern life had dramatic implications for the continued transmission of traditionalist values and for the future of community, social cohesion, and consensus. "If the fate of twentieth century man is to live with death," Norman Mailer wrote in 1959, then "the only life-giving answer is ... to divorce oneself from society, to exist without roots."[2] Most Americans would not follow Mailer into his existentialist bubble, but a vital and dynamic cohort of young Americans would find it attractive.

The Holocaust, once its full dimensions became revealed, seemed like something altogether new in the long history of man's inhumanity to man. Except for the sheer numbers, it wasn't. Every continent on the globe had witnessed genocide in various forms at different times. Many a people have been lost to

---

[2] Norman Mailer, "The White Negro," in *Advertisements for Myself* (Putnam's, 1959), p. 338.

history, victims of mass "liquidation," perhaps beginning with the extermination of the Neanderthal by the Cro-Magnon, supposedly the first *homo sapiens*.
But it came as a shock that such barbarism could occur in the twentieth century,
more than 150 years after the "Age of Enlightenment" had supposedly ushered
in a new era of rational human discourse. It was numbing that the Holocaust
could occur within the bounds of the European civilization, within "Christen-
dom," which long had regarded itself as having ascended to moral heights far
above those ever achieved by more "savage" people.

It was, indeed, not merely the number of humans exterminated in "the final
solution" – Hitler's term for his methodical killing of 6 million Jews, 1.5 million of them young children. Nor was it just the 4 million other civilians caught
in one or another spasm of Nazi spite or vengeance. Rather, what literally stu-
pefied was the calculated malevolence of it, the high-powered ideological rationalization that underlay it, the meticulous organization of it, and the seemingly
complete absence of sympathy.[3] The executioners often stood close to their victims to command and to kill. They looked into their faces, before and after.
They had literally to get into their faces in order to extract the gold fillings from
their teeth. Many mocked and humiliated the doomed before putting them to
death, atrocities preserved on "home movie" film and in the perpetrators' own
photos for their own delectation years later – and for later generations to view
with horror. Most Americans did not believe reports of the Holocaust until the
war was all but over and when members of the armed forces came upon – even
then in disbelief – the horror of Dachau, and then Belsen and Mauthausen, and
Buchenwald, and Treblinka, ...[4]

The atom bomb also seemed like something incomprehensibly new in the
long history of humankind's capacity for indiscriminate killing. In only a limited sense, it was. The source and dimensions of the explosive power were entirely
new. But horrendous massacres executed by unseen and unseeing warriors who
hurled murderous devastation far from the scene had already become commonplace at least since 1914. It was during the First World War that the deliberate
victimization of innocent civilians became a technique of modern warfare and

---

[3] "Genocide, alas, is a common practice across the globe and across historical eras. But it has now
come to haunt Western consciousness in an especially unsettling way, for the obvious reason that
on European soil in the twentieth century it was implemented with a systematic rigor and an
ideological dedication that had not been seen before or elsewhere." Robert Alter, "Immodest Proposals," review of Claude Rawson, *God, Gulliver, and Genocide: Barbarism and the European
Imagination, 1492–1945* (Oxford University Press, 2002), in *The New Republic*, 23 March 2002.

[4] "When, as members of an advance British army unit, we came upon Bergen-Belsen, I recall vividly
the feeling of incredulity, even in 1945, that Germans, or anyone else, could have committed so vast
and monstrous an outrage on their fellow human beings." Brian Urquhart, "Shameful Neglect,"
New York Review of Books, 25 April 2002, p. 12.

when long-range artillery brought devastation to nonmilitary targets. It was then that the terroristic methods of the ancient and medieval conquerors – Roman, Gothic, Mongol, Saracen, Ottoman, and their like – emerged again in Europe after four centuries of comparative quiescence.

Perhaps most Americans in 1941 still suffered the anguish of the humane over the massacre of innocents. But such horror would soon become an enduring and perhaps even a distinguishing feature of the twentieth century. By 1944 or 1945, most Americans did not suffer to think about the quarter-million or more men, women, and children indiscriminately killed in the fire bombings of Hamburg, Dresden, and Tokyo. Nor did they reflect somberly on the nuclear obliteration of Hiroshima and Nagasaki – that was war. It had come to be assumed that the people of enemy countries deserved whatever suffering befell them; or in any event it couldn't be helped. The main thing was to win the war with the fewest American casualties.

President Harry Truman would later say that he never gave a second thought to using the atom bomb against Japan. "I regarded the bomb as a military weapon and never had any doubt that it should be used," he wrote later.[5] Maybe so; or maybe it was in the nature of postwar, post-decision bravado.[6] It was, however, consistent with the general consciousness of the war years. Most other policy makers, as well as the scientists who worked on the Bomb, generally agreed at the time and in their own memoirs that the overriding concern in 1945 was the war and how to end it quickly.

On the other hand, in April 1945 – about the same time Franklin D. Roosevelt suffered the stroke that killed him and made a failed haberdasher from Missouri the president of the United States – some of the scientists working on the Bomb were in Washington warning government leaders to consider seriously the political implications of actually using it. They emphasized what it would likely do to the prospects of avoiding a postwar nuclear arms race with the Soviet Union and the assured mutual destruction that such an arms race might portend. In fact, Truman appointed a civilian advisory committee on the subject, including many eminent scientists. More than a hundred nuclear scientists were secretly polled, a plurality of whom argued that an offshore demonstration of the Bomb might be sufficient to end the war. In June, government leaders considered a confidential report by some of the scientists who opposed using the Bomb. The scientists contended that to use on cities a weapon so indiscriminate and a million times more destructive than any previous weapon would sacrifice America's

---

[5] Harry S. Truman, *Memoirs by Harry S. Truman: Year of Decisions* (Doubleday, 1955), p. 419.

[6] However, Truman's successor, Dwight Eisenhower, decidedly viewed nuclear weapons as legitimate military equipment and contemplated using them in Korea and in Indochina.

moral position and, moreover, "prejudice the possibility of reaching an international agreement on the future control of such weapons."[7]

The wisdom as well as the humanity of using the Bomb would remain hotly debated for the rest of the century. Some would note that the incineration of Tokyo by conventional bombs left more people dead (90,000) than initially died in Hiroshima (50,000) and Nagasaki (30,000) taken together.[8] In fact, some generals, like Curtis LeMay, who headed the strategic bombing campaign against Japan, resisted using the atomic bomb because they believed that conventional bombs would be sufficiently effective, as demonstrated in Tokyo. That argument, however, implied that, without the Bomb and the accelerated surrender by Japan that it clearly induced, many hundreds of thousands more Japanese probably would have died in the prolonged warfare. The suggestion that an offshore demonstration might have been enough to induce surrender fails to consider that at the time the United States had only two Bombs, each of a different technology. There was no way to know if either or both might fail, so an announced demonstration would have been risky. As it happened, the Japanese gave no indication of a readiness to surrender after the first bomb destroyed Hiroshima. Resistance to surrender persisted in the Japanese government for days after the second bomb was used on Nagasaki and days after the Russians entered the war and broke through Japanese lines in Manchuria.

It was generally understood that even without the Bomb Japan would be forced to surrender within a year, perhaps by November or December. But it was calculated that Japanese civilian casualties would rise astronomically in the interim and also that American military casualties would rise substantially. Which American policy makers would have volunteered to explain to desolated American families why they chose not to use a weapon that almost certainly would have shortened the war and obviated the terrible losses they mourned? Then again, the Americans could have waited to drop the first bomb until the Russians entered the war against Japan, as Stalin had promised Roosevelt and Churchill at Yalta that they would within three months after Germany surrendered. Stalin reaffirmed the promise to Truman at Potsdam in July, and in this case he proved true to his word. Yet by the spring of 1945, tensions between Washington and Moscow were already high. With minimizing American casualties in mind, Truman had gone to Potsdam to secure Stalin's commitment to enter the war against Japan; however, after learning of the successful test of an

---

[7] Quoted in Daniel Kevles, *The Physicists* (Vintage, 1979), p. 335. See also Richard Rhodes, *The Making of the Atomic Bomb* (Simon & Schuster, 1986), ch. 18 ("Trinity").

[8] These estimates refer to initial deaths; many thousands died later. By some estimates, 197,000 died in Tokyo.

atomic weapon in Alamagordo, New Mexico, Truman turned his attention to the potential consequences of increased Soviet power in postwar China, Korea, and Japan. It is uncertain how heavily such concerns weighed in the decision to bomb Hiroshima. But even if they were the predominating factor (which no scholar has demonstrated), it would seem hard to fault a decision that precluded the risk of letting the Soviet Union dictate the terms of Japan's surrender and postwar reconstruction.[9]

In sum, the choices in the summer of 1945, like so many that Americans would face in the rest of the century, were not all good.

On the sixth of August, 1945, the first Bomb was dropped. The Soviet Union entered the war against Japan two days later. On August 9, the second Bomb fell. The Japanese leadership held out for another five days until finally, on August 14, the war ended. Most Americans were jubilant. At the end of the year, *Time* magazine made Harry Truman its "Man of the Year." But in an editorial it noted: "What the world would best remember of 1945 was the deadly mushroom clouds over Hiroshima and Nagasaki .... In such a world, who dared be optimistic?"

Not the jubilance over Hitler's death and the Nazi surrender in May, nor the spectacle of the Japanese formal capitulation in September on the deck of the battleship *Missouri* in Tokyo harbor, but instead the gigantic boiling cloud of radioactive ash, flattening and spreading at the top like a mushroom as it lost momentum five miles up – *this* would be the most memorable image of the war's final year.

---

[9] Cf. Barton J. Bernstein, "The Atomic Bombings Reconsidered," *Foreign Affairs* (Jan./Feb. 1995); Robert L. Messer, "New Evidence on Truman's Decision," and Gar Alperovitz, "More on Atomic Diplomacy," *Bulletin of Atomic Scientists* (1985), reprinted in William H. Chafe & Harvard Sitkoff, eds., *A History of Our Time* (Oxford University Press, 1995); and Gar Alperovitz, "Hiroshima: Historians Reassess," *Foreign Policy* (Summer 1995). These represent the continuing effort by critics of the use of the Bomb to justify their criticism, although without directly confronting the consequences of not using the Bomb. For a contrary view see Robert James Maddox, "The Biggest Decision: Why We Had to Drop the Atomic Bomb," *American Heritage* (May/June 1995).

4

The Inflation of Moral Possibilities

To contemplate the moral possibilities of the new world order at mid-century required a major mental adjustment. Power is never unlimited, wrote Alexis de Tocqueville more than a hundred years earlier. "Above it in the moral world," he claimed, "are humanity, justice, and reason." This had been a matter of long-standing faith in Western civilization. In the nineteenth century, much of Western society shared a strong moral consensus that permitted people to take for granted that moral scruples among "civilized" people invariably limited potential human barbarism. Some decades after Tocqueville, the American philosopher William James wrote that to argue that human beings enjoy free will is not to say "that everything that is physically conceivable is also morally possible. It merely says that of alternatives that really *tempt* our will more than one is really possible"; whereas, James argued, "Of course, the alternatives that do thus tempt our will are vastly fewer than the physical possibilities we can coldly fancy."[1]

For the witnesses of the Second World War and for their descendants, "vastly fewer" no longer appeared to apply. No horror, no cruelty seemed beyond human temptation. No quantity of civilian casualties, no number of innocent children or of aged, disabled, or helpless human beings, and no measure of human sympathy posed a limit on the indiscriminate death perpetrated in the course of the war. America's enemies – and, what was more chilling, Americans themselves – had shown both the technological and moral capacity for producing such devastation.[2]

[1] William James, "The Dilemma of Determinism," in *The Will to Believe and Other Essays in Popular Philosophy* (Longmans, Green, 1896), p. 157n.
[2] "While the worst atrocities were perpetrated by the Axis," wrote Barton Bernstein, the foremost expert on the decision to use the Bomb, "all the major nation-states sliced away at the [traditional]

Americans' moral capacity for the indiscriminate murder of innocents would, in the next quarter-century, grow to horrific dimensions. It may be briefly illustrated by their president calling U.S. Army Lieutenant William Calley "a national hero" after the man stood accused of the cold-blooded murder of more than a hundred women, children, and aged men in the Vietnam hamlet of Thuanyen (My Lai 4), an act that the convicted Lt. Calley casually claimed in court was "no big deal." The Army's own Peers Report – named after Lt. Gen. William R. Peers, director of the investigation begun in November 1969 – charged the Army with "individual and group acts of murder, rape, sodomy, maiming, and assault on noncombatants and the mistreatment and killing of detainees" in *addition* to the particular atrocities at My Lai.[3] "We grieve for an America," wrote the novelist William Styron, "which, 26 years after the end of a war to save the world for democracy, finds itself close to moral bankruptcy ... [as] symbolized by the Mylai [*sic*] carnage and by its flyblown principal executor, First Lieut. William Laws Calley."[4]

Was it "no big deal" because Americans were supposed to understand that such atrocities had become commonplace in the Vietnam War? Or was it "no big deal" because, in the struggle against world communism, traditional moral standards had to be put aside – and would be? In the 1980s, for example, the U.S. government deliberately covered up the massacre of several hundreds of women and children in the El Salvadorean province of Morazon in December 1981. The atrocities were carried out by El Salvadorean troops trained, equipped, and supported by an administration in Washington that had made fighting "communism" its sole priority in Central America. A U.S. embassy official in San

---

moral code .... By 1945 there were few moral restraints left .... America was not morally unique – just technologically exceptional. Only it had the bomb, and so only it used it." Barton J. Bernstein, "The Atomic Bombings Reconsidered," *Foreign Affairs* (Jan./Feb. 1995).

[3] The Peers Report (suppressed for three years, until 1974) revealed that what happened at My Lai was replicated at other nearby villages. An estimated 400 infants, children, women, and old men were killed in scenes similar to those witnessed by Holocaust survivors at Auschwitz and elsewhere. Only Lt. Calley was prosecuted. The quotation from the Report is taken from *Time* (25 Nov. 1974), p. 19. Most of the story had already been "leaked" and uncovered by astute reporters such as Seymour Hersh. See his *My Lai 4* (1970) and his later exposé of the Army's attempt to cover up the murders, "A Reporter At Large: Cover Up – I" and "Cover Up – II," *The New Yorker*, (22 & 27 Jan. 1972). See also *New York Times* (4 June 1972), pp. 1ff, reporting extensive excerpts leaked from the Report.

[4] Styron, in the *New York Times Book Review* (12 Sept. 1971), sec. 7, p. 1, reviewing Richard Hammer, *The Court-Martial of Lt. Calley* and *Lieutenant Calley: His Own Story*. Hersh's *My Lai 4* remains the definitive as well as original account, or exposé, of the incident. Calley was convicted of murdering 22 individuals. Originally given a 20-year-to-life sentence, he was paroled within two years, an outcome that led Gen. Peers to lament: "To think that out of all those men, only one was brought to justice. And now he's practically a hero. It's a tragedy." Quoted in *Time* (25 Nov. 1974), p. 20.

Salvador explained to a friend that he did not press the issue with his superiors
in Washington because, "You know, we're talking about people ... whose priorities were definitely not ... about getting at exactly what happened."[5]

---

[5] From Mark Danner, *The Massacre at El Mozote: A Parable of the Cold War* (Vintage, 1994),
quoted in Joan Didion, "'Something Horrible' in El Salvador," *New York Review of Books* (14
July 1994), p. 8. Following the U.S. invasion of Iraq 22 years later, and claiming the need to use unconventional methods to fight "global terrorism" (which had replaced "world communism" as the
centerpiece of U.S. foreign policy), U.S. government leaders dismissed the Geneva Conventions
with regard to the treatment of thousands of Muslim prisoners, including a few U.S. citizens. President G. W. Bush unilaterally declared them "unlawful combatants" and thus without any rights to
due process, holding them incommunicado in brutal prisons for years. Meanwhile "Abu Ghraib,"
a miserable prison in Baghdad, became the Iraq War's "My Lai" after photographs revealed disgusting mistreatment of prisoners by U.S. soldiers and intelligence agents. Subsequent revelations
indicated that similar mistreatment had become commonplace in numerous prisons. For many observers, including Americans, Bush's and defense secretary Donald Rumsfeld's public dismissal of
the Geneva Conventions bore at least indirect responsibility for the atrocities committed in Iraq in
2003–2004, in the U.S. prison in Guantanamo, Cuba, and in U.S.-occupied Afghanistan as well.

5

The Generational Chasm

However new to Americans such acknowledged callousness may have been, it was hardly a historical novelty. But there were other "firsts" that postwar society would have to cope with. Social and technological change had been accelerating for more than 200 years. By the mid-twentieth century it had become a fundamental fact of life. The British philosopher Alfred North Whitehead had remarked earlier in the century how the ordering force of tradition had always depended on the assumption that "each generation will live amid the conditions governing the lives of its fathers and will transmit those conditions to mould with equal force the lives of its children. We are living in the first period of human history for which this assumption is false."[1] "The simple security of the old orthodox assumptions," Whitehead noted, "has vanished .... The new situation in the thought of today arises from the fact that scientific theory is outrunning common sense."[2] The weakening of the force of tradition would take on new significance after 1945.

The conditions that would govern the lives of the postwar generations contrasted starkly with conditions for their parents. The values usually transmitted by custom and linking generations to one another would become increasingly tenuous. The first-person narrator in Wallace Stegner's 1971 novel, *Angle of Repose,* describes his son Rodman as a member of a generation "born without a sense of history." "To him," the narrator says, "it is only an aborted social science. The world has changed, Pop, he tells me. The past is not going to teach us anything about what we've got ahead of us. Maybe it did once, or seemed to. It

---

[1] Quoted in Clyde Kluckhohn, "Mid-Century Manners and Morals," in Bruce Bliven, ed., *Twentieth Century Unlimited* (Lippincott, 1950), p. 314.
[2] Alfred North Whitehead, *Science and the Modern World* (Macmillan, 1926), p. 166.

doesn't anymore." "That is no gap between generations," the novel's narrator goes on. "That is a gulf."[3]

The children of the generations of adults who had experienced the Depression and one or both World Wars would have to settle on personal values and social standards without obvious guidance from traditions. They were not altogether unique; their parents, too, had experienced a sharp break with a past that had become suddenly archaic by 1915. As the philosopher Charles Ayres wrote in the 1920s, the modernist critics of religion-based traditions could cheerfully dismantle the old order of the nineteenth century because they lived "at the height of Victorian propriety," when "morality was then in no danger of being wrecked." For the critics themselves, the traditional values they had absorbed in their youth still disciplined their lives. That was before the mind-numbing horrors of World War I and the rise of the Fascist and Bolshevist varieties of totalitarianism. "Today," Ayres remarked, "we know what the wreck of morality might mean."[4]

Even so, the ancient oppression of poverty and the urgent imperatives of war continued to give order to the lives of those who came of age before 1945. Confronting challenges to survival or subsistence has a way of focusing the mind and ordering the daily regime. In contrast, children of the 1940s and afterward would face the daily problems of choice virtually without imperatives, without urgent need, and – perhaps worst of all – without any standards they felt compelled to respect. At the end of the 1960s, social critic Daniel Bell would remark about this generation: "The sociological problem of reality in our time ... arises because individuals no longer follow inherited ways, are constantly faced with the problems of choice ... and no longer find authoritative standards or critics to guide them."[5]

The dissipation of authoritative standards had broad social and political as well as individual effects. Historically, Americans had given over to "competition in a marketplace environment" a major role in the allocation of social resources and rewards. Americans tended to assume that individual pursuit of an enlightened self-interest on a "free and fair field" that was governed by the rule of law would produce a just distribution of social goods. But without a consensus on standards or common experiences on which it could be based, the principle of self-interest and individualistic competition as a social regulator would lose its chief link to social justice. Law would come to be viewed less as the articulation of a just resolution of social conflicts and more as the mere institutionalization

---

[3] Wallace Stegner, *Angle of Repose* (Fawcett, 1971), pp. 11, 13.
[4] Charles Ayres, *Science, The False Messiah* (Bobbs, Merrill, 1927), p. 27.
[5] Daniel Bell, *The Cultural Contradictions of Capitalism* (Basic Books, 1978), p. 90.

of the dominant interests' preferences. The use of law to coerce rather than to mediate would become more important and even more urgent as a social regulator. Much of what would happen in the Sixties and thereafter – on the left and on the right – may well be traceable to a growing sense, in an increasingly polarized society, that law and government lacked legitimacy.

PART TWO

EIGHT REVOLUTIONS

The first revolutionary change that the American people encountered, beginning with 1940, was the transformation of the nation's role in world affairs from isolationism to global interventionism. It was a development initiated by the Second World War. It was carried forward more comprehensively by the Cold War that followed but also by dramatic transportation and communication advances that raised the importance of transnational business activities. The unprecedented ascendancy of the military to substantial influence in American life would follow more or less directly from those changes. Both would have important ramifications for a dramatic restructuring of American business.

Yet, in many respects, the most consequential of changes that Americans experienced after 1940 was the unprecedentedly rapid and broad growth in affluence. Postwar affluence arrived with such suddenness and with such magnitude as to constitute a social revolution in its own right. That development underlay the nation's rise to hegemonic influence in the world and its ability to fund an incomparable military. It also underlay the revolutions in racial and gender relations. It probably contributed significantly to the dramatic changes in sexual behavior as well as, arguably, a growing personal disregard for the value of privacy, even as new technology made it possible for government and private agencies to snoop into people's most private affairs.

By the 1960s, among the remarkable effects of the revolutionary rise to affluence was the country's policy makers' unprecedented concern for America's poor. Widespread abundance was not the sufficient factor for producing measures for reducing poverty and alleviating the hardships of the poor, but it was the necessary factor. Continued abundance during most of the last quarter of the century proved insufficient to sustain Americans' concern for the poor. That is an important story of its own, to be discussed in Part III.

6

Affluence

> The remarkable capacity of the United States economy in 1960 represents the cross-
> ing of a great divide in the history of humanity, especially ... in view of the fact
> that a number of other industrially advanced countries possessed similar capabili-
> ties. The full significance for all mankind lies in the possibility that poverty can be
> eliminated within the foreseeable future. "The poor are always with us" became a
> dated proposition in the 1950s.[1]
>
> Harold Vatter

The generation of Americans that endured the Great Depression gained relief
with the onset of the Second World War. War brought profound heartache for
some, but for most it brought a resounding sense of national triumph and, more
durably, a broad-based and rapidly increasing prosperity. Over the next thirty
years, the American people (and, in fact, most of the people living in the old and
the newly developing industrial nations) would experience the most sweeping
material progress in the history of the world. Within twenty years of the war's
conclusion, America's poor amounted to a small, scattered, and dwindling constituency with little evident political leverage. Even so, at precisely that time the
national government launched an effort, unprecedented in the nation's history,
to end or at least alleviate the effects of residual poverty in America.

Historically, poverty had been a mass phenomenon. In contrast, for the postwar United States – and also, by the mid-1950s, in Western Europe – it became a
problem for a dwindling minority. In 1939, about half of American households
dwelled in poverty. The war brought full employment and substantial increases
in personal income, but in 1947 a third of Americans still lived in poverty. By
1960 the figure had dropped to about one in five persons, and by 1965 to about

---

[1] Harold G. Vatter, *The U.S. Economy in the 1950s: An Economic History* (Norton, 1963), p. 1.

one in seven. In 1978 poverty affected an all-time low of about one in nine Americans and only 9 percent of U.S. families.[2] Affluence – and most particularly the rapid ascent to affluence – would be the most conspicuous general feature of American life in the third quarter of the twentieth century.

In the 25 years after 1947, real median income doubled; most American families gained more real disposable income in that period than in the country's previous 75 years. The proportion of American families with incomes substantially above the "comfortable" range increased by a factor of almost 6. In the already prosperous year of 1947, 6 percent of American families enjoyed an annual income of over $25,000 (in 1979 dollars); just thirty years later, almost 35 percent were in that income class.[3]

Even those figures showing the drop in the percentage of Americans living below "the poverty line" – nearly 50 percent in 1939, 32 percent in 1947, 20 percent in 1965, and 11 percent by the seventies – do not tell the full story, because in recognition of new standards of comfortable living the statisticians raised the poverty-line threshold by 30 percent during the two decades following the war. One can get a measure of the rising expectations from the fact that, within forty years, the median family income of 1950 would amount to no more than the real income of families near the bottom tenth of all income-earning American families. That is: by 1990, even after the economic slump of the 1970s and the growing inequality of income beginning in the 1980s, the real income of American families near the bottom tenth of all income-earning families was the equivalent of the median family income in 1950. Clearly, most Americans enjoyed a substantial rise in their living conditions and in their expectations as to what constituted a comfortable living standard.

Affluence made it possible for more Americans than ever before to afford extended formal education. The proportion of 17-year-olds earning high-school degrees rose from under 50 percent in 1939–1946 to over 75 percent by 1969–1976. By then, the proportion of persons aged 23–28 that completed at least four years of college more than doubled, while the annual number of college and postgraduate degrees more than quintupled. To look at the improved educational environment in another way, consider that in 1950 the mothers of 70 percent of the nation's children enjoyed less than a full high-school education, whereas by 1979 only 29 percent of the nation's children had such mothers. Moreover, by 1979 the mothers of almost 25 percent of American children had at least some college education, up from only 10 percent in 1950.

---

[2] U.S. Department of Commerce, Bureau of the Census, *Statistical Abstract of the United States, 1988*, p. 433.

[3] Figures taken from the U.S. Census *Statistical Abstracts*. See also Martin Feldman, ed., *The American Economy in Transition* (University of Chicago Press, 1980), ch. 6. For a less statistically laden and more popular account, see John Brooks, *The Great Leap: The Past Twenty-Five Years in America* (Harper & Row, 1966).

Taking such figures together with the stunning advances in communications and transportation, the improved education levels among individuals and in the home meant a liberation of another kind. Namely, the liberation that accompanies the opening of vistas, the charging of the imagination, and the introduction to possibilities, choices, and opportunities that once lay concealed beyond parochial horizons.

Americans in the third quarter of the twentieth century would witness dramatic gains for human freedom and dignity. That the bonds and indignities of poverty fell away for the great mass of the population was in itself one of those achievements. It contributed to others. Good times would make it easier to combat all kinds of bigotry. Religious intolerance, especially anti-Semitism, was the first to decline – helped along by Adolph Hitler, who made it unfashionable. For somewhat different reasons, anti-Catholicism, long an American blight, would all but disappear. Racism was more resistant, yet it too would abate significantly for the first time in modern history, not only in social practices but in attitudes. Women would gain emancipation from much of the gender stereotyping that for centuries had robbed them of personal, political, vocational, and economic choices and opportunities. That would have liberating effects for males as well. The greater access to education made possible by the rising affluence probably heightened Americans' humane sensitivities, although education is certainly no guarantor of either civility or humanity.

To a considerable extent, poverty is a relative matter. The living conditions of the median family in 1950 included small and even cramped housing space, modest to virtually nonexistent vacation and travel opportunities, limited expectations regarding higher education (especially in an elite private university) for themselves or their children, and limited access to modern medical technology and care. A typical family of four or more could still only hope to rent, or just possibly to own, an apartment or a house with more than two bedrooms – and almost never more than a single bath. By 1950, they would likely own one car, which was probably used and probably the first car in their immediate family. Without hand-me-downs in baby equipment, clothes, toys, and the like, the family budget would be extremely tight. A single radio, perhaps a "hi-fi" set with a phonograph turntable, a 10-inch black-and-white television, and possibly a clothes washer (but not likely a dryer) would round out most of the household "luxuries" in the family's possession. Most families that subsisted in such conditions typically considered themselves "comfortable" and belonging to the "middle class," and their position near the middle of all income-earning families justified that consideration. Forty years later, most families probably would have considered such conditions below the "comfort level" and akin to poverty.

Most of the increase in affluence for the great majority of Americans occurred during the first thirty years after the war, with the increase well under way by 1960. The dramatic reduction in the percentage of destitute households owed mostly to the rapid economic growth of the period, enabling most of the able-bodied and working poor to climb out of poverty. In fact, by 1960 many writers were commenting on how there were only "pockets of poverty" left in the country and how the prospects for further reduction of poverty seemed grim because so few suffered from it that they lacked political clout.[4] Their numbers seemed beneath general political interest. In 1956 the liberal historian Arthur Schlesinger wrote: "the central problems of our time are no longer problems of want and privation." For the future, he intimated, liberals should concentrate on improving the quality of American life.[5] As the "poverty level" was then defined, only 20 percent of Americans still lived below the line.

Yet this figure was nearly twice what it would be only twenty years later. The continued reduction in poverty owed mostly to direct government assistance to the poor that was initiated by Washington policy makers in the mid-sixties. And that is a remarkable story.

*   *   *

The postwar economic boom caught nearly everyone by surprise. A Gallup poll in January 1945 showed that nearly 70 percent of Americans expected a new depression. Economists agreed almost unanimously. The United States had known only economic decline, massive unemployment, and stagnation for ten years before the war began. Most economists had already developed elaborate theories to explain why the country – why the world's industrial nations – had reached a more or less permanent "stage" of stagnation, or at best a gently sloped plateau of slow economic growth.

One theory was that industrial nations eventually but inevitably develop productive capacity beyond the capacity of their people to consume, thereby driving prices and profits down below incentives for investment. The great wartime expansion of productive capacity in most industries, including agriculture, was expected to make things only worse at the war's end.

Then there was the sharp decline in the birth rate, a phenomenon that economic theory also associated with advanced industrial societies. Industrialization led to the increase in urban, white-collar, mercantile, and professional middle classes that valued large families less than did farming families. In the United States, the birth rate in the 1930s had declined to a point where seemingly it might soon become hardly enough to maintain the population. Meanwhile, the National Origins Immigration Act of 1924 had reduced immigration to barely a

---

[4] See e.g. John Kenneth Galbraith, *The Affluent Society* (Houghton-Mifflin, 1958); Dwight Macdonald, "Our Invisible Poor," *The New Yorker* (19 Jan. 1963), pp. 130ff; Michael Harrington, *The Other America: Poverty in the United States* (Macmillan, 1962).

[5] Arthur M. Schlesinger, Jr., "The Challenge of Abundance," *Reporter Magazine* (3 May 1956), pp. 8–11.

quarter of the pre–World War I annual flow. With population growth dwindling, the United States would have to do without the stimulus that economists figured had accounted for almost two thirds of its economic growth over the course of its history.

Finally, there was the experience of the severe recession following the First World War – and, in fact, following most major wars. American engagement in the Second World War was twice as long and far more intense. It was reasonable to assume that the trauma of the post–World War II reconversion, and absorption of nearly 12 million servicemen into the peacetime economy, would be at least as bad. Unless government did something dramatic, most experts believed, a return to something like the conditions of 1939, when 8 million Americans were unemployed, seemed inevitable.

As it turned out, instead of an economic slump the country experienced a major postwar boom. Instead of a period of high unemployment rates, 12 million men mustered out of the military while unemployment remained under 4 percent.[6] In just two years, a third of the total labor force was reallocated from war production and services into the peacetime economy. Although take-home pay for wage workers declined once the war ended, steady paychecks plus wartime savings provided an expanding market for consumer goods, reversing the trend of the prewar decade. Tax rates also declined, but federal, state, and local revenues continued to exceed those of the prewar period, providing resources for employment at regular salaries for teachers, health-care workers, and other government agency employees at all government levels. In fact, it was in health care and education, mostly supported by public revenues at the state and local levels, that employment grew the fastest for thirty years after the war. Prosperity ensued, not recession.

In the closing years of the war and for a few years thereafter, a vigorous debate raged over the need for proactive government intervention in the economy in order to avert a new depression. For years, conservatives had been arguing that the New Deal had prolonged the Depression because deficit financing of government spending for public works, for work projects to provide jobs, and for unemployment relief had demoralized the financial community. But by the middle of the war, a progressive sector of the business community implicitly conceded that the New Deal had failed to restore prosperity because *it had not spent*

---

[6] About half a million women also served in the military, but it was not expected that their demobilization would crowd the job market. Actually, the total workforce, including those in military service, declined by 5.7 million. See Robert Higgs, "From Central Planning to the Market: The American Transition, 1945–1947," *Journal of Economic History* (Sept. 1999), p. 613. In part this was due to many women dropping out of the labor market – as did many men of retirement age who had continued to work during the war – while about a million ex-servicemen delayed their entry into the workforce by taking advantage of severance pay and the GI Bill's provisions for a free college education.

enough. The newly organized Committee for Economic Development (CED), a fragment from a more conservative group of business leaders that had been formed in 1933 to "advise" the federal government, acknowledged that the magnitude of wartime spending – almost 50 percent of gross national product (GNP) by 1943 – had done the trick in two years while the comparatively puny spending of the New Deal had failed after six.[7] In the important category of new construction, for example, the increase in federal expenditures during the 1933–1939 period barely compensated for the decline in state and local government expenditures after 1929. Moreover, the net contribution of federal spending to aggregate demand during the ten years after 1929 significantly exceeded that for 1929 only in 1936.[8]

Producing military goods was the perfect public works project. Government guarantees a market, the equivalent of virtually infinite demand, and such goods quickly become obsolete. "It would indeed be more sensible to build houses and the like," wrote the English economist John Maynard Keynes in his seminal opus, *The General Theory of Employment, Interest and Money* (1936), but "political and practical difficulties [stand] in the way of this." Keynes's theory for combating recession argued for extensive government intervention in the form of reduced discount interest rates by central banks (in the United States, the Federal Reserve Bank) and lower tax rates, even if reduced revenues required deficit financing for the hefty government expenditures for public works needed to put people to work and raise consumer demand. Without increased consumer demand, fiscal and monetary stimuli would fail to inspire investment, resulting in continued high unemployment rates.

By the end of the war, many leading figures of American business and politics had come to accept *some* of the principles of Keynesianism. Leading business groups such as the CED accepted fiscal manipulation, including lower taxes (though not a steeply graduated income tax), and even deficit financing of government needs. And they no longer fought income transfers through Social Security and emergency unemployment payments. But they vigorously fought public works projects except for some sectors of the infrastructure (e.g. highways). This attitude represented a partial acceptance of Keynes, what some historians have called "commercial Keynesianism."[9] Still, in conceding that government had a

---

[7] In 1933, the Business Council was organized among the CEOs of the country's major corporations. It had semi-official status with the federal government and was given free offices within the Department of Commerce. It enjoyed official status as an agency within the Commerce Department, although Commerce officials did not attend its meetings except when invited and had no control over membership or agendas. The CED gained similar access and status after its organization in 1942. See Kim McQuaid, *Big Business and Presidential Power* (Morrow, 1982), and Robert M. Collins, *The Business Response to Keynes, 1929–1964* (Columbia University Press, 1981).

[8] J. R. Vernon, "World War II Fiscal Policies and the End of the Great Depression," *Journal of Economic History* (Dec. 1994).

[9] The term was invented by Robert Collins, *Business Response to Keynes.*

major role to play in the business economy, they effected a radical change. Left to itself, the private sector and the so-called free market could not sustain prosperity or even stability. "We require," declared Beardsley Ruml for the CED, "for success in the attack by business and government on the danger of mass unemployment a commitment on the part of government that, through an explicit fiscal and monetary policy, it will act when business ... cannot act to sustain employment and effective demand." Although by the end of the 1940s this came to seem like a stale truism, in 1945 the sentiment marked very nearly a revolution in American business thinking. "We can't afford to go into another tail spin," said Eric Johnston, president of the once die-hard antigovernment U.S. Chamber of Commerce. "We can't afford to go into another depression which would mean the loss of our system."[10]

Some policy makers urged that government intervention should be thoroughly planned so that policy reflected long-range and comprehensive growth targets chosen for their social and national security value. Conservatives, fearful of letting the government intrude on the discretionary power of private corporate employers, rejected such proposals as "the road to serfdom." For a few years beginning in 1944, Americans enjoyed a rich debate on the subject.

The easy access that big business leaders enjoyed in government circles would almost certainly have tipped the outcome of the debate against a planning policy in any case. Given the pluralistic character of the American business environment, most business leaders were averse to entrusting agencies outside the economic arena to make crucial long-term decisions that could benefit their rivals, jeopardize their market advantages, or forestall their short-term profit opportunities.

But in any event, the unexpected and swift growth of the economic pie disarmed planning advocates. This was not because the theories about the need for government economic intervention were wrong. In fact, *government resources had just about everything to do with the boom*. The experts had simply failed to reckon with some important features of the war economy and with some prewar and wartime legislation.

First, wartime employment opportunities did actually redistribute income a bit downward, that is, more favorably for lower-income groups. Lower-income families of necessity usually spend close to all of their income, thereby boosting aggregate demand. But much of the wartime income had gone into savings, because rationing of most household necessities and consumer durables had produced surpluses in home economies. War-bond campaigns, including payroll deduction plans, had induced consumers and nonbank businesses to purchase $135 billion worth of interest-bearing savings. By early 1945, demand deposits at $69 billion were three times the pre-crash 1929 total, while cash in circulation

[10] Collins, *Business Response to Keynes*, p. 102.

($25 billion) was five times that of 1929.[11] When the war ended, releasing production for consumer goods, Americans were able to go on a spending spree that more than made up for the drop in federal spending, which plummeted from $99 billion in 1945 to $36 billion in 1946 and to $28 billion in 1947. Within two years consumer spending soared by 36 percent, from $117 billion in 1945 to $159 billion in 1947.[12]

With much of their industrial capacity destroyed by the war, Europeans depended for many years on imports of U.S.-made goods. Much of this was financed by loans and grants from the U.S. government, including the $17 billion dollars spent in five years on the Marshall Plan (1948–1952). Foreign aid programs to old industrial and newly developing countries further boosted demand for billions of dollars of American farm and industrial goods. The Export-Import Bank, a New Deal agency created in 1934, helped finance exports of American goods by expediting loans to foreign purchasers. American troops stationed abroad, together with other military aid, also contributed to foreign purchasing power for U.S. goods – as did loans from the International Monetary Fund and World Bank, both of which obtained most of their capital from the United States.

Meanwhile, the U.S. government acted vigorously to correct the failure of the market to produce a stable, growing economy. Federal legislation provided outright subsidies to large staple crop producers (increasingly, agribusiness corporations) and to legalized cartels designed to control output and raise profits in the dairy industry and some parts of the fruit industries. These measures left people in those sectors of the economy with a healthy share of disposable income. For example, by 1956 a single federal agency (the Commodity Credit Corporation) had paid $8.3 billion to hold wheat surpluses off the market in order to maintain profitable market prices.[13] Similar outlays were made for cotton, peanut, corn, tobacco, and rice producers. The Soil Bank Act of 1956 would pay certain farmers for land that they withdrew from cultivation. The oil and natural gas industries were similarly subsidized by generous tax write-offs for various industrial activities, by a tax on oil imports, and by government regulations that limited output.

Furthermore, although a precipitous decline in government outlays for the military accompanied demobilization, even at their postwar low point in 1948 they remained far above prewar levels. The outbreak of the Korean War in 1950, coupled with the financial and troop commitments to the North Atlantic Treaty Organization (NATO) and to Japan and Taiwan, more than doubled those outlays as a percentage of a growing GNP by the mid-fifties. At the same time,

[11] *Fortune* (March 1945), p. 124.
[12] Stanley Lebergott, *The Americans: An Economic Record* (Norton, 1984), p. 471.
[13] Joseph Finklestein, *The American Economy* (Harlan Davidson, 1992), p. 79.

wartime federal subsidies for increasing industrial capacity had presented private corporations with capital that could now be used for the mass production of consumer goods, especially durables, craved by the enriched postwar civilian population. The government, in other words, had provided in advance much of the extra capital needed to satisfy the inflated postwar consumer demand.

Meanwhile, the generosity of a nation grateful to its military men and draftees cushioned the expected impact of demobilization on employment. First, under the terms of the Servicemen's Readjustment Act – more popularly known as "The GI Bill of Rights" – the returning servicemen received a severance allowance of $20 per week for one year at a time when two thirds of all families earned less than $75 a week; that bonus induced many to defer entry into the job market while contributing to consumer demand. More important, with financing from the GI Bill, more than a million of them entered college. By 1956 the federal government had contributed almost $15 billion to educate nearly 8 million veterans (of the 15.6 million eligible). Of that sum, $5.5 billion enabled war veterans to enter and to graduate from college.[14] The Readjustment Act also provided low-interest loans to another million veterans who needed capital to open their own businesses.

Among postwar consumer demands, housing topped the agenda because of its importance to the economy and as one of Americans' priorities for achieving the good life. The potential demand was plentiful, since an estimated 3 million families were sharing abodes in 1945. With many more millions of soldiers returning to their brides or to wed, the housing demand would balloon. To make demand effective, supply had to be made affordable.

One New Deal agency, established in 1934, almost single-handedly underwrote the postwar housing boom. Until the advent of the Federal Housing Authority (FHA, originally called the Federal Homeowners Loan Corporation), state law and construction industry practices limited loans to only 60 or 70 percent of purchase price; such loans rarely exceeded five years, often requiring balloon payments at the end of their term. The FHA insured loans made by private financial institutions to home buyers (or to builders of apartment houses) for up to 90 percent, and it arranged for amortization at low interest rates for up to 25 years. Even such favorable terms could not inspire construction of more than 45,000 new housing units per year between 1935 and 1939, because high unemployment and low incomes during the thirties meant low effective demand. The steady wartime earnings and forced savings of a fully employed workforce corrected that.

The GI Bill went the FHA one better (as they might say in Levittown): it authorized the Veterans Administration (VA) to guarantee loans made to home buyers and eliminated the FHA's 0.5-percent insurance charge. As with FHA loans, the

[14] John W. Jeffries, *Wartime America: The World War II Home Front* (Ivan E. Dee, 1996).

government agency took the risks while private lenders took the profits. In addition, "tax expenditures" by state and federal governments in the form of permitting mortgagees to deduct interest from their taxable income further promoted the housing industry. It was an ingenious way for the government to provide for housing without the threatening stigma of "socialism."

Since FHA and VA rules superseded state laws that banned out-of-state lending, they had the important effect of creating an interstate market for mortgages. That, of course, further increased the willingness of financial institutions to issue loans. Meanwhile, the Federal National Mortgage Association (FNMA, popularly known as "Fannie Mae"), created in 1938, bought and sold FHA and VA mortgages – usually in bundles to hedge against individual forfeitures. This secondary market for mortgages provided still more liquidity to lenders who sought to make more loans.[15] "In effect, by the beginning of the 1950s, the whole system of housing credit was substantially underwritten by the government."[16]

State and local governments contributed their share to the postwar suburban housing boom. They put up tax money (or sold bonds) to finance land fill or drainage, water lines, county roads, sewers, parks, schools, and other community amenities that made the new developments both attractive and feasible. Such actions served essentially as subsidies to the real-estate and construction industries – and to prospective home buyers.

Additional federal encouragement of the construction industry came in the form of the National Defense Highway Act of 1941 (and its many successors). Thus began the building of the vast interstate highway network. Who could deny that good roads were needed to facilitate the mobilization of wartime resources? Who then would object that government financing of such roads might lead to socialism? (By contrast, most of the nation's railroads had been financed, operated, and maintained by private capital seeking profits.) That good roads would increase incentives to buy automobiles, boost the oil industry, add value to suburban real estate, and make cheap land on the periphery of cities accessible for large-scale housing developers was simply taken as happy incidentals.

Alert entrepreneurs responded by applying mass production techniques to housing developments. With loans insured at low interest by the FHA, they could begin by purchasing topographically uniform tracts of low-cost land outside of cities, minimizing the need for multiple designs. Then, laying concrete slabs for the foundation instead of digging cellars, substituting plywood and sheetrock for lath and plaster, using sprays instead of brush painting, and prefabricating forms for on-site assembly, developers dramatically reduced the cost of new housing to levels well within the war-swelled means of most lower–middle-class families.

[15] See Ned Eichler, *The Merchant Builders* (MIT Press, 1982), especially ch. 1.
[16] Vatter, *U.S. Economy in the 1950s*, p. 50.

With $700 to $1,000 down and an FHA or VA loan, a family could own a home with fixed monthly payments of $45 to $55 for 25 years – during which time inflation and escalating real wages would continually reduce the real costs. For the first time (perhaps the only time) in history, the purchase of a family home did not require a lifetime of saving for persons of average income.

The most remarkable of the new builders was William Levitt, who set the standard for the industry with the first Levittown (on Long Island, New York), a wholly planned residential development. There he sold two basic unattached home styles for about $7,000 and $9,500 each. Beginning with 300 homes in 1945, Levittown would eventually have 18,000 houses accommodating 82,000 residents. The typical home was a two-bedroom, 750-square-foot cottage with a front lawn, a living room 12 × 16 feet with a picture window facing a rear garden, a single bathroom, and an all-electric kitchen including a refrigerator and Bendix washing machine. Levitt planned every detail of the community, including the cherry, apple, and evergreen trees, the nine swimming pools, sixty playgrounds, ten baseball fields, bowling alleys, curved streets, and circumferential access roads. He also donated land for churches and synagogues.

Neither the homes nor the new suburban developments as a whole satisfied the aesthetic sensibilities of most architects or lesser social critics. One popular song mocked them as "Little Boxes made of ticky-tacky / And they all look just the same."[17] Nor, in their racial and income-class uniformity, did they encourage a liberal social or urban environment. Until 1949, FHA and VA rules for qualified loans required neighborhoods to be racially homogeneous – which meant "for whites only" – ostensibly in order to protect property values underlying the loans. Levitt, who personally opposed the racism that inspired the de facto housing segregation, is supposed to have quipped: "We can solve the housing problem or the racial problem, but at this time we cannot solve both." It was a sadly accurate statement. The U.S. Supreme Court declared such rules unconstitutional in 1948.[18] But that alone did little to bring most of the benefits of the GI Bill, housing, and other measures of the rising affluence to racial minorities who continued to suffer from official and de facto discrimination, especially in the South.

Yet, for all the shortcomings, without a doubt the new suburban developments satisfied the average American's vision of Utopia – at least for a time. (Levittown-type building would soon decline when the market for low-end housing dwindled.) More than one wag remarked that the Levitt home was to housing what the Model-T car was to the auto industry. Both at least provided low- and middle-income (white) American families with significant access to the American Dream.

[17] "Little Boxes," words and music by Malvina Reynolds (Schroder Music Co., 1962).
[18] *Shelley v. Kraemer* (1948).

Annual housing starts by 1950 reached nearly 2 million units, compared to the all-time prewar high of about 1 million in the mid-twenties. There were only 600,000 housing starts in 1940 and just 325,000 in 1945. It doesn't require additional statistics to make the point that the housing boom had an enormous economic ripple effect, from the production of household appliances to utility industry growth, the furniture industry, and the construction of schools, churches, synagogues, civic centers, and roads. And since most of the new suburbs were located away from existing interurban railway lines, the automobile would increasingly become the transportation mode of necessity as well as choice. It is not hard to imagine the stimulus to the auto industry and then, of course, to the oil industry, to service stations and repair shops, and to the burgeoning recreational industries associated with travel: motels, restaurants, and resorts. Add to this the boom in the building of shopping centers and malls – all deliberately designed to serve the automobility of the suburbs by offering convenient, cost-free parking. Such shopping facilities began to appear in the country in the early 1920s when some farsighted developers anticipated the centrifugal effects of public road building, suburban housing, and the low-priced automobile. After World War II, they proliferated. In 1949 there were 70 shopping centers nationwide; by 1954 there were more than 1,000 and by 1960 nearly 4,000.[19]

Within fifteen years of the end of the war, more Americans lived in suburbs than in the cities. Decentralization of defense plants during the war contributed to the postwar spread of industrial workers outside central cities and factory towns. But the postwar construction boom accelerated the trend. By 1966, half of all industrial workers lived in the suburbs. The American penchant for detached family homes, together with their economical availability, put 65 percent of all families in their own houses by the mid-sixties; over 70 percent by the seventies. And those figures rise to 85 percent when considering two-parent families headed by a person 45 to 64 years old and to 75 percent for families headed by a wage earner belonging to the AFL-CIO. "The labor movement," commented Walter Reuther, president of the United Automobile Workers, "is developing a whole new middle class."[20] No proletariat ever had it so good.

No matter that to own such homes sometimes required living even an hour or more from one's place of work, though the typical commute time was fifteen minutes each way. For most Americans by mid-century, the job in any event had ceased to define one's way of life. Some professionals, business proprietors,

---

[19] Paul William Davies, "American Agora: *Pruneyard v. Robins* and The Shopping Mall in the United States," Ph.D. dissertation, Department of History, University of California, Berkeley (2001), contains a comprehensive account of the development of shopping centers as well as a historiographical survey. There were a few shopping centers built as early as 1907 before the automobile became commonplace. After World War II, accommodation for cars dictated design.

[20] David Brody, *Workers in Industrial America* (Oxford University Press, 1980), p. 192.

entrepreneurs, and high corporate executives probably continued to view themselves in terms of their work, as did most artists, intellectuals, and many small farmers. But more broadly, in the modern industrial society one's job had long become simply a way to make a living, a means to the enjoyment of life that centered on the home and recreation. The government had made good roads nearly ubiquitous and nearly always free, while the banks and auto companies made car purchases seemingly painless via long-term monthly installment plans. Auto production soared from 2 million in 1946 to 8 million by 1955. As early as 1950, 60 percent of American households already owned a car and 7 percent owned two cars; within 25 years, 85 percent owned a car and nearly half of American households owned two. Commuting as much as two hours a day, a suburbanite could remain insulated in his own private space, a kind of portable piece of home.

Of all the innovations produced by technology since the beginning of the Industrial Revolution in the eighteenth century, the automobile unquestionably had the most liberating effect for the most people. A later generation would fret over pollution and traffic gridlock – and perhaps over the corruption and the miserly tax resistance that impeded the building of effective mass transit facilities that might have served to abate both pollution and traffic jams. But there should be little doubt about the enlarged horizons, the enhanced personal freedom, the broader access to jobs, and the immeasurably greater recreational opportunities that the privately owned automobile provided for the great mass of people.

Wartime government policies also had much to do with bolstering the labor unions and thus in furthering the widespread growth of real income. In order to achieve maximum industrial tranquility, Washington had encouraged a trade-off arrangement with the unions and business management. In exchange for a no-strike pledge, the unions received management's pledge that it would not interfere with the "maintenance of union membership." The unions did more than maintain their prewar membership. With 9 million members in 1940 (29 percent of the nonagricultural workforce), organized labor could boast of growing to nearly 15 million members in 1945, on the way to its all-time high of 17.5 million (36 percent) in the mid-fifties. Because unionized workers resist declining real income more effectively than do the unorganized, their postwar strength, especially in manufacturing, had much to do with maintaining a flow of purchasing power into the low- and middle-income ranks of the society. This helped significantly to sustain consumer demand. And after 1945, paid vacations became standard in many union contracts, boosting the fast-growing travel and recreation industries.

To cap the postwar economic effect of wartime savings and government stimuli, Americans began having children again as they hadn't done in more than half a century. The return of affluence made having children economically manageable, and more than two children per family became positively fashionable.

By 1947, the American birthrate jumped to a pace 25 percent higher than for the twelve years preceding the war, and it would remain at that level for another twelve years or so.[21] The so-called Baby Boom contributed to the postwar prosperity by providing a growing market not only for all the products traditionally associated with infancy and growing up but also for a plethora of new gadgets, toys, conveniences, and comforts produced to fit the fashionable preoccupation with children and child-rearing. Children's goods, moreover (like military goods), are highly destructible and quickly become obsolete, and this obsolescence accelerated as the tradition of hand-me-downs faded among young upwardly mobile parents in the increasingly affluent U.S. society.

Manufacturers, merchandisers, and investors did not miss the certainty of a dramatically expanding demand for products that were needed, or merely wanted, by young people. That fact put a commercial premium on "the youth market," where "youth" meant not those in early adulthood but rather those still in their teens (or younger). The commercial appeal to adolescents would help to transform the culture. Perhaps for the first time in history, being young and remaining young – that is, maintaining the lifestyle of a teenager – was valued distinctly above achieving "maturity." Rabbit Angstrom, John Updike's character in *Rabbit Run* (1960), plainly spoke for millions when he tells his friend how he has no desire to be mature because "as far as I can make out, it's the same thing as being dead."[22] Until the 1950s, children dressed and at least outwardly comported themselves as adults as early as possible. Beginning in the late 1950s, adults dressed and behaved as children for as long as appeared seemly and sometimes longer.[23] It is part of the story of the rebellious Sixties.

Finally, postwar expenditures for national defense pumped billions of government dollars into the economy. Continuation of the military draft (except for 1947–1949) relieved the job market of 1.5 to 3 million young men annually who were paid substantially more than the New Deal had disbursed to the unemployed. Even at its lowest point in the late forties, defense spending came to more than 5 percent of GNP, or about what it was in the late 1970s. By the early 1950s it exceeded 13 percent. As President Eisenhower told the public in his farewell address of January 1961, "We annually spend on military security more than the

---

[21] From 19.4 per 1,000 population in 1940 and 20.4 in 1945 to 24.1 in 1946 and peaking at 26.6 in 1947; then remaining at about 25 per 1,000 until 1961, when it began a sharp decline. Figures from the annual *Statistical Abstract of the United States*.

[22] John Updike, *Rabbit Run* (Fawcett, 1960), p. 91. Charles Reich, author of the best-selling *The Greening of America* (Random House, 1970), later reminisced of his own resistance in the fifties to "growing up": "Being 'adult' meant ... no more hope of excitement, no more fun." *The Sorcerer of Bolinas Reef* (Random House, 1975), quoted in Barbara Ehrenreich, *Hearts of Men: American Dreams and the Flight from Commitment* (Anchor, 1983), pp. 109–10.

[23] "We can all remember the 1960s when it was widely regarded as almost shameful to be an adult." Lawrence Stone, in the *New York Review of Books* (20 Sept. 1981), p. 13.

net income of all United States corporations." When military spending began declining after 1955, federal appropriations for defense-related space research and for construction of 41,000 miles of "interstate and defense highways" – costing over $100 billion in ten years – made up for most of the decline. This was no coincidence. By the mid-fifties, even the conservative and big-business–oriented Eisenhower administration recognized the need for a Keynesian response to impending recession; hence the federal appropriations for public works.

One additional factor may be considered, a factor that some conservative "free market" economists insist is most important of all. That is the restoration of confidence among business leaders that opportunities for profits would grow unhindered by either an unfavorable political climate or militant labor union activity. According to the conservative argument, business confidence rebounded from the slough of the Depression years when Roosevelt's wartime government brought in corporate executives to run most of the war-mobilized economy. With such friendly hands on the economic controls, investors could look forward to exploiting profit opportunities while the meddlesome New Dealers sat on the back benches. The same influence in Washington contributed to rapid demobilization and lower taxes immediately following Japan's surrender. The Republican congressional victory in November 1946 added more friendly influences, leading to still lower taxes and to the management-friendly, anti-union Taft–Hartley Act of 1947. Expectations of a favorable business climate thus led to a boom in investment. And according to economists who emphasize the supply side of economic behavior, it was investment, not consumer demand, that was the key to postwar prosperity.[24]

The argument has some merit, but its main thrust must be taken as an article of faith. The point about corporate executives gaining control of government levers during and after the war is well taken. Secretary of War Henry Stimson remarked about the recruitment of top business leaders into the government during the war: "If you are going to try to go to war, or prepare for war, in a capitalist country, you have to let business make money out of the process or business won't work."[25] The point about the importance of an environment of favorable expectations by businessmen about profit opportunities also deserves attention. But even granting the reassuring effect of a business-friendly federal government, it is fair to question whether a New Deal–type administration that might have imposed higher taxes on corporations and the wealthy while maintaining an environment conducive to a more successful labor union movement

[24] See e.g. Higgs, "The American Transition," pp. 600–23.

[25] Stuart D. Brandes, *Warhogs: A History of War Profits in America* (University of Kentucky Press, 1997); R. M. Abrams, "You Have to Let Business Make Money," *Reviews in American History* (June 1998), pp. 428–33.

would have forestalled efforts by private enterprise to exploit the profit opportunities of satisfying the massive postwar demand for consumer goods. That is to say, the evidence would appear to demonstrate that the demand pull was far more important to investors than release from some disincentives for supply. Moreover, the "free market" argument conspicuously omits consideration of the obvious role of government subsidies and tax incentives in augmenting consumer demand, which produced most of the profit opportunities under consideration.

That the prosperity continued apace during the ostensibly less friendly Kennedy and Johnson administrations suggests again the prime importance of the demand factor, although it is important to note that Kennedy's proposed investment tax credit – followed by a reduction in corporate taxes by 1964 – fit well with the "supply side" economic textbook. Liberal administrations, including the New Deal, never neglected supply-side policies (i.e., investment incentives) when attempting to maintain consumer demand.[26]

However one views it, the ripple effect of defense spending, government subsidies, foreign exports, and the housing, automobile, and baby booms, along with a confident business environment, catapulted postwar society into an astounding level of affluence. America had always been, relatively, a wealthy country. Even so, the emergence of the mass of the society from poverty and modest means to opulence within less than a generation was a radical event.

The general prosperity that was fueled by federal and state expenditures (subsidies) of various kinds that promoted the construction boom, a growing export market, and defense procurement accounted for most of the decline in poverty during the first fifteen postwar years. But in 1960 there remained in poverty millions of Americans for whom job opportunities remained slim or nonexistent and thus for whom the opportunity to rise from their condition of need remained elusive.

They included a widely disparate group of people. There were first of all the unemployables: mentally and physically disabled or ailing individuals. Second, there were the virtually unemployable people who were uneducated or under-educated and without basic tools for job seeking. Third, there were millions of workers without the skills that could earn them a living wage or who had little access to personal or family contacts that could put them in touch with good job opportunities. Fourth, there were the victims of racism, who made up outsized proportions of the second and third categories. Fifth, there were millions of single mothers for whom full-time employment was unfeasible even if they had employable skills, as many did not. And there were countless numbers of

---

[26] So-called conservative administrations, at least in the last quarter of the twentieth century, rarely showed such balance.

children who were born into such impoverished households. Finally, there were retirees who were not covered by Social Security or other pension plans or for whom retirement pay left them impoverished.

Meanwhile, by the end of the 1950s, millions of workers in both agriculture and manufacturing were forced from jobs by technological changes and growing foreign competition. Many lacked skills to move to other employment that paid a living wage. The changes affected especially farm areas where machines and chemicals raised productivity at three and four times the national rate. The displaced families were forced to migrate to the cities where, contrary to their hopes, above–poverty-level jobs were in short supply. They made up a substantial army of American workers who earned less than a living wage. A great many of the migrants were Southern Negroes who met a wall of racial discrimination that made them all but unemployable in their new urban abodes except at less-than-subsistence wages.

There was, in short, a "hard core" of poverty-stricken Americans for whom the indirect effects of economic growth did not and could not improve their condition. As the Council of Economic Advisors concluded in its 1964 Report to the President: "in the future, economic growth alone will provide relatively fewer escapes from poverty."[27] Public policy would have to devise more direct subsidies, such as were offered to certain farmers, exporters, oil producers, and the like. To alleviate the destitution of the "hard core" required a government program something like those in major European countries that could provide the poor, in cash or in kind, with a minimally comfortable income.

As of 1960, that seemed improbable. Taking on the elimination or reduction of poverty as a political cause in the United States entailed great risks. The poor provided office seekers with no effective constituency. They were a diverse and scattered part of the population and a tiny, mostly ineffectual part of the electorate. As the Harvard economist John Kenneth Galbraith noted in 1958 in his best-selling book, *The Affluent Society,* "Any politician who speaks for the very poor is speaking for a small and also inarticulate minority."[28]

On top of that, historically most Americans held firmly and longer than people in other industrial countries to the view that low status and poverty expressed moral flaws, "the penalty for and the proof of personal failure."[29] After all, America was the land of opportunity. If people could not make it in America, it had to be because they did not put effort into supporting themselves and their families. To be sure, widows and orphans and the disabled deserved some consideration,

[27] James T. Patterson, *America's Struggle against Poverty, 1900–1980* (Harvard University Press, 1981), p. 112.
[28] Galbraith, *The Affluent Society*, p. 328.
[29] David Potter, *People of Plenty: Economic Abundance and the American Character* (University of Chicago Press, 1954), p. 105.

but these were *marginal* problems and in any case should be the responsibility of family or friends, not of government. Since most Americans implicitly believed that vertical mobility to higher income strata was readily achievable, they assumed that for nonmarginal Americans poverty was a temporary problem and therefore not interesting; to probe it was to suggest that America was not America. For most Americans in the 1940s and 1950s, the belief in poverty's temporary nature seemed validated by having personally experienced their own dramatic rise to affluence in those years.

Contemporary polls showed some ambiguity in American attitudes, though evidently it was the phrasing of the questions that evoked the seemingly contradictory responses. Most answered that it was proper to aid "the needy." But to regard "the poor" as deserving of government largesse was widely viewed as un-American. In postwar, Cold War America, "un-American" took on the quality of being soft on communism. To make poverty a political issue ran the risk of playing into the hands of the communists at home and abroad by highlighting some things that might be wrong with America and with capitalism. In 1956, when a few political leaders dared to mention that poverty remained a problem for millions of Americans, Vice-President Richard Nixon called it "grist for the communist propaganda mill."[30]

Despite all these adverse factors, the 1960s would witness an unprecedented assault on poverty by the national government. Contrary to the expectations of "experts" and the political risks that were forecast, poverty did become a political issue. It would give rise to federal programs that within fifteen years helped to reduce the percentage of Americans suffering from poverty by still another 45 percent below the 1960's level.

The War on Poverty contained numerous parts. The Economic Opportunity Act of 1964 created the Office for Economic Opportunity;[31] a Job Corps (to make teenagers employable); a Neighborhood Youth Corps (to provide training and work experience for adolescent students and dropouts); a Manpower Development and Training Act (to retrain displaced workers); Head Start (to

---

[30] Quoted in Carl M. Brauer, "Kennedy, Johnson and the War on Poverty," *Journal of American History* (June 1982), pp. 95–119.

[31] The preamble to the Act read as follows: "Although the economic well-being and prosperity of the United States have progressed to a level surpassing any achieved in world history, and although these benefits are widely shared throughout the Nation, poverty continues to be the lot of a substantial number of our people. The United States can achieve its full economic and social potential as a nation only if every individual has the opportunity to contribute to the full extent of his capabilities and to participate in the workings of our society. It is, therefore, the policy of this Nation to eliminate the paradox of poverty in the midst of plenty in this Nation by opening to everyone the opportunity for education and training, the opportunity to work, and the opportunity to live in decency and dignity. It is the purpose of the Act to strengthen, support, and coordinate efforts in furtherance of that policy."

provide preschool education, especially for children of impoverished and under-educated families); Upward Bound (for talented but underperforming teenagers to prepare for college); free school lunches (especially for impoverished school districts); food stamps (to supplement the budgets of the poor and also to help subsidize agriculture); and legal services (to make litigation available to the great mass of the public that cannot afford legal fees). Amendments to the Social Security Act added Medicaid and neighborhood healthcare centers (medical services for the poor of any age) as well as Medicare (guaranteeing medical services for the aged as an extension of Social Security). Social Security benefits were significantly increased, to which Congress in 1975 added an automatic escalating cost-of-living provision. The Supplemental Security Income Act of 1974 added benefits for the elderly disabled, blind, and destitute. Thereafter, Americans covered by the Social Security system could generally look forward to comfortable levels of disposable income in their retirement. It had the dual purpose of rewarding people for a lifetime of labor and of sustaining overall demand for consumer goods in an economy of continually growing productivity.

By the mid-seventies, the proportion of Americans living in poverty shrank dramatically in spite of the increasing percentage of Americans over the age of 65 and jobless because of frailties or forced retirement and despite the high birthrate among low-income immigrant families. The continuing growth of the economy contributed to probably no more than half of the progress in reducing poverty. Although the postwar economic boom had, by 1960, reduced the incidence of poverty as a continuing problem to barely one in five Americans, the War on Poverty declared by President Lyndon Johnson during in his first State of the Union Address in January 1964 must be credited with further reducing the proportion of Americans living below the poverty line to the 11 percent low reached by the mid-1970s. Transfer payments, in cash and in kind, to Americans with sub–poverty-level incomes helped critically in reducing the suffering of the poor. Without greatly increased Social Security benefits, aid to families with dependent children (AFDC), unemployment and disability payments, food stamps, scholarships, Medicare, Medicaid, and other direct or in-kind payments, the entire bottom third of income recipients would have subsisted at or below the poverty level.

The direct attack on the existence of poverty in America was unprecedented in the country's political history. How did this happen? For many contemporaries, it seemed to come from out of the blue. When poverty was "rediscovered" after 1960, many scholars remarked on how little anyone knew about the phenomenon. There were few statistics and few scholarly studies. The Labor Department had not begun to collect unemployment statistics until the disastrous 1930s, and it had never collected systematic data on poverty. The government needed data on the unemployed mostly to know how much to appropriate for the emergency relief programs. In the thirties, joblessness and impoverishment became so widespread that it was commonplace for people to remark – then and while reminiscing later – that they didn't feel poor "because everyone was poor." But studying unemployment in the thirties did not shed much light on the problem of "core poverty." As one sociologist complained: "During the 1940s, the 1950s, and the first few years of the 1960s, the topic of poverty was virtually nonexistent in the sociological literature." The sociologist Daniel Bell recalled that, "[w]hen the poverty issue arose, nobody was really prepared, nobody had any data, nobody knew what to do."[32] "The words 'poverty' and 'poor' were not parts of the public language," wrote sociologist Hylan Lewis of the years immediately preceding the War on Poverty.[33]

Why did the poverty issue arise when it did? *Why, in the midst of a booming prosperity that had already reduced poverty to historically unprecedented levels, should poverty have become a major political issue?* Or, to ask the question political scientists and pundits would inevitably pose: Where was the voting constituency for such an issue?

The scattered poor had diverse interests and no organization. They made up a part of America that was politically easy to overlook. In 1962 Walter Heller, chairman of the Council of Economic Advisors, told President Kennedy that "[c]ontemporary poverty, to the extent it is peculiarly associated with nonwhite color, widowhood, old age, etc. – may be harder to overcome than the more generalized poverty of earlier generations."[34] Although they were a minority of the population, there were millions more Americans enduring poverty than there were farmers and millions more than there were labor union members, but they had no Farm Bureau or AFL/CIO to lobby for their interests in Congress. There were millions more of them than the combined population of at least a dozen states, but most of the poor did not live in those states, whose senators spoke for relatively well-subsidized interests. Mostly uneducated or undereducated, the poor had little ability to articulate their predicaments. Nor did a great many of them have the ability or inspiration even to vote.

What then inspired first John F. Kennedy and then Lyndon Johnson to take up the issue of poverty and promote the first national programs designed specifically to alleviate the problem? If the constituency was as small and scattered as liberal economists such as Galbraith had noted, what was there in the particular circumstances of the time that led political leaders to elevate the welfare of the poor to central national attention?

---

[32] Quotations from Patterson, *Struggle against Poverty*, p. 78.
[33] Quoted in Alice O'Connor, *Poverty Knowledge: Social Science, Social Policy, and the Poor in Twentieth-Century U.S. History* (Princeton University Press, 2001), p. 139.
[34] Quoted in Brauer, "War on Poverty," p. 105.

Part of the answer lies in the effect of affluence itself. Affluence helped to sensitize modern America to the problem of the harder core of poverty. This did not happen right away. The rapid rise to prosperity in the postwar period made it easy for most Americans to ignore the poor. As one historian has written: "Concern with poverty seemed remote and almost antiquarian during the war and postwar years."[35] Moreover, before the Sixties, the conventional association of poverty with immigrants and racial minorities had enabled most white Americans to relegate the problem to a corner of their mind. It was taken for granted that such people would be poor. In fact, the popular association of the poor with indigent blacks – and particularly with the rising and increasingly visible numbers of unmarried Negro mothers and jobless Negro males newly migrating to cities outside the South – first hardened opposition to public assistance generally. But then the civil rights movement, picking up momentum by 1960 on the strength of a rapid-fire series of Supreme Court decisions and a general sense of good will engendered by affluence, would make unacceptable the presumption that racial minorities were and would always be poor and thus unworthy of attention. The civil rights movement forced Americans to reconsider what they customarily took for granted.

Some of the same factors that inspired popular opposition to expanding welfare programs also served proponents of such programs. Although communist-baiting conservatives deplored attention to poverty in America because it might provide ammunition for Moscow in the competition for favor – especially in the so-called Third World countries – the obverse argument would also be made: Poverty in America could not be kept a secret, and unless public policy vigorously addressed the problem it would prove to be an embarrassment and a handicap in that very competition.

The thousands of southern poor who were forced by the postwar agricultural revolution[36] to migrate from the rural South into mostly northern and western cities put enormous pressure on urban welfare agencies. Although a majority of the migrants were white, it was the higher visibility of blacks and their concentration in a few cities that drew the most attention. Deep-seated racial prejudices mobilized white locals against extending assistance to the newcomers while those same prejudices blocked their employment. But liberal judges entrenched in federal courts beginning in 1960 ruled that assistance could not be denied to Americans merely on the basis of recent residency. In a sense, the issue was joined and awaited political response. The migration of the southern poor was a national problem and demanded national attention.

---

[35] Walter I. Trattner, *From Poor Law to Welfare State,* 2nd ed. (Free Press, 1979), p. 246.
[36] Agricultural productivity rose substantially faster than that in any other sector of the U.S. economy.

Although in an important sense the issue was triggered by its racial element, it was the agitation among white Americans that public policy first attended to. This was true in two senses. First, national input into urban welfare resources was needed to help allay concerns about the local costs to the mostly white natives of assisting the poor. Second, it was during the 1960 presidential campaign that the ultimately successful Democratic candidate, John F. Kennedy, first took notice of poverty as a serious American problem when he encountered it not in Harlem or South Chicago but in the virtually all-white, depressed coal-mining towns of West Virginia where Kennedy was campaigning for the state's delegates to the Democratic national convention.

Two major initiatives of the Kennedy administration indirectly gave further impetus to the emerging poverty issue. First, responding to a minor recession in 1960–1961 and fear of a recurrence in 1964, his administration pushed through a major tax cut that of course most benefited businesses and individuals with substantial incomes. Second, in response to the swelling movement for civil rights, Kennedy proposed in the spring of 1963 sweeping legislation against racial discrimination, a proposal that would materialize after his death in the Civil Rights Act of 1964. With these things in mind, some of Kennedy's advisors urged initiatives that would aid the poor, most of whom were white. They argued that, for political if not more worthy reasons, measures to alleviate poverty would offer "balance" to the measures that benefited the nation's well-to-do and the nation's racial minorities.

But there was nothing inevitable about such political considerations. "Balance" on behalf of a politically ineffectual constituency has not always been a policy choice. There were, however, a significant number of individuals in government with predispositions toward a social justice that included some redistribution of the society's resources. The growth of the federal government during the New Deal's struggles with the Depression as well as during the war had placed substantial numbers of social workers and liberal-minded economists in government agencies. From their bastions in the bureaucracy, they had access to policy makers in the executive and legislative branches of the government. Congress, too, had many socially minded members as yet uncorrupted by the need for massive campaign funds from rich special-interest clients.

In the 1950s, there had been a few efforts by some political leaders to legislate assistance for the nation's poor – most notably by Democratic Senator Paul Douglas, an internationally respected economist from Illinois. Douglas had sought legislation to "redevelop" rural and urban areas of the country that had fallen on hard times as changing technology and trade patterns undermined regional economies. But Douglas and his allies had made no progress against the alliance of Republicans and conservative Southern Democrats that dominated Congress during both the Truman and Eisenhower administrations.

By 1960, however, it was becoming clear that the Southern Democratic hold on the national party had weakened. Harry Truman had won the presidency in 1948 despite a three-way split in the Democratic party that included desertion of four of the eleven states of the Old South to "Dixiecrat" candidate Strom Thurmond of South Carolina. In the 1952 and 1956 presidential elections, several southern states broke ranks again to give their electoral votes to Republican Dwight Eisenhower. The Southern Democrats could continue to dominate the Congress, but if they hoped to enjoy the patronage of a Democrat in the White House then they would have to tolerate policies that had more national appeal than the southerners' race-based politics.

Meanwhile, the pain of poverty became all the greater for its increasing rarity and the inescapable awareness of its contrast with the general prosperity. "The reality of the new poverty," Michael Harrington wrote in 1965, "lies in its contrast to U.S. affluence, and it is heightened by the constant, often self-congratulatory talk about that affluence."[37] Harrington's 1962 book, *The Other America*, had helped bring hard-core poverty to the country's attention – in particular, to President Kennedy (who read perhaps only Dwight Macdonald's provocative and widely cited review in *The New Yorker*).[38] This apparently had a great influence on Kennedy. Access to television (over 90 percent of the poor owned TV sets by 1960) as well as the increased mobility of the population made the poor more conscious of their excluded condition. No longer was "everyone" poor. As the renowned Berkeley economist Robert Aaron Gordon wrote in 1965, a year in which poverty had already been made a major issue in the nation's politics: "I think it is fair to say that the outstanding fact about the problem of poverty in the U.S. today is our increased sensitivity to it. There is nothing new about poverty, it has always been with us. And by almost any criterion, there is less of it now than there was 25 or 50 or 100 years ago." But now, he added, "the taste of poverty is more bitter."[39]

And it was bitter not only for those who suffered poverty but also for the affluent who witnessed it. It may be too much to argue that the well-off on the whole became afflicted by pangs of conscience, but a great many Americans plainly became more receptive to notions of social responsibility: more responsive than most preceding generations and certainly more than the generations that followed. What is indeed a remarkable fact about American politics in the 1960s is the astonishing level of generosity shown by at least a decisively large minority of Americans during that decade in supporting – or at least not

[37] Patterson, *Struggle against Poverty,* p. 114.
[38] Macdonald, "Our Invisible Poor."
[39] R. A. Gordon, "An Economist's View of Poverty," in Margaret S. Gordon, ed., *Poverty in America* (Chandler, 1965), p. 3.

opposing – governmental measures that extended massive aid to the smaller minority of the poor, the underprivileged, the handicapped, the unlucky, and the historically oppressed. Although one survey in 1969 showed that 80 percent of Americans polled thought that "too many" (not defined) of the recipients "ought to be working," a remarkable 34 percent agreed with the statement: "Generally speaking, we are spending too *little* money on welfare in this country."[40]

The widespread benevolent spirit that bloomed in the Sixties did not come from some kind of mass spiritual conversion. But it is reasonable to infer that it owed much to an unaccustomed sense of plenitude that encouraged a non–zero-sum mindset – that is, a belief that one did not have to surrender anything important in order to contribute something to someone else. Nor were the architects of the poverty programs unaware of the opportunities, and the obligations, that economic growth presented. "Prosperity," wrote Walter Heller in 1966, "extends economic freedom, creating jobs, and enabling a President to battle the tyranny of poverty for some without wrenching resources away from others." Heller went on to say that "[p]rosperity adds economic rights to civil rights."[41] Americans eventually would, on the whole, reject Heller's remark about "rights," but for those in government who urged the poverty programs on Congress and the American people, it represented a genuinely held conviction that played a major role in their daring to face down the political risks.

In that respect, nothing is more important for explaining the attack on poverty in the 1960s than the role of what has to be called an activist elite. Unlike the civil rights movement after the mid-fifties, there was no mass agitation for an antipoverty program of any kind. Reform came not from a grassroots movement, but from the top. As one meticulous chronicler of the War on Poverty wrote, major legislation to assist the poor, such as the Economic Opportunity Act of 1964, "was the creation of the Executive Branch with little involvement of the Congress or outside constituencies like civil rights groups or the labor movement."[42]

And no individual was more important in the initiatives from the top than President Lyndon Johnson, nothing more important than Johnson's personal desire to crown his own political career by following up the work of Franklin Roosevelt thirty years earlier in alleviating the privations of those stricken by economic hardship. Like his economic advisor Walter Heller, Johnson understood

---

[40] Patterson, *Struggle against Poverty*, p. 172. When looking for signs of "generosity" in human behavior in the mass, one should never expect to find it among a majority. In any case, in politics especially, an informed or aware minority can be decisive in producing or supporting policy changes.

[41] Walter W. Heller, *New Dimensions of Political Economy* (Harvard University Press, 1966), p. 13.

[42] Robert F. Clark, *The War on Poverty: History, Selected Programs and Ongoing Impact* (University Press of America, 2002), p. 28.

the responsibility of leaders to lead, to educate, and to activate values that people avowed but neglected to act on from apathy, ignorance, preoccupation, or simple self-interest. Not well schooled himself, Johnson nevertheless understood the principle that, as one political scientist put it: "Political leadership and other such infrequent occurrences can perform a reconstitutive teaching function that may greatly alter the scope of what is feasible politically."[43]

Whatever the man's flaws as an individual or a politician, there should be no doubt about Lyndon Johnson's genuine commitment to "doing good." And in his mind, doing something for the nation's poor had high priority. His concern reflected his personal and political background, having experienced a measure of poverty as a youth in rural Texas during the Great Depression. For Johnson, Franklin Roosevelt had been a political idol and the New Deal a model beginning for a liberal future. "Some men want power," he told one young biographer, "simply to strut around the world and to hear the tune of 'Hail to the Chief.' Others want it simply to build prestige, to collect antiques, and to buy pretty things. Well, I wanted power to give things to people – all sorts of things to all sorts of people, especially the poor and the blacks."[44] Although Lyndon Johnson could be cynical, crude, and disingenuous, most of his biographers have credited that self-appraisal as basically true.

It helped that Johnson's martyred predecessor had already prepared to make poverty in America an issue in anticipation of the 1964 campaign. The assassination lent extraordinary weight to measures associated with Kennedy, giving them political momentum that it is unlikely they would have enjoyed had Kennedy lived. Johnson felt strongly that he should follow up on Kennedy's initiatives. And probably nothing interested him more keenly than the poverty issue. Shortly after he took office, Johnson told some friends at dinner, "I have to carry out the Kennedy legacy. I feel very strongly that that's part of my obligation." "So," one of the friends present at the time related, "he came to this poverty program – making it nationwide." "That's my kind of program," Johnson said to Walter Heller around the same time. "We should push ahead full tilt on this project."[45]

Some students of the issue prefer to emphasize the great urban riots that burst forth in the mid-sixties. A remarkably accelerated increase in AFDC disbursements began in 1964 and would continue to rise for most of the next decade. In this view, the War on Poverty was inspired by fear of social disorder, and particularly what some radical sociologists called "the increasing political trouble

[43] Hugh Heclo, "The Political Foundations of Antipoverty Policy," in Sheldon H. Danziger & Daniel H. Weinberg, eds., *Fighting Poverty* (Harvard University Press, 1986), p. 312.

[44] Robert Dallek, *Flawed Giant: Lyndon Johnson and His Times* (Oxford University Press, 1998), p. 6, citing Doris Kearns, *Lyndon Johnson and the American Dream* (New American Library, 1977). See also Kearns, pp. 192ff.

[45] Dallek, *Flawed Giant*, p. 61.

caused by blacks."[46] The interpretation is common among those who find reforms in a capitalist society in general (and welfare programs in particular) to be primarily "instruments of social control." But there appears to be little evidence in the diaries, memoirs, or communications among the policy makers that historians have so far culled indicating that the so-called ghetto wars ever came up directly in conjunction with the antipoverty programs that were developed.[47]

In sum: Poverty became a major political issue in the 1960s – in the midst of the country's greatest increase and broadest spread of wealth ever experienced and despite the absence of a significant political constituency that demanded reform – as numerous, mostly unrelated developments came together. Among them were (a) a general good-spiritedness and a generous, non–zero-sum popular mindset, both arising from the unprecedented onset of abundance; (b) demographic changes that put pressure on urban welfare resources, thereby calling attention nationally to the problem of poverty; (c) the civil rights movement, which put to an end Americans' customary dismissal of poverty as something that racial minorities "naturally" endured; (d) a broad-based increase in sensitivity to the plight of the poor that was a by-product of the very affluence sweeping the country during the postwar period, along with a readiness (or at least a passive willingness) to use public revenues to do something about poverty; (e) a significant sector of the national bureaucracy, developed during the struggle against the Great Depression, that was in place and prepared to promote reform from within the government; (f) the fortuitous control of the presidency at this historical junction by a person with a genuine commitment to attacking poverty head-on while the nation's political conservatives foundered in disarray; and (g) the historical accident of an assassination that lent sympathetic force to reforms with which the martyred president had been associated.

✳   ✳   ✳

The story of the last quarter of the twentieth century, however, presents a sharply different scene. That difference underlines the vital importance of top-down leadership.

Between 1980 and 1986, the percentage of American families living beneath the poverty line rapidly increased by over 40 percent, reaching almost one in six, or about 16 percent. It then stabilized at slightly below that level, even during the sustained prosperity of the 1990s, although by some calculations it dropped again to about 12 percent by the year 2000. At the same time, the gap between

---

[46] Frances Fox Piven & Richard A. Cloward, *Regulating the Poor: The Functions of Public Welfare* (Vintage, 1971), p. 222, see also pp. 185ff. Actually, the Watts riot, usually referred to as the first of the major urban disturbances of the Sixties, did not erupt until 1965.

[47] Cf. Patterson, *Struggle against Poverty*, p. 163; Danziger & Weinberg, *Fighting Poverty*, pp. 298ff; Brauer, "War on Poverty."

the well-off and the working and nonworking poor grew to levels unmatched since the early part of the century. From 1947 to 1980, the relative shares of the nation's income enjoyed by the top 5 percent and by the bottom 40 percent of American families had remained about the same, with the share of the top 5 percent actually dipping slightly. But within ten years, beginning in 1981, the share of the nation's income received by the richest 5 percent soared from 15 percent to over 20 percent – a 33-percent gain – while the share of the poorest 40 percent of American families dropped from 17 percent to 14 percent.[48] To the further disadvantage of the poor, between 1974 and 1987 the median rent for low-income renters rose by 49 percent (compared with only 16 percent for all renters). Five years later, conditions were no better. A 1992 report of the General Accounting Office, the independent research agency of Congress, reported: "Rising costs, declining real wages, and a decreasing number of affordable homes have put a decent place to live beyond the reach of millions of families."[49]

Furthermore, statistics on family income include cash transfer (welfare) payments to lower-income families, but they omit income for the well-to-do from capital gains as well as the implied income of health benefits that are typically enjoyed proportionately more by those families in the "comfortable" to upper income brackets. If such capital gains and benefits were included, the gap between the richest 5 percent and the poorest 40 percent would widen significantly.

More important than the changes in the *shares* of total income received by families and households[50] was the drop in real income, or spending power, for those in the lower quintiles. After 1979, according to U.S. Labor Department figures issued in 1995,[51] the poorest 20 percent of American households suffered a 9-percent decline in real income and the second-poorest 20 percent suffered a 2-percent decline. In the same period, the richest 20 percent of American households enjoyed a 26-percent gain in real income, with most of the gain going to the top 5 percent.[52]

---

[48] Figures taken from Paul Ryscavage, *Income Inequality in America: An Analysis of Trends* (M.E. Sharpe, 1999), and the U.S. Census *Annual Demographic Survey,* among other sources.

[49] Housing and Development Report (23 July 1990), vol. 18, no. 10, p. 178, cited by David Erickson, unpublished paper. GAO report, "Housing and Community Development Issues," cited in David Erickson, "Community Capitalism," Ph.D. dissertation, Department of History, University of California, Berkeley, ch. 5.

[50] "Households" are defined as two or more related individuals living together (families) plus individuals who live alone or who reside with nonrelated persons. The Census began keeping separate data on "households" in 1967 when it became apparent that an increasingly large number of older and young individuals were not residing with families for the simple reason that, especially beginning in the Sixties, two- and more-earner families had become commonplace while more young people (e.g., college students) and elderly (widows, widowers, retirees) were living on their own, typically with low incomes.

[51] Cited in *New York Times* (9 Jan. 1997), p. 10.

[52] Similar figures appear in U.S. Census: Housing and Household Economic Statistics Division, Historical Income Tables – Families, Revised (13 May 2005).

To be sure, being poor wasn't what it used to be.[53] Declining wages and rising housing costs had put "decent housing" out of the reach of millions of Americans, but "decent" implied much higher-quality accommodations at the end of the century than it did in the seventies. By the nineties, almost half of America's poor lived in homes or apartments that had air conditioning – deemed minimally necessary in the country's south and in crowded cities like New York and Chicago, where disproportionate numbers of the poor lived and where, as late as 1960, air conditioning was still rare. Thanks to Medicaid, improved medical practices and education, food stamps, and other measures that came to make up the common social environment after the Sixties, infant mortality rates dropped by more than half during the last quarter of the century (although the United States still did poorly compared to other industrial countries). By the end of the century, twice as many families in the bottom fifth of the income strata owned a car as did in 1970, and only a quarter as many Americans lived in "crowded" abodes (i.e., more than one person per room) as had earlier. Moreover, during the last quarter of the century the proportion of adults who had failed to complete high school dropped by half, and more of the poor gained access to a college education than had been common earlier. All these facts say much about the momentum of the remarkable spread of affluence throughout the country during the third quarter of the century and about the new expectations that affected even conservative political administrations thereafter.

And yet, though many more young Americans earned college degrees, the greater investment in education did not necessarily produce higher incomes. In 1979, about 18 percent of college-age Americans earned bachelor's degrees; by 1997, their numbers grew to 27 percent. But during that same period the average entry wage for college graduates actually dropped by 2 percent. It was still economically important to earn a college degree, because high-school graduates lost much further ground; by 1999, new college graduates earned 80 percent more than high-school graduates, up from only 35 percent more twenty years earlier. In all, beginning wages for high-school graduates in 1997 were only 76 percent of what they had been in 1979. That union membership among male high-school graduates dropped by almost half during the period (from 38 percent to 21 percent) suggests one important reason, considering that union workers typically earned about 15 percent more than similarly employed nonunion workers.[54]

---

[53] See Nick Eberstadt & Sally L. Satel, *Health and the Income Inequality Hypothesis: A Doctrine in Search of Data* (American Enterprise Institute, 2004).

[54] *New York Times* (1 Nov. 2000), p. A25, an article by Richard Rothstein citing, among other sources, "The State of Working America," a semi-annual report issued by the Economic Policy Institute. The drastic cut in mostly unionized manufacturing jobs during the last third of the century in the face of automation, movement of plants to labor-unfriendly states in the South and Southwest, and low–labor-cost foreign competition resulted in the evisceration of union strength throughout the country.

The losses of middle-income families during the last quarter of the twentieth century actually tend to be understated. Between 1975 and 1995, median family incomes remained virtually unchanged, but the average wife by 1995 was working fifteen more weeks, or 600 more hours, per year than she did in the 1970s.[55] By 1995, 55 percent of all women with children under 2 years old were working full- or part-time, up from 31 percent in 1975. From this it is easy to calculate that, between 1975 and 1995, real hourly income for working families truly plummeted. In fact, despite all the additional hours of labor, middle-income families between 1973 and 1996 gained barely $550 in real annual income. In comparison, households at the bottom of the *top* 5 percent gained more than $25,000 each during this period.[56]

In short, although conditions improved marginally for middle-income families in the last five years of the century (before the stock market bust in 2001), the "prosperous 1990s" was largely a delusion for them. For most of the families that managed to maintain or improve their standard of living, doing so came at the cost of substantially intensified labor. Median-income two-earner families worked 256 hours (32 days) more in 1999 than in 1989 just to pull down barely $300 more in real income than in 1989 ($44,500 versus $44,200 in 1989). Accompanying these developments was a dramatic decline in money available for leisure activities for working families. Figures collected by the Labor Department's Consumer Expenditure Survey show that the proportion of family income spent on necessities such as housing, utilities, and health care rose from 33 percent in 1973 to 46 percent in 1993.

Meanwhile, employees' benefits shrank. More and more, employers were withdrawing support for their workers' health insurance, driven in part by soaring premiums. In 1980, employers for 54 percent of workers in medium to large firms paid the full cost of their employees' family health insurance. By the mid-nineties, that figure had fallen to 20 percent.[57] In order to avoid paying benefits, more and more employers resorted to hiring temporary workers or people who worked as private contractors. During the last twenty years of the century, the proportion of temporary workers in the economy rose by over 400 percent.[58]

While state and federal governments stood by, the country's major corporations used generous bankruptcy laws and unchallenged mergers to shed pension

[55] Lester C. Thurow, "The Boom That Wasn't," *New York Times* (18 Jan. 1999). See also Louis Uchitelle, "Were the Good Old Days *That* Good? Maybe Not, but the Standard of Living Was Climbing Much Faster," *New York Times* (3 July 2005), sec. 3, pp. 1, 7.

[56] Ryscavage, *Income Inequality*, p. 68. See also Cathie J. Martin, *Shifting the Burden: The Struggle over Growth and Corporate Taxation* (University of Chicago Press, 1991), especially pp. 159, 190–1; Bennett Harrison & Barry Bluestone, *The Great U-Turn: Corporate Restructuring and the Polarizing of America* (Basic Books, 1988), especially pp. 6–7.

[57] Charles Lewis, *The Buying of the Congress* (Avon, 1998), p. 4.

[58] See Jeff Madrick, "How New Is the New Economy?" *New York Review* (23 Sept. 1999), p. 49.

and medical coverage obligations for their employees, sometimes cheating long-time employees of all or major portions of their anticipated pensions. Removing such obligations served to raise stock values and to make corporations attractive partners in the massive consolidations that characterized the reorganization of American business during the decade.[59] Meanwhile, senior management enjoyed skyrocketing compensation for often dubious services. While scores of bankruptcies at the end of the century revealed years of unethical and illegal deals and accounting practices, chief executive officer (CEO) remuneration rose from 42 times that of the average American worker in 1980 (already an astonishing figure) to 531 times in 1999, a fact that stunned counterparts in all other industrial countries.[60] Altogether, the average earnings of corporate executive officers rose from 29 times the pay of average workers in *their own* companies in 1979 to 107 times in 1999. This was a phenomenon unmatched in any other industrial country.[61]

As the 1990s waxed and the stock market indices rocketed to successive record heights, the media and politicians exulted in the unprecedentedly prosperous economy and the low levels of reported unemployment. And it was true that, by the late nineties, the real income of those one tenth of the way up the income ladder approximately equaled the real income of the median household forty years earlier. Although most of that progress had been achieved by 1975, and despite the decline in their real income since that year, even those near the bottom of the income ladder continued to enjoy improvement in their standard of living. All things are comparative, and comparisons condition perceptions. Perhaps it is for this reason that one poll in 2000 reported that 16 percent of Americans believed that their incomes put them in the top 1 percent of income recipients!

Popular misperceptions aside, the figures unfortunately omit a crucial part of the story. The spread in income inequality had some seriously disadvantageous effects on those in the bottom 60 percent of income recipients and especially on those in the bottom 40 percent. The problem has to do with what economists call "lumpy goods," that is, goods that cannot be consumed in small units but must be bought whole. This category includes housing, medical care, and educational expenses. In the last quarter of the twentieth century, consumer costs for such goods rose far beyond the overall rate of inflation; this means that, when measured by their purchasing power *for those goods,* middle- and lower-income

---

[59] *Wall Street Journal* (28 Dec. 2000), p. A1, describes at length how GE and other corporations – through mergers, down-sizing, and other financial manipulations – left thousands of their former and retired employees in poverty. This was before the scandal broke on the great Enron, WorldCom, and other notorious bankruptcies of 2001–2002 that left still more thousands of workers impoverished while top management cashed in on tens of millions of dollars.

[60] "CEOs: Why They're So Unloved," *Business Week* (22 April 2002), p. 118.

[61] These lower figures are based on accounts by John Cassidy, "Who Killed the Middle Class?" *The New Yorker* (16 Oct. 1995), and Ryscavage, *Income Inequality.*

families were far worse off than figures stating their overall real income might suggest. Among other things, income inequality caused housing prices in preferred locations to rise disproportionately. Those with disproportionate gains in wealth – those in the top 20 percent, and especially the top 5 percent, of income recipients – bid against each other for center city locations. That forced middle- and lower-income families to move farther and farther out of town, leaving them in less desirable locations that required more unpaid time devoted to commuting to work sites and well as higher transportation costs. It also impelled Americans to spend greater proportions of their income on the basic need for housing. Between 1980 and 2000, the number of American families that spent over half their income for housing (or who lived in substandard housing) rose from 7.2 million to 13.7 million, or from 9 to 14 percent of all families.[62] It isn't clear how much the inflation in housing costs contributed to the conspicuous growth of homeless Americans who were forced to "camp out" on city streets or in miserable, often dangerous municipal shelters.

The "lumpy goods" effect similarly constricted access to what might be called social goods, goods that contribute to the quality of life. Vacation trips, sports events, and access to recreational facilities and the performing arts all became disproportionately expensive and beyond the reach of the lower quintiles of income recipients, as those enjoying income advantages could afford to pay ever more for them.

Meanwhile, in the 1970s the newly wealthy generation of Americans rebelled against paying taxes. Even though Americans paid, on a per capita basis, the lowest taxes of citizens living in any of the world's advanced industrial countries (except perhaps for Japan), in the 1970s they claimed to feel oppressed. With well-financed statewide initiative campaigns, they succeeded in winning sharply reduced property taxes, locking in their achievements against legislative revision with constitutional amendments. In the 1980s the federal government followed the trend, slashing income taxes – the nation's main source of revenue – especially for those in the upper income brackets. It did the same for corporate income taxes, which slid to their lowest levels since the 1930s. By the nineties, at only about 1.2 percent of GDP such taxes brought in less than 10 percent of federal tax revenues, down from 28 percent at the end of the fifties. Altogether, during the last two decades of the century, total income and corporation tax revenues dropped dramatically, a first in recent history for a growing economy.

While revenues declined, the nation's political leaders pushed up the national debt in order to finance a fourfold increase in military expenditures, and by the

---

[62] Michael Stegman, "The Fall and Rise of Public Housing," *Regulation* (vol. 25, 2002), pp. 64–70. Thanks to David Erickson for calling this source to my attention. Conventional economic thinking suggests that prudent families should spend only about a third of their gross income on housing, a figure that mortgagers typically will look for.

mid-1980s they reached record peacetime levels. President Ronald Reagan also intensified the "war on drugs," a campaign generated far more by moral convictions than by health or economic considerations. Among other huge enforcement costs, the antidrug campaign greatly increased the prison population, doubling it to nearly 2 million within a short span of years and at an average cost per prisoner of about $40,000 per year (in 2001 dollars). With that expense plus a major increase in the portion of the federal budget devoted to paying the interest on the national debt, government funding for the nation's domestic concerns plummeted. For many of the architects of the Reagan administration's tax reductions, this was not an unintended consequence.[63] For example, federal regulatory mechanisms were weakened even further than the levels mandated by the deregulation movement that blossomed in the mid-seventies. In addition, public services declined while subsidies to the arts, humanities, education, and even scientific research and development shriveled.

By the end of the 1980s, total revenues (federal, state, and local) would climb back to earlier levels, mainly on the strength of regressive sales and excise taxes and, most of all, higher payroll taxes: Medicare, Social Security, disability, and unemployment insurance payments. While Congress in the 1980s reduced income and corporation taxes, it incrementally raised the regressive Social Security tax on seven occasions and also dipped into the Social Security fund in order to simulate a "balanced budget." That three fourths of Social Security contributors paid more to Social Security than they paid in income taxes underscores the steeply regressive nature of the tax system inaugurated in the eighties.[64]

Even though total taxation regained 1980 levels by 1989, both federal and state revenues failed to keep pace with the country's increasing population and new government responsibilities. Enforcement of affirmative action guidelines and of environmental regulations, for example, as well as overseeing consumer and employee safety protection, were tasks mandated to the federal government only in the 1970s, precisely when rising antigovernment sentiment led to cuts in federal civilian jobs. Insufficient revenues led local, state, and federal governments to cut back on such public services as libraries and schools, park maintenance and management, urban transit, and even important parts of the nation's infrastructure. All over the country, bridges, roads, railway lines, and water systems deteriorated. California, which pioneered in the so-called Tax Rebellion in 1978, dropped from tenth to forty-sixth among the states in per capita expenditures for its public schools. As the quality of public school education deteriorated,

---

[63] See David Stockman, *The Triumph of Politics: How the Reagan Revolution Failed* (Harper & Row, 1986). Also, Haynes Johnson, *Sleepwalking through History: America in the Reagan Years* (Anchor, 1991).

[64] Edward Berkowitz, *America's Welfare State: From Roosevelt to Reagan* (Johns Hopkins University Press, 1991), p. 83.

the well-to-do put their children in private schools. Meanwhile, lack of adequate state and federal funds closed down thousands of hospital emergency rooms on which the poor and uninsured especially are forced to depend for medical care. Politically, raising taxes was not an option.

The country increasingly moved toward "use taxes" to finance services and amenities. Americans resisted paying for services they did not personally use or used rarely. Bond issues for public schools went down to defeat in numerous communities across the country where childless and elderly voters predominated. One governor of Wisconsin even proposed exempting retired people from state taxes targeted for public schools on the grounds they didn't use the schools. Gone was the notion of commonweal, whereby a well-educated public benefits all citizens. At the same time, admittance to museums, zoos, and aquariums as well as national, state, and even some municipal parks ceased to be free or accessible for nominal entrance fees. The new admission charges put such public goods out of the reach of millions of low- and middle-income families. Reduced government subsidies to the performing arts translated into higher ticket prices, which also put theater and concerts further beyond the financial range affordable by millions of American families. Similarly, city and state colleges and universities were forced to abandon long-standing tuition-free education. Although need-based scholarship and fellowship programs increased (owing largely to private sources), they failed to keep pace with the increased demand for higher education, particularly among lower-income families.

Although so-called conservatives attacked welfare payments as creating millions of "dependency-addicted" families, these moralists were silent when state after state repealed its laws against gambling in order to supplement dwindling treasuries with money from poor people enticed into spending their pay on lottery tickets and on slot machines in newly legalized casinos. But who can blame the lottery clientele? Given the transformation of the economic system since the mid-seventies, the chances of improving one's living standards by hard work seemed not much better than the chances of winning a lottery. (Richer folk put their money in the stock market, which proved after its collapse in 2000 to be yet another form of legalized gambling.)

In sum: Americans paid the lowest per capita taxes of citizens in any modern industrial country, yet they complained more loudly and insistently about "high" taxes than any people in the world; during the last quarter of the twentieth century, lower- and middle-income families suffered a considerable decline in their access to the public goods that sustain the quality of a nation's life.

To compound the problem, during this quarter-century the newly wealthy Americans financed a political attack on the so-called welfare state. The term "welfare" did not include government subsidies of various kinds to business corporations, and neither did it include the free award of exclusive radio and telecommunications wavelengths to commercial enterprise, property that could have brought in billions of dollars in federal revenues if properly auctioned.[65] Nor did it include federal payoffs to wealthy savings and loan (S&L) bank customers – whose deposits of more than $100,000 exceeded insurance coverage – when a combination of fraud and embezzlement, government deregulation, mismanagement, and extraordinary loans to bank managers' friends and political benefactors led to the S&L's industrywide collapse in the 1980s. Nor did "welfare" include government-financed marketing abroad for select American manufacturers, especially airplane and weapons manufacturers. Nor did it include government-sponsored research and development in the pure and applied sciences, whose achievements certain commercial enterprises – from the computer industry to the pharmaceutical and telecommunications industries – were permitted to appropriate for their private profit.

Neither did critics of "welfare" object to direct federal payments to farmers, based on acreage and regardless of need, which in 2000 amounted to $28 billion for the country's 1.6 million farm entities. Farmers were usually pictured as models of rugged individualism and self-sufficiency, but they prospered (if at all) on government checks no different in kind from those received by welfare mothers (except that welfare mothers faced a means test). In the year 2000, payments to individual and corporate farmers constituted 100 percent of all farm income in eight different states. Giant corporate farms received most of the subsidies (payments to a single farm entity were "capped" at $550,000), while small family farmers received little.[66] The payments were supposed to compensate farmers for their failure to make money in "the free market," although the subsidies applied even to profitable farms. It may be useful to understand that most of those fortunate private enterprisers resided in sparsely populated states that were thus overrepresented in Congress by senators who regularly railed against "welfare" and "big government."

For payouts of such government largesse, the media and politicians declined to use the word "welfare," to which public discourse had given a pejorative meaning. When opponents attacked the welfare state, they reserved the dirty word

---

[65] According to estimates made by the Department of Commerce, the government in the 1980s gave away about $46 billion worth of electromagnetic spectrum rights to telephone and broadcasting companies. Only in 1993 did Congress finally authorize the FCC to auction spectrum rights for telecommunication firms, although Congress decreed that spectrum for high-definition television, estimated by the FCC to be worth about $70 billion, should be granted free to the networks. Sen. John McCain (R-AZ) called this giveaway "one of the great rip-offs in American history." John McMillan, *Reinventing the Bazaar: A Natural History of Markets* (Norton, 2002), pp. 81, 85.

[66] In 2002, Congress fought to a virtual standstill over whether to limit payments to $275,000, a cut in the cap that would affect barely 1 percent of all farmers. *New York Times* (8 Feb. 2002), p. A16; *Wall Street Journal* (8 Feb. 2002), p. A12. The subsidies went to farms producing staple crops: corn, wheat, rice, soybeans, and cotton. Peanuts and tobacco also received subsidies.

instead for the checks made to those indigent Americans – including disproportionate numbers of the nation's minorities – who were unable to work or to hold
jobs that offered a living wage. They included the unpensioned or inadequately
pensioned elderly, the ill, the uneducated or undereducated, the mentally and
physically disabled, some single mothers with dependent children, and the simply unlucky.

We have developed some understanding of why, in the sixties, the national government initiated a war on poverty in an astonishingly affluent environment and
at a time when income inequality had reached a half-century low.

But there remains the puzzling question: Why did Americans reverse course
in their political response to poverty during the similarly prosperous 1980s and
1990s, when income inequality reached nearly unprecedented levels and when
the percentage of American families struggling with incomes at or below the
poverty line rose significantly? Before the mid-seventies, the rise to affluence was
steep and broad. After 1980, however, there was at last statistical support for
the longtime leftist accusation that the rich were getting richer while the poor
got poorer. What political agitation there was on the poverty issue after the
mid-seventies was actually directed toward *reducing* government aid to the poor
and the disadvantaged. In contrast to the 1960s, when real incomes were soaring
and income inequality remained stable, Americans in the prosperous though increasingly inegalitarian eighties and nineties witnessed (and often participated
in) an unprecedented and effective "war on the poor."

How can we explain the paradox? Why was there no clamor for a campaign
to alleviate poverty and to reduce income inequality during the last quarter of
the twentieth century, when both were growing conspicuously? The question
requires close attention to chronology, to a confluence of events that led to the
development of the seemingly unlikely. It was, in fact, a part of the story of
the post-Watergate reaction and the decline of the liberal Democratic coalition,
which we will examine in Part III.

7

From Isolation to International Hegemonic Power

> In the United States [during the postwar period] were statesmen of wisdom, author-ity and courage who wrought a revolutionary change in their country's traditional policies. There was to be no withdrawal into isolationism as after the first World War.[1]
>
> Anthony Eden

> For we have won great wars and assumed to ourselves great powers. And we have thus become the least free of all peoples.[2]
>
> George Kennan

America emerged from World War II as the world's greatest power, economi-cally, politically, and in some respects even militarily despite almost immediate demobilization. Unlike its major allies, Britain, France, and the Soviet Union, it suffered virtually no damage at all besides its comparatively small losses in man-power. Its strength, however, imposed on the country the burden of enormous responsibilities that were quickly put to the test, responsibilities that most Amer-icans resented and resisted. It took extraordinary leadership at the top to move U.S. policy into line with its responsibilities as a major international power.

Unlike the aftermath of World War I, the second postwar era proved to be one of those rare and wonderful moments in history when a policy-making elite moved with foresight and dispatch to meet impending human and political disas-ter, even, it must be said, in the face of considerable popular domestic resistance.

In the environment of the war, liberal internationalism had risen triumphant over the nation's long-standing tradition of unilateral nationalism. Not long after the U.S. entry into the war, it became conventional wisdom that America's

---

[1] British Foreign Secretary Anthony Eden quoted in Richard M. Freeland, *The Truman Doctrine and the Origins of McCarthyism* (Schocken, 1974), p. 7.
[2] George Kennan, *Sketches from a Life* (Pantheon, 1989), p. 123.

unwillingness to take on a leadership role after the First World War and in the 1930s had contributed in major ways to both the Depression and the ascendancy of world fascism. During the First World War, the United States had declined even to be included among "the Allies," preferring "Associate" status in its relations with Britain, France, Russia, and Italy. After that war, it refused membership or any kind of official relationship with the newly founded League of Nations. In 1931, it intensified its isolationist political and economic posture with the Hawley–Smoot protective tariff, thereby contributing to the trade wars that worsened the disasters of the Great Depression. Passage of two Neutrality Acts in the 1930s expressed the refusal of Congress to choose between fascist and republican belligerents. Most Americans chose instead to close their eyes to the rise of totalitarianism and to deny American resources to those abroad fighting against it.

With the fall of France in May 1940, America began its shift toward taking on international responsibilities. At President Franklin Roosevelt's urging, Congress mandated the first peacetime military draft in anticipation of possible involvement in the European conflagration. By the smallest of margins, Congress in early 1941 also agreed to fund the president's Lend-Lease program, which enabled Britain to obtain supplies while it stood alone at war against Hitler and Mussolini and while bracing for attack by Japan on Britain's possessions and Commonwealth nations of the East – from Australia to Singapore, Burma, and India. The Lend-Lease program was extended to the Soviet Union a few months after Hitler invaded in June 1941. It is not clear that much of this had substantial support from the American public generally. What is clear is that the country's political leadership saw its simple wisdom.

A strong sense of responsibility lay at the center of liberal humanism, which was enjoying a new ascendancy courtesy of its stark contrast with fascism and communism. That sense had everything to do with why, in spite of urgings to the contrary by America Firsters and other isolationist groups in 1940 and 1941, the United States continued to support England throughout the long dark thirteen months after the epochal evacuation of British and some French troops from Dunkirk in May 1940. That was a grim time, when the Soviet Union was still joined with Germany in the Nonaggression Pact it had signed in August 1939 (prelude to the dual invasion of Poland the following month); when Italy and Japan were formally allied with Germany as the Axis powers; when France, beaten on the battlefield, threatened to put itself, its empire, and its navy at Hitler's service; and when many conservative and fearful Britons as well as Americans (notably the popular hero, Charles Lindbergh) were urging an accommodation with Hitler. Yet after the war, many (probably most) Americans – unaccustomed to leadership in world affairs – chafed at the expenditure of resources for foreigners once the war emergency had ended. If not prodded by the country's leaders, especially those in the executive branch who wielded the threat of "world communism" as a persuasive weapon, it seemed that most Americans would have preferred a return to traditional isolationism.

The nation and its leaders faced a dual challenge once the war was over. First was the challenge of using America's resources to help reconstruct the devastated countries of Europe and Asia. Among most policy makers there was the felt obligation to restore or to promote human freedom and dignity abroad. This contrasted with the American consensus after the First World War. That was when Europe had suffered the agony of revolutionary and civil war, massive economic turmoil, widespread starvation, and a devastating flu epidemic while the United States, the richest country in the world, had retreated into the "normalcy" of isolation. The memory of Americans' post-1918 irresponsibility lay as a shadow across the mind of policy makers in the years following the Second World War.

The second challenge was that of Soviet power. Having gained an enemy in common after Hitler invaded the Soviet Union (on June 22, 1941) and declared war on the United States (on December 11 of that year), the United States, the United Kingdom, and the Soviet Union joined in a wartime alliance of convenience. Many people hoped the convenience might lead to real amity. But even before the war ended, leading Americans perceived (as they had before the war) that Stalin's Soviet Union was a brutal, totalitarian regime ideologically committed to the unlimited expansion of its influence and to the ultimate defeat of liberalism by communism. In 1944 President Roosevelt had remarked: "We either work with the other great nations or we might some day have to fight them." But by March 1945, even Roosevelt had become agitated about Stalin's intransigence over Poland and other matters concerning Eastern Europe.[3]

Although bloodied by four years of war mainly on its own most populous territories, at war's end the Soviet Union stood at the peak of its power. It possessed the world's largest land army and was within easy reach of the major industrial countries of Europe and Asia. It did not wholly demobilize. Tensions between the wartime allies mounted swiftly as each perceived aggressive intentions by the other. The Western allies fretted over (among many things) Stalin's determination to annex, or at least to dominate politically and economically, all the countries on his prewar western borders and some beyond as well. Soviet leaders, on the other hand, were convinced that the Americans were intent on using their power to isolate the Soviet Union while expanding their capitalist interests across the globe. In fact, each side correctly understood the other's intentions. And the power that each side possessed dictated that each stand firm for what it viewed as essential to its vital interests.

---

[3] See e.g. Robert Dallek, *Franklin D. Roosevelt and American Foreign Policy, 1932–1945* (Oxford University Press, 1979), especially pp. 523ff.

At the conclusion of history's most extensive and destructive war, then, the two largest countries in the world, still formally allies, moved ominously toward belligerency. A few Americans, like the nationally popular news broadcaster and columnist Walter Winchell, stridently urged a preemptive war against the Soviets at the earliest possible moment. Few could stomach such a prospect, but the country and the world would hunker down for a long, cold relationship between the world's two biggest powers for what appeared to be the indefinite future.

By 1945, the nation's statesmen were determined to commit the United States to vigorous political, military, and economic intervention wherever liberal institutions seemed threatened or could be advanced. They took the initiative in promoting the principle of collective security through the United Nations; in establishing an international system of currency control through the founding of the International Monetary Fund (IMF); in underwriting economic development with its own resources and through agencies such as the International Bank for Reconstruction and Development (usually called the World Bank); and in establishing a General Agreement on Trade and Tariffs (GATT) that worked toward founding an international trade organization to reduce trade barriers and to adjudicate trade disputes. Finally, they set up the United States as the principal shield against the perceived threat of an expansive Soviet Union. Within a few years of the war's end, the liberal internationalists would go so far as to dismiss George Washington's venerated warning and to join an "entangling alliance" with more than a dozen European nations, an alliance called the North Atlantic Treaty Organization (NATO) though it included the strictly Mediterranean countries of Italy, Greece, and Turkey. In 2004, a dozen years after the collapse of the Soviet Union, NATO would be expanded to include the former Soviet-bloc countries of Poland, the Czech Republic, and Hungary.

Establishment of the United Nations actually introduced transnational agencies far beyond the policing function implied by the concept of collective security. Through international organizations such as the United Nations Educational, Scientific, and Cultural Organization (UNESCO), the United Nations Children's Fund (UNICEF), the World Health Organization (WHO), the Court of International Justice (World Court), and the Food and Agriculture Organization (FAO), the UN provided multiple means for nations throughout the world to communicate with one another. These agencies aimed at the exchange of information as well as at the peaceful resolution of various conflicts of interest between or among nations. They also worked to deal with problems that cannot be contained within national borders, such as disease, crime, famine, economic distress, and natural disasters. The United Nations Relief and Redevelopment Agency (UNRRA) preceded by some years the work of the IMF and the U.S. Marshall Plan in helping to reconstruct Western Europe's economic system. Implicit in all these agencies were the seeds of a political and social globalization to parallel the globalization of business that was already under way.

In the decades following the war, military forces under UN commanders served as peacekeepers in a dozen or more places in the world where armed buffers seemed necessary to prevent bloodshed between neighboring nations. They weren't always successful and often were insufficiently armed to be entirely effective. But they represented a big step forward in fostering a sense of international responsibility for human welfare. As the noncommunist world's biggest military power, the United States usually made up the most important part of such military expeditions, especially in providing logistical and financial resources.

By the 1990s, in response to genocidal violence within nations in various parts of the globe, a transnationalist ethos inspired multinational military action that challenged the 350-year-old concept of international law know as "national sovereignty." The intervention by NATO forces to halt the one-sided assault against Bosnian Muslims by Bosnian Serbs (aided by the Serbian army) and against Albanians in the Serbian province of Kosovo was a remarkable example of an multinational force acting to limit brutality – "crimes against humanity" – within the borders of an independent nation. Multinational interventions had occurred many times before: the suppression of the Paris Commune in 1871, the attempted reversal of the Bolshevik Revolution by British and French troops after World War I, and the intervention in the Spanish Civil War by Germany and Italy in the 1930s are a few (not altogether praiseworthy) examples. But the Bosnian and Kosovo interventions seemed to reflect simpler humane objectives rather than a will to impose some preferred regime on a people.

In the more immediate postwar era, "Munich" became the great foreign policy lesson for liberal internationalist political leaders. "Munich" referred, of course, to the 1938 agreement concluded in that Bavarian city whereby Britain and France conceded to Hitler borderland territories of Czechoslovakia in the interest of "peace in our time." The British prime minister, Neville Chamberlain, actually described the agreement as an "appeasement" that he hoped would satisfy Hitler's expansionist appetite. The agreement came to symbolize the irresponsible retreat of great powers in the face of aggressors. Once the United States had been drawn into the European conflagration, it highlighted the wrongheadedness of U.S. isolationism. Citing "Munich," postwar American policy makers took on the responsibility for monitoring, and influencing, what happened or seemed likely to happen in almost every part of the globe, especially if the outcome of some political change appeared likely to enhance the power or influence of the Soviet Union.

With communism replacing fascism as the perceived aggressor, liberal internationalists found that American conservatives, long the stalwarts of isolationism, were eager converts to internationalism. It was a limited sort of internationalism, to be sure, but liberals found it politically useful or at least necessary. This proved especially important as the liberal internationalists perceived the first postwar crisis in U.S.–Soviet relations. That occurred during the winter of 1946–1947, when Britain issued an official plea for U.S. aid in holding back a communist-led insurgency in Greece. There, a small contingent of British troops had been fighting to bolster the slatternly Greek government's resistance. The European winter had been a ferocious one and a disaster for Britain's economy, which still had not recovered from the war's devastation. The British told the American president that they no longer had the resources to continue their fight. If the Americans did not take over at least financially and with materiel, then Greece would be lost to the communists and Soviet influence would grow immeasurably in the eastern Mediterranean, an area crucial for access to the oil resources of the Middle East.

President Truman and his advisors responded positively to the plea. On 26 February 1947 Truman, Secretary of State George C. Marshall, and Under Secretary Dean Acheson met in the Oval Room of the White House with the leaders of Congress in order to persuade them to accept the transfer of the burden borne so far by the British. It was not going to be an easy task. The elections of November 1946 had produced a Republican majority in both houses of Congress, and the veteran isolationist Arthur Vandenberg of Michigan was the new chairman of the Senate Foreign Relations Committee. The Republican leaders in Congress had firmly established their primary interest in reducing taxes and in putting an end to government activism both at home and abroad. They promised the most unfriendly scrutiny over any expansion of American commitments to foreign causes. Many of the Republicans had not even yet become fully reconciled to the involvement of the United States in the war against Hitler, and they had resisted establishment of the International Monetary Fund, the World Bank, and the United Nations.

The president opened the session with a short statement informing the congressmen of the problem and of its seriousness. British aid would be ended and the troops were to be withdrawn within a few months. If, as expected, the Greek government fell because it no longer had the resources to fight the revolutionaries, it would expose Turkey to hostile governments on both its eastern and western frontiers. The defense of the eastern Mediterranean against the spread of pro-Soviet regimes and influence would have to be assumed by the United States; there was no one else. Truman concluded by telling all assembled that he hoped they would go along with the decision he had made to provide aid to Greece and Turkey.

Secretary of State Marshall followed with a plea for a show of generosity to take on responsibilities that others, far less well endowed, had shouldered for so long. He appealed to principles of common humanity and of loyalty to former comrades-in-arms. When he finished, it was obvious that he had persuaded no one. Vandenberg and his fellows squirmed uncomfortably in their seats. How much was it going to cost? one asked. What kind of long-term commitments would we be making? another carped. Sensing that the cause was all but lost, Acheson asked to speak.

"Our interest in Greece," he reassured the congressmen, "is by no means restricted to humanitarian or friendly impulses." If the communist-led rebels should win in Greece, all kinds of dominos would probably fall. Turkey would be surrounded and would likely succumb to Soviet pressure. (Stalin had already made it known that he wanted a naval base on the Turkish Straits.) That would jeopardize Euro-American interests in the Middle East, from which Europe drew most of its oil and American oil companies much profit. In general, Western civilization's defenses against the darkness of communism seemed on the brink of crumbling. "Like apples in a barrel infected by one rotten one," Acheson warned, "the corruption of Greece would infect Iran and all to the east. It would also carry infection to Africa through Asia Minor and Egypt, and to Europe through Italy and France, already threatened by the strongest domestic Communist parties in Western Europe." The United States, and only the United States, had the resources to avoid calamity. "It is not alarmist to say," concluded Acheson to the alarm of his listeners, "that we are faced with the first crisis of a series which might extend Soviet domination to Europe, the Middle East and Asia." This was what the "British withdrawal from the eastern Mediterranean offered to an eager and ruthless opponent."

As the story is told by several who were present, Acheson's presentation was followed by an awed silence. Finally, Vandenberg cleared his throat and said, in words variously reported: Mr. President, if that's what you want, there is only one way to do it. You must personally go before the Congress, and scare the hell out of the American people.[4]

However he phrased it, Vandenberg's advice to the president represented a clear condition of his support. If the Republicans were going to return to their tightfisted and largely isolationist constituents with a half-billion-dollar invoice for helping foreign nations, they wanted Truman and the Democrats to make it clear that the issue was Soviet communism and not any New Deal, do-gooder program for promoting prosperity and social welfare abroad.

Truman seemingly had no quarrel with that. On 12 March 1947 he appeared before a joint session of Congress to lay before it "the gravity of the situation

---

[4] This account is taken from Joseph Jones, *Fifteen Weeks* (Harcourt, Brace, 1965); Dean Acheson, *Present at the Creation* (New American Library, 1970); Charles L. Mee, Jr., *The Marshall Plan* (Simon & Schuster, 1984); and Eric Goldman, *The Crucial Decade – And After* (Vintage, 1960), pp. 59–60.

which confronts the world today." He presented the case for military and economic aid to Greece and Turkey in classic liberal terms. "The seeds of totalitarian regimes are nurtured by misery and want," he said. He proposed that "our help should be through economic and financial aid which is essential to economic stability and orderly political processes." He pointed out that "a fundamental issue in the war with Germany and Japan" was their attempt "to impose their will, and their way of life, upon other nations." He proposed now that a fundamental source of contention with the Soviet Union (never named in the address) was its attempt to impose its will and way of life on other nations. "The people of a number of countries of the world have recently had totalitarian regimes forced upon them against their will," he said, specifying Poland, Rumania, and Bulgaria.

Then he went on to sketch the prospect of falling dominos, providing the note of impending disaster that Vandenberg and his colleagues required. It was a "fateful hour," Truman said, with dire implications "far reaching to the West as well as to the East." "I believe," he continued with perhaps the most fateful part of his address, "that it must be the policy of the United States to support free peoples who are resisting attempted subjugation by armed minorities or by outside pressures." The president concluded with a liberal internationalist peroration: "The free peoples of the world look to us for support in maintaining their freedoms. If we falter in our leadership, we may endanger the peace of the world – and we shall surely endanger the welfare of our own nation."

In laying out the principles of the "Truman Doctrine," as journalists dubbed the policies outlined in the address, Truman defined American obligations in terms that would soon beleaguer and eventually cripple the liberal approach to foreign relations.

First, Truman appeared to globalize American obligations to "free peoples" everywhere, when all that the moment required was aid to two embattled countries of some particular strategic value to U.S. and West European interests. This had two consequences: (1) it placed U.S. interests at risk whenever and wherever policy makers perceived an expansion of Soviet interests or influence; and (2) meeting such a global responsibility required a substantial military buildup and creation of a significant military establishment of some permanence.

A second difficulty was that Truman himself admitted that the two governments at issue, those of Greece and Turkey, fell far short of democratic ideals ("No government is perfect," Truman said in his speech). And so the definition of "free peoples" settled with uncomfortable force solely on its simple contrast with communism.

Finally, by presenting the case for international leadership in the context of great fear, Truman helped ripen a phobic anticommunism at home that came to overshadow all efforts to deal intelligently with international as well as domestic problems. By agreeing to "scare the American people," Truman helped release the genie of anticommunist madness.

In its short-term purposes, the Truman Doctrine speech was outstandingly successful. The Democratic administration gained an invaluable ally in Senator Arthur Vandenberg, who was pleased to become important in what was billed as a fight for freedom against world communism. His aid was indispensable not only for passage of the $500 million Truman requested for Greece and Turkey but also for the more than $15 billion in economic assistance to rebuild Western Europe over the next five years under the terms of the Marshall Plan. Throughout most of the third quarter of the century, Congress – though dominated by conservatives – made vast amounts of money available for foreign commitments, including grants to encourage economic growth and to fight poverty in underdeveloped parts of the world. But liberal internationalism would pay a price for this, as a simple (and simplistic) "anticommunism" came to replace the more complex and progressive reasons for the projection of U.S. power abroad in the postwar world.[5]

Until at least the end of the 1960s, the United States took on a hegemonic role in the non-Soviet world. Its international leadership was comparable to, and in many ways exceeded that of, the British in the nineteenth century. Technology as well as economic power gave America the ability to influence global developments well beyond what the British could have hoped to do even at the height of the globe-girdling British Empire.

Within ten years of the war's conclusion, nearly half a million U.S. military personnel were again stationed abroad: in South Korea, Japan, West Germany, Greece, Turkey, and remote islands in every ocean of the globe.[6] The direct and massive military intervention in Korea following the invasion of South Korea by the Communist North in June 1950 contrasted starkly with the cautious prewar "wait and see" policies of the Western democracies during the fascist expansion in the 1930s: Germany into Czechoslovakia, Japan into Manchuria and China, and Italy into Albania and Ethiopia. Similar considerations regarding what was perceived as Communist aggression brought the U.S. military into Indochina, culminating in the long, hot, and disastrous war in Vietnam (1963–1975). Meanwhile, covert U.S. actions, some mainly financial but others paramilitary in nature, decisively altered political outcomes in places like Iran, Italy, Greece, and Guatemala.

---

[5] Richard M. Abrams, "American Anticommunism and Liberal Internationalism," *Reviews in American History* (Sept. 1982), pp. 454–67.

[6] By 1970, about a million U.S. troops were abroad. See Bruce M. Russett & Alfred Stepan, eds., *Military Force and American Society* (Harper, 1973), p. 4.

Until the end of the 1960s, America's overwhelming economic power had served to stabilize and even dictate the terms of an international economic regime that encouraged free trade, unrestricted currency convertibility, the commercial development of nonindustrial countries, and multinational investment. In pursuit of such liberal capitalist objectives, U.S. policy makers persuaded the American people to accept important short-term sacrifices. When the IMF's resources proved insufficient to meet Western Europe's postwar economic difficulties, America responded with the Marshall Plan providing grants, not loans, that amounted to more than $15 billion over five years (about $150 billion in post-2000 dollars). In the 1950s the United States encouraged organization of a European Payments Union and later the European Economic Community (EEC) – or Common Market – which discriminated against American exports but stabilized intra-European trade and currency exchanges. In 1956 and 1967, when war in the Middle East cut off oil supplies to Europe, America accommodated Europe's needs with its own surpluses. After 1949, when China went Communist and the Chinese market seemed off-limits to Japan's industry for the indefinite future, the United States persuaded Western Europe to give Japan most-favored-nation status as a trading partner. Japan already had access to an open market in the United States – without entirely reciprocating to American exporters and investors. As the political economist Robert Keohane summed it up: "So the United States farsightedly made short-term sacrifices in giving financial aid and in permitting discrimination against American exports in order to accomplish the longer-term objective of creating a stable and prosperous international economic order in which liberal capitalism would prevail and American influence would be predominant."[7]

After the sixties, U.S. international power declined. Not that the United States lost its leadership role. But power is a comparative thing, and when some become more powerful, others become comparatively less powerful. In adjusting to the new circumstances, many Americans perceived their country to be in an absolute fall. The seventies were years in which Americans, or at least American pundits, wrangled over the causes of the country's "failure," a word that came into common use by the end of the sixties with reference to everything from liberal internationalism to the civil rights movement and the War on Poverty (see Chapter 16).

To be sure, the seventies marked the end of the rapid increase in Americans' rise to affluence. Productivity growth fell. American manufacturers found themselves in a losing rivalry with foreign producers in many merchandise sectors, even in the domestic market. For the first time in more than half a century, the

---

[7] Robert Keohane, "Hegemonic Leadership," in William P. Avery et al., eds., *America in a Changing World Political Economy* (Longman, 1982).

merchandise balance of trade turned negative; that is, the country began paying more for imported goods than it received from exports. Real family income continued to rise in the 1970s but at a dramatically slower rate. For example, real income for middle-class families rose by 13 percent between 1970 and 1980 and by only 11 percent for the 1970–1990 period, compared to 39 percent for the sixties and over 100 percent between 1950 and 1970. That two-earner families had become increasingly commonplace by the 1970s made the relatively small rise in real family income especially troubling.[8] The contrast – the ending of the postwar revolutionary increase in affluence and the blow to expectations that it all implied – seems to have had a demoralizing effect.

The United States remained the dominant power in the non-Soviet world, but within increasingly perceptible limits. Its failure to defeat the campaign by the North Vietnamese communist regime to annex South Vietnam and dominate neighboring Laos and Cambodia shattered postwar illusions about America's military omnipotence. For a time, some feared that the Vietnam debacle had weakened the effectiveness of the American shield against the expansion of Soviet communism. The appearance of weakness was magnified in 1979, four years after the U.S. withdrawal under fire from Vietnam, when Iran's newly established revolutionary regime took the entire U.S. Embassy staff in Teheran hostage and taunted the world's greatest military power in its helplessness.[9] What both the Vietnam defeat and the Teheran standoff demonstrated was that – in the face of suicidal military tactics, terrorism, and the use of hostages as a weapon of war – American military might would prove largely ineffectual.

Meanwhile, U.S. economic leadership had gone into partial eclipse. This was more important than the military factor. Following America's lead, international trade barriers had come down. World trade grew spectacularly as the industrial and industrializing nations became increasingly interdependent. On U.S. prompting, GATT conferences gradually reduced tariff and import quota barriers to virtual insignificance (except for agriculture). Between 1963 and 1973,

---

[8] U.S. Census Bureau, Housing and Household Economic Statistics Division, as revised 13 May 2005.

[9] It was in an important sense a self-imposed helplessness that rested on Americans' humane considerations for the lives of both the hostages and innocent Iranians. A less scrupulous power could have used its ample technology to obliterate Teheran. It may be instructive to consider George Orwell's essay, "Reflections on Gandhi," reprinted in *A Collection of Essays* (Doubleday, 1954), pp. 177–85. Orwell credited Gandhi with success in freeing India of British rule by an extreme pacifist tactic, but he notes how ineffectual the tactic would have been if Gandhi had been dealing with Hitler or Stalin (or any of the later dictators, from Idi Amin to Augusto Pinochet and Sadaam Hussein). "It is difficult to see," Orwell wrote, "how Gandhi's methods could be applied in a country where opponents of the regime disappear in the middle of the night and are never heard of again." Gandhi's methods might work well in dealing with even a limited liberal regime, but not hardly, Orwell judged, "when you are dealing with lunatics" (pp. 184–5).

merchandise trade among industrial countries quadrupled and then more than doubled again in the next ten years – and then doubled still again during the following decade.[10] In three decades after 1960, the proportion of U.S. GDP derived from overseas trade more than doubled, from its long-standing historic average of just under 10 percent to 22 percent by 1992.

Americans were witnessing the rise of the global business firm that "outsourced" manufacturing processes in multiple countries for assembly and then sold the finished product, usually back home or in another of the advanced industrial countries; likewise, parts of a product might be shipped from diverse sources for overseas assembly and then reshipped back to a home market. One effect was to reduce the American manufacturing workforce, eliminating millions of high-paying jobs but also reducing consumer costs. Another effect was to stimulate economic development in impoverished countries, pulling significant portions of their populations out of poverty.

But the success of its policies in rehabilitating and stimulating industrial growth in Western Europe and Asia eventually diminished America's hegemonic power. The strength of West European and East Asian competition in foreign and domestic markets raised protectionist sentiment in the United States and also among its trading partners, whose greater economic strength emboldened them to resist U.S. pressure for extending the range of free trade. Although formal tariff protectionism remained low, nontariff barriers to trade proliferated. These included a variety of techniques: (a) product quality standards; (b) licensing requirements; (c) traditionalist business arrangements among networks of home-country suppliers and distributors (e.g., in Japan the *keiretsu*; in Korea the *chaebol*); (d) government subsidies and protection for favored domestic industries; (e) "trigger mechanisms" designed to activate tariffs against "unfair dumping" of foreign exports; and, if all else failed, (f) import quotas.

By the 1960s, U.S. policies designed to provide liquidity to European capital markets by covering payment deficits with chits or IOUs began to run out of control. The IOUs circulated or were put into credit accounts as "eurodollars." The deficits resulted from five major dollar outflows: (1) foreign aid programs, (2) support of U.S. troops abroad, (3) tourist spending, (4) foreign investments by U.S. businesses, and (5) increased imports of foreign goods. The latter was especially important because, as the U.S. positive merchandise trade balance shrank, the payment deficits rose sharply. Moreover, the American merchandise trade surplus was the main support for European confidence in the soundness of the eurodollars. As international confidence eroded in the early sixties, the United States faced a major challenge to its leadership.

[10] Joan Spero & Jeffrey Hart, *The Politics of International Economic Relations,* 5th ed. (St. Martin's, 1997), ch. 3.

The dollar had been the international medium of exchange as well as the standard of value against which the West European and Asian trading partners fixed their currencies. Foreign countries accepted lines of credit in dollars because U.S. exports dominated international trade; every country figured it could always use dollars, because either it or its trading partners would ultimately need dollars to buy American goods. But by the early 1960s, European and Japanese exports began to rival those of the United States. As the American merchandise trade balance dwindled, some countries (notably France) began calling on the United States to pay its debts with gold rather than with more credits. By that time it was already evident that the value of the U.S. export balance would no longer come close to covering all claims on the dollar. But to pay in gold, priced then at a fixed $35 an ounce, would have quickly stripped the United States of all its gold reserves.

As early as 1963, the Kennedy administration's promotion of the Interest Equalization Tax Act signaled acknowledgment of the change. It reversed earlier policy by aiming to *reduce* incentives for American investment in foreign securities and property assets. It proved insufficient. By 1971, the Nixon administration moved to meet the rising deficit problem by taking the United States off the international gold standard. That effectively devalued the dollar by allowing the price of gold to float free. (It rose in a short time to over $800 an ounce, then settled back in subsequent decades to fluctuate mostly between $200 and $350.) For a hegemonic state to devalue its own currency symbolized the decline of its power.

But devaluation did not alter a more basic problem, which was the increasing competitiveness of European and Asian industrial exports. For example, in 1950 Americans were buying only 4 percent of their automobiles from foreign manufacturers, but by 1979, 27 percent of American-owned vehicles were manufactured abroad. Americans were importing 14 percent of their steel in 1979 versus 4 percent in 1960. Americans preferred foreign to domestic sources for more than half their electronic products, up from less than 6 percent in 1960; almost half their textile machinery, up from less than 7 percent; and more than a quarter of their metal-cutting machine tools, up from less than 4 percent.[11]

The failure of American manufacturers to keep pace with modern production and merchandising techniques – especially in steel and automobiles, but also in consumer electronics and in the crucial areas of machinery and machine tools – compounded the problem. So did the fact that modern communications and transportation technology had made it possible for American manufacturers to move production facilities to low-wage and environmentally heedless countries abroad, notably Hong Kong, Singapore, South Korea, Taiwan, and Mexico. The

---

[11] Spero & Hart, *International Economic Relations,* ch. 3.

multinational corporations created jobs abroad while reducing manufacturing employment at home.

Meanwhile, many American consumers perceived a sharp decline in the quality of goods made in the United States. There seemed to be widespread discontent among American workers. It is not clear whether the discontent resulted from managerial abuse or from a deterioration of the work ethic among a generally prosperous and possibly overpaid industrial workforce.[12] The fact remains that the annual rate of growth in American productivity for the two decades after 1960 amounted to only half that for the previous two decades, and in some years it was negative. In the 1960–1973 period, U.S. productivity improved by an annual average of 2.8 percent. That was already the lowest rate of growth in the non-Soviet industrial world; for the rest of the 1970s, it grew by less than 1 percent.[13]

All these factors helped make American-made goods uncompetitive in world markets. By 1972, for the first time in the twentieth century the balance of merchandise trade between the United States and the rest of the world turned unfavorable. By 1981, Americans were importing $28 billion more in foreign goods than they were exporting. The deficit would grow to $500 billion in the next seven years. In 1969, imports represented just 14 percent of U.S. GNP that originated in manufacturing, but by 1986 that portion had grown to 45 percent.[14] By the mid-eighties the dollar, once the international standard of value, had begun a steep decline; it became merely another currency, whose value in relationship to Japanese and West German currency, for example, dropped by as much as 50 percent. In order to maintain its economy, the U.S. resorted to borrowing heavily abroad.

It was primarily massive Japanese and German investments and purchases of U.S. Treasury bonds in the 1980s that kept the Reagan economy from going bust after his administration reduced taxes while raising military expenditures fourfold. By the mid-1980s the United States – once the world's creditor – had become the world's largest debtor nation, owing a quarter of a trillion dollars to foreign lenders and paying them annually more in interest than it was able to appropriate for its own federal housing and education budgets combined. Meanwhile, American industry also found it necessary to go abroad for its investment

---

[12] Some economists speculated that antidiscrimination regulations under the Civil Rights Act of 1964 deterred management from effective testing of potential employees' suitability for important jobs and that this depressed productivity. For a balanced assessment of the many reasons for the decline in productivity, see Edward F. Denison, *Trends in American Economic Growth, 1929–1982* (Brookings, 1985), especially ch. 3, "The Slowdown in Growth."

[13] Ira C. Magaziner & Robert Reich, *Minding America's Business* (Vintage, 1983), pp. 32–6. See also Spero & Hart, *International Economic Relations.*

[14] Cathie J. Martin, *Shifting the Burden: The Struggle over Growth and Corporate Taxation* (University of Chicago Press, 1991), p. 161.

capital. Foreign-held assets of U.S. properties outstripped American-held assets abroad by another $250 billion.[15]

❊   ❊   ❊

In the 1940s, then, Americans had to adjust to living in and being part of the world's richest and most powerful country. As Henry Luce had urged, the U.S. belatedly became a world leader. Reacting to the acknowledged costs of their own earlier aloofness, Americans – or at least their policy makers – took on the burdens they deemed commensurate with their power, their ideals, and their ambitions. For better and in some cases for worse, the United States had tremendous influence on people in a wide variety of ways and in almost every corner of the globe.

Americans had to adjust to the responsibilities that their riches and power, and that the country's liberal internationalist leaders, had thrust upon them. Most of the people of postwar Europe and Asia sought nothing more than peace, stability, and prosperity, and they looked to the United States for leadership. Unlike the aftermath of World War I, America took on that role, becoming the "leader of the free world," arbiter for the noncommunist world of standards of legitimate political and economic behavior, underwriter of economic development, stabilizer of international markets, and in general the hegemonic power in the international political economy. That influence and power came with a price. Americans would pay materially to help rehabilitate Western Europe's and Japan's postwar economy; to throw back North Korea's invasion of South Korea; to reverse Iraq's military conquest of Kuwait; to attempt to impose some respectable order on a brutally corrupt and inept regime in Haiti; to try to restore a semblance of order amid murderous anarchy in places like Lebanon and Somalia; among many other interventions.

But Americans did not always use their power wisely or humanely or according to principles of international law. Guatemala, Nicaragua, Honduras, Panama, El Salvador, Iran, and Chile remain places associated with some of Americans' less respectable interventions. But it was America's military intervention in Indochina that would prove both beyond Americans' power and beyond their moral stamina. The barbarism of the effort would do lasting damage to the country as a liberal society and to Americans' self-respect, while its cost was doing like damage to the nation's economy.

And so, in the 1970s, Americans would have to adjust again, this time to their country's sharply reduced power, to its status as a major net importer and

---

[15] *Wall Street Journal* (18 Jan. 1988), p. 1. For a more complete account of the growing stake by foreign investors in U.S. companies and assets by the mid-eighties, see Martin Tolchin & Susan Tolchin, *Buying into America: How Foreign Money Is Changing the Face of Our Nation* (Times Books, 1988).

debtor, and – in large measure because of the Vietnam disaster – to its diminished moral standing as well.

If, as is generally understood, World War II was the most transforming event of the twentieth century, then for the United States the Vietnam War was the crucial event of the second half of that century. It divided liberals and propelled a polarization of American thought and politics (already slowly underway) that had no parallel since the Civil War era. More than anything else, what produced this outcome was the increasingly brutal and inhumane manner with which the war was fought and the unpersuasive and largely disingenuous manner with which it was defended.

The altogether too frequent misuse of power would foster a profound disillusionment among many Americans, as well as among people abroad, about the promise of America as a beacon of hope and a model of democratic decency. In fact, by the 1970s a remarkable number of distinguished Americans began expressing their growing doubts that the America they had cherished unquestioningly in their youth as the herald of all good things for the world could any longer be so regarded.

"In 1960," wrote one eminent political economist in 1979, "I had not even questioned the general superiority of American society and American institutions .... By 1975 I found myself ... wondering what had happened to America."[16] Only 27 years after Henry Luce had proclaimed "The American Century," Andrew Hacker, one of the country's leading political scientists, proclaimed *The End of the American Era* in his book by that title, and he asked Americans "to acknowledge candidly that we are no longer capable of being a great power."[17] In 1976, the venerable diplomat and historian George Kennan expressed his own grave disappointment. "I grew up," he wrote, "with a certain faith in American civilization and a certain belief that the American experiment was a positive development in the history of mankind .... Now I do not think that U.S. civilization of these last forty to fifty years is a successful civilization."[18]

Shortly before he died in 1974, the renowned political columnist Stewart Alsop wrote in his journal: "For weeks now I have been haunted and depressed by a sense that the American system, in which I have always believed in an unquestioning way, the way a boy believes in his family, really is falling apart; by a sense that we are a failed nation, a failed people." Around the same time he remarked to his fellow journalist brother, Joseph Alsop: "You know, I sometimes thank God you and I were born Americans so long ago – for although I don't

---

[16] Ezra Vogel, *Japan as Number One* (Harper, 1979), p. ix.

[17] Andrew Hacker, *The End of the American Era* (Atheneum, 1970), p. 227.

[18] George Kennan, in *Encounter* (Sept. 1976), p. 104, quoted in William Pfaff, *The New Yorker* (6 June 1977).

enjoy getting older, I begin to suspect we have seen the best times in this country."[19] The eminent historian Henry Steele Commager may have summed it up
around the same time when he asked: "Who now believes that America is the
model for the world?"[20]

In 1941, William Saroyan had written a play that celebrated America as, in
his words, "a happy nation, a free and growing people ... whose casual everyday humanity is stronger than any other power in the world." Forty years later,
Time editorialized, "It has been a while since Americans have felt that way about
themselves."[21]

Even so, for the rest of the century most of the world, sometimes resentfully,
would continue to look to the United States for leadership. Only the United
States had the resources and the will (however attenuated by the mid-seventies)
to carry out major international endeavors. Invariably it was to the United States
that the world turned in order to contain diverse calamities, from natural catas-
trophes to potential and on-going genocidal violence. It was to America that
Palestinians and Israelis came when seeking a way out of their decades-long
cycles of mutual violence. It was to America that the British turned in hope
of ending the mindless conflict between Northern Ireland's Catholic and Protestant thugs. It was to the United States that the governments of Germany, Britain,
France, and Italy turned before anything effective could be done to end the mutual massacres among the Serbs, Muslims, and Croats in the former Yugoslavia.

It was, moreover, the example of American liberal democratic institutions
that, for the postwar world, made liberal democracy an almost universally accepted model for legitimate government. That was something new, because for
at least the half-century before 1945 much of the world had searched for alternatives to liberalism, such as fascism and communism. When the United States
came under criticism for misusing its power, the standards on which the criticisms were based typically were those that Americans themselves had established
and promoted. Indeed, at home, the disillusionment of people like Kennan and
Commager came from a profound sense of betrayal of their birthright.

In the nineteenth century, Britain's Lord Acton famously quipped: "Power
corrupts, and absolute power corrupts absolutely." During the Vietnam War,
Senator William Fulbright of Arkansas echoed that thought as he warned his
country about "The Arrogance of Power," the title of a major address to the
Senate that was later published as a book. With the collapse and disintegration

---

[19] Comment to Joseph Alsop is quoted in Robert W. Merry, *Taking on the World: Joseph and Stewart Alsop – Guardians of the American Century* (Viking, 1996), pp. 529–30. The other remark is
in Stewart Alsop, *Stay of Execution: A Sort of Memoir* (Lippincott, 1973), p. 298.

[20] Henry Steele Commager, *The Defeat of America: Presidential Power and the National Character*
(Simon & Schuster, 1974), p. 117.

[21] *Time* (23 Feb. 1981).

of the Soviet Union in 1991, the United States became the world's sole and in-comparable superpower. The country's heavy expenditures over the decades for military technology and transport had meanwhile made it possible for America to project unprecedented military might to virtually any part of the globe; in many respects, it possessed "absolute power." Two years into the twenty-first century, Lord Acton's and William Fulbright's words appeared to take on new cogency.

The belligerence and the unilateralism of America's postmillennium policies would evoke still more disillusionment at home and abroad. Inspired by its unchallenged military power, the administration of George W. Bush began by trashing several international treaties and protocols. It followed up by snubbing the International Criminal Court and expressing contempt for the United Nations. When it acted on its newly minted doctrine of "preemptive war" to invade Iraq despite its failure to gain support in the United Nations for that method of fighting international terrorism, the United States became something of an international pariah. In response to criticism by the governments of France and Germany, two of America's major trading partners and its crucial allies during the Cold War, U.S. officials dismissed their importance as "Old Europe." To justify bare-knuckle treatment of prisoners taken in "the war on terror" in violation of the Geneva Conventions, administration officials ridiculed the Conventions as "quaint" and "obsolete." In response to international complaints that U.S. military officers and CIA agents were using torture in their interrogation of prisoners, administration officials exonerated themselves by offering a redefinition of "torture."

Once more, distinguished Americans who had never questioned their pride in being Americans felt impelled to express their dismay. One was the eminent historian John Higham, who, shortly before he died in 2003 at the age of 82, wrote to a friend how disturbed he had become by the shift in America's international standing. "I feel," he said, "that everything I have stood for is being undermined and that I must get back to work instead of brooding about what seems like a long term failure of the promise of America."[22]

But this takes the story a bit beyond the purview of this book.[23]

---

[22] In the *New York Review of Books* (23 Oct. 2003), p. 62. America's image would continue to deteriorate. On Memorial Day weekend 2005, *New York Times* columnist Bob Herbert – expressing a view spreading rapidly around the world – wrote sadly about how ours was "the country that was once the world's most brilliant beacon of freedom and justice." Now, he noted, "the image of the United States has deteriorated around the world. The U.S. is now widely viewed as a brutal, bullying nation that countenances torture and operates hideous prison camps [overseas] ... where inmates have been horribly abused, gruesomely humiliated and even killed." *New York Times* (30 May 2005), p. A19.

[23] However, see Chapter 21.

8

The Rise of the Military in American Society

A standing force ... is a dangerous, at the same time that it may be a necessary, provision. On the smallest scale it has its inconveniences. On an extensive scale its consequences may be fatal. On any scale it is an object of laudable circumspection and precaution.[1]

James Madison

Safety from external danger is the most powerful director of national conduct. Even the ardent love of liberty will after a time, give way to its dictates .... To be more safe, [people] at length become willing to run the risk of being less free.[2]

Alexander Hamilton

The country's reversal of its historic isolationism would bring a change of potentially prodigious significance for the place of the military in American life. For over half of its history, America's geographic advantages had permitted the country to do without a sizable military. Probably even more important, the nation's political orientation had served to keep the military weak. Partly from their colonial experience, the post-Revolution leaders of the new nation were wary of the dangers and particularly the expense of a large standing army. The Founding Fathers gave over to the citizen-soldier the chief burden of national security. They relied on conscription of able-bodied male citizens into state militias when necessary to meet security needs. Furthermore, a nation that was dedicated to the proposition that "all men are created equal" could not readily accept the rigid hierarchy of status and authority implicit in military organization. Nor did the American presumption that the state existed to serve private economic ambitions leave much room for military values, military matters, or military

[1] *The Federalist Papers* (Modern Library, 1937), no. 41, p. 262.
[2] Ibid., no. 8, p. 42.

ways.[3] Throughout most of U.S. history, there remained a long-standing cool-ness between the military and American businessmen, whose concern for costs usually trumped all supposed imperatives of glory or honor. Finally, the na-tion's scientists and scholars, who as a group placed individualism and inde-pendent thought high among their social priorities, viewed the military and its regimented, conformist discipline as an alien and at best simply a necessary presence.

After 1949, all the historic barriers to a large military establishment eroded.

On the whole, the military had fared badly in American life. The literature on U.S. military history is filled with lamentations over the stepchild treatment accorded the professional military. One historian noted that, "until the respon-sibilities of world power in the 20th Century brought a new rapport between the Army and people, the Regular Army was sufficiently isolated to resemble sometimes a monastic order."[4] Sociologist Morris Janowitz, a leading expert on the professional military, concluded in 1960: "In the United States the military profession does not carry great prestige .... In contrast to the public acclaim ac-corded individual heroes, officership remains a relatively low-status profession."[5] Political scientist Samuel Huntington invented the phrase "business pacifism" to describe the attitude of American society at the height of its commitment in the late nineteenth century to capitalist individualism, industrial growth, and lib-eral economics.[6] Indeed, Americans' historical commitment to the materialist objectives of private business enterprise made them fundamentally averse to mil-itary ideals, a point which Huntington drove home – and deplored – in the close of his classic study, *The Soldier and the State*. There he starkly contrasted the "disorderly" and crass aspect of Main Street with the symmetry and serenity of West Point. That such a sentiment was put forward in 1957 by a "mainstream" Harvard scholar with liberal Democratic credentials may have been a sign of the increasing attractiveness of things military to Americans in the Cold War era.

Until at least mid-century, formidable forces remained to subdue any ten-dency Americans may have had to exalt the military as either a central American institution or as a model for designing the Good Society. Geography still played a role in diverting attention from military virtues, as Americans continued to re-gard the Atlantic and Pacific Oceans as sufficiently protective moats. Reliance

---

[3] See: Thomas C. Cochran, *Business in American Life* (McGraw-Hill, 1972); J. Willard Hurst, *Law and the Conditions of Freedom in the Nineteenth Century United States* (University of Wisconsin Press, 1956); Stuart Bruchey, *Enterprise: The Dynamic Economy of a Free People* (Harvard Univer-sity Press, 1990); Richard Hofstadter, *The American Political Tradition and the Men Who Made It* (Vintage, 1954).

[4] Russell Weigley, *History of the United States Army* (Indiana University Press, 1984), p. 158.

[5] Morris Janowitz, *The Professional Soldier* (Free Press, 1960), p. 3.

[6] Samuel Huntington, *The Soldier and the State* (Vintage, 1957), pp. 222–6.

on conscription during threats to national security meanwhile served to assure that the enlarged military would consist mostly of civilian-oriented personnel. For some draftees, two years of compulsory service had the prospect of producing a lasting antimilitary animus (although it is true that many draftees would regard their army stint as the proudest experience of their life). The tradition among the general officers, moreover, remained committed to civilian superiority and to keeping clear of partisan politics. The intellectual leadership of the country, Professor Huntington notwithstanding, retained a strong preference for the disorderliness of Main Street over the serene symmetry of West Point. Finally, when one enumerates the reasons for Americans' traditional repression of a strong professional military establishment, the role of the business community must rank at the top.

Postwar events would weaken all of these subduing forces. With the advent of nuclear energy, supersonic transportation, intercontinental ballistic missiles (ICBMs), and planet-circling satellites, America's geographic advantages all but vanished. As the Cold War intensified, Americans poured a substantial share of their economic resources into military supplies, services, and personnel and into weapons procurement and development. The size of the new and by then permanent military force countered all previous American experience. The ten-year average for 1947–1957 was just under 3 million men, about ten times the 1939 total. National defense outlays during that period absorbed about a third of all American government expenditures (federal, state, and local), and about 60 percent of federal expenditures. That did not count appropriations for aerospace; veterans' benefits and services; general research and development, probably at least half of which was for military purposes; outlays for the Atomic Energy Commission, which funded nuclear weapons research and procurement;[7] and foreign loans and grants, which also contained large defense and defense-related sums.

Inevitably, particular sectors of the business and wage-earning communities developed vital stakes in expenditures for such things. Congressmen competed vigorously among themselves to obtain military contracts for companies in their districts and to establish military facilities there. They enjoyed active support not merely from the giant corporations that held the principal contracts but also from labor unions and small business subcontractors, as well as from chambers of commerce and real estate boards that hoped for increased mercantile and property transactions. Such developments went a long way toward creating a network of businesses within American society with a special interest in perpetuating a wartime economy. As Senator William Proxmire of Wisconsin argued in a subcommittee report in 1969: "The danger to the public interest is that these

---

[7] In 1974, these functions were folded into the newly created Department of Energy.

firms ... have a community of interest with the military itself. They hold a narrow view of public priorities based on self-interest. They have a largely uncritical view of military spending .... Fortified by self-interest ... they may see only military answers to exceedingly complex diplomatic and political problems."[8]

The political pressures for new expenditures for the military provoked President Dwight Eisenhower, in his valedictory address to the nation in January 1961, to warn of the growth of a "military–industrial complex," which he implied might already have acquired "unwarranted influence" in the councils of government. "[The] conjunction of an immense military establishment and a large arms industry is new in the American experience," Eisenhower warned. "The potential for the disastrous rise of misplaced power exists and will persist .... *We should take nothing for granted.*"[9]

Eisenhower went further, warning of the "prospect of domination of the nation's scholars by Federal employment, project allocations, and the power of money." Much of the necessary military and military-related research was already being done at universities and government-funded research centers. The arrangement was a carryover from initiatives taken by the nation's universities and research institutes for the development of weaponry during the war. After Japan's surrender, America pursued rapid demobilization and in general sought a separation from arrangements necessitated by the war. But plans had already been made to sustain close ties between the military and academia. In June 1941, President Franklin Roosevelt had issued an executive order creating the Office of Scientific Research and Development, which for the first time endorsed systematic federal support of basic research by university scientists and engineers. Toward the end of the war Edward L. Bowles, science adviser to Secretary of War Henry Stimson, called for "an effective peacetime integration" of the military with the resources of higher education. "Not only is there a great opportunity to underwrite research for its direct contribution to the nation's welfare," he wrote, "but the opportunity [also] exists to encourage the training of brilliant minds and to instill in them a consciousness of their responsibility to the nation's security."[10]

The onset of the Cold War assured that government leaders would stress higher education's obligation to service national security needs. Meanwhile, the

---

[8] Proxmire quoted in Carroll W. Pursell, Jr., ed., *The Military–Industrial Complex* (Harper & Row, 1972), pp. 253–63.

[9] "Farewell Address" (17 Jan. 1961), in *Public Papers of the President of the United States, Dwight D. Eisenhower, 1960–61* (Government Printing Office, 1961), pp. 1035–40. The address is reprinted in numerous anthologies, including Pursell (ibid.); emphasis added.

[10] Quoted in Clayton R. Koppes, *JPL and the American Space Program: A History of the Jet Propulsion Laboratory* (Yale University Press, 1982), p. 26.

heavy federal funding needed for modern scientific research more or less guaranteed that university faculty would be receptive. Some major universities – such as the University of California, the Massachusetts Institute of Technology, and Johns Hopkins – won long-term contracts to administer and provide staff for government-owned military research and development (R&D) facilities; for example, the nuclear weapons research facilities run by the University of California at Los Alamos (New Mexico) and Livermore (California) and the Applied Physics Laboratory run by Johns Hopkins under contract to the U.S. Navy. Several independent R&D institutes served essentially as affiliates of one or another of the armed services, such as RAND Corporation's relationship with the Air Force. With the intensification of the Cold War, those ties became much firmer.[11]

For the most part, the militarist effects of the so-called military–industrial–academic complex remained limited by popular pressures to keep taxes and the power of an activist government at a minimum. After the 1950s and until at least the 1980s, total outlays for the military continued to grow slowly, while the proportion of government expenditures for the military in fact declined significantly. Total federal expenditures for all goods and services remained fairly constant at about 20 percent of gross national product (GNP) throughout the 1950–1980 period. As the proportion of expenditures for social services (Medicare, Social Security, education, welfare, and other transfer payments) increased, national defense expenditures dropped to less than 50 percent of total federal spending by 1960 and to about 25 percent by the mid-seventies. Department of Defense contributions to the nation's R&D dropped significantly below the contributions of the National Science Foundation and the National Institutes of Health. As a percentage of GNP, defense appropriations fell from a postwar high of about 13 percent during the Korean War (1950–1953) and remained below 9 percent thereafter, hitting a low of about 5 percent in the post-Vietnam seventies and reaching a half-century low in the 1990s. Even during the unprecedented peacetime military buildup during the Reagan administration, defense spending barely reached 7 percent of GNP.[12] By this time there was little opposition in the country to the maintenance of a powerful and permanent military establishment.

There remained the question of the increasing role of professional military officers in shaping public opinion and in the policy-making councils of government. Liberals as well as conservatives could not deny that the problem presented

---

[11] See Richard M. Abrams, "The U.S. Military and Higher Education: A Brief History," *Annals, AAPSS* (March 1989), pp. 15–28.

[12] See Edward Reubens, "The Peace Dividend: Potentials, Resistances, and Planning for Military/Industrial Conversion," *In Depth* (Fall 1992 special issue), p. 204. In 1990 dollars, average U.S. military expenditures in 1980 amounted to $208 billion. Reagan raised that precipitously to $284 billion by 1984 and to $324 billion by 1986, leveling off slowly to $299 billion by 1990.

by fascism in Europe and Asia had had to be solved by military means, not by the liberal preference for negotiation and compromise. Hence even liberals, who might have been expected to stress economic and diplomatic means, gave over to military leaders – and in some cases to the military as an institution – a prime role in facing up to the postwar problem presented by Stalin's Soviet Union.

One reason was that, given the novelty of the nation's postwar international posture, there were few people available with the skills that many military leaders had. In his book *The Power Elite* (1956), the social critic C. Wright Mills noted, no doubt reluctantly: "As a coherent group of men, the military is probably the most competent now concerned with national policy."[13] It was not without significance that General George C. Marshall, wartime chief of staff of the Army, became President Harry Truman's Secretary of State and later Secretary of Defense (for which Congress had to waive the ban on a military person holding that post) as well as Truman's most trusted foreign policy adviser during both his administrations; nor that Truman tried to persuade General Dwight Eisenhower to accept the Democratic nomination for president in 1948 and again in 1952.

Mills was, in fact, probably the first scholar to remark on the entry of the professional military into the top circles of the American "ruling elite." In his pathbreaking work, he called attention to the millions of dollars expended by the U.S. military to build a positive image for public appreciation. "The content of this great effort," as Mills saw it, was "to define the reality of international relations in a military way, to portray the armed forces in a manner attractive to civilians, and thus to emphasize the need for the expansion of military facilities. The aim is to build the prestige of the military establishment and to create respect for its personnel, and thus to prepare the public for military-approved policies, and to make Congress ready and willing to pay for them. There is also, of course, the intention of readying the public for the advent of war."[14] "Never before," wrote military sociologist Charles Moskos, "had uniformed officers been so characterized in American society."[15] But as early as 1949 Hanson Baldwin, the *New York Times*'s leading military specialist, had sharply warned: "the influence of the military on public opinion – a necessary influence in the atomic age – has reached the point today where it is time to call a halt."[16]

[13] C. Wright Mills, *The Power Elite* (Oxford University Press, 1956).
[14] Mills, *Power Elite*. Most of the book has been put on the Internet; the quoted passage can be found at ⟨http://www.thirdworldtraveler.com/Book_Excerpts/MilitaryAscendancy_PE.htm⟩.
[15] Charles C. Moskos, Jr., "The Military–Industrial Complex: Theoretical Antecedents and Conceptual Contradictions," in Sam C. Sarkesian, ed., *The Military–Industrial Complex: A Reassessment* (Sage, 1972), p. 10. Two books also published in 1956 made similar observations about the unprecedented ascendancy of the military in American life: Arthur A. Ekrich, *The Civilian and the Military* (Oxford University Press, 1956); and Walter Millis, *Arms and Men* (Putnam's, 1956).
[16] "When the Big Guns Speak," in Lester Markel, ed., *Public Opinion and Foreign Policy* (Council of Foreign Relations / Harper, 1949), p. 119.

There would be no halt. By the end of the sixties, a number of scholars made strong cases for the argument that military leaders had come to wield political power independently of both the civilian bureaucracy and private-sector business interests and had thus become prime movers in policy making.[17] The Pentagon would continue to finance lobbying efforts in the halls of Congress (illegal, but never challenged) on behalf of weapons procurement and budgetary advantages.[18] Corporations hoping for military contracts purposefully put high-ranking retired military officers on their payrolls to help with lobbying federal procurement agencies. As of 1970, more than 2,000 such officers were employed by the 100 companies that were awarded two thirds of all defense contract dollars.[19]

In truth, the more serious effect of the newly enlarged military establishment on American society during the second half of the twentieth century concerned the growing propensity among *civilian* leaders to seek military solutions to international problems – simply because so much military power was available and paid for and because so much financial power lay behind it. In making military power available and in paying for it, the U.S. government created a strong core of civilian interests with a more or less permanent stake in maintaining a preponderant military establishment. This would prove to be no small matter: it contributed to giving the military a highly significant role in national policy making, one that contradicted more than 150 years of American tradition and practices. Whether the role of the military in policy making came primarily from uniformed military officers or from government or bureaucratic people influenced by the new and hefty military presence has been disputed by the specialists, but there can be little doubt of the tremendous change in circumstances for American society.

To sum things up so far: The heavy reliance of American society on the military to provide security in a threatening world, when combined with the stake that the business and academic communities came to have in a sizable military establishment, inevitably diminished the historic resistance of those communities to a powerful military role in American life. So, too, would the ending of military conscription in 1973. In fact, that event might prove to be the most crucial of all in revolutionizing the role of the military in American society. Congress had authorized the draft again in 1949, a year that featured the first successful Soviet testing of an atomic bomb and the communist victory in China. In

---

[17] See Richard J. Barnet, *The Economy of Death* (Atheneum, 1969); John Kenneth Galbraith, *How to Control the Military* (Signet, 1969); Robert Heilbroner, "Military America," *New York Review of Books* (23 July 1970).

[18] See e.g. Willaim J. Fulbright, *The Pentagon Propaganda Machine* (Liveright, 1970).

[19] Those same corporations, however, earned most of their profits from nondefense products and services. See Albert D. Biderman, "Retired Military within and without the Military–Industrial Complex," in Sarkesian, *Military–Industrial Complex,* pp. 110–11.

a (largely successful) effort to defuse campus protests against the war in Vietnam, President Nixon announced the end of conscription in 1970, to take effect in 1973.[20] He emphasized the justice of a volunteer system in a free society while noting that "our likely military needs in the future will place a special premium on the services of career soldiers."[21]

Revoking the draft and going to an all-volunteer military – during a period of serious international tensions that required millions of military personnel – decidedly broke with the tradition of a citizen army. "The expanded 'peacetime' all-volunteer military introduced in June 1973," wrote military expert Morris Janowitz, "constituted a completely new development in the United States."[22] It raised the prospect of a professional military that could develop in isolation from the rest of the society, with its own traditions, its own elan, its own ethics, its own commitments.

In fact, in 1998, in upholding the right of the military to exclude homosexuals, the courts effectively confirmed that prospect. In *Able v. U.S.*, a federal appellate court declared that the "equal protection" clause of the Constitution does not apply to military personnel because they voluntarily subject themselves to an authority that "is characterized by its own laws, rules, customs, and traditions, including numerous restrictions on personal behavior, that would not be acceptable in civilian society."[23] In short, the advent of the "all-voluntary" military created the potential for a military establishment like those that had repressed or threatened democratic forces in most countries for most of the world's history.

"The great modern fact [for Western civilization]," wrote the renowned political theorist Gaetano Mosca in his classic study, *The Ruling Class*, "is the huge standing army that is ... obedient to the orders of civil authority and has very little political influence." But that fact, he continued, "represents a most fortunate exception, if it is not absolutely without parallel in human history. Only a habit of a few generations' standing, along with ignorance or forgetfulness of the past, can make such a situation seem normal." Mosca went on to warn: "It is not at all impossible that different historical circumstances that are now maturing may end by weakening, or even undoing, the complex, delicate and sagely elaborated mechanism of the modern army."[24] As Eisenhower had cautioned in his "military–industrial complex" remarks of 1961, Americans "should take nothing for granted."

---

[20] For the libertarian and "free market" arguments that underlay the decision to end conscription, see Martin Anderson, *The Military Draft* (Hoover Press, 1979).

[21] Quoted in Anderson (ibid.), p. 606.

[22] Morris Janowitz, *The Reconstruction of Patriotism* (University of Chicago Press, 1983), p. xiii.

[23] The decisions in that case and one other were not appealed to the U.S. Supreme Court. *Able v. U.S.*, 2d Circuit, vol. 155, F.3d (1998), p. 628; *Thorne v. U.S. Dept. Defense*, vol. 139, F.3d (1998), p. 893.

[24] Gaetano Mosca, *The Ruling Class* (McGraw-Hill, 1939), p. 229.

Little of this potential would be realized by the 1990s, despite the large military buildup during the Reagan administration and Reagan's exceptional attention to extolling military values and professional personnel. At least in the media advertising, recruiting for the all-volunteer services nearly always emphasized the civilian uses of skills that an enlisted man or woman could gain in a brief hitch with the military. In an important way, the recruiting technique suggested that "volunteer" is not exactly descriptive of the new military; "mercenary" might be more appropriate. Most recruits were not responding to a call to duty as good citizens but instead were selling their services for economic rewards, current and future, which the military recruiters took pains to emphasize. It fit well with the market-oriented (or "privatization") approach to policy that gained favor in the seventies.[25]

Until at least the 1980s, leaders of the military establishment continued for the most part to be individuals whose own training had specifically emphasized traditional deference to civilian control. By the last decade of the century, however, Americans had reason to note that the generation so trained had passed. In 1993, when General Colin Powell (head of the Joint Chiefs of Staff) publicly challenged President Clinton by hinting that he might resign over an issue of military personnel policy – specifically, the president's proposed order to end the exclusion of homosexuals from the military – it seemed to many people a dangerous confrontation of the country's civilian commander in chief by a high military officer, a noteworthy departure from the traditional civil–military relationship. In 1948, when President Truman had ordered an end to racial discrimination in the military,[26] Army chief of staff General Omar Bradley was quoted the following day as saying that the Army "is not out to make any social reform." Truman publicly rebuked Bradley, whose status as a war hero was nearly as exalted as General Eisenhower's. Bradley apologized, saying he had not known of Truman's order when he made the statement and never intended it to suggest defiance. Eisenhower, too, opposed the order but never said so publicly, although opponents of desegregation continually embarrassed him by quoting a comment he had earlier made to the Senate Armed Forces Committee: "I do believe that if we attempt merely by passing a lot of laws to force someone to like someone, we are just going to get into trouble." Truman pushed ahead, with eventual success, against some congressional disapproval and determined

---

[25] "The military services are the only employers today who don't have to compete in the job market," Nixon argued in his address to the nation announcing the new policy. Quoted in Anderson, *Military Draft,* p. 606. Once combat danger rose after the invasion of Iraq in 2003, recruiters fell short of quotas and so job opportunities in the military went begging.

[26] Executive Order 9981: "It is the declared policy of the President that there shall be equality of treatment and opportunity for all persons in the armed services without regard to race, color, religion, or national origin."

resistance from the officer corps.[27] President Clinton found it impossible to take similar action.

When he was president, Eisenhower had insisted that, once the commander in chief makes a decision, every officer in the service was duty-bound to support it. To do otherwise, he said, "is damn near treason." Every officer has "an absolute duty" to speak frankly when questioned by Congress, but taking the initiative to approach Congress or the press and contradict the president, Eisenhower claimed, was "insubordinate" and required "correction."[28] By the 1990s, there was no one of stature in the military who would publicly endorse Eisenhower's claim.

By the mid-nineties, the tendency of a volunteer military establishment to develop a sense of isolation from the civilian sector – and specifically, a sense of aggrieved isolation – showed elements of realization. As Morris Janowitz had noted 35 years earlier in his classic study *The Professional Soldier,* military ideology had always stressed disapproval of the lack of discipline and disrespect for authority that had historically characterized American society. By the 1990s, the "countercultural" challenges to authority and traditional decorum that blossomed in the Sixties had become a source of widespread public agitation, particularly as traditionalist sectors of the polity focused on publicly expressed and debated sexual practices and preferences. Traditionalists aggressively confronted the cultural insurgency that they blamed for the country's high crime and divorce rates, the rising number of out-of-wedlock births, and growing welfare costs. Political partisans exploited the issue, contending that American society was gravely engaged in a "culture war." With the ending of the Cold War, an influential number of retired and active officers in the new, volunteer, professional military began to articulate a role for themselves in the multicultural ferment of the nineties.

Directly challenging the military's long tradition of abstinence from public posturing, a popular military analyst and two Marine reservists probably summed up a lot of thinking among the new professional military leaders in an article in *The Marine Corps Gazette* in 1994:

---

[27] Stephen Ambrose & James A. Barber, Jr., eds., *The Military and American Society* (Free Press, 1972), p. 191; Adam Yarmolinsky, *The Military Establishment: Its Impacts on American Society* (Harper & Row, 1971), p. 341; Richard M. Dalfiume, *Desegregation of the U.S. Armed Forces: Fighting on Two Fronts 1939–1953* (University of Missouri Press, 1969), pp. 167, 172. Eisenhower would offer variations on that theme for the next twelve years, and throughout his presidential administration, against urgings that he be more aggressive in enforcing the Supreme Court's desegregation decisions.

[28] Stephen E. Ambrose, *Eisenhower* (Simon & Schuster, 1984), vol. 2, p. 561, citing notes of a telephone conversation taken by Eisenhower's secretary, Ann Whitman. See also Brian Duchin, "President Eisenhower and the 1958 Reorganization of the Department of Defense," *Presidential Studies Quarterly* (Spring 1994), pp. 243–61, especially p. 251.

Starting in the mid-1960s, we have thrown away the values, morals, and standards that define traditional Western culture. In part, this has been driven by cultural radicals, people who hate our Judeo-Christian culture. Dominant in the elite, especially in the universities, the media, and the entertainment industry ... the cultural radicals have successfully pushed an agenda of moral relativism, militant secularism, and sexual and social "liberation." This agenda has slowly codified into a new ideology, usually known as "multiculturalism" or "political correctness," that is in essence Marxism translated from economic into social terms .... The next real war we fight is likely to be on American soil.[29]

Whereas historians had found that few professional military personnel before the middle of the twentieth century had engaged in politics even to the extent of voting, by the 1990s this had changed significantly. Two decades of the volunteer military meant the rise to the top of a wholly different breed of officers, a corps of men and some women increasingly inclined to regard themselves as special and especially as superior to the civilians they had grown apart from. According to several close observers of the military, there appeared to be a sneering, condescending attitude among them toward "ordinary Americans" in the civilian sector and especially toward the "effete elite" they charged with bringing about the decline of "traditional values." The inconclusive war in Korea and the defeat in Vietnam aggravated tensions between military officers and the American polity. Many U.S. officers responded to their sense of frustration by putting blame on civil institutions, some of which were central to the American political tradition.

A decade before the introduction of the all-volunteer military, scholars had noted the sharp divergence in the attitudes of military personnel toward civil society. One expert on the military wrote, "Brought up in a conservative tradition, their scapegoats have tended to be the civilian politicians and the democratic political process .... Their panacea," Harold Stein found, "has been double-headed: a political process of sufficiently authoritarian character, and a shift of strategic concentration from the actual or potential battlefield to the enemy within."[30]

As the new millennium opened with the onset of America's "war on terrorism" – to which a hard-right, "conservative" president promised an indefinitely long and open-ended engagement – Americans might have had reason to be apprehensive about where the unprecedented ascendancy of the military in American life might lead. Some observers, indeed, began writing of how the United States was becoming "a military society" in which not only foreign relations but also domestic politics had become "militarized."[31] The American president

---

[29] Quoted in Thomas E. Ricks, "The Widening Gap between the Military and Society," *Atlantic Monthly* (July 1997), pp. 66–78.

[30] Harold Stein, ed., *American Civil–Military Decisions: A Book of Case Studies* (University of Alabama Press, 1963), p. 14.

[31] See e.g. Andrew J. Bacevich, *The New American Militarism: How Americans Are Seduced by War* (Oxford University Press, 2005).

declared himself "a war president," demanding loyalty to him as commander in chief rather than as the leader of the nation's civil society. The nation's foreign policy became increasingly militarized with over 700 official military bases abroad, nearly as many as on its own territory. One astute commentator noted how American civilians had even begun purchasing military service vehicles ("Humvees") as family cars, while "only in America do soldiers and other uniformed servicemen figure ubiquitously in political photo ops and popular movies." It would seem that "war and warriors have become the last, enduring symbols of American dominance and the American way of life."[32]

[32] Tony Judt, "The New World Order," *New York Review of Books* (14 July 2005), p. 16.

9

The Reorganization of American Business

> [The] increasingly democratic structure of English commerce is very unpopular. It prevents the long duration of great families of merchant princes ... who are pushed out by the dirty crowd of new little men from the rough and vulgar crowd.[1]
>
> Walter Bagehot

> A few hundred industrial megacorporations under the potential control of an even smaller group of financial institutions today represent the central core of economic power. Furthermore, these dominant industrial and financial institutions are tied together with overlapping boards of directors drawn from a limited pool of several thousand unrepresentative men and a few women with the same backgrounds, values, and affiliations.[2]
>
> Phillip Blumberg

The spread of a military–industrial complex – that is, the growth of a significant military stake in the midst of the private business sector – represented just one feature of a more general transformation of the American business system. In the late 1950s, the conglomerate and the multinational megacorporation bloomed to alter the American business system as nothing had since the "corporation revolution" of the late nineteenth century. The result was what can be called the "second business revolution."

There were two major parts to the radical restructuring of the American business system in the decades after the Second World War: first, the conglomerate merger mania beginning in the late fifties and sixties; second, the rapid spread of multinational corporations throughout the era. Both were stimulated

---

[1] Walter Bagehot, *Lombard Street: A Description of the Money Market* (1873), quoted in Roy C. Smith, *The Money Wars: The Rise and Fall of the Great Buyout Boom of the 1980s* (Truman Talley, 1990), pp. 3, 11.

[2] Philip Blumberg, *The Megacorporation in American Society* (Prentice-Hall, 1975), p. 174.

by remarkable advances in technology, especially communications and transportation technology that globalized business transactions. But cultural and political changes also played a role.

Accompanying the changes, and in many respects enabling them, was the unprecedented growth of billion-dollar professionally managed pension funds that inspired and helped finance the colossal corporate turnovers. And few of these developments would have been possible except for the invention of novel business entities and new forms of debit contracts designed by hundreds of tireless lawyers and accountants. Most of them were young, recently out of elite law and business schools, and unconstrained by prevailing business conventions. They constituted virtually an entirely new class of entrepreneurs. Some of them self-consciously sought to replace the great banking and "merchant prince" families as dominant figures in the American business establishment. They came armed with computers that could provide lightning-fast financial calculations as well as, by the 1980s, virtually instantaneous global communications. The new technology permitted them, moreover, to turn business firms into almost infinitely divisible and readily marketable parcels.[3] Meanwhile, a growing number of venture capitalists entered the business world, supporting remarkably innovative technology and astonishing opportunities for rapid capital gains. The newcomers sought the age-old goal of accumulating wealth, but their style was more aggressive than had become commonplace within the old business establishment and was reminiscent of the upstart capitalists of the late nineteenth century who had fashioned the corporation revolution.

Propelled by innovative financial instruments produced by the new entrepreneurs, the stock market rose to become the principal allocator of capital, creating new and amazingly profitable business for stock brokerages, investment bankers, and other financial intermediaries. Profit opportunities beckoned only secondarily from the efficient production and distribution of goods and services. The young "number crunching" geniuses discovered that faster profits could be netted by pushing stock prices up through securities transactions and then reaping capital gains. Law firms all over the country established oversized departments devoted exclusively to mergers and acquisitions. All this contributed to what Alan Greenspan, chair of the Federal Reserve Board in the 1990s, called "excessive exuberance" in the securities markets, foretelling the calamitous collapse of stock-market prices in 2001.[4]

---

[3] See Alfred Chandler, "The Competitive Performance of U.S. Industrial Enterprise Since the Second World War," *Business History Review* (Spring 1994), especially p. 22.

[4] Greenspan used that phrase in an early warning about the bubble developing in the securities markets in the late nineties. But his remarks were dismissed as premature and viewed as perhaps a dangerous incitement to a bear market.

Tying much of the income of senior corporate executives to stock prices by including stock options in salary contracts provided incentives for executives to maximize the firm's operating efficiency, but the options also tempted them to pump up stock prices by concealing liabilities and reporting inflated profits.[5] This they accomplished with the aid of global accounting firms that coveted the business of the new entrepreneurs and their megacorporations, especially the business of serving as "consultants" in addition to their responsibilities as auditors. Meanwhile, "free market" enthusiasts newly appointed to the Federal Reserve Board by President Ronald Reagan agreed to override the Glass–Steagle Act of 1933 (without prior congressional action), permitting commercial banks to engage in the investment banking business.[6] The conflicts of interest in both industries were obvious to all who cared to look, but few did. Partly because the deregulation mania of the eighties and nineties rendered watchdog agencies ineffectual, investors would not learn of how widespread and enormous the fraud was until the stock market collapsed in 2001.[7]

Meanwhile, more than ever before, the U.S. economy came to be "market driven." More than ever, business activity aimed at maximizing *business efficiency,* generating short-term personal profits, and focusing on "the bottom line" (especially for the financial community and senior corporate executives) with only secondary attention to production, employment, innovative research, or public usefulness. In an important sense, *economic efficiency* – that is, providing for innovative production of consumer goods and services at optimally minimal unit costs – took a back seat. The public-policy theorists who shepherded these developments, especially from the seventies on, insisted that all desired production of goods and services, long-term consumer interests, innovative research, and maximal employment were best served by maximizing the private pursuit of profits unrestrained by any concept of a *public* interest. A generalized suspicion of authority and government that bloomed in the seventies after Watergate and Vietnam effectively silenced challenges to that notion while serving to permit the reversal of much of nearly half a century of advances in public scrutiny of corporate behavior.[8]

---

[5] In 2005, a study by Moody's Investors Service indicated a clear correlation between high stock-option pay packages for senior executives and a greater risk of business failure: Floyd Norris, "Stock Options: Do They Make Bosses Cheat?" *New York Times* (5 Aug. 2005), p. C1. See also Dow Jones News Wires, "Moody's Finds Link between High Pay and Credit Risk" (25 July 2005), ⟨http://news.morningstar.com/news/DJ/MO⟩.

[6] See Davita Silfen Glasberg & Dan Skidmore, *Corporate Welfare Policy and the Welfare State: Bank Deregulation and the Savings and Loan Bailout* (De Gruyter, 1997).

[7] See Jacob M. Schlesinger, "What's Wrong: Fourth in a Series – The Deregulators," *Wall Street Journal* (17 Oct. 2002), pp. A1ff.

[8] Just how it came about that the post-Watergate mood of the country would serve reactionary rather than progressive impulses is one of the issues covered in Part III.

Arguments about defining "public interest" have always impeded efforts to direct private energies toward liberal and humane goals. Furthermore, some analysts at the time credited the withdrawal of government oversight of corporate behavior with reviving business profits and productivity following the "stagflation" of the seventies. Few have doubted, however, that the relaxation of government controls permitted an epidemic of extraordinary corporate fraud and corruption, which was exposed after the market collapse and the ruin of hundreds of thousands of employees and pensioners as the twentieth century came to a close.

The Industrial Revolution of the last quarter of the nineteenth century had transformed America's primarily agricultural and artisan economy into one featuring factory-organized manufacturing by wage labor for the mass production of goods for a mass market. In the process, the small-unit, private proprietary business enterprise gave way to the large-scale, multidivisional, multifunctional public corporation. As it evolved, ownership became separated from control of the business firm; the typical business corporation came to be owned by thousands, sometimes millions, of mutually anonymous stockholders and run by professional managers, none of whom typically owned a significant share of the firm. Proprietary capitalism had given way to managerial capitalism. Ownership became reduced to a claim on a firm's earnings, and then only on that share of earnings that management deemed appropriate to release in the form of dividends.

The concentration of economic resources at the turn of the century in the hands of a relatively small group of corporate managements provoked the creation of federal government agencies that were intended to constrain the behavior of the new instruments of power. In most cases, the main forces behind the new agencies were smaller, mostly proprietary businesses that faced overbearing competition from the giant corporate entities. But in spite of the great reforms of the Progressive Era, domination of the economy by the large-scale public corporation had come to stay, and to increase. By 1936 Arthur Burns, who would later become chairman of the Council of Economic Advisors for President Dwight Eisenhower and then chairman of the Federal Reserve Board during the Nixon administration, was impelled to write: "The rise of the 'heavy industries,' changes in methods of selling, and the widening use of the corporate forms of business organization are bringing, if they have not already brought, the era of competitive capitalism to a close."[9]

---

[9] Arthur Burns, *The Decline of Competition* (1936); quoted in Glenn Porter, *The Rise of Big Business, 1860–1920*, 2nd ed. (Harlan Davidson, 1992), p. 90.

Despite such an informed and indeed accurate observation, conventional economic and political wisdom continued for the next seventy years to assume that "competitive capitalism" was alive and well and that therefore Americans should leave the allocation of resources and rewards to "the free market" – that is, to the ambitions and choices of individuals exercising freedom to exploit all economic opportunities for their own private benefit.[10] Although government regulatory agencies grew (albeit fitfully) in size and scope, the efforts to channel private profit–motivated power toward socially responsible goals remained handicapped by unapt economic theory and by a legal system that for the most part continued to treat megacorporations (giant entities of collectivized capital) as if they were private family firms. Competition of a sort would continue to determine some market outcomes, but it would be of an oligopolistic kind that was itself further cramped by intricate webs of interlocking directorates, shared corporate ownerships, and joint ventures rather than the "free field" that market theory originally presumed.

Neither the Great Depression of the 1930s nor the Second World War altered the large-scale public corporation's domination, even though both crises required the government to intervene in the private-market sector in order to redirect and redistribute economic resources in the interest of economic efficiency. None of the government's intermittent efforts during the first half of the twentieth century to reduce the concentration of power in the private sector proved effective. Moreover, at no time did any of the reforms serve to restore to stockholders any measure of the power that owners once had to influence the management of their firms. In fact the courts, the Congress, and state legislatures went decisively the other way, reinforcing corporate managers' power to make policy – as "stewards" of the properties – with minimal interference from shareholders. As one Wall Street consultant wrote in 1991: "Today, boards of directors exercise virtually unlimited discretion in the conduct of corporations because, under what's called the business judgment rule, the courts presume that they are acting in the interests of the shareholders unless there is explicit evidence of fraud or self-dealing."[11]

How much self-dealing passed the test? Consider the case of chief financial officer Heidi Miller, who left the megaconglomerate Citigroup to become CFO

---

[10] "The community's enduring belief in the existence of competitive market structure capitalism is partially explained by the fact that basic economic beliefs are religious in nature and, being so, are difficult to modify." John R. Munkirs, *The Transformation of American Capitalism: From Competitive Market Structures to Centralized Private Sector Planning* (M.E. Sharpe, 1985), p. 49.

[11] Harvey Segal, *Corporate Makeover: How American Business Is Reshaping for the Future* (Penguin, 1991), p. 13. Some corporate charters required that dissident shareholders win 80 percent of a vote to pass a shareholder-initiated resolution. Apparently it was not unusual for managements to ignore majority votes of shareholders, there being no legal requirement that they do otherwise. See e.g. *Business Week* (22 April 2002), p. 16: "Northrop's Odd Take on Takeovers."

of Priceline.com in 2000. Shortly after assuming her new office, Priceline's stock prices plummeted, rendering her stock options in the company nearly worthless. As Priceline hurtled toward bankruptcy, the company's board of directors restored Ms. Miller's fortunes by "forgiving" a $3.3 million "loan" they had made to her from the company's dwindling assets. Priceline's shareholders, also devastated by their company's stock collapse, were permitted to say nothing about such "business judgment"; nor would the courts consider a remedy.[12]

One irony in this is that, according to the law, the interests of shareholders nearly always trump the interests of other stakeholders – namely, employees, suppliers, consumers, and community interests generally. But it was left to management to decide on and to define shareholder interests. And by the 1950s, the practical status of shareholders had been reduced to that of unsecured creditors. This was not altogether a new phenomenon, but as one economist observed: "During the 1950s, the subjugation of the shareholder by corporate management to the position of quasi-creditor, as long ago noted by Joseph Schumpeter, seemed to have reached an extreme."[13] During that decade, the percentage of sales distributed as dividends dropped precipitously, while the share of corporate profits retained by management doubled.

As powerful as a relatively small number of megacorporate managers had become in the United States during the first half of the century, the further concentration of private economic power would be an outstanding feature of the postwar economy. Government actions during World War II achieved some dispersal of market power in a few industries (e.g. aluminum) but, beginning especially in the 1950s, concentration resumed and accelerated. Over the next few decades a dwindling percentage of American corporations would account for a continually increasing percentage of net (after-tax) corporate income. By the end of the 1960s, the 100 largest industrial corporations held a greater share of total assets than the 200 largest in 1950, and the largest 200 held about the same share (61 percent) as the largest 1,000 did in 1941. Between 1955 and 1970, the "Fortune 500" largest nonfinancial public corporations increased their share of total employment, profits, and assets from about 40 percent to about 70 percent.[14]

With the ascendancy of free-market ideology in the last quarter of the century, business consolidations and monopoly power would accelerate. Antitrust

---

[12] *New York Times* (31 Dec. 2000), sec. 3, p. 1.

[13] Harold G. Vatter, *The U.S. Economy in the 1950s: An Economic History* (Norton, 1963), pp. 207–8.

[14] Phillip I. Blumberg, *The Megacorporation in American Society: The Scope of Corporate Power* (Prentice-Hall, 1975), pp. 24ff. By some measures, since the 1970s a result of divestitures is that large corporations can be seen as constituting a smaller percentage of GDP than they did earlier. But how one defines a single firm when determining the weight of a corporate conglomerate has become much more complex.

laws went into abeyance. "The merger boom of the 1980s," wrote one ex-investment banker, "differed from those that preceded it." Among other things, "same-industry mergers occurred in the oil and gas, foods, drugs, finance, and numerous other industries .... Such concentrations had not been allowed since the early days of antitrust enforcement at the beginning of the century."[15] By the nineties, a handful of megacorporations would dominate numerous industries, from food and petroleum to print media and telecommunications. That a mere four corporations accounted for 82 percent of all cattle slaughtered in the United States by the end of the century, more than double the 1980 figure, typified what was happening.[16]

*   *   *

In addition to the growing market power of the largest corporations, it was significant that after the 1950s the growth was taking place not through a natural expansion of sales and production but rather through mergers with, or takeovers of, other corporations. And more and more of the mergers crossed industrial lines. Alfred Chandler, widely regarded as "the dean" of American business historians, observed: "By 1969, the drive to growth through merger and acquisition in unrelated industries had become almost a mania."[17]

Here is an abbreviated account of just one string of takeovers of the kind that began to take place in the 1950s and proliferated later:

Esmark (until 1973 Swift & Company ... the nation's largest food company) expanded enthusiastically in the 1960s and early 1970s into related food products. In the mid-1970s its CEO, Kelly, undertook many large acquisitions in non-food products and spun off the Swift Meat-Packing Division as an independent company, Sipco. In 1983, he acquired another large food-based conglomerate, Norton Simon, which had businesses in cosmetics, liquor, wine, soft drinks, and car rentals. In May 1984, Kelly's Esmark was purchased by Beatrice after a failed bid by Kelly and the LBO specialist Kohlberg Kravis Roberts (KKR) to take over Beatrice. (That enterprise had been a well-run dairy and food products company until a new CEO took it on a diversification binge during the early 1980s.) Before the end of the next year, however, Kelly, after engineering a huge $6.5 billion LBO with the assistance of KKR, acquired Beatrice. He immediately began a massive sell-off. In 1987 Kelly formed E.H. Holdings, consisting of the undivested pieces of Beatrice, and used the new company to target American Brands, the highly diversified successor to American Tobacco. Kelly netted another handsome profit when American Brands responded by purchasing EH for $2.7 billion. The dismemberment of the original Beatrice empire was completed in 1990, when ConAgra purchased its remaining business for $1.34 billion .... In 1981, Standard Brands ... merged with Nabisco, and in 1985 the enlarged

[15] Smith, *The Money Wars*, p. 106.
[16] *Wall Street Journal* (13 March 2002), p. A20. There were similar developments in the hog, grain, and broiler chicken industries.
[17] Chandler, "Competitive Performance," p. 18.

enterprise combined with the even more aggressively expanding R.J. Reynolds Tobacco. After four years of continual buying and selling of companies ... these financial activities culminated in 1989 in a $25 billion LBO engineered by KKR, followed by a large-scale sell-off to reduce the private company's huge debt.[18]

From 1949 to 1968, the 200 largest industrial corporations acquired 3,900 companies with assets of $50 billion (about $300 billion in 1999 dollars).[19] By the 1960s, almost all large manufacturers operated in more than five industries, and more than thirty were engaged in more than ten separate industries.[20] Between 1961 and 1968, a mere eleven firms acquired over 500 companies.[21] In the twenty-year period between 1954 and 1973, a stunning 214 of the country's top 500 nonfinancial corporations disappeared, cannibalized by fellow corporations; 197 of them disappeared in only the seven years after 1966.[22] Perhaps most significant for how the country used its savings, by 1968 the cost of acquiring companies represented 55 percent of total expenditures on new capital investment, up from only 3 percent during 1948–1952.[23]

The emergence of the conglomerate business corporation signaled a reorganization of the American business system comparable to that which occurred during the industrial and corporation revolutions of the late nineteenth century. The old large-scale public corporation typically had many divisions that performed diverse economic functions – for example, providing raw materials, transportation, manufacturing, processing, marketing, and financing, all within the same firm – but it generally confined all those functions to a single industry, such as steel or automobiles, packaged foods, or chemicals. The modern conglomerate corporation, on the other hand, operates across industrial lines and owns subsidiaries that may be only remotely related (if at all) to each other. And whereas the nineteenth century corporation revolution in the United States led to the separation of ownership from control, the 1960s revolution most often caused a separation of top management from middle management; the CEOs of the parent company became distanced from the executive officers of the operating companies and their production, finance, and marketing divisions.[24] Indeed,

---

[18] Ibid.

[19] Blumberg, *Megacorporation*, ch. 2.

[20] Elliot Brownlee, *Dynamics of Ascent* (Dorsey, 1988), p. 325.

[21] Alfred Chandler & Richard Tedlow, *The Coming of Managerial Capitalism* (Irwin, 1985), p. 737. "Case 28: The Conglomerates and the Merger Movement of the 1960s," pp. 737–75 in that volume, contains an excellent description and explication of the conglomerate movement.

[22] Willard F. Mueller, "The Celler–Kefauver Act: 16 Years of Enforcement," *A Staff Report to the Antitrust Subcommittee of the Committee on the Judiciary of the U.S. House of Representatives* (Government Printing Office, 16 Oct. 1967), pp. 37ff.; Blumberg, *Megacorporation*, p. 22.

[23] John F. Winslow, *Conglomerates Unlimited: The Failure of Regulation* (Indiana University Press, 1970), p. 4.

[24] See Chandler, "Competitive Performance."

when corporate scandals broke over various forms of fraud – from the antitrust violations of GE, Westinghouse, and Sylvania in the 1950s to the financial frauds of Enron, WorldCom, HealthSouth, and others of 2001–2002 – many CEOs pleaded innocent on the grounds that they didn't know what was going on in their own corporate divisions.

Most Americans remained indifferent to or unaware of the radical nature of the transformation of the American business system. The media were busy covering the spicier racial and sexual challenges to conventional norms, the Cold War, the Vietnam War, the diversionary rhetoric of partisan rivalries, the antics of professional entertainers vying for attention, and other serious and nonserious preoccupations. But the transformation did not go unnoticed among professionals monitoring the economy. A former staff member of a U.S. House antitrust subcommittee wrote in 1970: "The unique features of the merger wave which began to intensify in the 1960s are so important and incongruous with what had happened before that they have forced reappraisal of status, power, how a business should be run, the meanings of value, and so forth."[25] The *Wall Street Journal* expressed its worry a year earlier:

Unchecked expansion of conglomerates would eventually reduce competition and impair the efficiency of our approximator of a free market economy. When ties among large corporations get too widespread and too unwieldy, it seems to us that they will impede the free movement of prices and capital even if the merged corporations are not in the same field. Certainly, the consolidation of various corporations into conglomerates could invite a vastly increased concentration of power, which gives us pause on both economic and social grounds.[26]

The *Journal*'s reference to "social grounds" is noteworthy, especially given the editors' traditionalist view of political economy. A common nineteenth-century theory held that American democracy depended crucially on a multitude of property owners competing for advantage. Although it is not often understood, at its origin U.S. antitrust policy aimed more at protecting competitors than at protecting consumers.[27] A competitive multitude not only checked the concentration of power in the country but also served – according to prevailing theory – to build individual character, upon which the success of a self-governing people vitally depended. "Only through the participation by the many in the responsibilities and

---

[25] Winslow, *Conglomerates Unlimited*, p. 5.
[26] *Wall Street Journal* (26 March 1969).
[27] The literature on antitrust is voluminous, but on congressional intent regarding protecting competitors see, for example, Hans Thorelli, *The Federal Antitrust Policy: Origination of an American Tradition* (Johns Hopkins University Press, 1955), and William Letwin, *Congress and the Sherman Antitrust Law, 1887–1890* (University of Chicago Press, 1956). As Olivier Zunz observed in *Making America Corporate, 1870–1920* (University of Chicago Press, 1990): "The fight against bigness was part of a larger goal of maintaining the heterogeneous character of society" (p. 36).

determinations of business," wrote Louis Brandeis, an early twentieth-century champion of proprietary capitalism, "can Americans secure the moral and intellectual development essential to the maintenance of liberty."[28] The *Wall Street Journal* had come to accept the submersion of private proprietary capitalism by the corporation revolution, but it had not yet adjusted to the conglomerate revolution.

In addition, many old-line corporate managers and Wall Street financiers were uncomfortable with the free-wheeling acquisitions of properties across industrial lines, which seemed to violate conventional assumptions about the culture of a firm and its relationship with employees, creditors, customers, and suppliers. There was indeed something of a class element in the matter. The acquisitors were nearly all postwar Baby Boomers and almost all newcomers to the world of corporate finance, brashly challenging the "stodgy" practices of the old corporate establishment.[29] A high percentage of them were Irish Catholics, Jews, Italians, and children or grandchildren of other "non–Anglo-Saxon" immigrants.[30] They were social and economic newcomers who emerged far from the wood-paneled board rooms of the major corporations. As one historian noted in his study of the telecommunications conglomerate, ITT: "The Charles Francis Adamses of this world didn't relish the idea of being displaced by such as [Harold] Geneen. In their own way they were even more strongly opposed to the conglomerates than were the liberal reformers." Adams, the descendant of two U.S. presidents, was president of Raytheon and Geneen's superior there before Geneen left in 1959 to take over as head of ITT. Geneen was a first-generation American, born in England of Russian and Italo-English parents and brought to the United States at the age of 1. His father deserted the family when Harold was 5.[31]

In an important sense, the conglomerate movement represented the apotheosis of managerial capitalism. Managers built empires that enhanced their power to hedge against cyclical downturns in different industries, to move capital into parts of their empire that offered the best profit opportunities at the moment, and in general to exploit economies of scope. Empire building also highlighted corporate leaders' deal-making prowess, an important feature of the new culture of the modern corporation and an essential element in pumping up "value"

---

[28] Louis D. Brandeis, dissenting in *Liggett v. Lee*, 288 U.S. 517 (1933).

[29] See e.g. Smith, *The Money Wars*, p. 228.

[30] The youth and "outsider" ethnic character of most of the new financial dealers stands out in the many accounts of the massive Wall Street scandals of the 1980s. See e.g. James B. Stewart, *Den of Thieves* (Simon & Schuster, 1991); George Anders, *Merchants of Debt: KKR and the Mortgaging of American Business* (Basic Books, 1992); Dennis B. Levine with William Hoffer, *Inside Out: An Insider's Account of Wall Street* (Putnam's, 1991).

[31] Robert Sobel, *ITT* (Times Books, 1982), pp. 165–6, 257.

in the stock market. Largeness also magnified a corporation's leverage with suppliers and retailers. To counterbalance that leverage, suppliers and retailers in many industries found it necessary to merge, thereby propelling the economy further away from "competitive capitalism."

Not least important was the much greater influence that a conglomerate operating in numerous geographic and economic markets could wield politically, especially with its huge financial resources for lobbying and campaign contributions. A company with steel interests in Pennsylvania and West Virginia and oil interests in Texas and Oklahoma, for example, was in an excellent position to lobby a multitude of congressmen on behalf of protective tariffs for the steel industry and enhanced depletion allowances for the oil industry. Such power as resided within a conglomerate corporation could serve to improve *business* efficiency – that is, to raise profits and to expand perquisites for top management, although not necessarily to benefit local or state economies – or to improve consumer services or reduce consumer costs.

The conglomerate movement downgraded production and service operations into secondary features of the capitalist economy: financial deals became the primary feature. In retrospect, later analysts would attempt to calculate the cost in *economic* efficiency. In 1983 the eminent economist Robert Lekachman would conclude: "Conglomerates are little more than mutual funds perpetually shuffling resources out of some subsidiaries and into others with scant heed to the production of anything more useful than paper claims."[32] That same year, two economists for the financial reporting firm of Dow Jones echoed the thought: "Too many of the activities associated with current business combinations," they remarked, "have little or nothing to do with the creation of real economic value."[33]

The conglomerate reorganization took many forms, some of them not greatly different from the more commonplace diversification that accompanied the corporation revolution of the late nineteenth century. When Coca-Cola bought Minute Maid, it crossed over from soft drinks to frozen fruit beverages, but the two businesses required much the same kind of marketing. The same could be said of Reynolds Tobacco buying Nabisco (maker of packaged cereal food products) to become RJR Nabisco, and of Philip Morris taking over Kraft Foods and Miller Beer. Apart from siphoning off some of the operating profits of the acquired companies, the holding companies gained leverage with supermarkets in their demand for shelf space against those of competitive brands. But when Pepsi-Cola renamed itself "Pepsico" and bought into major trucking corporations and

---

[32] *New York Times Book Review* (24 April 1983), p. 18, in a review of Robert Reich, *The Next American Frontier* (Times Books, 1983).
[33] *The Collegiate Forum* (Dow Jones, Fall 1983), p. 3.

when Mobil Oil bought Montgomery Ward (which had already been merged with a major container corporation and renamed "Marcor"), the contrast in holdings was more conspicuous. Their promoters justified such cross-marketing mergers as a form of diversification to minimize the risks of remaining in a single, possibly declining industry. When in the late sixties ITT – an international telecommunications corporation – bought Hartford Life Insurance, Avis Car Rental, Bobbs-Merrill Publishers, William Levitt & Sons homebuilders, Hostess bakeries, and the Sheraton hotel chain (among other diverse companies), it showed the full potential of the new business behavior.[34] By the 1970s, there were scores of companies like ITT, many also featuring initials rather than a proper name: for example, PPG (formerly Pittsburgh Plate Glass) and FMC (once Food Machinery Corporation). For a while, there was even a company named the National General Corporation, which said it all.

Ironically, an effort by Congress in 1950 to close a loophole in the antitrust law indirectly encouraged conglomerate mergers. Because, for a time, horizontal mergers with competitors became more difficult, corporate managers on the prowl to grow by acquisition looked across industrial lines. But beginning in the 1980s, amid the deregulation enthusiasm of the Reagan era, horizontal mergers among megacorporations resumed while antitrust agencies of the federal government looked away. The word "synergy" was invented to describe how both kinds of mergers would bring "efficiency" to related industries, increase shareholder value, and make life easier for consumers through "one-stop shopping" and the like. But increasingly from the late sixties onward, the mergers had far more to do with financial deals, with the profits to be made from the deals, and perhaps most of all with the increase in share value on the stock market that usually followed deal making. Reducing consumer costs for improved services or products rarely came into the picture – in fact, quite the contrary. In the 1990s, for example, the mergers of the Mobil Corporation with Exxon, Chevron with Texaco, Phillips with Conoco, and British Petroleum with Sohio, Amoco, and Arco were quickly followed by the reduction of workforces, the closing of "redundant" service stations, constricted refinery output, and the raising of prices.[35]

---

[34] As did many other multi-industry conglomerates, ITT later sold off some of its acquisitions (e.g. Avis).

[35] In the San Francisco Bay area, the closing of service stations had clear effects on competition and thus on prices. Although the area had major oil refineries, gasoline prices typically were higher than elsewhere in the country. When asked by a reporter why prices were higher than elsewhere, an oil company representative answered simply: "Because we can get it." *San Francisco Chronicle* (16 May 2000). For an extensive account of the effect of mergers in the oil industry on consumer prices and service and on independent gasoline retailers, see "Pumping It Up," *Wall Street Journal* (24 Jan. 2002), pp. 1ff.

Nor could it be said that mergers were always designed to produce cost savings for improving returns to shareholders. The telltale evidence may be found in the collapse of many merger negotiations because of disputes over which corporate executive from which of the merging corporations would end up in control of the new entity. Shareholders be damned! if a CEO found that a proposed merger required yielding his personal power. The end of talks between British Airways and KLM in September 2000 is one outstanding example of the phenomenon.[36] Management often took to rewriting the corporation's charter – inserting a "poison pill" provision – in order to make it unattractive for a "hostile" takeover bid; the outside bid might enhance value for stockholders, but the incumbent management was more interested in keeping control.

To be sure, shareholders of targeted companies usually gained from the premiums paid for their stock by the raiders. In that sense, the mergers were "good for shareholders." But most studies of merged corporations showed that the advertised profit advantages of the takeovers failed to materialize.[37] On average, shareholders of especially the acquiring firms did poorly.

The ascendancy of a "free market" mindset among policy makers by the end of the seventies suppressed virtually all effective resistance to the growing monopoly power of a relative handful of corporate managers. By the 1990s, the consolidation of megacorporations became so commonplace that it hardly raised comment, much less attention from the government antitrust agencies. During the Clinton administration, the federal government did attempt to prosecute the Microsoft Corporation (on the urgings of its few remaining competitors) for documented violations of an earlier consent decree about its illegitimate business practices as well as new violations of antitrust law. This drew a lot of attention and much of the resources of the understaffed federal enforcement agencies, but most of the government's suit was undone by the succeeding administration, whose free-market ideology led it to turn a blind eye to monopoly power. Although it was a bit more vigorous than most in enforcing antitrust laws designed to free the market of monopoly power, the Clinton administration chose to ignore the mergers of the nation's leading banks, oil companies, power distributors, and especially media firms.

---

[36] *Wall Street Journal* (22 Sept. 2000), p. 1. In 1999, the original negotiations for merging Chevron with Texaco fell through when Peter Bijur, CEO of Texaco, "had wanted the combined board to decide who would head the merged company," but Kenneth T. Derr, Chevron's CEO, "was not willing to share power with Mr. Bijur." *San Francisco Chronicle* (3 June 1999), p. C1; *New York Times* (3 June 1999), pp. B1ff.

[37] See e.g. Smith, *The Money Wars*, pp. 107–8. Smith, a former investment banker with Goldman Sachs (a leading underwriter of mergers), presents a detailed defense of the merger movement and of leveraged buyouts. He acknowledges that researchers show that "on average" the mergers failed to deliver as promised, but he dismisses "average" outcomes as ignoring the successes.

Were the megamergers justified by economic gains, for the nation's economic growth, or even for shareholders? Reporting on some careful studies concluded in 1999, *The Economist* (a conservative British financial weekly) noted that "over half of them had destroyed shareholder value, and a further third had made no discernible difference" – except, that is, for the difference most of them made to discharged employees and bereft cities and regions. *The Economist* further observed: "As every employee knows, mergers tend to mean job losses." This often had consequences not only for the employees and their communities but also for the merged companies, since some of the best managerial talent tended to migrate, "often taking a big chunk of shareholder value with them." The report concluded with the example of the merger of Travelers Insurance with Citibank, which "reaped big profits from cost-selling [laying off employees], though rather less from its original [putative] aim of cross-selling different financial services to customers." In other words, Citibank cut costs by firing thousands of workers, consumers got little discernible benefit, and stockholders got doubtful returns. But the ruling corporate managers, their brokers, and their "financial advisors" nearly always banked outsized profits.[38]

In short, during the last quarter of the century, corporate managements' primary energies and attention drifted increasingly toward buying up properties and/or merging with other corporations for a number of reasons unrelated to productivity or other measures of economic efficiency. In some cases, companies were taken over for the income they already provided – a straight-out investment in a money machine, without contributing significantly to economic growth. In other cases, takeovers achieved profits by writing off losses to reduce tax liabilities. Tax laws provided incentives for tax-free mergers by means of share exchanges rather than buyouts, which could incur taxes on capital gains.[39] Since by the seventies most of the takeovers were financed by heavy borrowing, deductions for interest payments on the debt further reduced a company's tax burden. Once the acquisitions were completed, the new management might sell off parts of the acquired firms to help pay off debt or, in some cases, to take tax losses.

[38] *The Economist* (22 July 2000), p. 19: "How Mergers Go Wrong." These findings were confirmed two years later by a *Business Week* study that concluded, among other things, that 61 percent of the acquisitions "destroyed shareholder wealth": "The Merger Hangover: How Most Big Acquisitions Have Destroyed Shareholder Value," *Business Week* (14 Oct. 2002), p. 60.

[39] "International oil and minerals companies with unusual foreign tax credits acquire companies whose incomes can be 'sheltered' by those credits .... A central motive behind Container Corporation's union with Montgomery Ward to form Marcor was to defer payment for several years of more than $60 million a year of federal income taxes by taking fuller advantage of Ward's ability to defer taxes on profits arising from installment credit sales." Oil companies enjoying depletion allowances "acquire high-profit firms for the same reason." Chandler & Tedlow, *Managerial Capitalism*, p. 747.

Nor is it possible to ignore the immediate profits that management executives could garner for themselves in the merger deals, either from the bonuses and fees they took for themselves for managing the mergers and/or from the rise in stock prices that enabled them to cash in on the options they also had awarded themselves before the mergers. When the corporate and accounting industry scandals broke in 2002, it was revealed that several major investment banking houses and brokerage firms (e.g., Citibank and Merrill, Lynch) awarded huge financial benefits to individual corporate executives as incentives for winning the business of underwriting acquisitions. By the end of 2002 it had become clear that the formation of giant financial conglomerates had led to a fulsome corruption of American capitalism. As *The Economist* editorialized:

During the '90s, America's financial institutions transformed themselves into giant conglomerates, offering credit, equity, insurance, fund management, analysis, and just about everything else. It is increasingly clear that this model pushed the limits of the law, hurt the average investor, and distorted both debt and equity markets. In the name of efficiency and synergy, the financial conglomerates indulged in egregious conflicts of interest.[40]

This may do some injustice to those few conglomerates that served to bring within a single management team a variety of functions that had mutually reinforcing features. For example, merged research and development (R&D) divisions could cut unit costs and facilitate the transfer of information for innovations. That seems to have motivated consolidations in some industries. But in practice, the rationale for mergers generally focused on marketing strategies. A film corporation such as Disney could use its ownership of a magazine (i.e. *Talk*) to promote articles that would serve as seeds for motion pictures or, conversely, to plant articles promoting the films of Disney subsidiaries.[41] Conglomerates like Viacom – which owned both the CBS network and MTV, the world's most popular entertainment channel for teenagers – produced programs that were simply merchandising vehicles for displaying its own many products (including videos to be sold through Viacom's Blockbuster subsidiary) or those of its advertising clients. On the other hand, most of the predicted "synergies" failed to materialize. Media companies seeking to bolster their relatives often were saddled with failing shows or with publications that produced declining or negative revenues.[42]

A conglomerate could conceivably speed the spread of new management practices by exploiting modern computer technology. In the words of economist Neil

---

[40] *The Economist* (9 Sept. 2002), p. 156.
[41] For example, Miramax, a division of Disney, developed movies based on magazine articles in *Talk* magazine, which Disney owned in partnership with the Hearst corporation. *Talk,* however, folded in 2002. See "*Talk* Collapses Just as Strategy Was Taking Root," *Wall Street Journal* (21 Jan. 2002), p. B1.
[42] See e.g. "How NBC Defies Network Norms – To Its Advantage," *Wall Street Journal* (20 May 2002), pp. A1ff.

Jacoby, modern technology "created opportunities for profits through mergers that remove assets from the inefficient control of old-fashioned managers and placed them under men schooled in the new management science."[43] Computerizing intrafirm communication and accounting practices as well as bringing fresh ideas to production techniques and shop-floor design did much to streamline business operations. As the United States began to regain competitive strength internationally after the rough years of the seventies and eighties, many economists credited the gains at least partly to the economies they attributed to the conglomerate mergers and "the new management science."

Not all economists and financiers agreed. John Shad, the Reagan-appointed and staunchly conservative chair of the Securities & Exchange Commission, concluded: "The theory that contested takeovers discipline incompetent managements is of limited veracity .... [On the contrary], the increasing threat of being taken over is an inducement to curtail or defer research and development, plant rehabilitation and expansion, oil exploration and development, and other programs which entail current costs for long-term benefits."[44]

By way of cutting current costs, the new management science also commonly meant ruthless cost-cutting wage and benefits reductions, "downsized" workforces accompanied by labor speed-ups, and outsourcing production and management functions to countries with low labor costs and lax or nonexistent environmental safeguards. America's business rivals in Japan and Western Europe were constrained by law and custom from implementing the brutal takeover and labor policies that by the 1980s had become commonplace in the United States. "Far more successfully than their Japanese and German rivals," wrote economist Robert Lekachman in 1981, "American corporations have resisted union participation in management, nonhierarchical organization of work in factories and offices, effective regulation and legal limitations upon layoffs and plant closings."[45] This put the Europeans and Japanese at a competitive disadvantage, which would begin to reverse the position of the rival economies by the late eighties. American labor productivity rose significantly in the last quarter of the century, but most of the rise took place in the nineties and then as much at the cost of intensified work as from new technology.[46] While paid vacation time for

---

[43] Neil Jacoby, "The Conglomerate Corporation," *Center Magazine* (Spring 1969), reprinted in Chandler & Tedlow, *Managerial Capitalism,* p. 746.

[44] Quoted in David A. Vise & Steve Coll, *Eagle on the Street* (Scribner's, 1991), pp. 187–8. Shad's remarks, made in a widely reported speech, led to a campaign by ideologues within the Reagan administration to "neutralize" him.

[45] Robert Lekachman, "How to Succeed in Business," *New York Times Book Review* (7 June 1981), p. 24.

[46] The growth in U.S. labor productivity, last among the major industrial countries, declined through most of the eighties and turned negative in 1986. "Productivity Growth Lags Normal Pace," *Wall Street Journal* (15 June 1985), p. A1. See also Bennett Harrison & Barry Bluestone, *The Great U-Turn: Corporate Restructuring and the Polarizing of America* (Basic Books, 1988), p. 145.

Europe's workforce continued to increase throughout the last half of the century, in the United States it began to shrink during the 1970s.[47]

The new management science also meant cutting investment in parts of a conglomerate enterprise that were most resistant to short-term profit maximization. That often meant cutbacks in R&D and in quality. Thus, when Lawrence Tisch of the Loews conglomerate took over the CBS radio and television network, he cut financing for the world-renowned but expensive CBS News division, turning it into an entertainment vehicle in which news gathering and serious commentary became secondary. Having built up "share value" in this fashion, Tisch then sold CBS at a profit to Viacom, another conglomerate that owned dozens of TV channels, movie theaters, video outlets, and publishing houses. In 1986 Jack Welch, CEO of General Electric, acquired RCA – mostly because he wanted its NBC subsidiary. He proceeded to sell off not only RCA's brand name but RCA's David Sarnoff Laboratories.[48] Then, like Tisch, he cut the budget for NBC News, constricting its newsgathering capabilities.

The self-promoting Jack Welch was not unique among the new breed of corporate titans in his devotion to cutting costs, but he was surely more zealous about it than most.[49] During his twenty-year chairmanship, he trimmed GE's American workforce by about 100,000 men and women while expanding overseas operations. Each year he set a standard for his division managers that required they show 10-percent cuts in their cost accounts. Each cut registered gains in value for GE stocks because reducing workforce signaled higher capital gains for stock speculators on Wall Street. Rising share prices also enriched top management, who typically held millions of dollars worth of stock options. Managers who failed to meet targets were summarily fired. "Before his [Welch's] tenure," one business reporter observed, "most GE employees spent their entire careers with the company, and knew they would be looked after when they retired. That company no longer exists."[50]

---

[47] Juliet B. Schor, *The Overworked American: The Unexpected Decline of Leisure* (Basic Books, 1991), pp. 2ff. Schor estimated from Labor Department figures that U.S. workers in manufacturing worked 320 hours per year more than their West German and French counterparts.

[48] Thomas McCraw, *American Business 1920–2000: How It Worked* (Harlan Davidson, 2000), p. 144.

[49] Welch's zeal for cutting costs did not touch his own pocketbook. In 2002 it was revealed that – in addition to his multimillion-dollar annual salary and hundreds of millions of dollars worth of stock options – he had contrived a secret contract with GE that obligated the company to pay him an annual $7.5 million pension in perpetuity in addition to all his postretirement housing costs, use of the company jet, and many other of his personal living expenses. See the *Wall Street Journal* (4 Sept. 2002), p. A1, and "Corporate America's Woes, Continued," *The Economist* (30 Nov. 2002), p. 60.

[50] John Cassidy, "Gut Punch: How Good Was Jack Welch?" *The New Yorker* (1 Oct. 2001), p. 83. On the new focus on short-term profits among top managements generally, see also Robert Hayes & William Abernathy, "Managing Our Way to Economic Decline," *Harvard Business Review* (July/Aug. 1980).

To achieve his profit and share-price goals, Welch – the son of Irish immigrants and one of the "new men" in the American corporate establishment – also slashed funding for research and development not only in the RCA division but within GE itself, although R&D had formerly been one of GE's great strengths. During Welch's twenty-year rule, the company that had pioneered in many areas of engineering failed to produce a single significant new product. This, too, would become commonplace in the new business system.[51] America would not cease to produce innovative products and technology, but increasingly the innovations were born in small, sometimes startup companies, many of which the megacorporations later bought out for the value of their patents.

The development of the giant conglomerates had major political implications. The great wave of regulatory reforms of the sixties and early seventies provoked political mobilization by the country's giant corporations. The authority of many of the new federal agencies – for example, the Environmental Protection Administration (EPA), the Occupational Health & Safety Administration (OSHA), and the Equal Economic Opportunity Commission (EEOC) – crossed many industrial lines, a new phenomenon for which the conventional corporate pressure group tactics proved inadequate. In 1971, a group of CEOs who described themselves as "action oriented members" of the Business Council, a private organization of big businessmen that had gained semi-official status within the U.S. Department of Commerce in the early 1930s, arranged what they called "the March Group." That group evolved into the new Business Roundtable. Initially, membership in the Business Roundtable consisted of the CEOs of the hundred leading corporations in the country. Later it was expanded to include two hundred.

The purpose of the Roundtable was to apply their members' economic power to counter the effectiveness of the new regulatory agencies. The new regulatory system, as Business Council advisor Murray Wiedenbaum put it, "makes it impractical for any single industry to dominate their regulatory activities in a manner of the traditional [industry-specific] model." The CEOs came to understand that they needed proactive collective means to control the new agencies. The method was to have each CEO actively lobby the senators and representatives in the districts where they had their heaviest investments. A hundred or so CEOs of the country's biggest conglomerates easily covered the entire political field.[52]

---

51 Chandler, "Competitive Performance"; William Lazonick, *Business Organization and the Myth of the Market Economy* (Cambridge University Press, 1991), especially pp. 50, 54ff; Anders, *Merchants of Debt*, p. 281.

52 See Kim McQuaid, *Big Business and Presidential Power* (Murrow, 1982), especially pp. 285–9. For a comparison with the more limited corporate political activity before the conglomerate revolution, see Edwin M. Epstein, *The Corporation in American Politics* (Prentice-Hall, 1969).

The impact of megacorporate influence on the media was particularly troublesome. For example, a CBS documentary on the tobacco industry in the 1980s was held off the air when the sale of CBS was pending because by angering the tobacco companies it could have jeopardized the sale.[53] The giant retailer Montgomery Ward had been a reliable contributor to campaigns for consumer safety laws; its contributions ceased when Mobil Oil took it over in the 1970s. The wide range of products that corporations such as GE,[54] Proctor & Gamble, Phillip Morris, and RJR Nabisco owned gave such firms outsized influence on media content because of their advertising clout. Moreover, any legislator – city, state, or federal – who might challenge one of the megacorporations or major industries would invariably face a barrage of advertising (some of it plainly mendacious) that would quickly terminate that legislator's political career.[55] The media corporations meanwhile induced the regulatory agencies to rescind an early requirement that air time be made freely available for rebuttals on political issues.

"As if monopolizing media time were not enough," wrote Max Frankel (former executive editor of the *New York Times*) in 1999, "some corporate behemoths have bought favor and protection simply by buying the media .... Not incidentally, that also gives them control over all the television news concerning their own conduct. That is why the giveaway of perhaps $70 billion worth of spectrum space ... was passed last year with hardly any public discussion. The television networks allowed no serious on-air debate of the possibility of auctioning off such a valuable public resource."[56] The control of the nation's television networks by a handful of giant conglomerates – Disney (ABC), Viacom (CBS, MTV), Rupert Murdoch (Fox), GE (NBC), AOL Time Warner (CNN) – meant reduced outlets for creative programming as well as for political dissent.[57] Insofar as the deregulation movement of the seventies and eighties freed the networks from restraints on programming and air time devoted to advertising,

[53] In addition, CBS CEO Lawrence Tisch's son was president of one of the major tobacco companies.
[54] Whether as a case of grim humor, tasteless bragging, or something else, shortly after the September 11, 2001, terrorist massacres in Manhattan and at the Pentagon, GE's newly appointed CEO Jeff Immelt had this to say about the extent of GE's empire: "My second day as chairman, a plane I lease, flying with engines I built, crashed into a building that I insure, and it was covered with a network [NBC] that I own." Quoted in *Newsweek* (1 Oct. 2001), p. 17. It is also noteworthy how Immelt, who owned only a small fraction of GE's equity, used the first person singular in referring to the giant corporation – as if he and GE were identical.
[55] Bill Moyers, "Free Speech for Sale," Public Broadcasting System TV documentary (June 1999). See commentary by Max Frankel, *New York Times Magazine* (13 June 1999), pp. 28, 30.
[56] Frankel, ibid.
[57] Throughout the eighties and nineties, right-wing federal judges appointed by Presidents Reagan and the first Bush further undermined limits on how many newspapers, television, and radio networks a single media corporation could own; the chair of the FCC, Michael Powell (appointed by the second Bush), declared himself opposed to any limits.

quality broadcasting faced virtual extinction in the commercial race to the bottom. Perhaps more seriously, it also meant narrower editorial commentary and news coverage. As one analyst of American journalism wrote in 2001:

In a world in which independent news organizations are being gobbled into [*sic*] giant international corporations like the Walt Disney Company or AOL Time Warner or General Electric – corporations whose primary business is something other than journalism – there is reason enough to be concerned about the loss of competing voices.[58]

The magnitude of the political influence of megacorporation ownership of the media approached ominous dimensions by the end of the millennium. With Republican advisor and former presidential confidante Roger Ailes running Rupert Murdoch's Fox News, the Fox network became an active arm of the Republican Party. With a confidence oozing over into outright cynicism, Fox's right-wing television pundits bragged about how their "reporting" turned the 2002 congressional elections into a Republican victory. "It was because of our coverage that it happened," exulted talking head Brit Hume. "People watch us and take their electoral cues from us. No one should doubt the influence of Fox views in these matters."[59] The heads of the other major news networks were more discreet about their slanted news coverage, but a researcher would be hard-pressed to discover any significant difference in how GE's NBC, Disney's ABC, Viacom's CBS, or AOL Time Warner's CNN covered political, economic, and social issues.

Economist Charles Lindblom wrote in 1979: "In American law the corporation is a 'person'; and in all the democratic market-oriented systems, corporations and other business enterprises enter into politics .... But these fictitious persons are taller and richer than the rest of us and have rights that we do not have. Their political impact differs from and dwarfs that of the ordinary citizen."[60] This had major implications for the health of democratic institutions, a fact that most Americans – scholars and ordinary citizens alike – continued to ignore. It may have had a role in the widespread cynicism and demoralization that led fewer and fewer Americans to participate in local and national elections as the century drew to a close.

※　　※　　※

The conglomerate movement declined briefly in the mid-1970s. It would revive with even greater vigor in the 1980s. But for a few years, enthusiasm for the "new wave of rationalization" cooled. In part this owed to some bad publicity surrounding some of ITT's acquisitions. That included disclosure that President Nixon had ordered his attorney general, Richard Kleindienst, to drop an

---

[58] Bill Kovach, "Out of the Pool," *New York Times Book Review* (23 Sept. 2001).
[59] Quoted in Paul Krugman, "In Media Res," *New York Times* (29 Nov. 2002), p. A33.
[60] Charles E. Lindblom, *Politics and Markets* (Basic Books, 1979), p. 5.

antitrust suit against ITT and memoranda from an ITT lobbyist surfaced that suggested that Nixon's order had followed some major contributions to the Republican Party.[61]

But the ultimate in paper shuffling would come in the late 1970s when the "leveraged buyout," or LBO, became the new game on Wall Street. By then, some keen watchers of businesses – mostly ambitious Baby Boomers making use of new computer technology – calculated that the virtual autonomy enjoyed by corporate management often induced risk-minimizing rather than profit-maximizing behavior. This fact, they supposed, was reflected in the stock market's apparent "underpricing" of many a firm's securities. A school of corporate raiders descended upon such "underperforming" firms in order to buy them out from under their current management and stockholders. Thus, the country would begin witnessing the phenomenon of little-known financial and legal sharpsters, operating out of small firms (of which many were little more than paper shells), gaining control over megacorporations of long-standing international stature.

The technique called for borrowing all or nearly all the money needed to acquire a controlling share of a corporation, usually ousting all or most of the original management, dumping the debt incurred by the buyout on the target firm, and then paying off the huge debt either from the target firm's own earnings or by dismantling the firm's assets and selling them off separately. Alternatively, the raiders would accept a payoff from the target company for backing away from the takeover, a practice that came to be known as "greenmail."[62] Sometimes, to protect themselves, corporate managements would arrange a "friendly takeover" by another corporation or financial group that would either leave the original management intact or provide a "golden parachute" of millions of dollars in bonuses to the top executives who were displaced. (Executives thus could profit by selling their own offices.)[63]

---

[61] The connection between the contributions and the action was circumstantial and probably not directly causal. But the public's assumption of a quid pro quo was entirely reasonable then and now, especially because Kleindienst (among others) would plead guilty to lying to the Senate Judiciary Committee in the matter. See Sobel, *ITT*, chs. 15 and 16; Anthony Sampson, *The Sovereign State of ITT* (1974), especially pp. 240–51.

[62] A classic example was a bid by raider Saul Steinberg in 1984 to take over the Disney Corporation. Disney protected itself by buying back the stock that Steinberg had acquired, paying an above-market price of $30 million plus $28 million in "fees" to Steinberg's financial backers. See Levine, *Inside Out*, pp. 132ff. Levine spent 17 months in federal prison for violating insider-trading law.

[63] "The top seven officers of Pacific Telesis stand to receive a total of up to $25.2 million in 'golden parachute' payments if they lose their jobs as a result of the proposed buyout of SBC Communications .... Investment bankers also stand to make millions on the merger. PacTel agreed to pay Salomon Bros. $26 million and SBC has agreed to pay Lazard Freres & Co. $15 million when the deal closes. These prices were negotiated based on similar sized deals, a PacTel spokesman said." *San Francisco Chronicle* (19 April 1996), p. B1.

One of the innovators in the LBO technique – Kohlberg, Kravis & Roberts (KKR), a partnership of only 20 individuals and associates – at one point owned numerous giant corporations, including RJR Nabisco (which the partners created by financing the consolidation of Reynolds Tobacco with the food packaging giant), Safeway, Owens-Illinois, and Duracell. Together, the KKR group controlled companies with sales larger than those of Chrysler, Texaco, or AT&T and that employed nearly 400,000 people.

Although the acquired company might continue to enjoy operating profits, often the debt burden would force the company into bankruptcy, as happened with Macy's Department Stores after its management used the LBO method to take over the company from its stockholders. Even when companies successfully fought off a hostile takeover bid, the battle usually left them mortally laden with debt that forced the sell-off of major assets. Although acquired by KKR in a "friendly" fashion, Safeway had to sell nearly all its stores in southern California and the Midwest in order to survive elsewhere, leaving, of course, its former customers with reduced competition among local supermarkets.

Running a profitable firm (like Safeway) no longer sufficed. If a firm did not maximize profits – if it did not squeeze its labor force to the extent of its endurance as well as its talents, or if it had branches that did not return optimal profits – then it could become a takeover target. After fifty years of the nurturing leadership of William Paley, CBS in the 1980s showed steadily positive but relatively low earnings and thus a depressed market price for its shares. Partly that was because Paley put lots of money into costly news services and high-quality but small-market programming that resulted in lower TV ratings. It became a ripe target for a takeover, which resulted in sharp cuts for CBS News and in reduced funding for all but high-profit programming. By the 1980s and well into the 1990s, "downsizing" – the fashionable term for reducing a firm's market outlets as well as its workforce at every level – became not merely the fashion but an absolute fad. In the media, "downsizing" would also mean "dumbing down."

The engineers of the merger and LBO phenomena benefited crucially from the emergence of billion-dollar pension and mutual funds administered by professional money managers. As late as 1952, only 4.2 percent of Americans held corporate securities. By 1980, more than half had stakes in corporate equity, mostly by entrusting their money to money managers in pension funds and money market accounts. By the end of the century, slightly under half of all Americans owned stock of their own, some of it through mutual funds.[64] To justify their management of such vast sums of other people's money, the fund managers needed at least to match the Standard & Poor Index of the performance of 500 "blue-chip" corporate stocks. To meet their targets, the fund managers

---

[64] *Wall Street Journal* (19 Jan. 2000); *New York Times* (19 Jan. 2000).

had to buy and sell securities in large batches (10,000 shares or more) in transactions made primarily for short-term gains. By 1990, such institutional agents
controlled 55 to 60 percent of all publicly listed securities.[65] Their investments
were made not with an eye to returns from a firm's profitable operations but to
speculation in capital gains from an ever rising stock market.

In some respects, because corporate raiders often sold off the various subsidiaries or branches of a firm's business to reduce the takeover debt (or simply
to loot the company), the LBO boom partially reversed the conglomerate movement. By 1977, conglomerate divestitures accounted for as much as 53 percent
of all corporate transactions.[66] Corporate raiding also shook up complacent
managements that lived off the fat of the corporations that they ran as if they
owned them. At their best, takeover firms like KKR forced management to return their attention to innovations and operating efficiencies, thereby helping to
restore a level of productivity that went some way toward rectifying the country's
declining international competitiveness. Some economists likened LBO specialists such as KKR to private "reconstruction finance banks" that created value
by identifying, buying out, and restructuring underperforming firms – indeed,
using market mechanisms as a substitute for the absence of governmental agencies capable of disciplining private business management. Some would argue,
too, that the LBOs restored to stockholders a measure of control over the productivity of their properties.

The downside, however, was that most of the LBO activity did less to sharpen
productive efficiency and U.S. competitiveness than it did to enrich a few individuals and investment bankers, who left scores of previously profitable and well-
functioning businesses strapped with debt and often forced into bankruptcy. The
broader costs of the reorganization of American business were not easy to perceive or to calculate. But there is little doubt that the cost cutting that inevitably
followed from the mergers and takeovers put long-term economic growth in
jeopardy. Bronwyn Hall, a leading expert on U.S. capital formation, concluded
unequivocally in 1990: "Leveraged buyouts and other private acquisitions of publicly traded manufacturing firms ... brought a decline in investment in plant and
capital equipment as well as in R&D."[67] Manufacturing megafirms that were

[65] The manager of Washington State's huge workers' pension fund was an important source of capital for takeover specialists such as KKR. Calpers, the California employees' pension fund, was
another source.

[66] Allen Kaufman & Ernest J. Englander, "Kohlberg Kravis Roberts & Co. and the Restructuring
of American Capitalism," *Business History Review* (Spring 1993), 52–97 (see p. 67).

[67] Bronwyn H. Hall, "The Impact of Corporate Restructuring on Industrial Research and Development," *Brookings Papers on Economic Activity: Microeconomics 1990* (Brookings, 1990), pp.
85–135. See also Alfred Chandler, "Competitiveness and Capital Investment: The Restructuring
of U.S. Industry, 1960–1990," *Business History Review* (Spring 1994), p. vii.

born from LBOs suffered substantial cuts in capital expenditures. Moreover, they averaged annually only one fourth the R&D outlays per employee of other manufacturing firms.

Altogether, between 1972 and 1992, total investment in the United States averaged only 3.1 percent of gross domestic product, a poor showing compared with the "Group of Seven's" 7.1 percent, Germany's 33 percent, and Japan's 25 percent. Nondefense R&D spending as a proportion of GDP in approximately the same 20-year period increased only 3 percent in the United States while increasing by 31 percent in Germany and 55 percent in Japan. Meanwhile, unit labor costs in the United States declined while those in Germany and Japan rose, evidence of the squeeze American employers had put on their workforce in attempting to keep pace with overseas rivals.[68] Even so, growth in U.S. productivity (measured by real GDP per worker) increased only 1.2 percent per year during the 1960–1983 period, compared to 3.7 percent for France, 3.4 percent for West Germany, 5.9 percent for Japan, and 2.3 percent for Britain.[69] These facts help explain America's partial eclipse by the revived and newly industrialized countries of Western Europe and East Asia during the seventies and eighties.

As a reporter for the *Wall Street Journal* concluded in his book about the LBO phenomenon: "The buyout specialists, for all their daring, hard work, and charm, never produced anything .... Instead, a new class of financier-industrialists grew astonishingly rich in the 1980s while having almost no lasting effect for good or bad on industrial progress."[70]

✻   ✻   ✻

American business corporations moved on a large scale not only across industrial lines but across national boundaries as well. There had been a few multinational corporations (MNCs) in the nineteenth century, but after the 1950s they became commonplace. In some measure, they responded to the vacuum left by the weakened postwar European and Japanese economies. But American corporations also went abroad with the forceful encouragement of the government. American policy makers favored foreign investment as part of their efforts to rebuild the Western European economy and to stimulate economic growth in the newly emergent nations. A substantial American business presence abroad, it was believed, also translated into U.S. political influence. The policy had the dual goals of building an economic bulwark against communism and stimulating the U.S. economy by providing healthy trading partners for American business.

---

[68] Joan E. Spero & Jeffrey A. Hart, *The Politics of International Economic Relations*, 5th ed. (St. Martin's, 1997), p. 69.

[69] William Baumol & Kenneth McLennan, eds., *Productivity Growth and U.S. Competitiveness* (Oxford University Press, 1985).

[70] Anders, *Merchants of Debt*, p. 282.

Government encouragement took many forms, including special tax advantages for overseas investments, exemptions from duties on certain goods re-entering the country after foreign processing or fabricating, and government-sponsored insurance against "the political risks of inconvertibility, expropriation, and political violence."[71] For example, during the East Asian financial crisis of 1997–1998, when many American investments were shattered and contracts with foreign governments aborted, U.S. firms stood to be reimbursed by the federal government under the coverage of the Overseas Private Investment Corporation.

The figures on American business expansion abroad showed a continuing acceleration throughout the last half of the century. Given the relative weakness of the other industrial countries in the postwar era, it is not surprising that America led the way. But by the last quarter of the century an increasing number of foreign corporations, nearly all from the well-developed industrial economies, joined American companies in transnational investments and enterprises. In 1978, Americans provided more than 41 percent of foreign direct investment globally, but within five years that percentage declined to 38 percent. Still, between 1971 and 1992, the value of U.S. foreign direct investment (FDI) rose from $86 billion to $423 billion.

Interestingly, the percentage of FDI in Third World countries declined steadily; most transnational investment took place among the major industrial nations, more than 75 percent by the mid-seventies compared with only 50 percent in 1960. Japan, with 10 percent of global foreign investment in 1974, was the exception; most Japanese overseas investments went to less developed countries – mostly in Asia, although much in North and South America as well.

The most rapid growth of foreign direct investment by U.S. firms took place in the third quarter of the century. As of 1950, U.S. FDI amounted to $11.8 billion; by 1960 FDI came to $31.8 billion and ten years later it totaled $78.2 billion. By the early seventies, overseas production by U.S.-based MNCs surpassed trade as the main part of America's international business. In 1950, there were 2,300 foreign subsidiaries of U.S. firms; there were 8,000 in 1970 and 10,000 by 1973. In 1960, U.S. corporate earnings abroad amounted to only 7 percent of total U.S. corporate earnings; by 1974, about 30 percent of all such earnings came from overseas operations. In 1957, overseas investment in plant and equipment came to 9 percent of total such outlays by U.S. firms; in 1970, 25 percent. As of 1960

---

[71] This was set up by the Foreign Assistance Act of 1969, Title IV. "Objectives: to insure investment of eligible U.S. investors in developing countries and emerging markets, against the political risks of inconvertibility, expropriation, and political violence." Specifically included: "petroleum exploration, development and production." See e.g. Mira Wilkins, *The Maturing of Multinational Enterprise: American Business Abroad from 1914–1970* (Harvard University Press, 1974), pp. 331–2 and ch. 8.

there were only 124 branches of U.S. banks abroad, but five years later there were 536 U.S. branch banks overseas. By then, U.S. firms with subsidiaries overseas were selling four times as much abroad as U.S. firms exported from home. By the 1980s, intracompany trade across national borders accounted for more than 40 percent of total U.S. imports and more than 30 percent of exports.[72]

Other industrial countries showed similar developments in the same 20-year period. The number of foreign branch banks in New York City increased from 49 in 1965 to 92 in 1974, while their assets grew from about $5 billion to $29 billion. By 1974, foreign banks in the United States had assets of $56 billion. Meanwhile, Germany's FDI rose from $7.3 billion to $186 billion; England's, $16.2 billion to $259 billion; Japan's, $4.4 billion to $251 billion.[73] Interlocking investments and joint international ventures became commonplace among firms based in all the industrial and many emerging nations. For example, nearly all the major automobile companies owned substantial, often controlling interests in one or more of their foreign rivals. But by the 1980s equity ownership was not the most important form of transnational business. Rather, it took the form of joint ventures, management agreements, service contracts, licensing, franchising, production-sharing agreements, and subcontracting. By the eighties MNCs – U.S. and foreign together – employed about 4 million people in developing countries and almost 30 million worldwide, including 40 percent of American manufacturing workers.[74] By the end of the century, it became difficult to determine which corporations owned or had controlling interests in which others.

In the past, U.S. firms had moved abroad either to get around diverse trade barriers set up by the host countries or to gain control of forest, mineral, and agricultural products unavailable or in short supply at home. Sometimes, as in meatpacking and auto manufacturing, the purpose was to penetrate foreign markets before local entrepreneurs did. Yet beginning in the 1960s, multinational operations more typically involved moving materials to countries where labor costs were low and environmental regulations were few in order to manufacture cheaply goods that were then exported back to the home country or on to other industrial countries. By 1981, Ford Motor Company was producing more cars abroad than it did in the United States.[75]

---

[72] Spero & Hart, *International Economic Relations*, pp. 101, 114; Robert Gilpin, *The Political Economy of International Relations* (Princeton University Press, 1987), p. 239; Wilkins, *Multinational Enterprise*, pp. 330, 394.

[73] Spero & Hart, ibid., p. 103.

[74] Michael J. Webber & David L. Rigby, *The Golden Age of Illusion: Rethinking Postwar Capitalism* (Guilford, 1996), pp. 2ff.

[75] World Motor Vehicle Data (*Det. Motor Vehicle Mfr. Assn. v. U.S.*, 1982), cited in Munkirs, *Transformation of Capitalism*, p. 213.

One effect of the spread of MNCs was the weakening of the ability of national governments to control their domestic economy. Collecting taxes and securing a stable currency were just two of the problems faced by the nation-state in the last third of the century. Internal charges, or "transfer pricing" within the same firm, enabled MNCs to concentrate profits in the lowest tax venues. Efforts (e.g., in California) to capture revenues by enacting a "unitary" tax system failed because of the ease with which companies could move to low-tax states. Meanwhile, effective lobbying by the multinationals prevented a uniform national tax system. A protocol fashioned by the Organization for Economic Cooperation & Development (OECD) in 1979 sought to prevent transfer pricing that evaded legitimate taxes, but it had only advisory impact.[76] Although not the only reason, tax evasion opportunities by MNCs contributed to the decline in the share of national revenue accounted for by corporate taxes, from more than 25 percent in 1960 to less than 10 percent by the end of the century.

Monetary actions designed to cool or stimulate an economy could often backfire because of the ease with which capital could travel globally. For example, reducing interest rates to encourage business and reduce unemployment could lead to a flight of capital to higher-interest opportunities abroad. A rise in interest rates designed to deter inflation might invite capital inflows that could prove inflationary. International capital flows ballooned throughout the last quarter of the century. Net new bank loans across national lines grew by more than a factor of 5 just between 1973 and 1981.

A related consequence was the massive exporting of jobs. Many studies showed that, beginning especially in the 1970s, America's largest manufacturing companies were drastically reducing their domestic workforces while building them up overseas. The U.S. auto industry cut a quarter of a million American workers from the payrolls during the 1970s while the major auto companies entered into production agreements and partnerships abroad. Much of the job loss owed to the introduction of automated technology, but about half came from the export of jobs. In a few cases, partnerships with foreign corporations sustained production in the United States, as in GM's venture with Toyota in the Nummi Corporation to assemble autos in Fremont, California. Such cases aside, Americans in the neopatriotic 1980s would face a wonderful bit of irony: While

---

[76] Spero & Hart, *International Economic Relations,* p. 139. With a little help from friendly congressmen and presidents, MNCs benefited enormously from various accounting tricks that made overseas offices useful for tax-dodging purposes. Just one example: To accommodate tax evasion, special U.S. tax treaties with political entities such as Luxembourg and Barbados enabled corporations to transform taxable profits into expenses deductible from their U.S. taxes. Eligible expenses include interest payments to the overseas company, royalties for use of the company's logo, and fees for "management advice" from the overseas company. See e.g. *New York Times* (16 April 2002), pp. A1, C2.

pleading with American customers to "buy American," Ford, Chrysler, and GM imported 30 to 60 percent of their auto parts from abroad and in many cases marketed cars as their own (e.g., the Dodge Colt) that were made wholly abroad in joint ventures with foreign manufacturers.

The shrinking of global geography made multinational operations inevitable and necessary. Modern air transportation and satellite communications made international buying and selling as convenient as interstate operations had become fifty years earlier, and not much less convenient than interstate or even local trade currently was. If American companies did not go abroad, their products would have been forced out of U.S. markets by foreign imports. Increasingly they were anyway, as the growing merchandise trade deficit after 1972 clearly demonstrated. Failure to respond as American corporate leaders did to the globalization phenomenon would have seriously impaired the country's economic welfare. At the same time, the multinational revolution, like the conglomerate revolution, greatly empowered small groups of corporate managers to operate beyond the oversight and restraints of American democratic institutions.

But then business leaders, for better and for worse, had usually operated beyond the constraints of democratic institutions and preferences. The industrial and corporation revolutions of the nineteenth century had been propelled primarily not by legislative action but by the nation's courts, which changed tort, property, and corporation law, often directly contrary to popular sentiment.[77] The changes wiped away traditional constraints on business practices and facilitated the technological, managerial, and organizational innovations that produced a modern growth economy. In the course of those revolutions, a new business leadership – then and subsequently described as coarse, vulgar "robber barons" – swept by the old "merchant princes." They were, for the most part, callous, self-absorbed, sometimes cruel, and ethically challenged. Their innovative practices produced great long-term benefits but also great human costs, which might have been avoided or at least reduced with more attentive statesmanship such as belatedly emerged in the Progressive Era.

There seems to have been a parallel development in the last quarter of the twentieth century. The new business barons, drawn from the Baby Boom generation, showed much of the same competitive disregard for community interests and ethical conventions that their nineteenth-century counterparts did. In

---

77 J. Willard Hurst, *Law and the Conditions of Freedom in the Nineteenth-Century United States* (University of Wisconsin Press, 1954); J. W. Hurst, *The Legitimacy of the Business Corporation in the Law of the United States, 1780–1970* (University Press of Virginia, 1970); Morton J. Horwitz, *The Transformation of American Law, 1780–1860* (Harvard University Press, 1977); Richard M. Abrams, "Legal Change and the Legitimacy of the Corporation in America," *Stanford Law Review* (April 1972), pp. 765–77; Alfred D. Chandler, *The Visible Hand* (Belknap, 1977), especially pp. 499–500.

his book entitled *The Paradox of American Democracy* (2000), journalist John B. Judis noted the disappearance since the early seventies of an active, public-spirited business elite such as had provided leadership in promoting the progressive domestic and international achievements of the previous half-century. Although many business leaders became politically active, they embraced, Judis wrote, "a kind of irresponsible individualism that was antithetical to the spirit of twentieth-century elites." Herbert Stein – lifelong Republican and senior fellow of the conservative American Enterprise Institute; member of the business leadership group, the Committee for Economic Development (CED); and one-time head of President Nixon's Council of Economic Advisors – ruefully told Judis shortly before he died in 1999: "I think there was a period when there were businessmen outside the government who had some authority and who were respected, and who had a genuine national patriotic concern with the problems of the country. I can't think of a single name now of such a person."[78]

*   *   *

At the beginning of the twentieth century, the great maverick economist Thorstein Veblen noted the transformation of the American business system that had taken place over the previous quarter-century. He made the observation that there had come to be a major functional distinction between what he called "industrial and pecuniary employments." That is, he called attention to the distinction between the producing of goods and services on the one hand and the making of money on the other. The latter, he noted, made particular individuals rich but contributed little to the welfare of the nation.[79] There have been few Veblens among modern economists, but it does not take a Nobel Prize winner to acknowledge the remarkable shift in the attention and energies of modern business corporations.

On Wall Street, as the conglomerate and LBO waves crested, some brokers liked to tell the story of the merchant who was persuaded to buy a crate of newly arrived canned herrings by his wholesaler, a shrewd old Scot. (It seems there must always be an ethnic dialect in the punch line.) While the Scot was diverted by another buyer, the merchant opened one of the cans and was repelled by an awful stench. When the wholesaler returned, the merchant angrily complained: "These kippers y'sold me are stinkin' foul." "Ah, laddie," replied the Scot, "yuh dunnah unnerstan'. These kippers are nah fer eatin'. They're fer buyin' and sellin'."[80]

[78] John B. Judis, *The Paradox of American Democracy: Elites, Special Interests, and the Betrayal of Public Trust* (Pantheon, 2000), p. 237, citing a personal interview.

[79] Thorstein Veblen, *The Theory of Business Enterprise* (Scribner's, 1904).

[80] Taken from Segal, *Corporate Makeover*, pp. 44–5.

10

The Revolution in Racial Relations

> Almighty God created the races white, black, yellow, malay and red, and He placed
> them in separate continents. And but for the interference with His arrangement
> there would be no cause for such marriages. The fact that He separated the races
> shows that He did not intend for the races to mix.[1]
>
> Virginia trial court judge in 1959

In September 1953, on learning of the unexpected death of Fred Vinson, the chief
justice of the U.S. Supreme Court, Justice Felix Frankfurter remarked to two
of his law clerks: "This is the first indication that I have ever had that there is a
God." Frankfurter did not intend to sound cruel or acerbic, nor did he especially
dislike his chief, however little respect he had for his abilities. It was rather that
the Court was about to hear re-argument in the most important and nettlesome
case it had been asked to decide in perhaps a century. And all signs indicated
that, with Vinson's ineffectual leadership, the Court was about to divide 5-4, an
outcome that the justices agreed would be a national calamity.[2]

The case, of course, was the challenge to the constitutionality of racial segregation in public schools. The suit was brought by citizens in several states and
included the suit by the parents of Linda Brown of Topeka, Kansas. The cases
had been consolidated for purposes of the Court's review. Four of the justices,

---

[1] Virginia trial court judge, sentencing Mildred Jeter Loving and Richard Loving for violating the
state criminal law barring whites from marrying a person with "any trace of non-Caucasian
blood." The Virginia statute excepted the descendants of the legendary Pocahontas, in whom Vir-
ginians held much pride. Quoted in the U.S. Supreme Court decision overturning the law as a
violation of the U.S. Constitution: *Loving v. Virginia* (1967).

[2] Quoted in Bernard Schwartz, *Super Chief: Earl Warren and His Supreme Court – A Judicial Biography* (New York University Press, 1983), p. 72. Some accounts speculate that the vote would have
been 7-2 for desegregation, but Frankfurter had guessed 5-4.

including Chief Justice Vinson, were inclined to deny that the Court had a basis in law to overturn a social institution of such long standing, an institution that had enjoyed repeated confirmation by both the nation's judicial and legislative systems. Like the chief justice, Justice Robert Jackson had told his colleagues in an early conference that, under strictly legal tests, "I would have to say it [segregation] *is* constitutional." He had no doubt that segregation was wrong, but it was, he thought, "a question of politics, [and] ... I don't know how to justify the abolition of segregation as a judicial act." Four other justices believed they knew how, and two, including Jackson, *wished* that they knew how. All realized that a split court on a case with such profound social and political implications would carry little authority. That would mean jeopardizing the standing of the Court in public regard as well as the civil peace.

That was the situation when President Dwight Eisenhower, less than a year into his first term, paid off a political debt by appointing California's governor, Earl Warren, to replace the late chief justice. A favorite son candidate for the Republican presidential nomination in 1952, Warren had released his convention delegates to Eisenhower after Senator Richard Nixon had covertly led a defection in favor of Eisenhower from within the California delegation. That ended the candidacy of the then-leading contender, Robert Taft. Eisenhower would eventually rue the appointment, because Warren's social views proved to be substantially more liberal than the president's. But at the time of his appointment, Warren's background suggested rather mixed leanings on current social and political issues.

Warren grew up in the small, disorderly town of Bakersfield, where he inherited his Republicanism from the prevailing partisan loyalties. In his early career he generally shared the locals' suspicions of big government. "Big government" had long been conservatives' code words for the use of government revenues for social services and regulatory agencies – as opposed to using government revenues for military procurement, road building for lumber companies and real-estate developers, and subsidies for oil producers, tobacco growers, and numerous other business and agricultural interests. But the environment of his home town also produced in him a lasting distaste for corruption of both the personal and political kinds. In addition, he harbored a visceral sympathy for labor causes.

An education at the University of California in Berkeley and a law degree from its Boalt Hall may have done something to broaden his outlook still more. As district attorney for Alameda County he would display a commitment to the principles of the Bill of Rights that was uncommon among Americans generally until the 1960s. That may have helped win him the Democratic as well as the Republican endorsement in his campaign for attorney general, which California's cross-filing election laws at the time permitted. As governor he moved further from his provincial political roots, fighting for a variety of social programs that included, decades ahead of its time, a statewide employer-financed health-care program. (That program was defeated amid the inevitable charges of "socialized medicine" and "communism.")

But Warren also had absorbed the prevalent racial prejudices that white Californians of the first half of the century adopted more or less as an inborn reflex. Although his work as Alameda County's district attorney and as state attorney general earned him national recognition for his effectiveness and his fairness, historians are bound to highlight his willful role in the internment of Japanese-Americans during World War II. Two months after Pearl Harbor, as California's attorney general, Warren told a congressional committee: "We believe that when we are dealing with the Caucasian race we have methods that will test the loyalty of them .... But when we deal with the Japanese we are in an entirely different field and we cannot form any opinion that we believe to be sound." As governor in 1943, when the tide of the war had turned and there seemed no longer a reason to fear an enemy attack on the coast, he still opposed ending the internments. "If the Japs are released," he insisted, "no one will be able to tell a saboteur from any other Jap." Warren, observed Carey McWilliams, editor of *The Nation* and a fierce critic of the internment, "was entrapped ... by ... a kind of political environment out of which he came in California .... The sad truth ... is that you could count on the fingers of two hands the number of so-called public personages in California who opposed mass evacuation of the Japanese."[3]

But during the next ten years much changed, including Earl Warren. By the time he took his seat at the head of the conference table in the Supreme Court following the rehearing on *Brown v. Board of Education of Topeka* in December 1953, there was no doubt in his mind that racial segregation was incompatible with the nation's basic commitment to freedom and human dignity. At the outset of the discussion, Warren stated his position: "the more I've read and heard and thought," he began, "the more I've come to conclude that the basis of segregation and 'separate but equal' rests upon a concept of the inherent inferiority of the colored race." The *Plessy* case[4] that in 1896 had established the "separate but equal" doctrine, Warren said, could have been based on no other theory. If that still-prevailing doctrine were to be reaffirmed now 58 years later, it would have to be upon that basis. And that was unacceptable. "I don't see how in this day and age we can set any group apart from the rest and say that they are not entitled to exactly the same treatment as all others."[5] With that as the keynote for

---

[3] The quotations are from Schwartz, *Super Chief,* pp. 72, 14–16.

[4] *Plessy v. Ferguson* (163 U.S. 537, 1896).

[5] Schwartz, *Super Chief.*

the discussion, Warren won unanimous support from his brethren for declaring racial segregation in public schools unconstitutional. Forced separateness on the basis of race, the nine justices declared, is inherently unequal. In the decade that followed, the Court would explicitly overrule *Plessy* (which concerned segregated railroad cars) and extend the judgment of unconstitutionality to nearly all forms of adverse discrimination based upon race.

What had happened to make "this day and age" different? First and most important, by the 1940s most scholars and scientists had thoroughly discredited the idea that the physiological traits commonly used to define "race" had anything to do with character and behavioral traits. Although millions (probably a majority) of other Americans still didn't get it, Warren, his colleagues on the Court, and most of the nation's intellectual leadership by then did. Second, the war against fascism – and against especially the Nazis' murderous ideology of Aryan racial superiority – had helped greatly to identify racism with evil, even though most Americans during the war period itself expressed a heightened racially laden hostility toward Japanese people. (Sympathy for the Chinese people, Japan's victim and America's wartime ally, did soften the strictly racial feature of the anti-Japanese animus.) Third, by 1950 the Cold War with the Soviet Union was building fiercely, and racism in America plainly subverted the country's efforts to thwart the communists' courtship of Asian, African, and Latin American peoples.

Until this junction in history, Americans' commitment to the ideal of equality had almost always taken a back seat to other political priorities, especially economic growth, social order, and national security. But now, at last, equality served not only a liberal agenda but a premier national security policy objective favored by conservatives: containment of the Soviet Union.

Meanwhile, the Second World War had brought tens of thousands of young black men out of their mostly impoverished Southern rural environment and into military service. There the contrast between the wartime propaganda about "democracy" and their shabby treatment in segregated military units could not have been more stark or more provocative. "You must put yourself in the skin of a man who is wearing the uniform of his country," wrote James Baldwin, "and who watches German prisoners of war being treated by Americans with more human dignity than he has ever received at their hands."[6] The contrast between the propaganda and the disfranchisement of their families back home was equally provocative. In addition to the military experience, tens of thousands more Negroes migrated from their rural enclaves in the South to cities where wartime job opportunities beckoned. There they discovered something about

---

[6] James Baldwin, *The Fire Next Time* (Dell, 1963 [1962]), p. 76.

the power of voting, especially in such electorally important states as New York, Illinois, and Missouri.

Around the same time, a small but growing class of professionals among black Americans, especially those coming out of law schools such as at Howard University, had discovered the new effectiveness of lawsuits. The Supreme Court, newly constituted with liberal appointees during Franklin Roosevelt's twelve-year presidency, had already indicated its willingness to break from a long tradition against intervening in state criminal cases when it appeared clear that procedures were tainted by racial bigotry. In 1940, for example, a unanimous Court had reversed the murder convictions of four young Florida black men whose "confessions" had been brutally extorted from them in an environment of racist terror. As it set out on a new, activist course, the Court declared: "Under our constitutional system, courts stand against any winds that blow as havens of refuge for those who might otherwise suffer because they are helpless, weak, outnumbered, or because they are non-conforming victims of prejudice and public excitement."[7]

By the time *Brown v. Board of Education* first reached the Supreme Court in 1952, the legal branch of the NAACP, headed by the young Thurgood Marshall, had achieved several important victories against Jim Crow practices. That included outlawing racially exclusive state university graduate and law schools as well as voiding racially restrictive neighborhood and housing covenants. By this time, too, President Truman had ordered an end to racial discrimination in the U.S. armed forces. A momentum against racial oppression was slowly building both among the victims and in some vital sectors of white America.

Still, millions of Americans just didn't get it; and if desegregation had been left to the democratic political process, such as Justice Jackson initially believed it required, then those millions – concentrated in locales where the greatest number of the nation's racial minorities lived – would have blocked every gesture of change. In this as in several other areas of social change, it was the judicial system and not the democratic legislative process that made reform possible.

In fact, the historical evidence indicates that the most important gains made in the United States on behalf of a humane society during the third quarter of the twentieth century came not from grassroots pressures upon the political system, since most such pressures were directed quite otherwise, but from the efforts of a liberal elite fortuitously entrenched in key social, political, and especially judicial positions. As many modern scholars have come to recognize, much necessary reform in democratic societies has required proactive initiatives by members of the civil services or government bureaucracy. Especially in times of serious social tensions, Harvard political scientist Theda Skocpol has noted, "collectivities

[7] *Chambers v. Florida* (309 U.S. 227, 1940).

of career officials relatively insulated from ties to currently dominant socio-
economic interests, are likely to launch distinctive new state strategies."[8] Such,
in fact, appears to describe what happened during the third quarter of the century, not only in racial relations but in other areas of American life as well.

*   *   *

It is no exaggeration to say that, during the third quarter of the twentieth century,
the Supreme Court was the chief agency of state leading Americans finally out
of the nineteenth century. On vital issues concerning the protection of human
freedom and dignity, the political processes had stalemated. Democratic processes could hardly help oppressed minorities who were barred by discriminatory
election laws from even participating in the process. Those who did participate
had a special interest in keeping the bar. Nor could those processes rectify the
widespread and blatant violation of the constitutional requirement that election
districts be realigned to conform to shifting demographic patterns, especially the
urbanization of the population. Those elected from the anachronistic rural districts had a compelling interest in maintaining their underpopulated fiefdoms.
Only after the U.S. Supreme Court intervened in 1962 (*Baker v. Carr*) did that
blight on the American democracy begin to be remedied.

Nor could democratic processes alone safeguard the civil liberties of political dissidents or social outcasts during a period of intense anxiety over public safety and national security. "Dissidence" and "outcast" by definition refer
to minorities that are defenseless politically against democratic majorities. It
took Supreme Court intervention to protect American dissidents' right to speak,
print, and assemble from popular repressive government policies and slanderous
congressional pseudoinvestigations. Nor would democratic processes protect
the poor, racial minorities, and others marginalized from mainstream America
from abuse by local police. A populace frightened by, or simply suspicious of,
Americans whose appearance did not fit preconceived models of "good citizens"
generally were prepared to give police every benefit of doubt. It took Supreme
Court interventions to protect Americans against unwarranted searches of their
home, their property, and their person (*Mapp v. Ohio, 1961*); to require that
those accused of crimes be informed of their legal rights before they could be ar-
raigned (*Miranda v. Arizona, 1966*); and to have the right to legal representation
before and during trial (*Gideon v. Wainwright, 1963*).

The most conspicuous social change that Americans would experience in the last
half of the twentieth century would be in racial relations. Segregation and adverse

---

[8] Theda Skocpol, "Bringing the State Back In," in Peter B. Evans, Dietrich Rueschemeyer, and Theda
Skocpol, eds., *Bringing the State Back In* (Cambridge University Press, 1985), p. 9.

discrimination on the basis of race would cease to be official policy. More than that, adverse racial discrimination ceased to be commonplace in most of the private sector as well. With a series of Supreme Court decisions beginning in the late forties, the force of government in America for the first time would swing against racism.

The Court decisions were a principal cause but also an effect of a significant shift in social attitudes. The changed force of government greatly intensified – but also was partly inspired by – a civil rights movement that had been percolating through the nation's federal courts since the Second World War and that first gained significant national attention with a citywide bus boycott in Montgomery, Alabama, led by the young Martin Luther King, Jr., beginning in December 1955. That boycott was itself inspired by (and, one could argue, would not have occurred without) the U.S. Supreme Court's revolutionary decision in *Brown v. Board of Education* as well as a Fourth Circuit Court of Appeals ruling in July 1955 that reversed the dismissal of a case brought by a Negro woman against segregated seating in the Columbia, South Carolina, bus system. Nor was it likely that the Montgomery boycott would have succeeded if not for the Court's decision in November 1956 that affirmed the unconstitutionality of segregated transit systems.[9] The court-ordered desegregation of Little Rock's Central High School in 1957 required a reluctant president to send a thousand National Guardsmen to enforce the order against the Arkansas governor's defiance. The civil rights movement blossomed in the 1960s especially after the successful sit-ins at segregated lunch counters by Negro students, beginning on 1 February 1960 in Greensboro, North Carolina.

By noting the indispensable role of the courts in launching the success of the civil rights movement, I do not intend to belittle the role of the protesters, whose heroism needs little elaboration. Nor do I wish to suggest that the judges' decisions enjoyed ready compliance or implementation. Both the court actions and the street demonstrations were necessary. By analogy, one can think of the courts as the artillery and the demonstrators as the infantry. Before the infantry could begin to move in, the artillery had to prepare the way, which included inspiring the morale of the ground troops.[10]

---

[9] The U.S. Supreme Court, in *Gayle v. Browder* (352 U.S. 903, 1956) affirmed a lower federal court ruling (*Browder v. Gayle* 142 F.Supp 707, D.C. Alabama, 1956) that overturned efforts by Montgomery officials to break the bus boycott on the grounds that segregated buses violated the constitution. In affirming the Fourth U.S. Circuit Court's decision, the U.S. Supreme Court confirmed that the "separate but equal" doctrine established by the Court sixty years earlier in *Plessy v. Ferguson* had been overturned. For a meticulous account the sequence of events leading to the success of the bus boycott, see Robert Jerome Glennon, "The Role of Law in the Civil Rights Movement," *Law & History Review* (Spring 1991).

[10] By the end of the twentieth century, a lively debate developed over the importance of the *Brown v. Board of Education* decisions (1954 and 1955, the latter containing the controversial

Toleration, the byword of the 1940s, would give way in the 1960s to *integration* as the nation's preferred objective. In other words, the social message changed from one urging a smiling acceptance of differences among Americans to one arguing that, in social outlook as well as in law, no significant differences in either social or legal standing should exist on racial grounds. (By the late 1980s, when the idea of America as a "multicultural" nation gained popularity in some sectors of the society, *diversity* tended to displace *integration.* This was particularly so on college campuses but also among ambitious political leaders, for whom ethnic and racial differentiation and distinctiveness offered a means of access to the benefits of affirmative action programs.)

For the racially sensitive, at least among whites, the shift from *toleration* to *integration* had long held threatening implications regarding miscegenation; indeed, the changed message reflected changed attitudes on that subject. Although interracial marriage would not become commonplace,[11] neither would it evoke the shock and even horror that was nearly universal in the forties and fifties. The essence of the Southern rationale for racially segregated schools had always targeted interracial relationships. "If we white Southerners submit to [school desegregation]," declared a White Citizens Council report in 1956, "the malignant powers of mongrelization, communism and atheism will surely destroy this Nation from within. Racial intermarriage has already begun in the North and unless stopped will spread to the South."[12]

California's Supreme Court did not declare the state's antimiscegenation law in violation of the state constitution until 1949.[13] The state's civil code, upheld as recently as 1948,[14] had read: "No license may be issued authorizing the marriage of a white person with a Negro, mulatto, Mongolian, or member of the

implementation clause "with all deliberate speed"). Some argued that (a) it did not clearly establish implementation procedures and that (b) in any case it led to little compliance. For this view, see Gerald N. Rosenberg, *The Hollow Hope: Can Courts Bring About Social Change?* (University of Chicago Press, 1991), and Michael J. Klarman, *From Jim Crow to Civil Rights: The Supreme Court and the Struggle for Racial Equality* (Oxford University Press, 2004). For the most comprehensive narrative of the epic, see Richard Kluger, *Simple Justice: The History of Brown v. Board of Education and Black America's Struggle for Equality* (Knopf, 1975; revised 2004). For an incisive and balanced review essay on the most recent takes on the role of the courts, see Cass R. Sunstein, "Did *Brown* Matter?" *The New Yorker* (3 May 2004), pp. 102ff.

[11] At the end of the twentieth century, black–white marriages made up only about 0.5 percent of all marriages. Rodger Doyle, "The Progress of Love: Americans Are Discarding Taboos against Mixed Unions," *Scientific American* (October 2003).

[12] From Robert Patterson's 1956 annual report to the Mississippi Association of Citizens Councils. Quoted in Sara Diamond, *Roads to Dominion: Right-Wing Movements and Political Power in the United States* (Guilford, 1995), p. 73.

[13] California Civil Code, sec. 69.

[14] *Perez v. Sharpe* (32 C.2d 711 & 712, 1948).

Malay race." At the time, some thirty other states forbade whites to marry non-whites. "Black," "brown," "red," and "yellow" individuals could freely marry among themselves.

A 1965 Gallup poll found that 48 percent of American adults surveyed still favored criminal antimiscegenation laws.[15] It was only in 1967 that the U.S. Supreme Court belatedly declared such laws unconstitutional (*Loving v. Virginia*), reversing nearly two centuries of law requiring that a couple's liberty of contract and right to privacy yield to what the state regarded as a greater social interest – specifically, the interest in "racial purity." Although fifteen states repealed their antimiscegenation laws between 1949 and 1967, 72 percent of Americans polled by Gallup in 1968 still opposed interracial marriage.[16] But by that time, impelled by the leaders of the major professions – notably the media, education, science, and the law – the tide had clearly turned.[17]

Before then, powerful informal sanctions had generally supported the formal dictates of the law. The behavior of the privately controlled media is informative on the subject. For example, before the 1960s, themes in film, television, or the theater that might touch on interracial romance were regarded as impermissibly provocative, even when a recognizably white actor or actress played the role of the nonwhite protagonist. Such scenarios were as rare as nudity. In 1967, the black actor Sidney Poitier played the fiancé of Katherine Hepburn's and Spencer Tracy's daughter in *Guess Who's Coming to Dinner*. Although the film showed no on-screen smooching, a barrier had come down. By the 1970s, a couple of popular TV "sitcoms" included mixed racial family relationships.[18] It was by then finally possible for a white master of ceremonies on a national television variety show to greet or congratulate a female black star performer

---

[15] Robert Sickels, *Race, Marriage and the Law* (University of New Mexico Press, 1972), p. 42.

[16] Until nullified by the U.S. Supreme Court in 1967, sixteen states still outlawed interracial marriage. Interestingly, if "same-sex" marriage were to become legal in the United States, it would require the same sort of leadership from the judiciary. As of 2004, a majority of Americans, including the president, opposed legal marriage by gays and lesbians, even though Canada and the Massachusetts judiciary had ruled that the legislative bodies of those political entities could not ban it – on the constitutional grounds that all citizens deserved equal protection of the law.

[17] The same year of *Loving v. Virginia*, Secretary of State Dean Rusk, a Georgian, offered to resign "to protect" President Johnson's political flanks when he learned that his daughter planned to marry a black man. According to Defense Secretary Robert McNamara, whom Rusk consulted, Johnson simply offered Rusk his congratulations. Robert S. McNamara, *In Retrospect: The Tragedy and Lessons of Vietnam* (Vintage, 1995), pp. 282–3; also, Thomas W. Zeiler, *Dean Rusk: Defending the American Mission Abroad* (Scholarly Resources, 2000), p. 91.

[18] Most notably "The Jeffersons." Such programming disappeared by the 1980s. Although racial, ethnic, and also religious intermarriage continued to increase, some public leaders among Afro-Americans, Catholics, Jews, and other groups strongly criticized intermarriage as threatening the prideful identity of each group. "Diversity," in the view of these critics, required a sort of voluntary segregation. The media, sensitive to such complaints, seemingly responded.

with an embrace or kiss, something he would always have done with white performers. Previously, a handshake was all that was permitted.[19]

The most telling change had to do with the altered role of government. Except for sporadic interventions at the higher federal court levels, before the 1950s bigotry could usually find support in government policy and law. This was true not only among state governments but at the federal level as well. For example, until 1949 the Federal Housing Authority officially discouraged loans for houses in racially mixed or black neighborhoods and explicitly encouraged restrictive neighborhood covenants to maintain all-white areas. The U.S. Supreme Court declared such covenants unconstitutional in 1948 (*Shelley v. Kraemer*). Then in 1954 the Court's decision in *Brown v. Board of Education* began the long series of decisions, supplemented by legislation, that banned racial discrimination in most public facilities and many privately owned facilities as well.

Only after the nation's courts cleared the way did the democratic agencies of government move effectively against racial injustice. Court actions were followed by the Civil Rights Act of 1964 that essentially established a national standard for equal protection under the law of all Americans regardless of race, sex, age, religion, or national origin; by the Voting Rights Act of 1965, which placed access to the polling booth under federal supervision; and by President Lyndon Johnson's Executive Orders 11246 (1965) and 11375 (1967), which commanded all federal agencies, all government contractors, and all private institutions, agencies, or companies receiving federal money to engage in "affirmative action" to overcome the effects of historic adverse discrimination against women and designated racial and ethnic groups.[20] The nation's courts, moreover, began accepting suits by women and members of the specified minorities who sought financial damages against private companies where discriminatory personnel policies had deprived them of jobs and promotions. More than that, the courts began ruling that proof of such discrimination could be inferred from quantitative measures even in the absence of explicit company policy. It was the courts that implemented the principles of affirmative action; it was the courts that ordered school busing in order to overcome the de facto school segregation arising from long-standing neighborhood and housing patterns that followed racial lines. The courts also acted to overcome legislative efforts to preserve segregated schools by redrawing school district lines.

---

[19] In the 1950s, when the great Ella Fitzgerald sang duets on TV with Bing Crosby, and another time with Frank Sinatra, the white males stepped away and bowed stiffly at the end; not even a hand-kiss.

[20] The groups specified in Johnson's E.O. 11246 were Negroes, Asian-Americans, American Indians, Pacific Islanders, Filipinos, and Hispanics.

To highlight the contrast with conditions in mid-century, by the 1970s many white Americans would be complaining that affirmative action recruitment of black and other minority persons (and of women) for employment, political appointments, and college enrolment constituted "reverse discrimination."[21] There is little doubt that, if left to democratic processes, much less would have been achieved in alleviating the evils of America's racist past. The work of the courts and of the leaders of the nation's professions in promoting the ideal of racial equality enjoyed great success. Although the country would experience a reactionary backlash during the last quarter of the century that took a heavy toll on progressive political forces, the power of the new consensus on racial justice prevented any significant rollback in that area. Besides, conservatives found no difficulty in recruiting ideological kin among women and the designated minorities. So, for example, President Reagan would appoint the first woman, Sandra Day O'Connor, to the U.S. Supreme Court, and the first President Bush would name black American Clarence Thomas – a man who vowed to reverse most of the Warren Court decisions – to replace Thurgood Marshall on the Court. The diversity of political views among minorities and women, and uses to which it was put by conservatives in support of a broader agenda, assured the irreversibility of civil rights gains at least in public life.

By the seventies, meanwhile, Deep South cities such as Hattiesburg, Selma, Birmingham, Atlanta, and New Orleans – veritable bastions of American racial bigotry – would elect black mayors; so would Philadelphia, Los Angeles, Oakland, Cleveland, Detroit, and Washington, DC. Chicago, whose riotous resistance to desegregation was described in 1966 by Martin Luther King, Jr., as worse than almost anything he had encountered in the Deep South, elected a black mayor only sixteen years later. So, too, would New York City. (Unhappily, the electoral success of minority politicians appeared to do little more to improve the lot of most urban minorities than did their white predecessors.)

In 1976 California, the state most responsible for the racially motivated wartime internment of 80,000 Japanese-American citizens in 1942, would elect (Republican) S. I. Hayakawa to the United States Senate. By the 1990s, there would be a black governor of Virginia. Willie Brown, an Afro-American born into poverty in a small Texas town, became California's most powerful legislator, serving as Speaker of the State Assembly for an unmatched fifteen years (1980–1995),

---

[21] See e.g. Nathan Glazer, *Affirmative Discrimination* (Basic Books, 1975), and Carl Cohen, *Naked Racial Preference* (Madison Books, 1995). In 2000, Glazer changed his mind about opposing affirmative action. Most ironically, the University of Texas Law School, which was ordered by the Supreme Court in 1950 (*Sweat v. Painter*, 339 U.S. 629) to end its all-white admissions policy, in 1994 was sued over its affirmative action program for discriminating against whites (*Hapgood, et al. v. Texas, et al.*).

after which he became mayor of San Francisco for eight years. One-time white supremacist southern governors, congressmen, and senators (e.g., George Wallace of Alabama and Strom Thurmond of South Carolina) tailored their politics and campaigned vigorously for the support of the newly registered black voters who had become indispensable for their re-election.

One need not deny that racism was still alive and well in many parts of American society at the end of the century in order to acknowledge that racial relations had become transformed quite beyond what any adult American in 1945 could have anticipated. Blacks, Hispanics, and some other minorities would still suffer in disproportionate numbers from poverty as the century approached its conclusion. For many, conditions would become even worse as demographics and the structure of the economy changed. But the problem by the 1970s was as much a matter of class as of race.[22]

Disproportionately large numbers of Hispanics and Afro-Americans suffered from low educational achievement at the same time that good-paying low-skill jobs were disappearing as the economy turned toward information technology.[23] And this correlated with an increasingly high incidence of single-parent female-headed families, producing tens of thousands of children who, in most cases like their mother, would have little education and low expectations. By 1980, 55 percent of all black children lived with unwed mothers, 85 percent of whom lived without the father or any man in the household. A high proportion of the single mothers were teenagers at the time of their first birth. By 1990, the percentage of black children living with single mothers reached 70 percent. Among Hispanics, single-parent families in the 1980s were increasing by 7 percent per year, twice the national rate.[24] Unhappily, this tells much of the story. Low educational achievement coupled with single motherhood had a circular effect, producing a poverty trap.[25]

---

[22] See William Julius Wilson, *The Declining Significance of Race,* 2nd ed. (University of Chicago Press, 1980), and *The Truly Disadvantaged: The Inner City, the Underclass, and Public Policy* (University of Chicago Press, 1987). Cf. Bart Landry, *The New Black Middle Class* (University of California Press, 1987) for a slightly different take on the role of class and of race in the relative fortunes of Afro-Americans. See also "The Failure Syndrome: Civil Rights" in Part III of this volume.

[23] For example, a report issued in 2002 by the Public Policy Institute of California indicated that, in the aggregate, Mexican-Americans earned significantly less than Euro-Americans even after three generations because they stayed in school less than did Euro-Americans and, indeed, less than almost all other racial and ethnic groups in the country. *San Francisco Chronicle* (22 May 2002), p. A19.

[24] U.S. Census Bureau, reported in the *San Francisco Chronicle* (30 Jan. 1991), p. A2; Lawrence L. Wu & Barbara Wolfe, eds., *Out of Wedlock: Causes and Consequences of Nonmarital Fertility* (Russell Sage, 2001), especially the Introduction and ch. 10; also, Mark Abrahamson, *Out-of-Wedlock Birth: The United States in Comparative Perspective* (Praeger, 1998).

[25] In July 1998 it was reported that a 30-year-low 7.6 percent of unmarried Afro-American women gave birth in 1996, continuing a downward trend after a steady upward trend in the 1980s. But

The demoralization that had arisen from generations of racist brutalization and impoverishment apparently lay so deep for black Americans that, at least for a large minority of them, the remarkable achievements of the civil rights movement made little progress against it. Only a minority of blacks seemed encouraged enough by the advances against racism to act on a belief that education might lift them out of the morass of poverty. Insistence by militants that the civil rights movement was a "failure" and that racism was as prevalent as ever contributed to their disbelief. Whatever the reasons, as late as 1985 less than a quarter of young blacks in the 18–21 age group – most of them women – made it into a four-year or even a two-year college,[26] and only half of them stayed long enough to earn a degree. The crucial nature of this fact may be grasped by knowing that, by the mid-1990s, men with a college degree earned almost 90 percent more than men with only a high-school degree; that was up from only 49 percent more in 1979, just fifteen years earlier. Inadequate scholarship funding and new tuition charges in city and state colleges contributed to the difference. But finances were not the big problem; inadequate preparation for college, both at home and in the neighborhood schools, loomed larger. At least in part, inadequate preparation owed to the negative attitude toward achievement in school by blacks, especially black males, of many low-income families.[27] Another reason was the bare-bones funding of Head Start and follow-up programs. These were measures begun as part of Lyndon Johnson's War on Poverty in the Sixties that were designed to help 3–5-year-olds to overcome unfavorable conditions at home.

But those minorities who did gain the skills demanded by the modern political economy found that racism presented few unmanageable barriers. One indicator of this was that, by the mid-seventies, the average annual income of black college graduates under 35 living outside the Old South equaled or surpassed that of comparable nonblacks.[28] In 1945, by contrast, the income of black college graduates averaged less than that of whites who had no more than an eighth-grade education. There was, in short, a polarizing effect among Afro-Americans:

---

that 7.6 percent amounted to 69.2 percent of all black children born in 1996. Overall, 4.5 percent of unmarried women of all ethnicities of child-bearing age had children in 1996. In 1990, 11 percent of unmarried black teenagers aged 15–19 bore children; that declined to about 9 percent by 1996: *San Francisco Chronicle* (1 July 1998). Figures for the Mexican-American population showed similar problems. The incidence of unmarried Euro-American mothers also rose, but the biggest increase was among middle-class women cohabiting with a mate.

[26] That was still a higher figure than for all Englishmen; and not grossly lower than for Euro-Americans.

[27] See e.g. Hugh Pearson, *The Shadow of the Panther* (Addison-Wesley, 1994), pp. 341ff and elsewhere in the book.

[28] John Bound & Richard B. Freeman, "What Went Wrong? The Erosion of Relative Earnings and Employment among Young Black Men in the 1980s," Working Paper no. 3778 (July 1991), National Bureau of Economic Research.

between 1969 and 1980, the proportions of black men with income below $5,000 and above $25,000 (in 1980 dollars) *both* grew.[29]

After the mid-seventies, the ratio of black/white earnings began to fall, though it never approached the pre-sixties levels. There were a number of reasons for the decline, virtually none of which were specifically related to race. A decline in good-paying manufacturing jobs, especially in the auto and steel industries of the Midwest, hit black Americans disproportionately hard because they held a disproportionately high number of those jobs. The weakening power of unions also hurt, especially because it occurred in much the same high-paying job areas. The deterioration of inner-city economies also was a factor.[30]

Young black college graduates actually earned slightly more than young white graduates by the mid-seventies and were as likely as whites to become managers or professionals.[31] Afterward, however, the advantages declined as many more black Americans earned college degrees and began competing for fewer jobs. Then again, after 1980 the reduced enforcement of affirmative action guidelines – coupled with court decisions that made it harder to prove racial discrimination in employment – probably contributed to the deterioration of black/white earnings ratios. Finally, beginning in the late seventies a sharp rise in the jailing of young black men, especially among high-school dropouts, accounts for a significant drop in employment among such men and a corresponding drop in the aggregate black/white earnings ratio.[32] The conspicuous involvement of young black males in crime, or alleged crime – some of it clearly an effect of racism – affected the employment opportunities of many who had no such involvement, a consequence of a kind of "racial profiling" by potential employers.

During the same period, the black/white earnings ratio for women remained steady. Moreover, the apparent deterioration of relative earnings among Afro-American males after the mid-seventies by no means erased the substantial gains for Afro-Americans generally during the third quarter of the century. Although in 1940 fully 85 percent of black families subsisted in poverty, by 1980 that figure had declined to 26 percent. Of that 26 percent, the majority were single-parent families. Meanwhile, as of 1980 almost half of black Americans owned their own home, and there was virtually no difference in income between black and white

---

[29] "Thus black men at the top of the distribution were doing progressively better while blacks at the bottom [nearly a quarter of all black men aged 25 to 55] were doing progressively worse." Wilson, *The Truly Disadvantaged,* p. 45.

[30] See e.g. Wilson, *Declining Significance.*

[31] See Christopher Jencks et al., *Inequality: A Reassessment of the Effect of Family and Schooling in America* (Basic Books, 1972), and C. Jencks et al., *Who Gets Ahead? The Determinants of Economic Success in America* (Basic Books, 1979).

[32] Bound & Freeman, "What Went Wrong?" The high numbers of imprisoned black males reduced the availability of marriageable men and surely contributed to the disproportionately high percentage of single black mothers.

married couples under the age of 35 – after adjusting for the fact that more than 55 percent of all black families still lived in the low-income South.[33]

Although various people continued to insist that "nothing had changed" and that the disproportionate poverty of black Americans in the country owed to "racism," past and present, such arguments suggested either an abysmal ignorance of how bad American racism had once been or a level of militancy too high for facts to reach; maybe both. "There remains," Cynthia Tucker wrote in 1998, "a stubborn cottage industry of pessimists and nay-sayers whose stock-in-trade is bad news about race relations in America – even if their conclusions don't add up." The Afro-American editorial page editor of Atlanta's premier newspaper, *The Constitution,* noted how Vernon Jordan was hauled before a grand jury investigating President Clinton because the black man was personally so close to the president that he might have been privy to something Clinton said or did that might have confirmed the zealously partisan prosecutor's theory that the president might have committed perjury. She also noted how Texas cattlemen tried (unsuccessfully) to sue the popular TV hostess Oprah Winfrey, claiming that her casual remark about the perils of eating beef had driven down prices. Thirty years earlier, Tucker asked, what black woman could have been thought to have such influence? "Class," Tucker concluded, "is now more important than race. If you don't think so, look again at Oprah Winfrey and Vernon Jordan."[34] One might add, look also at Cynthia Tucker.

Look, too, at Toni Morrison, who won the Nobel Prize for literature; at Pulitzer Prize winning playwright August Wilson; at Motion Picture Academy Award winning actor Denzel Washington; at Alvin Ailey, whose dance company helped make New York City the dance capital of the world. Indeed, as the century ended it was possible to see that the three most popular and most universally liked and admired Americans had African genes. If he had chosen to run, retired general Colin Powell might have captured the Republican Party nomination for president in 1996 and might well have defeated incumbent President Bill Clinton

---

[33] A 1998 study by the Census Bureau showed that nationwide (not adjusting for regional residence or age) the median income for a black married couple in 1996 was $41,963, or roughly 83 percent of the median income of white married couples ($50,190); that was up from 80 percent in 1990. But only 46 percent of Afro-American families were headed by a married couple, as compared with 80 percent of white families. Single-parent families headed by a black woman typically earned less than $16,000, compared to $24,700 for the median single-parent family headed by a white woman. Not surprisingly, 26 percent of black families in 1997 had incomes below the poverty line (down from 31 percent in 1993). After the 1970s, Afro-American poverty levels ranged between 26 and 33 percent; for white families it ranged between 6 and 11 percent. U.S. Bureau of the Census, reported in *San Francisco Chronicle* (30 July 1998), p. A2. See also Katherine S. Newman, *Declining Fortunes: The Withering of the American Dream* (Basic Books, 1993), p. 33.

[34] Cynthia Tucker, "As I See It," syndicated editorial reprinted in the *San Francisco Chronicle* (6 March 1998).

in the national election that year. Probably no television personality was more popular across the nation, or earned more money, than Oprah Winfrey. No sports figure could command as high a fee from advertisers as Michael Jordan, whose product endorsements were sought after all over the globe. And not far behind was the superstar of golf, Afro-Asian-American Tiger Woods.

By the first years of the new millennium, there was more than ample evidence of the abatement of racial and religious prejudice. The ultra-conservative administration of Bush *fils* had among its leading foreign policy makers Colin Powell as Secretary of State and Condaleeza Rice, former Stanford University provost, as head of the National Security Council (later replacing Powell as Secretary of State). In the nineties J. C. Watt, a black congressman from Oklahoma, chaired the Republican House Caucus. Meanwhile, several black Americans and Hispanics had risen to CEO or other top executive positions in major corporations, such as Coca-Cola, Merrill Lynch, American Express, the multinational investment conglomerate Carlyle Group, and AOL Time Warner.[35] Numerous Jews and Irish or Italian Catholics, long excluded from most business and educational leadership positions, similarly rose to the top of megacorporations (e.g., Citigroup, Time Warner, DuPont, Chrysler, Monsanto, the New York Stock Exchange) with hardly a stir. The same applied to the nation's most prestigious universities (e.g., Yale, Columbia, Princeton, Penn, Michigan, U.C. Berkeley, and the statewide University of California system).

Whatever the degree of racism that still plagued American society at the end of the twentieth century, it is impossible to gainsay the remarkable and truly revolutionary changes that had taken place since the 1940s. Dick Gregory, a nationally popular black comedian who once was jailed for his radical activism against racism, summed it up when he remarked in 1995: "No country in the history of this planet has made the progress we made. Race relations will never go back to that era."[36]

---

[35] Namely: at Coca-Cola, Hispanic Roberto Goizeta; Merrill Lynch, Afro-American Stanley O'Neal; American Express, Afro-American Kenneth Chenault; Carlyle Group, Afro-American William Kennard; AOL Time Warner, Afro-American Richard Parsons.

[36] Quoted in the *New York Times* (15 Dec. 1995), p. B12.

11

The Revolution in Gender-Based Roles

> In a great number of societies men's sureness of their sex role is tied up with their right, or ability, to practice some activity that women are not allowed to practice. Their maleness, in fact, has to be underwritten by preventing women from entering some field or performing some feat.[1]
>
> Margaret Mead

> Humanity is now in the early phases of a transformation in the meanings of gender and the place of women and men in every society. The general direction of the change is clear: the lives and personalities of women and men are becoming more similar.[2]
>
> Daniel Levinson

The new way in which white Americans regarded racial minorities was matched in the seventies by a dramatic change in attitudes toward women, and by women, about social roles based on gender. For the first time in modern history, maybe in all history, challenges to assumptions about women's place in society – in the family, in their relationship to their husbands and children, in the business and professional world, in government and politics – enjoyed significant success. Before 1970, it was common for both men and women to argue that women must be treated differently than men in law and in manners, that they must have different ambitions or aspirations, and, moreover, that women had of necessity unique social and family obligations. After 1970, such views would drift outside the mainstream.

In many ways the change was truly revolutionary. Almost certainly no one in the fifties would have predicted it. As one commentator reflected at the end of the century after studying all kinds of predictions for the year 2000: "Futurists

---

[1] Margaret Mead, *Male and Female* (Morrow, 1949).
[2] Daniel J. Levinson, *The Seasons of a Woman's Life* (Knopf, 1995), quoted by Diane Johnson in *New York Review of Books* (28 Nov. 1996), pp. 22ff.

of the 1950s could easily imagine astronauts working on the moon, but not their own wives working outside the home."[3] In 1964, when Congress included "sex" in the epochal Civil Rights Act among the personal categories for which discrimination was outlawed, most Americans seemed to take it as a joke (as the cynical sponsor of the inclusion reputedly thought it would be, hoping it would help defeat the measure). A *New York Times* editorial joined most of the press and politicians in mocking the inclusion. *The New Republic,* a liberal periodical, thought it was "a mischievous joke." An airline official wondered what he should do if "a gal walks into our office, demands a job as an airline pilot and has credentials to qualify."[4] No doubt the quip produced the expected guffaws.

By the end of the seventies, women outnumbered men in the professions and were competing for jobs in sectors once regarded as exclusive male preserves, including the military, the police, construction work, trucking, politics, and corporate management. The idea of gun-wielding women on police forces; women climbing poles to repair telephone and power lines; women sailing as regular crew members on naval warships; women piloting giant passenger planes – such developments lay truly beyond Americans' imaginations in 1945, even for those who had come to accept "Rosie the Riveter" as a wartime phenomenon. By the end of the 1970s they would stir little commentary. In 1986, Barbara Ehrenreich would remark: "some of us are old enough to recall when the stereotype of a 'liberated woman' was a disheveled radical, notoriously braless, and usually hoarse from denouncing the twin evils of capitalism and patriarchy. Today the stereotype is more likely to be a tidy executive who carries an attaché case and is skilled in discussing market shares and leveraged buyouts."[5] One business school dean went so far as to propose that feminists helped sustain American capitalism by making success in the business world a criterion of their own liberation, just at a time when capitalism was under heavy fire from the young rebels of the Sixties.[6]

The governmental scene offered probably the most conspicuous changes. By the 1980s, women as mayors and legislators, in the president's cabinet, in both houses of Congress, in statehouses, and on the nation's highest courts no longer attracted astonished note. In fact, one study completed in 1995 showed that, by 1990, women held 59 percent of all U.S. public official positions, up from 24 percent in 1970; moreover, 27 percent of all lawyers and judges in the country in

---

[3] Rachel Emma Silverman, "Futurology," *Wall Street Journal* (31 Dec. 1999).

[4] Ruth Rosen, *The World Split Open* (Penguin, 2000), pp. 72–3.

[5] Barbara Ehrenreich, "Strategies of Corporate Women," *The New Republic* (27 Jan. 1986), p. 28.

[6] Dean Earl F. Cheit of the University of California (Berkeley) School of Business Management, at a conference, "The Humanist as Business Practitioner," on alternative careers for history Ph.D.s (16 Oct. 1981).

1990 were women, as against 6 percent in 1970.[7] Some other changes were just as dramatic. For example: between 1970 and 1990, the percentage of industrial engineers in the country who were women soared from 3 to 27; the percentage who were economists rose from 14 to 44; and the percentage who were police officers and detectives increased from 5 to 13.[8]

The government also contributed to the revolution in a more direct way. In December 1961, President Kennedy set up a Commission on the Status of Women. The move in fact was aimed at sidestepping a renewed interest among some women's groups for an Equal Rights Amendment (ERA) to the Constitution. Other women's groups and most labor unions, important constituencies of the Democratic Party, opposed the ERA because they feared it would jeopardize various labor laws, including some specifically designed to protect women. The commission's report came out in 1963, just as many other developments had begun to challenge all kinds of social conventions. Although it made the expected references to women's obligation to stem "the erosion of family life," the report also cataloged the multitude of inequities that women suffered in law and in the job market. When put together as the report did, the long list of inequities had a powerful impact. Among other things, it led various states to set up similar commissions. The injustices and abuses suffered by women could no longer be ignored. Eventually, the norms governing "women's place" in society would be challenged and overturned.

The revolution had its limits. That women gained access to prestigious and high-paying jobs and careers traditionally reserved for men was in itself revolutionary, but by the end of the century only a small minority of women actually attained such positions and careers. Meanwhile, by the mid-seventies they faced growing resistance. Some of the resistance was newly generated, a part of the widespread backlash against the cultural upheaval of the Sixties generally. Some of it was residual. Geography, education, and class conditioned acceptance of women's liberation. It met stiff resistance among non–college-educated men and women; among evangelical religious sects, particularly from the Bible Belt and other rural regions; and, to a lesser degree, among low-income families.

It met further resistance as feminism moved from an emphasis on equal rights (equal pay, equal access to opportunity, equal respect) to a critique of conventional lifestyles. The adoption by the National Organization for Women (NOW) and other feminist groups of the right to abortion on demand as a feminist cause

---

7 "Women's Work: What's New, What Isn't," *New York Times* (22 April 1995), p. A12, citing a study by the Program for Applied Research at Queens College, New York. "Public official positions" includes school boards, city and town councils, civic center administrators, etc.

8 Ibid.

turned many women against the movement on religious grounds. The demand for the right to choose lesbian lifestyles had similar negative effects on men and women who remained uncomfortable with divergences from more traditional lifestyles. Feminist arguments that their personal rights trumped family or community norms activated opposition from many conservatives who, until 1970 or so, had sympathized with the equal rights movement as well as with some family planning objectives.[9] Reagan Republicans would mobilize these constituencies in the 1980 election campaign in their broadscale counterattack against the liberal achievements of the Sixties, and the same constituencies would remain politically active and influential for the rest of the century.

By the end of the seventies, further gains for equality would come only incrementally, mostly through litigation and court decisions – most notably, of course, *Roe v. Wade* in 1973. That landmark decision gave constitutional protection within certain guidelines to a woman's right to choose an abortion. Again, the measure of the revolution taking place would depend heavily on nondemocratic agencies.

Still, by the seventies much of the energy that had propelled the gender revolution had dissipated. Although polls through the seventies showed that nearly two thirds of Americans favored the Equal Rights Amendment, its association with radical feminist demands for unconventional lifestyles did it in politically, especially in the predominantly rural states that were needed for ratification. The attack from well-financed religious, economic, and political interest groups with broader conservative agendas defeated it just three states short of passage and even persuaded five mostly rural states to rescind their earlier ratification. (Curiously, probably the most effective anti-ERA arguments focused on how the proposed amendment would lead to drafting women for combat duty; yet within the next 25 years, conservative Republican presidents would send military women into combat zones in Kuwait and Iraq with virtually no special media attention to battle fatalities.)

The same conservative interest groups promoted publicity campaigns designed to discredit "feminism." In the 1980s the media, in search of "news" – or, to put it another way, in its readiness to promote new fashions – would persistently highlight stories about the costs of women's liberation from traditionalist constraints. Much ink was spread announcing "the Cinderella syndrome" whereby once-liberated women ruefully discovered the misery that their newly won independence had brought.

A cynic might remark that if one "followed the money" – normally a good guide in a capitalist society – one would expect to find articulate women enjoying

---

[9] Patrick Allitt, *Catholic Intellectuals and Conservative Politics in America, 1950–1985* (Cornell University Press, 1993), ch. 5.

ready media outlets and wide notoriety for marketing tales of liberation woe. By the eighties and early nineties there appeared no shortage of women publishing such Cinderella tales and denouncing feminism as "the Great Experiment That Failed." Such publicity fit in well with the political conservatism that swept through the country in the eighties.[10]

To be sure, the power that liberation provided carried with it burdens that many women even at the end of the century found daunting. They faced difficult choices. The choice of pursuing both a family (children) and a career implied a lifestyle that featured high levels of stress, especially since husbands pursuing their own careers in traditional fashion rarely contributed proportionately to household needs. Still, polls throughout the last quarter of the century showed that most women continued to emphasize the opportunities that liberation offered, not the burdens that conservatives preferred to exaggerate.

Apart from active opposition from traditionalist rural and parochial sources, the change also met more subtle resistance in the more "urbane" sectors of the population. In the business world, many women complained of a "glass ceiling" that limited their advancement. Even by the end of the century only a mere handful of women had ascended to chief executive officer of a major corporation. In general, women would remain underrepresented in the prestige professions and in the upper levels of corporate management. Job discrimination, unequal pay for working the same or equivalent jobs, insidious sexual intimidation, and other expressions of the traditional ethic between the sexes would continue to plague women in the workforce.

Not all the limits were set by men. A poll taken in 1959 revealed that more men than women said that they could vote for a woman for president.[11] Probably most women supported demands for equal economic and educational opportunity, but even at the end of the century only a small minority of them seemed to accept the arguments for significant changes in gender-based roles. For example, in 1978 Dr. Rosalyn Yalow, a 1977 Nobel Laureate in medicine and a mother of two, told an interviewer: "I think if a husband feels like doing things, it's fine, but I think that running a house is a wife's responsibility .... A husband's responsibility is not to run a house."[12] Although among educated families women

---

[10] Kay Ebeling, "The Failure of Feminism," *Newsweek* (19 Nov. 1990), p. 9. For a scathing indictment of the media and advertising industries for imputing a "Cinderella syndrome" retreat among women, see Susan Faludi, *Backlash: The Undeclared War against American Women* (Crown, 1991). The image of a failed revolution would be another product of the "failure syndrome" discussed in Part III.

[11] Rosen, *World Split Open*, p. 19.

[12] *New York Times Magazine* (9 April 1978), p. 29. Taking a position not uncommon among professional women, but one that angered many feminists, Dr. Yalow insisted that women need not demand role changes in order to pursue their own ambitions although certainly they must fight

faced far less pressure to restrain their own talents and ambitions in deference to a husband's pride, in general the man–woman relationship remained remarkably stable throughout the era. As one commentator would write in 1986, "It's all so strange .... I can't believe so little has changed when so much has."[13] The remark had equal validity fifteen years later. Few could doubt that this was largely due to the lack of agreement in general or among feminist reformers in particular as to how far to press the requirement of equality between the sexes and just how "womanhood" should be defined so as to include full parity among all human beings while acknowledging the unalterable differences.

All the same, by the 1970s there was also no doubt that the rules of the game had changed, no doubt that traditionalism was on the defensive, and little dispute that historic definitions of the "proper" roles of men and women were anachronisms entirely unsuited for a modern and equitable society.

*   *   *

The most noticeable changes at first had to do mainly with women's sharply increased participation in the workforce, beginning in the 1950s. In the 25 years from 1950 to 1974, the number of women in the workforce about doubled: from 17.8 million to about 35.2 million, and from about 29 percent of the civilian workforce to about 39 percent. Those figures, however, tell only a small story. More significantly, as a proportion of all women over 16, women employed outside the home increased from about one third to about one half. By the 1990s, the proportion would reach 60 percent – an extraordinary level considering that the percentage of all women who were over 65 was increasing.

Meanwhile, as a proportion of all working women, married women accounted for 62.3 percent in 1974, up from 36.4 percent in 1940. In other words, in the last prewar year about two in three married women remained at home (most of them presumably fully employed as housewives), whereas 35 years later the proportions were exactly reversed: almost two in three married women were employed for pay outside the home. Moreover, by 1974 married women with husbands present accounted for 58 percent of all working women, as compared to about 30 percent in 1940. By then, too, working wives made up over 40 percent of the total workforce, compared to just 24 percent in 1950.

---

against adverse discrimination. In her Nobel Prize acceptance speech she said: "We still live in a world in which a significant fraction of people, including women, believe that a woman belongs and wants to belong exclusively in the home; that a woman should not aspire to achieve more than her male counterparts and particularly not more than her husband .... The world cannot afford the loss of the talents of half its people." Yalow's Nobel Prize address can be found on the Internet. Eugene Straus, *Rosalyn Yalow: Nobel Laureate* (Plenum, 1998), is a modest biography by a friend and colleague that alludes to her traditionalist views of a woman's role as wife.

[13] Anne Taylor Fleming, "The American Wife," *New York Times Magazine* (26 Oct. 1986).

Not incidentally, married women's employment for pay often doubled family income.[14] In fact, by the 1970s two earners had become increasingly necessary for a family to maintain its income-class status. In 1972, families with only one earner accounted for only 25 percent of families in the top fifth by income, down from 39 percent in 1950; nearly half the families in this top fifth required two earners to maintain their "upper middle" income status,[15] a portion that would grow considerably in the next two decades.

Even more striking, by the mid-seventies, 55 percent of all mothers with school-age children were in the workforce (only 31 percent in 1948), and 37 percent of all mothers with *preschool* children were employed (13 percent in 1948). In 1990, more than half of all new mothers were reported in the workforce.[16] Working wives had become the norm, a sharp reversal of the housewife norm of barely 32 years earlier. Indeed, by the 1970s any young, well-educated married woman – with or without young children – who held no paying job might have to endure some measure of scorn or condescension from her peers.

These facts are all the more remarkable in the context of the general and increasing prosperity in the quarter century following the Second World War. In the past, most women took paid jobs because they *had* to work to avoid poverty, either because they were unmarried or because their husbands could not fully support the family or had left them. Largely for these reasons, the urban middle-class ideal of the family required married women to remain *out* of the workforce (unless they worked for their own family in or out of the home). That most nonfamily jobs available to women were arduous, low-paying, and associated with subservience (e.g., factory and domestic labor) or with underclasses (immigrants and racial minorities) reinforced the determination of status-conscious husbands to keep their wives at home. It also helps to account for the willingness of wives to comply, even at the cost of boredom and substantial economic hardship.

The fashionableness of working wives arose from a number of changes that began to converge by the mid-1950s. Among other things, there was a great increase in the availability of jobs at which a woman could work while maintaining all the outward appearances of gentility. The rapidly increasing importance of the service sector of the economy (compared with that of the industrial sector)

---

[14] In 1970, average annual earnings of full-time employees amounted to about 1.5 times what it was in 1950, while *family* income rose by a third more: figures gathered from the Bureau of the Census, *Historical Statistics of the U.S., Colonial Times to 1970.* See also Clair Vickery, "Women's Contribution to the Family," in C. Vickery, *The Subtle Revolution – Women at Work*, ed. Ralph E. Smith (Urban Institute, 1979).

[15] Vickery, *Subtle Revolution*, p. 168.

[16] *New York Times* (4 Dec. 1991), p. A11, citing a Census Bureau report. See also *Wall Street Journal* (15 Nov. 1988), p. A1.

meant more white-collar jobs, and real wages in those industries rose sharply after 1940. Moreover, office positions and sales work in often posh department stores and smaller apparel shops, required little physical labor, brought women in contact with usually genteel customers, clients, and fellow workers, and permitted women to earn money while wearing more fashionable clothing than they were likely to feel comfortable in at home. The additional income became all the more important as middle-class status concerns drove more and more married couples from the center cities into the suburbs. There they faced heavy loan repayments on the new house, on the new car, and perhaps on the second car as well as costs for membership in the local country club, community center, church, or synagogue. By the 1950s, in other words, it was affluence and the changed character of the American economy, not poverty, that served to draw women into the job market.

So, in fact, it *was* economic need – of the new, middle-class sort – and not a major change in feminist outlook that accounts for the developments up through the 1960s. For all the increase in the proportions of well-to-do women in the job market during the fifties and most of the sixties, virtually nothing major had yet happened to masculine–feminine role definitions or behavior. The overwhelming number of women working held traditionally low-paying, low-status "female jobs," many of them part-time. Among the married women, their role remained the traditional one of backing up their husband's career and social aspirations, in particular by supplementing the family income. Although by the end of the century 39 percent of mothers with children would be working *full time year round*, in 1969 only 17 percent did.[17]

At the beginning of the sixties, fewer women appear to have thought of full-time careers than did so even a half-century earlier. At the time, for example, a smaller percentage of women held law or medical degrees, or were in college or graduate school, than in 1920. Women held only the same fraction (28 percent) of college faculty positions in 1960 as they had in 1920. In the fifties and perhaps the sixties as well, it was still a whispered bit of popular wisdom that a woman might do well to drop out of college lest too much education reduce her chances of marriage.

Contrary to some popular misconceptions and images of Rosie the Riveter, the wartime employment of women in nontraditional jobs appears to have had little lasting impact. With the conclusion of World War II, more than 3 million women immediately dropped – or were rudely forced – out of the workforce to make room for 12 million returning servicemen. How many of especially the younger women simply wanted out of the workforce for other satisfactions cannot be ascertained, but it would not be unreasonable to estimate that at least

[17] *Wall Street Journal* (1 Sept. 1998), p. 4.

half did.[18] Certainly women appeared in no great rush to return to the job market. In numbers alone, working women did not reach the wartime peak of 19.3 million again until 1955, and in percentages of all women over 16 not until the late 1960s.

This should not be surprising. In the immediate aftermath of the four-year-long war, it is easy to imagine how attractive the prospects of marriage and devotion to children and traditional family life in general must have appeared to young women, especially amid the warm glow of an unaccustomed material prosperity. Nor should it be difficult to understand how women reared in a culture given to the rigors of the work ethic could have enjoyed the luxury of not having to live by it, of not having to strain after a career or a livelihood, and of being able to leave such stressful tasks to their men. Indeed, the apparent contentment of most American women in their subordinate, dependent roles through the fifties was a source of irritation to Betty Friedan, who complained in *The Feminine Mystique* (the book that helped trigger the new feminist movement): "I wonder if a few problems are not somehow better than this smiling empty passivity."[19]

On top of this, of course, women were strongly encouraged to stay out of the workforce by the traditional social ethic that defined their complete fulfillment as marriage and motherhood. Before 1960, even those who spoke for women's causes tended to present the argument for equality in terms of the equal worthiness of the sexes' different social responsibilities. So, for example, in 1950 Agnes Meyer, who had led the criticism of the government for its failure to provide child-care services for working women during the war, wrote in an article entitled "Women Aren't Men" that women "have only one vocation – motherhood." "Women," she said, "must announce that no job is more exacting, more necessary, or more rewarding than that of housewife and mother."[20] In 1958, eight years later, the renowned anthropologist Ashley Montague presented the same argument in his article, "The Triumph and Tragedy of the American Woman." "Being a good wife, a good mother, in short, a good homemaker," Montague wrote, "is the most important of all the occupations in the world." He added, "I put it down as an axiom that no woman with a husband and small children

---

[18] One estimate is that 2.25 million women voluntarily left wartime jobs while about 1 million were laid off. Women over 45 tended to remain in the workforce. But between 1945 and 1950, about 2.75 million women newly entered the workforce at least in part-time jobs. Carl Degler, *At Odds: Women and the Family in America from the Revolution to the Present* (Oxford University Press, 1980), p. 422. See also Natsuki Aruga, "Private Rosies and Public Housewives," in Hitoshi Abe, Hiroko Sato, & Chieko Kitagawa Otsuru, eds., *The Public and the Private in the United States* (Japan Center for Area Studies, 1999).

[19] Betty Friedan, *The Feminine Mystique* (Norton, 1963), p. 57.

[20] Agnes Meyer, "Women Aren't Men," *Atlantic Monthly* (Aug. 1950). Mrs. Meyer was the mother of Katherine Graham, future publisher of the *Washington Post*.

can hold a full-time job and be a good homemaker at one and the same time."[21]
As late as 1962, in the first edition of *The Other America* (a book credited with
helping to inspire the Kennedy–Johnson War on Poverty), Democratic Socialist
Michael Harrington wrote: "[The] tremendous growth in the number of working wives … will be paid for in terms of the impoverishment of home life, of
children who receive less care, love, and supervision. This one fact … might well
play a significant role in the problems of the young in America."[22] It is indica-
tive of the great attitudinal changes that would begin to occur later in the decade
that Harrington omitted this passage from later editions of the book.

In the meantime, up through the mid- to late sixties, there appeared to be
virtually no change measured against attitudes of fifty years earlier when, for
example, Mrs. Samuel Gompers – wife of the head of the American Federation
of Labor (AFL) – berated working wives and declared that "A home, no matter how small, is large enough to occupy [a wife's] mind and time." And in the
same era the Federal Women's Bureau similarly attacked married women who
entered the labor market, asserting: "The welfare of the home and the family is
a woman-sized job in itself."[23] As Betty Friedan would remark in *The Feminine
Mystique*: "Over and over women heard … that they could desire no greater des-
tiny than to glory in their own femininity. In the fifteen years after World War II,
this mystique of feminine fulfillment became the cherished and self-perpetuating
core of contemporary American culture."

As Friedan saw it, the pressure of the cultural conditioning militated against
change. The media, the schools, and the laws all promoted the "mystique." It
was as if women were constantly subjected to brainwashing that removed from
their very imagination even the possibility of different lifestyles. Still, Friedan
was ready to accept an alternative explanation. "In the last analysis," she conceded, "millions of women in this free land chose, themselves, not to use the
door [that] education could have opened for them. The choice – and the responsibility – for the race back home was finally their own."[24]

So powerful was the traditionalist fix on women's role that as late as 1967,
while pondering what American society might look like in the year 2000, the eminent sociologist David Riesman could remark: "If anything remains more or less
unchanged, it will be the role of women."[25] In a much-noted scholarly article

---

[21] Ashley Montague, "The Triumph and Tragedy of the American Woman," *Saturday Review* (27
  Sept. 1958), pp. 13–15. For additional quotations of the same sort see Rosen, *World Split Open*,
  pp. 40ff.
[22] Michael Harrington, *The Other America: Poverty in the United States* (Macmillan, 1962), p. 191.
[23] Quoted in Peter Filene, *Him/Herself* (Johns Hopkins University Press, 1974), p. 121.
[24] Friedan, *Feminine Mystique*, p. 173.
[25] Quoted in Victor Navasky & Christopher Cerf, *The Experts Speak: The Definitive Compendium
  of Authoritative Misinformation* (Pantheon, 1996).

published in 1968 on the prospects for a transforming women's movement, historian Carl Degler observed: "Most American women have been interested in jobs, not careers .... [Like men, the American woman] shuns like a disease any feminist ideology." To bring about the changes that might produce real equality, Degler argued, required "a rationale, an ideology." But, said Degler, that was not going to happen. "Most American women simply do not want work outside the home to be justified as a normal activity for married women .... They like to think of it as special and exceptional."[26] That same year, a study of women and the law concluded:

Remarkably, the persistence of legal inequality between the sexes has in recent years engendered little excitement. In marked contrast to the spirit of the suffragist movement, still within living memory, and the current drive of American Negroes toward equal legal status,... no Americans have recently marched, picketed, sat-in, or otherwise dramatically demonstrated their opposition to legal expressions of sex discrimination .... Most American women don't appear to be greatly exercised by the persistence of inequities in their legal status.[27]

This, on the very eve of the blooming of the ideological challenge to traditionalist gender relations.

The historian William O'Neill wrote in 1972: "The ideological failure ... [of women until the late sixties] consisted largely of an inability to determine where their interests lay. Because they could not clearly define their problem, they could not devise a successful strategy for solving it."[28] The statement, however, stands on the presumption that most women found their roles to be unsatisfying. But, as Friedan suggested in her *Feminine Mystique* reference to the cultural conditioning of women through the fifties, that might be a false presumption. Years later, Friedan herself recalled that until she started writing her book, "I wasn't even conscious of the woman problem."[29] It required a different drum beat that would make women focus on a perceived inequity implicit in subordination. Feminist firebrands such as Kate Millett conceded, in her book *Sexual Politics* (1969), that many women do not recognize themselves as discriminated against. For her, however, no better proof could be found of the totality of their oppressive conditioning. Similarly, Alice Rossi complained with reference to Henrik Ibsen's 1879 drama, "A Doll's House" (about an independently minded wife's unhappiness), "There are few Noras in contemporary society because women

[26] Carl Degler, "Revolution without Ideology: The Changing Place of Women in America," *Daedalus* (Spring 1968), reprinted in R. M. Abrams & L. W. Levine, eds., *The Shaping of 20th Century America* (Little, Brown, 1971), pp. 116–33.
[27] Leo Kanowitz, *Women and the Law* (University of New Mexico Press, 1969), p. 2.
[28] William O'Neill, "Feminism as a Radical Ideology," *Dissent* (Feb. 1972).
[29] In Daniel Horowitz, "Rethinking Betty Friedan and the Feminine Mystique," *American Quarterly* (vol. 48, 1996), pp. 1–42, quote at p. 4.

have deluded themselves that a doll's house is large enough to find complete fulfillment in it."[30]

But it may be simply ahistorical to assume that the choices women made in the postwar period came from self-delusion. As one early feminist observed: "Change always hurts, but change in sex roles hurts women more than men."[31] Caroline Bird knew what choices she preferred. But the pain of having to make such choices was, at least until the late 1960s, not something most American women – or even a substantial minority of them – seemed prepared to accept. Perhaps it was not that most women were unable "to determine where their interests lay" so much as that they determined that their interests lay in accepting their traditional roles. It may even be that they were unwilling to surrender what the feminist historian Ann Douglas called "power through the exploitation of their feminine identity as their society defined it" – what in the late nineteenth century Harriet Beecher Stowe termed "Pink and White Tyranny."[32]

Ideological changes occur when enough contemporaries begin to reject the premises from which people customarily proceed to reason. Until the Sixties, American attitudes toward authority and tradition militated against challenges to basic social conventions and roles. Throughout the 1950s, intent upon enjoying material prosperity and cowed by the tensions produced by the Cold War abroad and anticommunist red-baiting at home, most Americans showed a distinct preference for stability over change. In the decade that produced Norman Vincent Peale's best-selling *The Power of Positive Thinking* (1953) and numerous secret-to-success clones, a powerful consensus impelled individuals toward adjusting their needs to fit society's values rather than working for changes in the social environment to fit the needs of individuals or of emergent groups.

Women's discontent with the constraints on their talents, ambitions, and independence imposed by timeless definitions of their obligatory roles had shown up periodically in American history, from Abigail Adams's muted complaints in the eighteenth century to the women reformers of the suffrage, abolitionist, and prohibition campaigns. But as Betty Friedan astutely noted, the struggle for women's equality did not move in a straight-line progression. It seemed, rather, to grow and recede with important changes in the society generally. In the nineteenth century, by making food and clothing inexpensive enough to be bought rather than produced at home, the Industrial Revolution seemingly diminished women's importance by making much household labor unnecessary, leading some pundits to speculate that this may have contributed to expressions

---

[30] Quoted in William Chafe, *The American Woman* (Oxford University Press, 1972), p. 223.
[31] Caroline Bird, *Born Female* (McKay, 1968), p. xiii.
[32] Ann Douglas, *The Feminization of American Culture* (Avon, 1977), pp. 6–7.

of boredom and discontent with "the doll's house." If that were so then the advance of technology, which provided goods and needs that could not be produced at home but required entry into the money economy, may have prompted more women to leave the household in order to obtain money and the goods. Such motivation must have become magnified with the rapidly growing affluence after World War II.

Industrialism and urbanization also produced disincentives for large families while scientific and medical advances extended longevity. Unlike women throughout most of history, whose motherhood often occupied the majority of their adult lives (and often severely abbreviated them), most women born after 1930 could look forward to living for decades after the last child had left the nest. The opening manifesto of NOW in 1966 stressed this fact:

It is no longer either necessary or possible for women to devote a greater part of their lives to child-rearing; yet childbearing and rearing, which continues to be a most important part of most women's lives, still is used to justify barring women from equal professional and economic participation and advance.

In short, modern technology, medicine, longevity, education, humanistic sensitivity to personal rights, and other related changes had formed most of the imperatives underlying the modern women's movement, or at least the restiveness – what Friedan called "The Problem That Has No Name" – that arose in the 1960s. But they were not sufficient.

A significant change in the definition of gender-based roles required, as Degler argued, something of an ideological leap. Among other things, it required thinking about women less as women than as human individuals. It required, as Betty Friedan put it, "a drastic reshaping of the cultural image of femininity." Such a reshaping would incur risks and costs in family stability, in personal relationships, in economic security, and in one's self-image and self-respect. By the late 1960s, more and more women prepared to accept the risks of transforming the standards by which they measured self-respect.

That the drastic reshaping began to take place in the late sixties should not be surprising. That was when the great uproar over racial injustice, the bitter and bloody struggle for civil rights, and most particularly the moral and military debacle in Vietnam made millions of Americans receptive to challenges to traditional customs, roles, values, and sources of authority. The message of Norman Vincent Peale – happiness and success lay within the self – no longer resonated. This generation saw too much that was unacceptable in the society and in its institutions, conventions, and morals for individuals to seek adjustment to society's norms as a remedy for discontent. To the contrary, more convincing now was the message of Paul Goodman, who argued in the popular *Growing Up*

Absurd that the young could find no cues from the society in which they grew up to make "adulthood" and "maturity" a rational choice.[33] If many among the young were given to antisocial behavior, like the "juvenile delinquents" of the fifties, then the fault – it came to be seen in the rebellious environment of the Sixties – lay not with them but with the irrational and inequitable structures of the society to which it seemed even irresponsible to adapt. The time was ripe for a wholesale assault on conventional principles.

And by the late 1960s, there were a great many well-educated and economically comfortable young women who were ready and eager to attack. Most were college students or at least of college age, and many were active in the civil rights movement. They were joined by increasing numbers of older women, a large proportion of whom had high-school and college diplomas. Most of them had held jobs during the Second World War, perhaps before they began having the children who were themselves coming of age by the late sixties. Some of these mothers had been made to feel guilt over their "idleness" in a work- and money-oriented society. Many had begun to find unacceptable the tensions of boredom, of life at home, sparring day in and day out with infants and children, and of envying the challenges of life "out there" where men competed in the economic and political arenas – and where men might encounter opportunities to participate, however covertly, in the sexual freedom that was gaining sensational attention ever since the appearance of Alfred Kinsey's studies on human sexuality in the forties and fifties. The 1962 near-proselytizing best-seller, *Sex and the Single Girl* by Helen Gurley Brown, and her transforming of *Cosmopolitan Magazine* into a not altogether subtle counterpart to Hugh Hefner's *Playboy*, all but urged women (married and unmarried) to join in the rebellion against the staid, restrictive, "Victorian" rules about what women might do for work and for pleasure. In this environment, the formerly anticipated and once-felt pleasures of a homebound life, free of the stress of cultivating a career and producing a livelihood, began to turn stressful and unfashionable.[34]

---

[33] Paul Goodman, *Growing Up Absurd* (Vintage, 1956). See also Edgar Z. Friedenberg, *Coming of Age in America* (Vintage, 1963), and R. D. Laing, *The Divided Self* (Tavistock, 1960).

[34] Fashion may play a bigger role than we are accustomed to grant it in these matters. For example, boredom and alienation had become fashionable among males, too; an apparent source of "the rebels without a cause" who emerged as a "type" in the fifties (and were celebrated in the 1955 film by that name in which James Dean – the sexy, sulky social misfit – made his film debut). See e.g. Kenneth Keniston, *The Uncommitted* (Harcourt Brace, 1964), and *The Young Radicals* (Harcourt Brace, 1967). Evidently, some of the same things that transformed life for women in the sixties and seventies affected men, who also sought "liberation" of a somewhat different sort. Barbara Ehrenreich, in *Hearts of Men: American Dreams and the Flight from Commitment* (Doubleday, 1983), details the growing flight from "maturity" and especially family responsibility among young males that developed in the fifties.

By the 1970s, a growing minority of Americans would become entirely estranged from the traditional conventions regarding gender roles. They came primarily from upper- and middle-income groups, held college degrees, lived in metropolitan areas, and tended toward liberal religious and political outlooks. Many of the older women had become sensitized to how badly conventional norms fit with the liberal principles they had almost absentmindedly absorbed during the Second World War and in their youth. Some of the younger women had been "radicalized" by the antibourgeois, existentialist literature of the "Beats" as well as by the civil rights movement. Most of them would find it hard to grasp how earlier generations of educated men and women could possibly have accepted, and even cherished, the traditionalist gender role models. For many of them, it would come to seem incomprehensible that men and women could actually prefer separate roles and distinctive aspirations. It would appear inconceivable that men and especially women could believe, moreover, that society's institutions – including the law, education, and job structure – *should encourage* the distinctive roles. It would become for feminists beyond understanding that a woman might glory in being, specifically, *feminine*, which (as the traditional culture defined the term) was to say physically alluring, perhaps a little coquettish, yet sexually diffident and chaste as well as wifely, motherly, outwardly passive, and pseudo-dependent ("pseudo" because the traditional mores required bright, independent women to avoid overt behavior that might seem to belittle their husbands). The disdain among the insurgents for these features of the received culture represented a dramatic intellectual as well as generational gulf.

The insurgent minority would remain still more estranged from their own contemporaries among blue-collar men *and* women for whom the traditional authority patterns continued to have powerful personal meaning.[35] For many wage-earning men, who typically spent each working day in a position subordinate to bosses, their sense of personal integrity depended importantly on their "being the boss" at least in their own home, while many a wage-earner's wife found it necessary to cultivate that "manly" posture to satisfy her own pride in marriage. Indeed, such traditional thinking still prevailed among the majority of all women through the remainder of the century. A Gallup poll in 1991 revealed, for example, that only 37 percent of women over 16 described themselves as

---

[35] In *Women's Place* (Basic Books, 1978), author Sheila Rothman observed: "In no simple sense has this latest [reform movement] been able to benefit all women in all social classes; it certainly has not promoted a more harmonious or cohesive social order .... [T]o the contrary: there is ample reason to believe that the politics of women's liberation, with its vigorous expression of its members' rights, has ... sparked conflict" (p. 9).

"feminists," while 57 percent explicitly rejected the label.[36] In the 1970s, "Ms." had become a major symbol of feminist insurgency, and yet a 1980 poll revealed that four out of five women preferred "Miss" or "Mrs." Twenty years later, the numbers had not significantly changed.

Meanwhile, feminists struggled to define what it was that they sought in their quest for gender equality. In the 1950s, what stood for "progressiveness" in the demands for women's rights emphasized women's distinctive gender, nature, and place. Lynn White, the male president of the all-women Mills College, derided the notion of those feminists who measured equality in terms of "acceptance of the masculine scale of values as the human scale" and who assumed that, to achieve equality, women must accept male values and lifestyles as the norm.[37] This kind of thinking became a ready target for the rebels of the sixties and seventies, who used it to point out how notions of gender difference underlay – and served as an instrument of – female oppression. In this context, some feminists insisted on a program that would ultimately make gender irrelevant, a nonfactor in role formation or character assessment. If gender were understood to be merely a social construct, then genetic and physiological differences could be seen as having no significant implications for behavioral traits or role assignments.

The attack on traditionally ascribed roles could be carried rather far from the straightforward quest for equal rights, especially among those who focused on gender relations as an angry contest for power. In her provocatively argued *Sexual Politics* (1969), Kate Millet wrote: "Nearly all that can be described as distinctly human rather than animal activity (in their own way animals also give birth and care for their young) is largely reserved for the male." And again: "Even the modern nuclear family, with its unchanged traditional division of roles, necessitates male supremacy by preserving specifically human endeavor for the male alone, while confining the female to menial labor and compulsory child care."[38] Such language went beyond arguing for men to take on an equal part of household burdens to begging the question, as one critic put it: "Why is the male's enforced labor at some mindless task [in a factory or office] 'distinctly human' while the woman bringing up her child is reduced to an 'animal' level?"[39]

---

[36] *Washington Post National Weekly* (20–26 Jan. 1992), p. 15. The responses may have been skewed by the success that conservatives had achieved in the media in identifying "feminism" with "liberalism," which by then had come to be associated with a number of unpopular developments and attitudes; see Chapter 16. That in the 1990s the president of NOW (Patricia Ireland) was an avowed "bisexual," living apart from her husband and with another woman, tended to equate "feminist" with "lesbian."

[37] Quoted in Chafe, *American Woman*, p. 207.

[38] Kate Millett, *Sexual Politics* (Avon, 1970 paperback edition [1969]), pp. 35, 224.

[39] Irving Howe, "The Middle-Class Mind of Kate Millett," *Harper's* (Dec. 1970), pp. 110, 129.

The argument for "sameness" had the virtue of simplifying the demands for "equality." The problem, however, was that such a theory defied the reality that for many (indeed, probably most) men and women alike, the idea of a gender-less society seemed unappealing. For a majority of American men and women, even in the 1970s, masculine and feminine remained categories of identity, not of oppression. Conservatives exploited this fact, identifying "feminist" with those who belittled motherhood, family life, and (among the more radical feminists) any kind of relationships with men. It was an effective tactic, especially because the strident rhetoric of some feminist leaders had put on the defensive those women without careers who had found satisfaction in lives with husbands and children.[40]

Inevitably, feminists had to respond by modifying their language. In *The Second Stage* (1981), Betty Friedan sought to repair some of the damage caused by "the many women [who] flinch at the women's movement as a threat to the family" and equally by the many other women who "flail at the family as enemy of women's very self." "Part of the conflict over motherhood today," Friedan argued, "and part of the conflict that feminists feel about the family and that younger women will feel about feminism, if it has to keep denying the power of the impulse to love, motherhood, family – is a hangover from the generations when too great a price was paid." The price, she continued, was still high, especially for women who had to maintain the household and to bear and rear children while cultivating a career on terms set by men and without equal household help from men. But it was time to recognize that the feminist movement had lowered the costs and made choice possible.[41]

By the 1980s, with a little help from the well-financed campaigns of conservative groups, the costs of liberation gained increasing media attention. Meanwhile, liberal scholars as well as journalists and conservative TV talking heads had begun to note some serious unintended consequences of the changes. One was the tremendous strain on young women who had to perform as "Super Moms" in order to mesh career with homemaking ambitions. A spate of articles began appearing in the press in which women complained that "liberation"

[40] *Ms. Magazine,* co-founded by Gloria Steinhem in 1972, drifted in the seventies increasingly though by no means exclusively toward expressing various lesbian views of liberation. It became an easy political target for conservatives and, judging from letters to the editor, troubled many feminists as well.

[41] For women, insisted Friedan (herself a wife and mother), independence and equality as a person must include the choice of marriage and motherhood with or without a paying job or career outside the home. "Surely," she wrote, "that very choice of motherhood is basic to their identity as women today, even though it no longer has to or even can define it totally." *The Second Stage* (Summit, 1981). See also B. Friedan, "How to Get the Women's Movement Moving Again," *New York Times Magazine* (3 Nov. 1985).

had inflicted on them such dual burdens, while others protested the pressures to "abandon" their families for careers.[42] Colette Dowling's *The Cinderella Complex,* published in 1981, described the agonies of an independence for which women's education and socialization from childhood had not prepared them. "We were not trained for freedom at all, but for its categorical opposite – dependency," complained the author. Women might work at a job or even a career, but deep inside they awaited the day when "someone will come along to rescue you from the anxiety of authentic living." Although the book celebrated those women who (like the author herself) overcame their fear of "authentic living" and became truly emancipated, it explained with sensitivity why many women of her generation preferred "scurrying into retreat – back where it's safe, familiar, known."[43]

One undeniable fact – possibly related to anxieties induced by the radical social changes – was the accelerating rate of divorce, which was accompanied by the rising impoverishment of single mothers. At mid-century, the typical American family as depicted in film and television consisted of a once-married husband and wife who were white, middle-class, and (probably) churchgoing Protestants, with the father as sole breadwinner, the wife as homemaker, and two or three children. By 1980, such families amounted to less than 10 percent of all American families. Between 1970 and 1980, single-parent families jumped from 11 percent to 17 percent of all families and to 40 percent of all black families. Meanwhile, the proportion of never-married women heading households increased from 7 percent to 15 percent.[44] No-fault divorce laws, which proliferated among the states in response to the gender revolution, aimed at improving equality between men and women. Instead, they worsened the lot of a great many women, especially in widening the income gap between the sexes. Some sociologists referred to divorced women and their children as a new American underclass. Meanwhile, by some estimates men typically enjoyed as much as a 40-percent increase in their economic condition after divorce.[45]

There were emotional as well as economic costs. One scholarly study concluded: "The traditional law embodied the partnership concept of marriage by rewarding sharing and mutual investments in the marital community. Implicit in the new laws, in contrast, are incentives for investing in oneself, maintaining

---

[42] Just one example of the many articles that began appearing in the popular press by the 1980s: Joyce Colony, "Diary of a Glad Housewife," *New York Times Magazine* (6 Dec. 1981).

[43] Colette Dowling, *The Cinderella Complex* (Summit, 1981), pp. 14f.

[44] Charlotte Saikowsky, "Women Today," *Christian Science Monitor* (Nov. 1978), p. 5; *Wall Street Journal* (28 Aug. 1980), p. 1.

[45] Leonore Weitzman, *The Divorce Revolution: The Unexpected Social and Economic Consequences for Women and Children in America* (Free Press, 1985), pp. ix–xviii and ch. 10. See also Fleming, "American Wife."

one's separate identity, and being self-sufficient. The new stress is on individual responsibility for one's future, rather than the partnership assumption of joint or reciprocal responsibilities." Ironically, although the revolution in attitudes toward gender roles inspired the dramatic reforms of divorce law in the seventies, in their consequences the reforms fit well into the groove of modern conservatism and its stress on personal responsibility. "[A]s rising divorce rates demonstrate," Leonore Weitzman observed in her exhaustive account of the reforms, "the strength of the husband–wife unit has declined and values of 'pure' individualism are emerging. The new divorce laws reflect this evolution in that they encourage notions of personal primacy for both husband and wife."[46] Indeed, Colette Dowling's ideal of "authentic living," as the modern woman acted to discard the Cinderella complex, required rejection of binding dependence on others, which meant virtually complete independence from personal commitment to others – husband, children, and family included.[47] This, too, would be an ingredient in why the seventies came to be called The Me Decade.

The changed role of women necessarily had its obverse side: the impact on the role of men, especially in family relationships. The entry of women into jobs traditionally reserved for men made fewer women economically dependent on male support. By the end of the century, the male was the sole provider for only about one in seven households that included a married couple. That fewer men could claim a distinctive identity based on their breadwinner role posed a challenge to some of the most durable beliefs about manhood and masculinity. If, as sociologist Kathleen Gerson put it, men were no longer the sole breadwinners and could no longer assert patriarchal privileges as the heads of their households, then how will they adjust their relationships with women and children? With the rising divorce rate and falling birth rate in the seventies, it became evident that many men answered the question by simply declining firm relationships with women and children.[48]

Debate would continue over how women and men might define their roles and their personhood, and whether to begin with a premise of *difference* or of *sameness*. The debate itself would mark an effect of the revolution. The fact remained that, by the end of the seventies, women had gained new options.[49] Both

---

[46] Weitzman, *Divorce Revolution*, p. 374.

[47] Arlie Russell Hochschild offers sharp commentary in *The Commercialization of Intimate Life* (University of California Press, 2003), especially pp. 19–29.

[48] Kathleen Gerson, *No Man's Land: Men's Changing Commitments to Family and Work* (Basic Books, 1993), especially chs. 2 and 7.

[49] Although the "glass ceiling" still limited women's access to top executive positions in major corporations, by the end of the century a number of women did break through. Women succeeded to CEO at Hewlett Packard (Carly Fiorina), which subsequently took over Compaq, at Xerox (Ann M. Mulcahy), and at Playboy (Christie Hefner). Consider, however, how few women had earned MBAs before 1975.

the law and attitudes had changed sufficiently to guarantee the durability of the revolution and the availability of the new options. They included the freedom for women to define for themselves the roles they would undertake as individuals, in the family, and in their careers without being destructively stereotyped or stigmatized.

That freedom was something new in history. Whether a particular woman would regard it as a relief and a joy or as a burden and a worry would depend on her own personal outlook or predicament. Still, as one historian – herself of the new generation – observed: "Surely this was not the first time in American history that daughters yearned to live lives different from their mothers .... What was unique for us – the generation coming of age in the sixties and seventies – however, was that we had the opportunity to act on these dreams and inspirations and to make them a reality."[50]

---

[50] Barbara Berg, *The Crisis of the Working Mother* (Summit, 1986), p. 40; quoted in Rosen, *World Split Open,* p. 40.

12

The Revolution in Sexual Behavior

> Sex is not a mere physiological transaction .... It dominates in fact almost every aspect of culture.[1]
>
> Bronislaw Malinowski

> Anyone brought up among Puritans knew that sex was sin .... [It embodied] the highest energy ever known to man, the creator of four fifths of his noblest art, exercising vastly more attraction over the human mind than all the steam engines and dynamos ever dreamed of; and yet this energy was unknown to the American mind .... Society regarded this victory over sex as its greatest triumph.[2]
>
> Henry Adams

It shouldn't take a rocket scientist, or even an anthropologist, to make this observation, but one anthropologist did feel impelled to comment in 1999: "The craving for sexual gratification is a primordial drive ... that has not changed its basic composition in some 70 million years." The poet W. H. Auden called it "that intolerable neural itch."[3] It is so powerful that men and women high and low and throughout history risked their careers, their fortunes, their reputations, and even their lives to satisfy it – from Paris of Troy and Dido of Carthage, to Mark Anthony and Cleopatra, Heloise and Abelard, on to the likes of Billy Swaggart, Jesse Jackson, and Ted Kennedy – not to mention presidents Thomas Jefferson, Grover Cleveland, Warren Harding, John F. Kennedy, and William Jefferson Clinton. The craving has enabled many a lowborn man, and also many a woman in a male-dominated world, to gain high place among royalty and other

---

[1] Bronislaw Malinoski, *The Sexual Life of Savages* (Harcourt Brace, 1929), p. xxiii.

[2] Henry Adams, *The Education of Henry Adams,* ed. Ernest Samuels (Houghton-Mifflin, 1973), pp. 384–5.

[3] Helen Fisher in "Just Do It," review of *Full Exposure* by Susie Bright, *New York Times Book Review* (12 Dec. 1999), p. 44.

sites of wealth and power. It should seem unarguable that sex is the dominant imperative, overriding all the others that historians have endlessly emphasized: the will to faith, the will to fame, the will to fortune, the will to power. God, gold, and glory have their force, but nothing, it would seem, trumps the will to sex.

And yet until the second half of the twentieth century, sex – this seemingly inexorable force, this "primordial drive," this "neural itch" – remained the least-studied natural phenomenon for which the technology and technique for study were readily available. The fact is, few in Western society, and particularly in American society, were willing to risk serious discussion of or even mere inquiry into the subject for fear of public attack, governmental censorship, and even legal action. Meanwhile, public or publicized transgressions against the narrowly conceived norms of sexual behavior, at least in the United States, brought punitive posses in dogged pursuit of the transgressors.

Nor did it save the sexual culprits that blatant hypocrites most often led the charge. Thus Henry Hyde, the Republican congressman and chair of the House Judiciary Committee who led the effort to impeach President Bill Clinton in 1998 for lying about an erotic dalliance with a young White House intern, was exposed by the press for himself having had an extended adulterous affair. Likewise Newt Gingrich, the Republican Speaker of the House who insisted on making Clinton's sexual escapades a campaign issue, was at that very time engaged in an adulterous affair. When Gingrich resigned, his successor Robert Livingston was forced to resign within a few weeks when he admitted that he, too, had had an adulterous affair.[4]

By the 1960s, sober interest in sex would begin to change radically. Not that hypocrisy lost its power; on the contrary, exposure of the sexual exploits of public figures would increasingly become political weapons for ad hominem destruction, as in the case of President Clinton. The vindictive pursuit of sexual miscreants was a paradoxical result of the increased public candor about sexual matters that permitted the media to "bare all," and with graphic enthusiasm. What changed was not only the public candor about sex but sexual decorum itself. It was perhaps inevitable that the same conditions underlying the racial and feminist insurgencies, conditions that weakened inherited conventions and structures of authority, would also contribute to a major collapse in sexual discipline. This would have many profound if not altogether obvious implications.

---

[4] The extremely partisan Republican majority in the House voted to impeach, but the Senate – also controlled by Republicans – declined to convict because not enough Republicans and conservative Democrats could be persuaded that Clinton's folly constituted an impeachable act.

First of all, sexual repression represented an integral part of a centuries-old Anglo-American identification of behavioral restraint with moral worth and superior culture. The "Victorian" ethic of restraint itself derived from a more ancient terror of surrendering to the impulses of the Devil, such as those that emerge within the body in the form of ungoverned "animal desires." Beyond this, sexual restraint had special significance in a society such as the United States, where for economic and political reasons voluntary personal contracts and transactions overshadowed the traditional ordering authority of the state and the church; such personal restraint was presumed to figure largely in maintaining the nuclear family as a basic unit of social education and control and for the transmission of traditional values.

Moreover, repression of erotic stimuli and behavior had long been thought to serve as a subtly powerful catalyst in the development of Western society's high-growth economy and hence of the cultural advances that accompanied such growth. Thus, the venerable historian of world civilizations, Arnold Toynbee, wrote in 1964 that societies that postponed rather than stimulated sexual experience among young adults had enjoyed the greatest progress. Bruno Bettleheim, the world-renowned psychologist, made the same argument: "If a society does not taboo sex, children will grow up in relative sex freedom. But so far, history has shown that such a society cannot create culture or civilization; it remains primitive."[5] Sexual repression, it was widely argued, played an especially important role in developing the ethic of self-discipline and postponed rewards that underlay the success of entrepreneurship, capital formation, and the industrial organization of work. "By curbing the fire of his own sexual passion," wrote Sigmund Freud, "[man] was able to tame fire as a force of nature."[6]

But among many of the young in the tumultuous Sixties, modern society's emphasis on materialism and economic growth came to be viewed as the main source of their own and the world's troubles. Freed so largely from fear of want by the spread of affluence, Baby Boomers saw little rationality in the "uptight" ethic of their elders or in a traditional lifestyle. And so sexual repression became a natural target for the rebels of the Sixties. Many hearkened to the messages of Herbert Marcuse and Wilhelm Reich, two older social critics with neo-Freudian roots, who castigated capitalism for inducing a crippling sexual repression in order to serve its oppressive needs. As historian Laura Umansky observed: "The counterculturalists of the 1960s quickly translated those ideas

---

[5] *New York Times Magazine* (10 May 1964), quoted in Charles Keating's dissent in the *Report of the President's Commission on Obscenity and Pornography* (Government Printing Office, 1970), p. 579.

[6] Sigmund Freud, *Civilization and Its Discontents* (Hogarth, 1949 [1930]), p. 51n.

into the vernacular. Declaring marriage and monogamy superfluous, hippies celebrated 'free love,' sex, and sensuality."[7]

In this context, a large-scale violation of sexual norms appeared as both symbol and substance of stinging social criticism.

One may argue over the appropriateness of the word "revolution" in the matter, but what occurred by the 1970s was a rather undeniable breakdown in traditional sexual decorum. Although sexual customs are always in a condition of change – and for the previous century had been changing, at least in the Western world, toward fewer and fewer ethical restraints – what occurred by the 1970s was distinctively new. For the Canadian writer J. B. Cameron, in 1976 there was no question about it: " 'Revolution,' like 'tragedy,' is a bit overused; but there can't be any doubt that we are in the course of … a revolution in sexual mores."[8]

To gauge the magnitude of the mid-century challenge to behavioral norms, it is useful to compare it to what happened in the 1920s, another era usually noted for sexual upheaval. At that time, assaults on standards of "legitimate" sexual behavior had been mounting for decades, spurred on by the diffusion of scientific thought, the spread of urban growth, the ascendancy of secular materialism, and industrialization. The declining influence of traditionalist religion in the late nineteenth century contributed its part. By the 1910s, popularized versions of modern psychology – especially the interpretation that Americans tended to give to Freudian insights about the sexual roots of neurosis – set the stage for the excitement of the 1920s.

Yet whatever did happen in the 1920s seems not to have had much to do with great changes in actual behavior. In the twenties, there was much pointedly open *talk* about sexual matters and even about sexual parts. A couple of "marriage manuals" – including Theodore van de Velde's fairly graphic 1926 best seller, *Ideal Marriage* – put into millions of homes illustrated information about the perils and pleasures of the marriage bed. For the unmarried, magazine writers, fashion designers, and advertisers promoted a variety of coquettish come-ons (e.g., cosmetics, short and skimpy skirts and dresses), a trend also encouraged by the film industry. There was some erosion of the double standard in judging women who had "affairs" or who took limited initiatives in the rites of courtship. But whatever seemed novel to the younger generation at the time in sexual *behavior* appears to have emerged much earlier, even by the 1890s. That was when covert premarital and extramarital sexual activity first appears to have gained

---

[7] Laura Umansky, *Motherhood Reconceived: Feminism and the Legacies of the Sixties* (New York University Press, 1996), p. 24.

[8] J. B. Cameron, "Sex in the Head," *New York Review of Books* (13 May 1976), pp. 19ff.

a significant foothold among middle-class women, together with a quiet social acceptance of the practice when engaged within the bounds of a real romantic relationship that eventuated in marriage. Even so, the double standard prevailed, and most of what was acceptable for men remained unthinkable for women. Chastity still defined "virtue" and "honor" for a woman. Adultery and casual sex for fun and recreation still invited general opprobrium.[9] The never-married mother invariably incurred pity and scorn. The very idea of voluntary single parenthood through childbirth simply didn't make it into the arena of public discourse.

Beginning in the late nineteenth century, most states had criminalized the manufacture and sale of contraceptive devices. The lawmakers insisted that sex had to be solely for procreation, not recreation, even for married couples. And so it was something of a breakthrough that in the 1920s the subjects of family planning and contraception did make their way into family magazines and newspapers. Still, one could not find there a candid discussion of abortion or of vasectomy, nor of the physiology of impotence or frigidity or of sexual tension and release. Although no intelligent person could seriously deny the overwhelming importance of the sexual urge for persons of every caste or class below and beyond the age of menopause, it remained outside the range of permissible inquiry. That plain fact had little effect on the certitude of prevailing opinions, particularly with regard to presumed limits and norms of female sexuality. Homosexuality was universally regarded as a perversion or an illness when it was publicly discussed at all, and all but two states treated homoerotic activity as a felony. Masturbation was condemned almost as universally, with warnings that it was both sinful and health threatening.

In brief, the so-called revolution of the 1920s left intact all the traditional conventions regarding (a) male–female sexual relations and roles, (b) homosexuality, (c) marriage and the family, and (d) the physiology of erotic stimulation. The conventions remained intact through World War II.

By 1975, something radically different had occurred. Within a decade of the end of the war, the defenses of the traditional sexual discipline would take a beating. An early blow was struck by Alfred Kinsey and his colleagues at Indiana University's Institute for Sexual Research. The biologist's unprecedented inquiries into Americans' sexual activities, published as *The Sexual Behavior of the Human Male* (1948) and *The Sexual Behavior of the Human Female* (1953),

---

[9] "Present day civilization gives us plainly to understand that sexual relations are permitted only on the basis of a final, indissoluble bond between a man and woman, that sexuality as a source of enjoyment for its own sake is unacceptable to it; and that its intention is to tolerate it only as the hitherto irreplaceable means of multiplying the human race." Freud, *Civilization,* p. 75.

hastened erosion of the authority of traditional sexual mores. Not that "every-one's doing it" constitutes much of a moral argument, at least to the logical mind, but it had that effect on the pragmatic and opportunistic mind of the average American, who tended to identify virtue with success and popularity.

What was stunning about the Kinsey reports was not merely their revelations about the extent of premarital and extramarital behavior among white middle-class Americans, male and female. They also revealed the prevalence of masturbation as a form of sexual release or recreation even among married men and women. Perhaps most disturbing of all was Kinsey's revelation that homoerotic experiences were not uncommon in general and occurred often even among those who led basically heterosexual lives – which, as we now know from exhaustive biographies, described Kinsey himself.[10] The point that no one could miss was that the boundaries of "sexual normality" would never again seem clear.

Relying on quantitative data gathered in interviews with more than 10,000 (mostly white) adult middle-class males and about half as many women, Kinsey estimated that – taken together over a lifetime (as only a quantifying scientist might put it) – only half the sexual climaxes achieved by American males arose from intercourse with their wives. This meant, Kinsey triumphantly pointed out, that more than half owed to activities that were "socially disapproved and in large part illegal and punishable under the criminal code."[11] He thus threw into doubt whether any concept of normality could be used to define what was moral.

Kinsey himself had few doubts. It was clear to him that nonmarital abstinence was *abnormal* and hence that sanctions intended to enforce it were indefensible.[12] He had, in fact, been telling his students at Indiana University since his very first lecture on marriage and the family in 1938: "There are only three kinds of sexual abnormalities: abstinence, celibacy, and delayed marriage. Think about this."[13]

Kinsey's pathbreaking research was followed by the astonishing clinical studies of sexual intercourse and autoeroticism conducted by Drs. William H. Masters and Virginia E. Johnson at the Reproductive Biology Research Foundation in St. Louis, beginning in 1955. The expressed primary purpose of their work was to help married people who failed to gain satisfaction in sex. They published their findings on sexual dysfunction in 1966 as *Human Sexual Inadequacy*. Ironically, as recently as 1944 an American anthropologist had commented that American

---

[10] See especially the definitive work by James H. Jones, *Alfred C. Kinsey* (Norton, 1997).

[11] Quoted in Paul Robinson, *The Modernization of Sex* (Harper, 1976), p. 76.

[12] Considering that Kinsey personally was a lifelong conservative who usually voted Republican with (as his wife and his colleagues described it) a nineteenth-century patriarchal, even auto-cratic, attitude regarding marriage and the family – in everything besides conjugal practices – his role in challenging the traditionalist "Victorian" ethos of modern industrial societies is truly remarkable.

[13] Jones, *Kinsey*, p. 333.

views on what was "obscene" in sexual matters were so firmly fixed that no empirical study of sexual interaction could ever be undertaken, even by medical doctors in a scientific laboratory. "Our cultural norms," he wrote confidently, "would scarcely tolerate such a situation."[14] Masters and Johnson began their work eleven years later.

For those who wanted sexual gratification without guilt, without personal commitment, without the inhibitions imposed by the powerful conditioning of the culture, the clinical and biological approach to sexual expression had especial appeal. It fitted perfectly the mood of a postwar, young, and affluent society. By the 1970s, few young Americans would know much about Kinsey, but they didn't have to; there had been many more salacious things to read about sex in the meantime. The message had become pervasive, cutely put by the young actress whom *Time* magazine quoted as saying: "To argue that one should not have sex without love is to argue that one should not ride in a car unless it's a Rolls Royce."[15] Years later, the *New York Times* in its weekly *Magazine* would highlight the opinion of one professed sex expert who, in commenting on monogamy, argued: "Sexual boredom is the most pandemic dysfunction in this country. Think of sex as an appetite. Now think about having to eat the exact same meal every day for the rest of your life – of course you'd get bored."[16]

That Kinsey could obtain major institutional funding for his research – and was permitted to publish it in an America that still embargoed *Lady Chatterly's Lover* – itself signified noteworthy attitudinal changes (although, bowing to conservative pressure, the Rockefeller Foundation withdrew its grant to the Kinsey Institute in 1955). So too did the ensuing spate of popular magazine articles, novels, and movies (e.g, *Peyton Place, Exurbanites, The Chapman Report*) that exploited the Kinsey findings. The budding movement for gender equality helped give legitimacy to "illicit" sex. Commenting on the sexual escapades of suburban women featured in film and fiction, Betty Friedan argued that such activity, if it occurred, must grow as a response to the "feminine mystique" that left open no other rewarding outlets for the achieving woman to do something daring, fulfilling, and satisfying yet independent of her husband.

There should be little doubt that while employing the techniques of scientific inquiry, Kinsey, Masters, and Johnson were engaged in advocacy of a radical change in attitudes toward sexuality. In this respect, they were following along the path paved by an earlier elite of sexologists (a term that dates from 1912),

---

[14] John J. Honigmann, in the *Journal of Criminal Psychopathology* (1944), quoted in Morton Hunt, *Sexual Behavior in the 1970s* (Playboy Press, 1974), p. 6.

[15] *Time* (4 April 1974).

[16] Quoted in Rebecca Johnson (contributing editor at *Vogue*), "Sex Advice for the Clinton Age," *New York Times Magazine* (4 Oct. 1998), p. 60.

most notably the Englishman Havelock Ellis. The public's obvious acceptance of Kinsey's studies also eased the task of Masters and Johnson. According to historian Regina Morantz: "No single event did more for open discussion of sex than the Kinsey Report, which put such matters as homosexuality, masturbation, coitus and orgasm into most [news]papers and family magazines."[17] Once there, it would be hard to establish new limits on either discussion or depiction. *Playboy,* the first full-feature magazine in America to present photographs of women mostly nude, made it to the newstands in 1953; in three years it had a circulation of half a million. (Marilyn Monroe was its first centerfold "Playmate of the Month.") More important than the nudity was that the magazine became an aggressive promoter of "sexual freedom."

By the 1970s it had become prevailing lore, especially among the well educated, that one's own sexual behavior and predilections were matters to be talked about freely and indeed that declining to talk about sex indicated one had "a problem." In 1978, for example, a sex therapist writing for the University of California's alumni magazine remarked: "It's still taboo for a lot of people even to admit they have a problem." Mental health, she claimed, required acknowledging the problem. Moreover, to admit that anything sexual might be offensive was to confess to inadequacy, neurotic repression, and unsophisticated obedience to irrational taboos.[18]

As the traditional barriers sagged, little was left to restrain sexual activity besides fears of disease and of pregnancy. But penicillin, developed during the Second World War, reduced the first; and the Pill (Enovid), certified as safe and effective by the Food & Drug Administration in May 1960, allayed the second.

In that year, the first children of the postwar Baby Boom reached adolescence. About 45 percent (and still rising) of the American population was under 25 years old, most of them uneducated to the personal discipline that emigration, war, or economic need had forced upon their parents.[19] The great majority would reach their sexually active years in a society that was experiencing massive racial insurgency, that was waging a barbaric war in Southeast Asia, that was in the process of becoming bereft of authoritative and respected political leadership, and that remained in the shadow of a nuclear arms race. It was also a decade of extraordinary economic growth that put money in the pockets of teenagers. Market specialists could not fail to target that money with media programming and print advertisements oriented toward teenagers' interests – preeminently their natural and intense interest in sex. Widespread affluence and

[17] Regina Markell Morantz, "The Scientist as Sex Crusader: Alfred C. Kinsey and American Culture," *American Quarterly* (Winter 1977), pp. 563–89.

[18] Nancy Friedman, "Bewitched, Bothered and Bewildered," *California Monthly* (July 1978), p. 15.

[19] "Projections of the Population of the U.S.: 1977–2050," *Current Population Reports,* ser. P-25, no. 704 (Government Printing Office, 1977).

the commercial imperatives of a teeming youth market combined to undermine whatever economic reasons remained for sexual discipline. On top of it all was women's push for social equality, their increasing financial independence, and their challenge to the double standard. The stage was set for a big change.

Responding to a poll on sexual attitudes in 1972, a 50-year-old mother replied: "Ten years ago I would have wanted my daughter to go with a fellow, fall in love, have a courtship and get married. Now, I only want to get across to her that what is important is to know when she is ready to handle sex ... and not to think that she has to marry some guy just because she's slept with him."[20] This was only the tip of the iceberg. It may once have been daring enough for a mass circulation journal to raise the question, "Should you have sex before marriage?" By the end of the century, the question had become, "Should you be married before having children?"[21]

Polls taken in the seventies indicated a substantial increase in nonmarital sex among women under 25. Although polls suggested that little else had changed among men and women (at least since Kinsey's report), there were more radical changes ahead that affected a broad spectrum of the population. In 1974 a veteran researcher on American sexual attitudes noted: "The average American now holds many opinions about sex that a generation ago were rarely held by any but highly educated big city sophisticates and bohemians."[22] The opinions covered the entire range of sexual activity, from spouse swapping and group sex to bisexuality and bondage.

So, in 1976, J. B. Cameron could write of what appeared to be "the complete repudiation of the dictates on sexual morality transmitted by the central tradition of our culture." He named "the Judeo-Christian proscriptions" against fornication, adultery, incest, homosexuality, "sexual connection with beasts," and prostitution. He neglected transvestitism and the nearly 2,000 transsexual metamorphoses that modern surgical techniques had already engineered (including the sex change of professional tennis player Renee Richards, née Richard Raskind, whose entry into women's competition created a small tempest on the tennis courts).[23]

For numerous celebrities, bisexuality became fashionable. The actress Maria Schneider, who co-starred with Marlon Brando in Bertolucci's avant-garde *Last*

---

[20] Quoted in Hunt, *Sexual Behavior*, p. 25.

[21] *Latina* (Jan./Feb. 2002), p. 91. Twenty-nine percent of those interviewed said No. Responding to the same inquiry, 35 percent of the 400 questioned said they could forgive "a partner" who had sex with someone else. The magazine expressed surprise that "a whopping 64 percent ... confessed to having just one sex partner in the last year." Ten percent, forty of those questioned, said they had more than ten partners within the year.

[22] Hunt, *Sexual Behavior*, p. 24.

[23] The first transsexual individual whom the media brought to public attention was Christine Jorgensen, a former GI who traveled to Denmark for the operation in 1952.

Tango in Paris (1972), announced: "I'm bisexual completely, and I've had quite a few lovers for my age .... Probably 50 men and 20 women." Maria Schneider was 22 years old at the time. Folk singer Joan Baez, who rose to renown in the early sixties co-starring at folk-rock concerts with her lover, Bob Dylan – and whose rendition of "We Shall Overcome" (1963) thrilled civil rights workers for a decade – was quoted in 1974 as saying: "If you swing both ways, you really swing. I just figure, you know, double your pleasure."[24] Feminist writer Barbara Grizzuti Harrison, author of *Unlearning the Lie: Sexism in School* (1974), complained in a 1974 article: "I find myself ready to believe that New York's sexual avant-garde may be entering the era of the closet heterosexual. Only a couple of years ago, I, like all feminists, found myself called upon to explain to every dim-witted or threatened antagonist that, no, we were not all lesbians .... But times have changed .... The question that vexes [the new avant-garde] is, 'If we really love women, why don't we go to bed with them?' And I find that scary, largely because no logical answer immediately presents itself." As John Updyke put it in his novel *Rabbit Redux* (1970), the great question of our time is, "Why not?"[25]

By the early seventies, even incest, sometimes described as "the last taboo," came in for detailed study and, for some, qualified approval.[26] The Kinsey research had found sibling incest to be fairly common and, like later confirming studies, found it to be almost certainly underacknowledged. Moreover, it was underacknowledged primarily because a mutually positive experience would likely remain unnoted: one survey of college students in the eighties indicated that three quarters of those who reported sibling relationships had engaged in them by mutual consent.[27] Some researchers ventured to suggest that even parent–child incest might sometimes be harmless or better.[28] Early in the decade, the Swedish legislature entertained proposals to decriminalize some familial sex. In 1973, Louis Malle's widely acclaimed *Murmur of the Heart* treated the subject

[24] *New York Magazine* (7 April 1974).
[25] By the early twenty-first century, the "why not" question extended to zoophilia (sexual connection with animals). "I think it's interesting and scary," commented a British filmmaker, who did a documentary for television on the subject. "Is it better," he added irrelevantly, "to beat your wife or abuse your child?" *New York Times Magazine* (3 March 2002), p. 69.
[26] For a report on public discussion regarding a modification of incest laws, see "Attacking the Last Taboo," *Time* (14 April 1980), p. 72.
[27] In addition to the Kinsey reports, see David Finkelhor, "Sex among Siblings: A Survey on Prevalence, Variety and Effects," *Archives of Sexual Behavior* (9 June 1980), pp. 171–94; Jones, *Kinsey*, p. 621; W. H. Masters, V. E. Johnson, & Robert Kolodny, *Masters and Johnson on Sex and Human Loving* (Little, Brown, 1986), pp. 421, 426–7.
[28] See e.g. Philip Nobile, "Incest: The Last Taboo," *Penthouse* (Dec. 1977), pp. 117ff; Masters et al., *Sex and Human Loving*, pp. 420–9; "Attacking the Last Taboo," *Time* (14 April 1980), p. 72; Janice M. Irvine, *Disorders of Desire: Sex and Gender in Modern American Sexology* (Temple University Press, 1990), p. 4.

sympathetically, as did the 1980 film *Luna*, filmed in Italy but featuring the Hollywood star Jill Clayburgh.

As Cameron had found, in modern sexual mores "virtually everything is interesting and nothing is grave (with the possible exception of forcing young people to engage in sexual practices against their will)." He concluded: "There are now in sexual matters no common principles of decorum .... Pretty much anything goes so long as it doesn't harm other people. What is to count as harm isn't easy to determine, for sadism and masochism are interesting too." Indeed, in 1981 the Public Broadcasting System would air a television documentary on "S&M" for the curious, the prurient, and the sympathetic – one consequence of which was to inspire the coroner's office in San Francisco to issue friendly advice to practitioners on how to avoid serious injury.

*   *   *

Inevitably, changed attitudes toward sex affected attitudes toward salacious or obscene speech and graphics, and toward pornography. All of it was tied into Americans' increasing interest in free speech and in civil liberties generally. At issue were the limits of the state's prerogatives to limit speech as opposed to the limits of an individual's right to speak. What boundaries might the state legitimately set in a free society for the purpose of maintaining public order? And what relevance did blasphemous, obscene, or pornographic expression have for that state purpose?

Finally, what words and images counted as "obscene" or "pornographic"? Were prolonged brutal beatings – as in, say, Elia Kazan's classic film *On the Waterfront* (1954) – obscene? How about blood and flesh splattered on the wall after a gun blast, a common feature of many "action" films? Or did the law recognize only verbal and pictorial representations of *sexual* action as "obscene"? Historically, and into the new millennium, most Americans answered Yes to only the last question.

Until 1957, the general obscenity rule in American law was that states could ban anything that tended "to deprave and corrupt those whose minds are open to such immoral influence, and into whose hands a publication of this sort might fall." The principle was established in England in 1868 and adopted into American law in 1871. By the 1940s, however, American courts began scrutinizing the issue of free speech and other First Amendment rights more closely. In some ways, the courts began moving the communicative freedoms alongside if not ahead of property rights as the central feature of a free society.

For example, in a 1944 case[29] the U.S. Supreme Court cited "the preferred place given in our scheme to the great, the indispensable democratic freedoms

---

[29] *Thomas v. Collins* (1944).

secured by the First Amendment." "That priority," Justice Wiley Rutledge went on, "gives these liberties a sanctity and a sanction not permitting dubious intrusions. And it is the character of the right, not of the limitation, which determines what standard governs the choice." The burden lay with the state to justify constriction of the right by demonstrating a "clear and present danger" to national security or public order. This represented a marked change from the historic view of the courts that federal and local governments could repress and punish certain kinds of speech without having to demonstrate any imminent danger.

Cold War tensions and fear of subversion and espionage by communists forced the courts to confront renewed efforts by federal and local governments to put limits on speech. In the short run, the standard that Justice Rutledge had sought to establish could not be sustained. In 1952, the Supreme Court upheld the conviction of eleven leaders of the Communist Party for "conspiring to advocate" the overthrow of the U.S. government by force or violence,[30] in effect reducing the "clear and present danger" test to "possible" or "probable" danger. Justice Frankfurter, in a concurring opinion, went so far as to claim that the Communists' formulaic and rote advocacy did not rise to the level of serious thought and therefore lay below the protection afforded by the First Amendment.

But the momentum would continue toward making free speech, especially political speech, a chief test of a free society. By the end of the eighties, an extremely conservative Supreme Court would extend protection to "symbolic speech," overturning the conviction of a man for burning the American flag in violation of a state law.[31] Jurists would continue to distinguish among types of speech that deserved First Amendment protection. That included re-examination of such speech as blasphemy, obscenity, lewdness, and slander, which most societies historically had regarded without question as beneath civil standards and undeserving of protection. The changes in postwar America society, including especially changing attitudes toward sexual matters, forced the courts to re-examine the line to be drawn between permissible and "unworthy" speech.

In 1952, the Court took the unusual step of voiding a book-banning statute in Michigan that forbade books containing obscene, immoral, or lewd language.[32] Justice Felix Frankfurter remarked in the Court's opinion that "[t]he incidence of this enactment is to reduce the adult population of Michigan to reading [only] what is fit for children." After this decision, the American Law Institute proposed a new standard intended to restore what in the 1990s would be called "traditional values." "Society," the Institute declared, "may legitimately seek to deter the deliberate stimulation and exploitation of emotional tensions arising from the conflict between social convention and the individual sex drive."

---

[30] *Dennis v. U.S.* (1952).
[31] *Texas v. Johnson,* 491 U.S. 397 (1989), p. 87.
[32] *Butler v. Michigan* (1952).

By 1957, with the sexual revolution underway, that formula already seemed quaint. In a new case, Justice William Brennan tried his hand at defining obscenity. The case concerned a U.S. Post Office decree banning what post office officials had decided were pornographic materials. Brennan proposed to add the clause: "material utterly without redeeming social importance" to the American Law Institute's reference to "deliberate stimulation and exploitation of emotional tensions arising from the conflict between social convention and the individual's sex drive."

Ironically for someone who would become one of the Court's most liberal justices in its history, Brennan began his opinion with an iteration of the old view that free speech must be justified in terms of state-determined bounds. "The dispositive question," Brennan began, "is whether obscenity is utterance within the area of protected free speech and press." Brennan thus seemed to return the issue to the state's prerogatives to restrict as opposed to individuals' prerogatives to act in the absence of a compelling state interest. And on these grounds Justices Hugo Black and William Douglas wrote vigorous dissents. The question to ask, the two justices argued, is what particular consequences that may be of interest to the state could be attributed to the allegedly pornographic or otherwise offensive materials? They insisted that First Amendment protections must be given the highest priorities and that therefore the state must bear the burden of demonstrating that a vital state interest was served by any proposed intrusion. But at the time they were alone in that argument.

The Court continued to be troubled by the issue. In 1959, the justices struck down a New York state attempt to bar a film version of D. H. Lawrence's *Lady Chatterly's Lover* on the grounds that the film tended to justify adultery. Justice Stewart found that to be preposterous, an attempt (as he put it) to create a category of "ideological obscenity" and to restrain advocacy of allegedly improper sexual values.

In 1964 the Court had to deal with another attempt to ban a film, this time Louis Malle's *Les Amants*. Here the Court split down the middle, but a plurality of the justices overturned the ban. The opinion by Justice Stewart contained the memorable lines: "I shall not today attempt further to define the kinds of material I understand to be embraced within [obscenity]; and perhaps I could never succeed in intelligibly doing so. But I know it when I see it, and the motion picture involved in this case is not that."[33]

In 1966, Brennan again tried his hand at defining censorable art, this time regarding a book popularly known as *Fanny Hill*.[34] Three elements must coalesce, Brennan ventured. "It must be established that (a) the dominant theme of

---

[33] *Jacobellus v. Ohio* (1964).

[34] The case is formally known as *"John Cleland's Memoirs of a Woman of Pleasure" v. Atty. Gen. of Mass.* (1966).

the material taken as a whole appeals to a prurient interest in sex; (b) the material is patently offensive because it affronts contemporary standards relating to the description or representation of sexual matters; and (c) the material is utterly without redeeming social value." Because the lower court had found *Fanny Hill* to have at least a modicum of social value, Brennan and five of his brethren overturned the ban.

But the same year, in separate cases including *Mishkin v. N.Y.*, Brennan wrote the majority opinion to uphold the conviction of two publishers, contending that the books were beneath the First Amendment's protection because they appealed to "a clearly defined deviant sexual group": gays, lesbians, and masochists.[35]

After these appallingly inconsistent and disorderly opinions, the Court apparently threw in the towel. In most such cases thereafter, the Court contented itself with overturning obscenity and pornography convictions without written opinions. Essentially, in the face of regionally popular legislative and prosecutorial preferences, the justices were confirming the sexual revolution.

Besides, by that time it was plain that there was money to be made in the revolution. In April 1968 the musical *Hair,* advertised as "the American tribal love-rock musical," opened on Broadway featuring lyrics that celebrated sex, drugs, and other symbols of young America's rejection of up-tight village culture. Its main theme was opposition to the war in Vietnam, but the antiwar message bore more encompassing social criticism.[36] For the first time in so-called legitimate theater – and for 1,750 performances to full houses through June of 1972 – male and female performers appeared together on stage entirely naked and sang (among many memorable numbers) of sodomy, masturbation, fellatio, and cunnilingus. A somewhat sanitized film version of *Hair* appeared in 1979, but within ten years Hollywood and moviemakers worldwide were routinely including sexual scenes that once could only be seen in so-called soft-core pornographic films.

Indeed, by the late 1960s it was possible to ask: *Why should* books or films whose "sole emphasis is on the sexually provocative," as Brennan had put it in *Mishkin* – or books that seek to arouse purely erotic excitement, or books that solely "appeal to a prurient interest in sex" – be regarded as having no redeeming social value? Furthermore, Brennan's earlier formula included the requirement that material had to be "patently offensive because it affronts contemporary

---

[35] *Mishkin v. N.Y.* (1966). "Fifty books are involved in this case. They portray sexuality in many guises. Some depict relatively normal heterosexual relations, but more depict such deviations as sado-masochism, fetishism, and homosexuality."

[36] The following year, *Oh! Calcutta!* – part play, part musical, and devoted entirely to sexual recreation while also featuring nude performers – opened in both New York and London. Mainstream artists such as John Lennon, Jules Feifer, and Sam Shepard, among others, contributed to its production. Like *Hair,* it ran for several years.

standards relating to the description or representation of sexual matters." That meant it was possible to say or publicly present something that was patently offensive and utterly without redeeming social value yet that was not restrainable under the Constitution because it had nothing to do with sex.

Such contradictions tend to explain why the Court gave it up. But by the seventies, village moralists regained ground as succeeding Court decisions narrowed some of the First Amendment protection achieved earlier. In two 1971 cases,[37] the Court upheld convictions of individuals for merely receiving sexually stimulating ("pornographic") materials through the mail. And in a 5-4 decision two years later,[38] the Court flatly rejected the argument that the state has no interest in telling adults what they may see or read. Chief Justice Warren Burger, whom Richard Nixon had named to replace Earl Warren, argued for a five-member majority that the government had the right to impose on all Americans its own definition of an acceptable tone and quality of life. Burger feared for the debasement of what he called "a sensitive, key relationship of human existence, central to family life." (In case it might be missed, he was referring to sex.) The four dissenting justices protested that receiving, reading, or viewing sexually stimulating materials concerned individual taste, and the state has no business regulating taste.

In general, because of the clear changes in modern American culture, it became more and more difficult for the purveyors of puritanical standards to win prosecutions against alleged pornographers. And the industry began to thrive as never before in history. Nevertheless, under the right-wing aegis of the Reagan and (first) Bush administrations, the Justice Department bypassed the law and the Constitution by instead assaulting the financial resources of book and magazine dealers. The federal government launched multiple suits against alleged pornographic distributors who did business in more than one state. Although a dealer might be acquitted in one state, the government quickly brought suit in another, thereby driving retailers out of business owing to legal costs – even when no conviction of any kind could be obtained, given the dubious constitutionality (or social policy presumptions) of the prosecution.

Public hypocrisy sustained the political popularity of the antiporn crusades. Americans publicly deplored porn and demanded laws to stamp it out, but privately they feasted on it. Sales of sexually stimulating materials in films, magazines, and Internet connections outpaced sales of just about every other form of graphic expression. According to one study, in 1989 there were 395 million rentals of adult video tapes, most of which were watched by two or more people. Women were equal-opportunity consumers, accounting for 47 percent of

---

[37] *U.S. v. Reidel* (1971) and *U.S. v. 37 Photographs* (1971).
[38] *Paris Adult Theatre v. Slaton* (1973).

all pornographic videos rented.[39] In 1988, there were 398 million such rentals. These figures do not include adult video sales, cable TV viewings, or adult theater attendance.[40] Major corporations – including AOL Time Warner, Comcast, AT&T, and Cablevision – regularly carried explicit sexual programming, while pornography accounted for up to 90 percent of pay-per-view receipts. Americans thereby demonstrated what they preferred to read and view for their own private gratification by their choices in the marketplace – conservatives' favorite agency for distributing social goods. Yet, through their representatives in Congress and in state legislatures, most of the same Americans publicly chanted their approval of government's interference with private preferences and forms of recreation – always on the assumption, of course, that it would be someone else's private preferences that were enjoined.[41]

As the new millennium opened, there was a continuing tug-of-war among the judges as to which principle should be given highest priority in deciding cases regarding personal behavior and private recreational or family choices. On the one hand, the state may constrain those choices that lack the sanction of history or traditional practice or a community's moral approval. Thus, in his 1986 concurring opinion that sustained a sodomy conviction, Chief Justice Warren Burger insisted that "the proscriptions against sodomy have very ancient roots ... [and] have been subject to state intervention throughout the history of Western civilization."[42] On the other hand, the state must demonstrate a compelling interest even when neither tradition nor history appear to provide protection for a personal behavioral choice. Thus Justice Blackmun, writing for three other dissenters in the same case, insisted that the case was not about sodomy. "Rather this case is about 'the most comprehensive of rights and the right most valued by civilized men,' namely, 'the right to be let alone.' "[43]

The first principle presumes that anything not specifically permitted by history or tradition cannot be treated as a protected right. Thus, Justice Byron White (writing for the majority in the same case) insisted: "The issue presented is whether the Federal Constitution confers a fundamental right upon homosexuals to engage in sodomy and hence invalidates the laws of the many States

---

[39] This might appear to contradict one of Kinsey's findings – namely, that women did not appear to be stimulated by visual images of sex. Perhaps the new evidence indicated further changes in sexual attitudes and sensibilities.

[40] Marcia Pally, *Sense and Censorship: The Vanity of Bonfires* (Americans for Constitutional Freedom, 1991), p. 32.

[41] In fact, in most states where antipornography legislation reached the voters in the form of referenda, the voters – secure in the privacy of the ballot box – rejected it.

[42] *Bowers v. Hardwick*, 478 U.S. 186 (1986).

[43] Ibid. Blackmun was quoting from the dissenting opinion of Justice Louis D. Brandeis in *Olmstead v. U.S.*, 277 U.S. 438 (1928), which concerned the use of wiretaps in a person's home to trap him in some criminal act.

that still make such conduct illegal and have done so for a very long time." The second principle presumes that, regardless of history or tradition, an individual is free to choose unless the state can demonstrate a compelling reason to intervene – implicitly, to prevent some material injury to the state or to private parties. Thus, dissenting justices in the same case cited the great jurist Oliver Wendell Holmes, Jr., who had written nearly a hundred years before: "It is revolting to have no better reason for a rule of law than that so it was laid down in the time of Henry IV. It is still more revolting if the grounds upon which it was laid down have vanished long since, and the rule simply persists from blind imitation of the past."[44]

The traditionalist principle asserts that it is legitimate for a state to impose a disadvantage on particular individuals or groups if only to express the majority's moral contempt for that group's practices – even when serving no other proper governmental purpose, such as protecting anyone's economic or security interests. Thus, Justice White declared that "majority sentiments about the morality of homosexuality" sufficed as a reason for state intervention. In other words, the majority may use the state to suppress speech or behavior that offends its moral sensibilities even in the absence of harm to others' personal economic, property, or security interests.

This was not a matter simply of the freedom to view pornography or to utter expletives. The future of private behavior – including contraception, abortion, and same-sex relationships, among other things – depended on which principle the courts would insist on. What is remarkable for present purposes is how far, even by the mid-eighties, a near majority of a strongly conservative Supreme Court had moved from traditional views about sexual behavior. In 2003, by a 6-3 majority, a still more conservative Court would reverse the 1986 antisodomy decision.[45]

*   *   *

Indeed, probably the most dramatic change accompanying the sexual revolution affected those who identified themselves, or were identified by others, as homosexuals. In some respects, this was the most unpredictable of developments. In fact, homophobic actions by both state and private agencies had been *intensifying* at least since the era of World War I, partly in reaction to the gradual lifting of the curtain of silence about sex in general and about homosexuality in particular. With the subject at least partly revealed, homosexuality attracted more aggressive hostility. After the Second World War, homosexuality became

---

[44] In Blackmun's dissent, citing Holmes's "The Path of the Law," *Harvard Law Review* (vol. 10, 1897).

[45] *Lawrence, et al. v. Texas,* 539 U.S. 558 (2003).

tied to communism as twin – and related – threats to America's national security, related because communists sought to undermine American manhood by
spreading "sexual perversion" and because homosexuals in government could
be blackmailed into serving as spies for the Soviet Union.[46]

By the sixties, most Americans could agree to disagree about the new per-
missiveness regarding sex. But if there was one thing at mid-century on which a
nearly universal consensus existed – in religion, science, medicine, law, and the
media – it was on the pathological perversity of homoerotic expression. In the
liberated atmosphere of the 1960s that consensus, too, began crumbling.

It may be ironic that the once progressive medical view that treated homo-
eroticism as a genetic deformity – as opposed to a depraved or immoral incli-
nation – may have contributed to inspiring a homosexual identity. According
to at least one historian of the gay movement after World War II: "Medical theories made homosexuality not a deed ... but a condition that described who
one was."[47] This may be an overstatement, since terms of identity like "homo,"
"fag," "fairy," and "queer" had a long history.[48] In any case, as some homosexuals began organizing in the early fifties, the leadership's use of Marxist analysis
served further to fix an identity and to raise consciousness among homosexuals as members of a distinctive oppressed class. Until at least the seventies,
this did little to gain acceptance for gays and lesbians in mainstream America,
or even among most of America's so-called elite. It also kept many gays and
lesbians from publicly declaring their personal attitudes and from joining the
movement.

Sympathetic treatment began in law, medicine, and the media during the late
1950s, almost certainly influenced by publication of Kinsey's findings, but also
as part of a general mood shift toward tolerance following the discrediting of
McCarthyism. Most Americans, however, still considered homosexuality to be
a deviance requiring correction as well as sympathy.[49] Most of the associations

---

[46] For contemporaries, the fact that many of the founders of gay organizations in the 1950s were or
      had been members of the Communist party seemingly lent substance to the linking of homosex-
      uality with communism.

[47] John D'Emilio, *Sexual Politics, Sexual Communities: The Making of a Homosexual Minority in
      the United States, 1940–1970* (University of Chicago Press, 1983), p. 21.

[48] According to the Oxford English Dictionary, the word "gay" as applied to homosexuals has a
      short history, apparently arriving in the early 1930s when the word was still more commonly as-
      sociated with people of dissolute character. The choice of the originally pejorative word by the
      Gay Liberation Movement parallels the choice of "black" by Afro-American civil rights leaders
      at the end of the 1960s.

[49] As late as 1977, in arguing that "positive incest" was an oxymoron, a leading psychiatrist from
      the Columbia Medical School declared: "I'd have to say that what's wrong with incest is the same
      as what's wrong with homosexuality. It's not necessarily wrong for the persons to do it if it gives
      them pleasure. But it implies that some wrong has already occurred – that there was not a nor-
      mal development." Similarly, Abram Kardiner, one of the world's leading psychiatrists and social
      philosophers, commented: "You will throw a monkey wrench into society by introducing the idea

formed by homosexuals after World War II (e.g., various Mattachine and Daughters of Bilitis societies) focused initially on helping members cope with their deviant proclivities in a hostile world and on fighting the malicious proclivity of the police for entrapping individuals in violation of sodomy laws. But at the end of the sixties, taking their cue from the "Women's Lib" and "Black is Beautiful" campaigns, thousands of people "came out of the closet" to join public marches and demonstrations for Gay Liberation.

The catalyst for this development occurred during the closing days of June 1969 outside the Stonewall Inn, a popular gay hangout in New York City's Greenwich Village. There, a major riot took place when police attempted to conduct what for them had become a routine mass arrest of gays, a sometimes violent ritual carried out with a variety of motives including simple blood lust and, of course, graft and extortion. Unlike previous raids, this time mobs of gays and sympathizers gathered in the streets and fought the police to a standstill. Rioting continued the following two nights. The Gay Liberation Front took shape there and in other cities in the immediate aftermath of the Stonewall riots. Gay and lesbian organizations thereafter pursued the goal of positive acceptance of homosexuality as the complete equal of heterosexuality, both legally and morally.

There is little question that this development had been germinating since World War II on the strength of new expectations that wartime propaganda had encouraged about the place and meaning of personal liberty in modern democratic societies. During the war against racist fascism, official condemnation of adverse discrimination against persons of particular identities – notably, the attack on anti-Semitism and anti-Catholicism – planted the seeds of such changes. The civil rights movement added emphasis to the power for change that individuals could wield when united to counter disadvantages suffered because of their ascribed personal identities, whether religious or racial. "Identity politics" was already well ensconced when the Stonewall riots served to mobilize people whose sexual preferences "described who one was."

For lesbians, activism followed directly from the movement for the liberation of women from narrowly ascribed roles as mothers and wives. Such liberation clearly had special importance for women whose preferences ran toward other women rather than toward potential husbands, and it had special meaning for their access to career and economic opportunities. As historians Estelle Freedman and John D'Emilio put it: "Without husbands to provide them a legitimate status, and uninterested in playing the part of the sexy girl who chased men, lesbians confronted squarely the limited options available to women."[50] Because

---

[of 'positive incest']. The family is in enough trouble already from homosexuality." Nobile, "The Last Taboo," p. 158.

[50] Estelle Freedman & John D'Emilio, *Intimate Matters: A History of Sexuality in America* (HarperCollins, 1988), pp. 316–17.

it gave ammunition to antifeminists in the popular domain, the participation of outspoken lesbians in the women's movement caused some hostility among other feminists. But at least this had the effect of strengthening the case for women's rights and also forcing modern society to face up to the legitimacy of individuals' personal choices in sexual behavior as in other expressions of individual liberty.

By the end of the seventies, the movement succeeded in establishing a new consensus among most educated Americans and in the major news and arts media – although not among the American public generally, especially outside the big cities. Included in the new consensus were: (1) that homosexuality should not be treated as a disorder, much less a perversion; (2) that it represented a lifestyle preference that all persons in a free society had a right to express; and (3) that – like women, blacks, the aged and the disabled, and ethnic and religious minorities – homosexuals deserved the protection of the law against adverse discrimination.

Attempts to include legal protection, however, continually failed in most states and in most respects at the federal level despite efforts by sectors of the judiciary, which again led the way on behalf of human rights. In one extreme reaction to the newly developing consensus on gays and lesbians, a popular referendum in Colorado, passed by the requisite two thirds of the state's voters, placed into the state constitution a permanent ban against legislation designed to afford protection against homophobic discrimination. Although the ban was struck down by the U.S. Supreme Court in 1996,[51] state governments and private businesses could, and some did, continue to fire employees who were discovered to be gay.[52] Of course, so did the United States military.

By the late seventies, the momentum toward legitimating gay lifestyles was slowed but by no means reversed. It was stalled by the traditionalist backlash against the rapid cultural changes that had been transpiring over the previous quarter-century, a reaction that brought Ronald Reagan to the White House. It took heavy blows from the onset of the AIDS epidemic in the early eighties, which in the United States spread most rampantly among sexually active gays. In fact, efforts to fund medical research to deal with the epidemic were impeded by the popular identification of AIDS with male homosexual life styles, an impression furthered by militant gay leadership in funding campaigns.

---

[51] *Romer v. Evans* (1996). With dissents from only the three most extreme conservatives on the Court, the majority opinion stated that the "sheer breadth [of Colorado's action] is so discontinuous with the reasons offered for it that the amendment seems inexplicable by anything but animus toward the class that it affects; it lacks a rational relationship to legitimate state interests." Nonetheless, Chief Justice Rehnquist and Justices Antonin Scalia and Clarence Thomas found the state's constitutional amendment to be entirely reasonable.

[52] See e.g. Urvashi Vaid, *Virtual Equality: The Mainstreaming of Gay and Lesbian Liberation* (Doubleday, 1995), pp. 3–10.

There continued, however, to be important signs that the general public had come to adopt a more favorable attitude toward gays and lesbians. One *Time* survey in 1989 reported that a substantial majority (65 percent) favored permitting homosexual couples to inherit each other's property, and 54 percent also favored domestic partner benefits. But a solid 69 percent opposed giving legal standing to same-sex marriages, and 75 percent opposed permitting homosexual couples or individuals to adopt children.[53] Moreover, although some polls in the nineties showed strong majorities opposed to discriminating against homosexuals in job opportunities generally, small majorities opposed gays and lesbians working in health care, education, and the clergy.

As already noted, in 1986 the U.S. Supreme Court (in *Hardwick v. Bowers*) upheld a state law that defined as a felony sexual acts between consenting male adults, even in the privacy of their own home. The five-member majority in the case declined to include such behavior among the personal liberties protected by the Constitution. Striking a blow against rising pluralism – or what modern progressives preferred to call "multiculturalism" and conservatives called rampant "moral relativism" – the Court asserted that, in a democracy, the majority had the right to legislate minimal standards of what it considered to be moral behavior.

Although rarely enforced, homophobic laws continued to prevail in most of the states of the Union through the end of the century. So, too, did a widespread animus against gay lifestyles. As the century ended, twenty states still had antisodomy laws, with Texas and five others defining acts between same-sex partners as criminal sodomy.[54] In spite of the positive attitudes prevalent among the well-educated and those in the media and most professions, homophobia generally prevailed in the political arena. At least through the nineties, the passionate opposition to accepting gays and lesbians translated into lavish funding of powerful pressure groups that successfully intimidated elected officials in most states.

A homophobic "macho" culture also worked for the traditionalists. The military's ban on homosexuals – a ban not against homosexual acts, but against homosexuals as a class – remained in place despite President Clinton's attempt in 1993 to have it rescinded. The idea that some fellows in their squad or company might be gay seemed to panic the heterosexual members of that institution, who ostensibly were prepared to brave live ammunition but were daunted by sharing showers with a gay person. Although some argued, as the newly designated

---

53 "Should Gays Have Marriage Rights?" *Time* (20 Nov. 1989), pp. 101–2.

54 Several other states' courts had ruled that such laws were unconstitutional. Still, New Hampshire and Florida made it illegal for same-sex couples to adopt children or for a single gay person to do so.

Secretary of Defense did in 1993, that a blanket ban of certain citizens as a class probably could not withstand a court challenge (it did), he warned the new Democratic president that even the heavily Democratic Congress would decisively oppose him on the issue. Whatever the merits of the case, the issue was not one that individual legislators were prepared to spend political capital on. Meanwhile, President Ronald Reagan and his successor George Herbert Walker Bush packed the Supreme Court and the nation's appellate courts with ultraconservative judges. The ban – modified, entirely ineffectually, by a "don't ask, don't tell" policy – outlasted the Clinton presidency.

Tested in the courts, it was upheld by conservative judges as within the discretionary power of the executive and legislative branches to assure national security and the "morale" of the military.[55] The courts ruled that the "equal protection" clause of the Constitution does not apply to military personnel who voluntarily subject themselves to the special discipline required by the military. The judges were apparently not impressed by the fact that the restriction applied not only to military personnel but also to civilians regarding their freedom to choose a particular career. The ban was on persons, not on behavior.

But the *Bowers* decision and the military's stubborn resistance to applying equal protection of the law to homosexuals represented a rearguard gesture made in the face of a strong tide of change. Justice Powell, who provided the swing vote in the 5-4 *Bowers* decision, only a few years later declared his vote to be the worst mistake of his judicial career. Although the ban on homosexuals in the military remained, in 2003 the U.S. Supreme Court reversed *Bowers*, with the usually conservative Justice Anthony Kennedy writing for the 6-3 majority and emphatically declaring Americans' right to privacy regardless of their sexual preference. "The liberty protected by the Constitution," Kennedy wrote in *Lawrence v. Texas*, "allows homosexual persons the right to choose to enter upon relationships in the confines of their homes and their own private lives and still retain their dignity as free persons."[56] The crucial issue, the Court majority declared, is that the laws in question seek to control a private relationship that is within the liberty of a person to choose without being subject

---

[55] *Able v. U.S.*, 2d Circuit, vol. 155, F.3d (1998), p. 628; *Thorne v. U.S. Dept. Defense*, vol. 139, F.3d (1998), p. 893.

[56] *Lawrence v. Texas* (2003): "Although the laws involved in *Bowers* and here purport to do no more than prohibit a particular sexual act, their penalties and purposes have more far-reaching consequences, touching upon the most private human conduct, sexual behavior, and in the most private of places, the home. They seek to control a personal relationship that, whether or not entitled to formal recognition in the law, is within the liberty of persons to choose without being punished as criminals" (pp. 3–6). In the 2003 Massachusetts case of *Goodridge et al. v. Department of Public Health,* the state Supreme Court ruled that the state could not ban same-sex marriage or deprive same-sex couples of the same pension, insurance, and tax benefits that were accorded heterosexual marriages.

to criminal punishment; and that the laws are therefore unconstitutional. The three dissenters, who on other days of the week would hold forth against "big government," saw nothing wrong with permitting government to control Americans' private relationships.

Once again, then, progress toward equal protection of the law for all Americans came from court actions in the face of popular, majoritarian opposition. The nation's judiciary would go further. In November 2003, the Massachusetts Supreme Court ruled that the state could not forbid same-sex marriage, overturning state law and contravening federal law passed in 1996. It did not go unnoticed that the Massachusetts action followed from the logic of the *Lawrence* case, even that expressed in Justice Scalia's vigorous and sarcastic dissent. "If moral disapprobation of homosexual conduct is 'no legitimate state interest',", Scalia argued, "what justification could there possibly be for denying the benefits of marriage to homosexual couples exercising 'the liberty protected by the Constitution'? Surely not the encouragement of procreation, since the sterile and the elderly are allowed to marry."

The Court's action provoked immediate demands by legislators and political candidates – in both congressional parties – for a constitutional amendment to overturn the decision. Responding to the populist outcry, President George W. Bush supported the demands, making "the sanctity of marriage" a centerpiece of his campaign for a second term. Many political analysts speculated that the issue played a major role in mobilizing religious conservatives in 2004 to help re-elect Bush.

All the same, bucking the conservatism of the overrepresented congressional and legislative districts of small-town America, gay lifestyles continued to become more open and more widely accepted. Many states repealed their anti-sodomy laws. Many states, universities, and major corporations adopted domestic partner pension and health insurance programs. Network television sitcoms, nationally distributed films, live theater, as well as major fiction and nonfiction increasingly featured homosexuality as part of mainstream life. In fact, by the nineties, although only a few nationally broadcast television sitcoms featured Euro- and Afro-American characters together and equally in the same show,[57] by the nineties several shows featured gay and lesbian characters in major roles on a par with "straight" characters. Some played lead roles. (Of course, Americans had long made homosexuality the target of humor; they found it funny and thus suitable for sit-coms. Americans rarely found mixed racial relations funny.)

The momentum of social change underlying *Lawrence v. Texas* and the Massachusetts court decision took its strength from a redefinition long in coming of the American idea of liberty. That idea once had focused primarily on free access

[57] This was not true of drama, especially police drama.

to economic opportunity through the private uses of property. By the middle of the twentieth century, the American idea of liberty had shifted to focus more on the communicative freedoms and on enlarged choices in lifestyle and social preferences. It was certain that sooner or later the social conservatism that had informed the *Bowers* decision would be forced to yield, as it finally did, to the new understanding of what liberties Americans could count on as constitutionally protected.

"It is remarkable," historian John D'Emilio wrote in the first year of the new millennium, "that, in the midst of a deepening conservative impulse in U.S. political life, this movement for social justice has marched forward .... It is not too much to say that, for millions of gay men and lesbians, the changes of the last three decades have been nothing short of revolutionary."[58]

There is little doubt that the revolution in sexual behavior permanently changed much in the character of modern life. In most respects it appears to have had a healthful, emancipating effect, overcoming much superstition and obviating unnecessary guilt and anxiety for millions of people.[59] But by the 1980s, the freestyle sexual activity that characterized the revolution in the late sixties and seventies began to subside. In 1994, the most thorough study of sexual practices completed since Kinsey found that despite the "widespread sexualization of American society," the data showed only "modest rates of partnered sex ... at least in contrast to the frequency of other everyday activities and the expectations created by media representations."[60]

Certainly the moderation of sexual activity reported by respondents in studies after 1980 owed partly to the onset of the AIDS epidemic that increasingly affected non–drug-addicted heterosexuals as well as gays and intravenous drug

---

[58] John D'Emilio, "Placing Gay in the Sixties," in Alexander Bloom, ed., *Long Time Gone* (Oxford University Press, 2001), p. 224.

[59] In an introduction to the second of two books, published seven years apart, that printed women's reports of their own sexual fantasies, Nancy Friday noted a striking difference. In the first book, *The Secret Garden* (Trident, 1968), "the greatest number of fantasies ... centered around themes of imaginary force and rape, abduction, domination, the anonymous man whom the woman never sees again – all of which are psychological strategies for allowing the woman to have the most thrilling experiences in her fantasies" while permitting her to say " 'It wasn't my fault.'... In other words, sexual guilt and its avoidance was the great emotion shared by most women" who contributed to the first book. The second book "reflected a whole new era of freedom of sexual expression .... I am struck by their pride in their sexuality .... They are not at all frightened by the sexuality of their earliest years. They aren't into guilt at all." *Forbidden Flowers* (Pocket Books, 1975), p. 17.

[60] Edward O. Laumann, John H. Gagnon, Robert Michael, & Stuart Michaels, *The Social Organization of Sexuality: Sexual Practices in the United States* (University of Chicago Press, 1994), p. 87. The observation refers to all partnered sexual activity, within and outside marriage.

users. The danger of contracting that mostly incurable and lethal affliction returned some of the caution that fear of venereal disease had instilled before penicillin. But the sexual revolution had other downsides as well.

What had happened succeeded in mostly dislodging the moral anchors of the old Victorian regime while offering little in the way of replacement. That left many people confused and anxious, indeed perhaps as "up-tight" in a new way as people felt before the liberation. "Ironically," wrote one sexologist, "the evolving sexual openness disclosed as much sexual misery as orgiastic revelry." Disappointment that sexual pleasure was not always easy to attain was aggravated by "the widespread belief that sex was crucial to personal and relational fulfillment."[61] But another part of the problem concerned the line to be drawn between freedom and irresponsibility. "At the end of the second millennium C.E.," wrote Roger Shattuck in his weighty tome, *Forbidden Knowledge,* "I believe we have arrived at a crisis in our lengthy undertaking to reconcile liberation and limits."[62] As one historian put it, writing about the "real" attitudes toward sex in the nineteenth century: "It may be useful to remind ourselves that the struggle for sexual freedom, at least in the lives of individual persons, requires considerable stepping over the bodies of others and that it is not only in political revolutions that crimes are committed in the name of liberty."[63]

By the 1980s, it was not just conservatives who began remarking on the difficulties induced by the new order. No one could ignore the near quadrupling of unmarried teenage pregnancy in the quarter-century between 1950 and 1976, which continued to increase until the early 1990s despite the availability of the Pill and other inexpensive contraceptives.[64] The new sexual freedom had led the television networks to feature prime-time sitcoms with often explicitly sexual dialogue in addition to on- and off-screen sexual action, but while the young liberated characters had their sexual frolics, the networks permitted no references in such programs to "safe sex" or contraception.[65]

---

[61] Irvine, *Disorders of Desire,* pp. 190–1.

[62] Roger Shattuck, *Forbidden Knowledge: From Prometheus to Pornography* (St. Martin's, 1996), p. 6.

[63] Steven Marcus, *The Other Victorians: A Study of Sexuality and Pornography in Mid-Nineteenth Century England* (Bantam, 1966), p. 160.

[64] Total live births to unmarried young women under 20 rose from 60,000 in 1950 to 235,000 in 1976. This included 3,200 live births to unmarried girls under 15 in 1950, rising to 11,000 in 1975: *The 1979 Hammond Almanac* (Hammond, 1979), p. 251. Source: U.S. Public Health Service.

[65] As one advertisement mailed out by Planned Parenthood put it: "They did it 20,000 times on television last year. How come nobody got pregnant?" According to the ad, in 1978 (even before sexual candor became overtly graphic on TV), researchers counted 20,000 scenes on prime-time network television – which doesn't count the usually steamy afternoon soap operas – without a single mention of the consequences of unprotected sex. See also Haynes Johnson, "Hypocrisy on

Meanwhile, feminists had begun noting how often it was women who were most victimized by their mates' wanderlust, which the new sexual freedom seemed to encourage. An extensive report commissioned by the *New York Times* in 1986 concluded: "The sexual revolution released us from a great many restraints, but we've paid a high price. Rather than bringing men and women closer to together, 'freedom' has alienated them." Long-term commitment to personal relationships, the report found, tended to yield to short-term gratification that loomed large amid the prevailing emphasis on sexual fulfillment howsoever satisfied. "Confusion over roles hasn't helped matters either. In the absence of givens, major renegotiations are called for at every turn of intimacy. No one seems quite sure what it is they want."[66]

As the historian Paul Robinson noted in his incisive study, *The Modernization of Sex*: "As moderns, we remain permanently divided between a Romantic past, whose repressions we would gladly rid ourselves of, and a de-romanticized future, whose emotional emptiness we fear even while we anticipate its greater freedom."[67]

Television: The Networks Will Sell Sex, but Not Condoms," *Washington Post National Weekly Edition* (2 March 1987), p. 25; also, *New York Times* (27 Jan. 1988): "A Study Has Found a Barrage of Sex on TV."

[66] Angeline Goreau, "Sexual Revolution," *New York Times* (18 Dec. 1986), p. 24.

[67] Robinson, *Modernization of Sex*, p. 195.

13

The Demise of Privacy

There is ... no doubt that a fundamental right of privacy exists, [and] that it is of constitutional stature. It is not just the right ... to be secure in one's person, house, papers and effects, except as permitted by law; it embraces the right to be free from coercion, however subtle, to incriminate oneself; it is different from, but akin to the right to select and freely to practice one's religion and the right to freedom of speech; it is more than the specific right to be secure against the Peeping Tom or the intrusion of electronic espionage devices and wiretapping. All of these are aspects of the right to privacy; but the right of privacy reaches beyond any of its specifics. It is, simply stated, the right to be let alone; to live one's life as one chooses, free from assault, intrusion or invasion except as they can be justified by the clear needs of community living under a government of law.[1]

Abe Fortas

If we don't sanction people who violate privacy, we can't expect the law to do much of that work for us. The point is that we should actually care about privacy, and it's not clear that we do.[2]

Robert Post

During an inquiry by the U.S. Senate into President Richard Nixon's "black bag" (burglary) operations aimed at finding something scandalous or incriminating on Daniel Ellsberg – the man who leaked the contents of the so-called Pentagon Papers that revealed much about the decision-making process during the Kennedy and Johnson administrations regarding Vietnam – the following

[1] U.S. Supreme Court Justice Abe Fortas, draft of an unpublished opinion for *Hill v. Time, Inc.* (1966), quoted in Bernard Schwartz, *Super Chief: Earl Warren and His Supreme Court – A Judicial Biography* (New York University Press, 1983), p. 644.
[2] Professor of Law Robert Post quoted in Jeffrey Rosen, *The Unwanted Gaze* (Random House, 2001).

exchange took place between Nixon's aide John Ehrlichman and Senator Herman Talmadge of Georgia:

"Do you remember," Talmadge asked, "when we were in law school we studied a famous principle of law that came from England and also is well known in this country, that no matter how humble a man's cottage is, that even the King of England cannot enter without his consent?"

To which Ehrlichman coolly replied: "I am afraid that has been considerably eroded over the years."

Talmadge retorted: "Down in my country we still think it is a pretty legitimate principle of law."[3]

Unfortunately, Erhlichman was correct.

During the last half of the twentieth century, American society went two ways in its respect for personal privacy. On the one hand, American jurisprudence – led by the U.S. Supreme Court during Chief Justice Earl Warren's tenure (1953–1969) – moved to enlarge personal freedom to include a constitutional right to privacy. As the political right wing complained, this was indeed a new direction for constitutional law. The Court fashioned new safeguards against unreasonable search and seizure, supposedly protected by the Fourth Amendment but commonly violated throughout the country. And it began – though only began – to treat matters having to do with sex and procreation as a private concern beyond the reach of the state. (One might have presumed that sexual matters would be ipso facto private. Not so for many Americans, whose puritanical insecurities regarding sex inclined them to use the state to pry, spy, and deny.)

On the other hand, mostly in the post-Warren decades, the courts progressively enlarged the prerogatives of the state and of private employers to intrude upon individuals' privacy. In addition, it gave broad license to the media to intrude into the private lives of Americans, celebrities and nonpublic persons alike. Some of these developments owed to what might be called the "principle of unintended consequences." In other cases, the erosion of privacy rights resulted from the country's pronounced shift toward a conservatism that was preoccupied with security, popularly referred to as "law and order."[4]

By the 1990s, courts began progressively to empower the government to use electronic devices in its search for incriminating evidence on individuals suspected of possibly illegal acts; to randomly stop and search people in cars and buses; to subpoena financial records, personal diaries, and other papers even of

---

[3] *New York Times* obituary for Talmadge (22 March 2002), p. C13.

[4] The suicide terrorist attacks of 11 September 2001 would produce a huge windfall for the conservative impulse to pry and control. Hysterical legislators rushed to empower police and military authorities, including the CIA and FBI, to spy on and detain Americans without prior scrutiny by judicial processes, all in the name of fighting terrorism.

persons suspected of no crime while investigating a targeted suspect; and even to arm acquaintances and false friends with devices to record supposedly confidential conversations between innocent persons in quest of incriminating evidence regarding a third person. In this respect, "privacy law" appeared to be stillborn. By the end of the century, Americans would have fewer protections against intrusive prying into their personal affairs than they had a century or even two centuries earlier.

Yet there was something still more telling about the demise of privacy. That is, Americans generally moved more or less voluntarily – in some cases one could say with giddy abandon – to surrender their personal privacy. For both profit and exhibitionist thrills, celebrities as well as sad sacks in quest of their "fifteen minutes of fame" exposed to prurient public inspection the most intimate details of their lives, their families, their bodies, and their souls. Television and computer Internet technology provided ready and inexpensive means for such exhibitionism. Meanwhile, further technological developments made it possible for both government and commercial profit seekers to intrude upon the privacy of that minority of innocent Americans for whom privacy still retained some value.

The idea that privacy should be included in the constitutional provisions protecting individual liberty began late in U.S. history. There was one lonely case decided by the U.S. Supreme Court in 1886 that referred to personal privacy as a "sacred right" of free people. In that case the Court declared:

The very essence of constitutional liberty and security is affected by all invasions ... [by] the government and its employees of the sanctity of a man's home and of the privacies of life. It is not the breaking of his doors, and rummaging of his drawers, that constitutes the essence of the offense; but it is the invasion of his indefeasible right of personal security, personal liberty and private property.

In concluding his majority opinion in *Boyd v. U.S.,* Justice Bradley asserted: "Any compulsory discovery [by the state] ... is contrary to the principles of a free government. It is abhorrent to the instincts ... of an American."[5] By the last quarter of the twentieth century, those instincts had withered.

Government and its employees were never the sole violators. In 1890, Louis Brandeis and his then law partner, Samuel Warren, published what was to become a "classic" article on the right to privacy. The article targeted the new journalistic practices of reporting on people's private lives. The authors complained: "To satisfy a prurient taste, the details of sexual relations are spread broadcast in the columns of the daily papers. To occupy the indolent, column

---

[5] *Boyd v. U.S.,* 116 U.S. 616 (1886), especially at pp. 631–2.

upon column is filled with idle gossip which can only be procured by intrusions upon the domestic circle."[6]

What inspired the article actually had nothing to do with sexual gossip. The two attorneys were incensed merely by an item in the Boston *Saturday Evening Gazette* that described a breakfast party that Warren had put on for his daughter's wedding. There was nothing scandalous or inaccurate about the article; what bothered Warren and Brandeis was the simple fact that a totally private party by a nonpublic figure had become game for strangers and gossipers. The right to privacy, they insisted, "implies the right not merely to prevent inaccurate portrayal of private life, but to prevent its being depicted at all." The authors worried more generally that new technology (i.e. photography), coupled with the new scandal-mongering journalism, was making it possible and frequent for individuals to suffer outrageous intrusions upon their privacy in both business and domestic affairs. The authors predicted that if the law did not change then it would soon be possible, as they put it, for all that "is whispered in the closet [to] be proclaimed from the housetops."

But no court or legislature took up the challenge to define a protected private space for American citizens. The *Boyd* case had arisen at a time when Americans, and the law, tended to define "liberty" in terms of property rights; the Court's decision in the case forbade invasion of a man's financial records in search of incriminating evidence because it violated his "indefeasible right of personal security, personal liberty and private property." There remained little acknowledgment of a right to privacy in the sense of personal space that is protected from public or private invasion.

After he became an associate justice on the U.S. Supreme Court, Brandeis attempted to bring the issue of personal privacy into constitutional law. In a wiretapping case in 1928, Brandeis sought to overturn a criminal conviction that had been won by the use of evidence obtained from several months of unauthorized wiretaps on a man's private telephone. The Court majority pretended that nothing had changed with modern technological advances and that, since the accused's home had not been invaded physically, there was no Fourth Amendment violation against unreasonable search. In his famous dissent, Brandeis sought to iterate the warnings of the Founders of the Constitution that "as against the Government, the right to be let alone ... [is] the most comprehensive of rights and the right most valued by civilized men." Not, however, for the Taft Court's five-member majority.

The Brandeis dissent in the Olmstead case appears remarkably prescient in view of subsequent developments. "The progress of science in furnishing the

---

[6] Samuel D. Warren & Louis D. Brandeis, "The Right to Privacy," *Harvard Law Review* (vol. 4, 1890), pp. 193ff.

Government with means of espionage," he wrote, "is not likely to stop with wire tapping. Ways may some day be developed by which the Government, without removing papers from secret drawers, can reproduce them in court, and by which it will be enabled to expose to a jury the most intimate occurrences of the home." Before the century ended, the arrival of Internet communications – and the covert means for intercepting them – turned what Brandeis saw as a possibility into stark reality.[7]

For a brief moment in the 1960s, the Supreme Court seemed to reverse the *Olmstead* decision. In 1967 (*Katz v. U.S.*), the Court ruled that the "Fourth Amendment protects people, not places." That the government had not physically invaded private space did not satisfy the Constitution's requirements against unreasonable search.

But in subsequent cases, a series of decisions exposed private citizens to various warrantless intrusions as well as to public revelations of their behavior, their casual comments, and even their thoughts. The courts used primarily three criteria to determine the legitimacy of a governmental or private invasion: (1) whenever some organ of the media might find a story "newsworthy"; (2) whenever an employer might seek to control a "moral" working environment; and (3) whenever an individual did not have a reasonable expectation that his or her privacy might be secure against governmental or private monitoring.

Suits by celebrities and some not-so-celebrated persons against the media for using telescopic lenses or supersensitive audio devices in order to gain salacious photos or recordings of private conversations proved to be futile, ostensibly on the grounds that the state should not interfere with the judgment of the press about the public's "need to know." And the courts came to define the "need to know" as whatever the press regarded as newsworthy. For the media, which subsist on commercial advertisements, what is "newsworthy" is whatever will likely enlarge readerships and audiences. "Need to know" readily drifted into whatever a prurient public was simply curious to know.

A key decision in 1967 seemingly bent the twig in the growth of privacy law. In his sole appearance as an attorney before the U.S. Supreme Court – between his defeat for the presidency in 1960 and his election in 1968 – Richard Nixon represented the Hill family in a suit for invasion of privacy against Time, Inc. *Life* magazine, a Time publication, had published a story that identified the Hills as the family on whom a Broadway play, *The Desperate Hours,* was based. The photo-story claimed that the play was a true and accurate account of the family's imprisonment in their own home by a couple of escaped convicts. Actually, the play fictionalized the story in a few important ways, including depictions of violence and threats of sexual molestation directed at the captives' teenage

---

[7] *Olmstead v. U.S.,* 277 U.S. 438, 478 (1928).

daughter. The event, massively covered by the press at the time, had occurred several years before the play appeared, and in the meantime the Hills had remained adamant in refusing any publicity or providing any details of their ordeal, including whether their daughter had in fact been threatened or molested. They claimed that Time, Inc. caused them severe mental anguish by representing the play as accurate and by identifying them by name, going so far as to film scenes from inside the Hills' one-time home. Nixon, and the Hills, lost the case.

It is a remarkable paradox, requiring close attention to historical context, that some of the Court's fiercest defenders of personal liberty – namely, William Douglas, Hugo Black, and William Brennan – made up part of the 5-4 majority against the Hills. In fact, the justices were initially inclined, 7-2, to vindicate the Hills. But the Court had only recently established an important precedent for freedom of the press in a libel case filed by Alabama law enforcement officers against the *New York Times*.[8] In 1967, supersensitive to efforts by racist officials in the South to silence the press by bringing repeated libel suits against their critics, Justices Black, Douglas, and Brennan found in the Hill case that freedom of the press trumped claims of privacy rights.[9]

Elsewhere in the private sector, some of the assaults upon privacy came as an unintended consequence of the campaigns against "sexual harassment." The Civil Rights Act of 1964 outlawed injurious discrimination on the basis of sex. In pursuit of criteria by which to measure violations of the Act's provisions, a series of court decisions invited litigation that shredded the privacy not only of alleged violators but of third parties who might have had a relationship with the accused. By defining "harassment" and "hostile working environment" as forms of "discrimination" and by making employers liable for violations by employees, the decisions provoked employers to set up intrusive mechanisms for monitoring and constricting their employees' personal behavior on the job and in some cases off the job as well. University administrations and business corporations won the right to peek into the paper files and computer files of all employees and to use what they found – even offhand memos expressing a momentary complaint – in order to discipline or to discharge. Essentially, as the law developed, employees could expect no privacy of any kind while on the job, with the possible exception of when they visited a toilet.

Even a company's written pledge not to monitor e-mail became no guarantee of privacy. In a 1990s case involving Pillsbury,[10] the baking company broke such a promise without warning. A Pennsylvania district court upheld the company's right to so monitor its employees' behavior, ruling that Pillsbury's "interest in

---

[8] *N.Y. Times Co. v. Sullivan*, 376 U.S. 254 (1966).

[9] *Time, Inc. v. Hill*, 385 U.S. 374 (1967).

[10] *Smyth v. Pillsbury*, F.Supp. ED Pa. (1996).

preventing inappropriate and unprofessional comments ... over its e-mail system outweighs any privacy interest the employee may have in those comments." As the legal scholar Jeffrey Rosen remarked in wonderment: "That just can't be right."[11] Nonetheless, as the century ended it remained as the law, at least in Pennsylvania.

In general, modern technology and especially computers made privacy, for those who valued it, almost entirely elusive. By the end of the century, hundreds of thousands of medical records of private physicians and hospitals wound up in the files of insurance companies. For-profit firms such as the Medical Information Bureau (MIB) built data banks of such information for sale to insurance companies, government agencies, and others for whom medical histories can help to reduce risks. In exchange for computer billing and other record-keeping and electronic services, thousands of physicians gave the Physicians Computer Network, an affiliate of IBM, access to the personal medical records of their patients. Increasing numbers of patients with medical histories, dire diagnoses (even those that prove to be mistaken), and genetic profiles indicating long-term health risks found it difficult or impossible to buy medical, life, and disability insurance, often facing employment difficulties as well.

Inevitably, computer hackers found ways to break into the records of medical, financial, and government data banks, thereby exposing credit cards, bank accounts, and all kinds of personal data to theft and abuse. There were no safe havens for any purposes related to privacy. As one *New York Times* reporter summed it up, following revelation of a massive break-in to a major bank's records: "If a person has held a job, held a lease, obtained a driver's license, carried a credit card, been fingerprinted, taken a drug test, gone to court, or simply received mail – odds are that those and many other of his or her recordable details are now stored in one or more consumer data bases and available for sale. Beyond fraud artists, the buyers might be landlords, prospective employers, or other customers of ChoicePoint, Lexis-Nexis and other big data brokers that offer one-stop shopping for clients seeking background data on tens of millions of individuals throughout the country."[12]

Use of the Internet further increased the likelihood of gross intrusions into the user's private life. By use of programs known as "cookies," private business firms and the government could track all Internet usage and discover a user's name, address, bank card, Social Security number, and virtually anything else they might seek to know, including credit histories, income, and employment records. Similar technology permitted access to any and all litigation or police records whether or not an arrest or indictment was involved. Through the

[11] Rosen, *Unwanted Gaze*, p. 74, quoting from the *Smyth v. Pillsbury* decision.
[12] Tom Zeller, Jr., "Breach Points up Flaws in Privacy Laws," *New York Times* (24 Feb. 2005), p. C1.

Internet, a person's medical records also became more or less readily available to anyone who really wanted to know. For fees, private "detective" agencies offered their computer skills for such access. Since certain computer software made it possible to retrieve virtually anything ever entered onto a hard disc, attempts to delete content – short of physically destroying the disc – became futile.

Although some states forbade recording of telephone conversations without the permission of both parties, legislators in 37 states and the federal government permitted corporations to record conversations secretly. The courts, moreover, found that citizens protected against secret recordings in their home state lost that protection when conversing with someone in a state that allowed such recording. Privacy held no trump cards.[13]

Efforts by corporations to reassure their "valued customers" about their privacy policy seemed little short of rank cynicism. For example, Macy's – a division of Federated Department Stores that held several giant retail chains – offered (in minute print) the following in the legally required notification of its "privacy" policy: "We collect personally identifiable information about you," such as "Information obtained online, including from 'cookies' (small pieces of data stored by your Internet browser on your computer) or other technology that may be used ... to help us track your website usage." Moreover, "We ... share all of the information described" with all subsidiaries, affiliates, service providers, joint marketing companies, as well as with financial services, "such as those offering insurance and investment products, and we may provide information to nonfinancial services affiliates ... offering consumer products." This, after the same notice led off by stating how much the company valued its customers' privacy.[14] All credit-card, banking, insurance, and similar firms issued nearly identical oxymoronic statements. Any individual who did not like it would find no financial agency to do business with.

Later court decisions further eroded privacy rights by stating that such rights depended on the reasonableness of a person's expectations that privacy would be respected. But since those using e-mail or the Internet could no longer reasonably expect confidentiality to be maintained, no one had any effective redress when personal information, comments, or behavior came to be observed, recorded, or

---

[13] See e.g. *San Francisco Chronicle* (3 April 2004), p. B3.

[14] This particular statement of the firm's privacy policy was issued in 2001, but it was virtually the same every year after federal law required a "privacy statement." A "privacy pledge" by Merrill Lynch the same year began by promising that the client's interests "always come first" and then went on to say: "We may disclose some or all of your personal information to our corporate affiliates, including transfer agents, banks, insurance companies and agencies, trust companies, mortgage brokers, securities broker-dealers, and investment advisers ...." In addition, "Merrill Lynch will, as necessary ... [provide your personal information to] nonaffiliated third parties." From enclosure with monthly statement, March 2001.

revealed to the public or to a government or commercial enterprise. Slip away for a weekend to a secret holiday retreat, or for a romantic rendezvous? Computer chips placed in private as well as rental cars, along with the emplacement of Global Positioning Systems to provide driving instructions, can record everything a driver did, from speed to routes and destinations chosen. Nor could anyone expect privacy to be respected when simply walking in the street or trying on clothes in department store changing rooms. In response to (and contributing to) the public's excitation over street crime, public officials in many cities began installing thousands of surveillance cameras in the streets. Storekeepers did the same to prevent shoplifting. Touted as ways of deterring crime and catching criminals, the cameras also caught innocent individuals in sometimes embarrassing postures, gestures, or acts. Although authorities and proprietors promised to hold the surveillance tapes exclusively for official use, inevitably they found their way to hawkers of salacious videos. If there is money to be made then entrepreneurs will find a way, whether through back alleys or otherwise. By the nineties, for about $15 voyeurs could buy tapes of or Internet access to films of lovers grappling in cars, couples engaged in arguments, women struggling with the wind to keep skirts down or undressing in changing rooms, victims of traffic accidents, even muggings. Targets of such peeping had no redress. In short, the complete erosion of legally protected privacy was well underway before the twentieth century ended. Justice Louis Brandeis' worst nightmares came to be fully realized in the 1990s.

In an incisive study of privacy law published in the first year of the new millennium, Jeffrey Rosen pointed out how far American law had fallen from principles established even before the nation was founded: "In the late eighteenth century, the spectacle of state agents breaking into a suspect's home and rummaging through his or her private diaries [on a general, nontargeting warrant] was considered the paradigm case of the unreasonable searches and seizures that the framers of the Bill of Rights intended to forbid." In that century, English law forbade the government to search, say, a dissident's home for materials that would indicate seditious libel; and in a famous case, a strongly disliked radical (John Wilkes) was exonerated because the government had violated that principle. A century later, the legal theorist most respected in the United States, Thomas Cooley, wrote: "It is not allowable to invade one's privacy for the sole purpose of obtaining evidence" – that is, to fish for incriminating material. As late as the 1890s, Rosen noted, "It was a matter of general agreement ... that the Constitution prohibited prosecutors and civil plaintiffs from rummaging through private papers in search of sexual secrets or anything else."

"It was during the 1970s and 1980s," Rosen went on to note, "that the principle that private diaries [or other private materials and files] couldn't be subpoenaed as 'mere evidence' in civil or white-collar cases, was quietly allowed to wither away. And it was during the 1980s and 1990s that the Supreme Court recognized sexually explicit speech and conduct that created a 'hostile or offensive working environment' as a form of gender discrimination, a development that made it increasingly difficult for lower courts and employers to distinguish consensual affairs from illegal forms of sexual coercion."

"The [Monica] Lewinsky investigation," Rosen continued, "might never have occurred ... if these two unfortunate legal trends hadn't converged with a third novel and illiberal law: the Independent Counsel Act, which encouraged a level of inquisitorial zeal in which ordinary prosecutors – constrained, as they are, by time, money, and public accountability – are less likely to indulge."

Using his unlimited resources and giving free rein to his partisan and ideological zeal, Independent Counsel Kenneth Starr went on an unconstrained fishing expedition among the personal belongings of a woman neither suspected nor accused of any crime or misdemeanor. Starr's object was to find incriminating material on the president of the United States. In the process, he successfully established precedents for trampling on the privacy rights of several third parties. His intrusions included subpoenaing Monica Lewinsky's diaries as well as bookstore records to discover Lewinsky's reading habits. He had Lewinsky's computer seized, from which he gleaned drafts of letters that she herself had never sent and had sought to expunge. He made use of illegally obtained tape recordings and then released them to the public. All this he presented to Congress, including numerous other intimate matters that had been revealed in grand jury proceedings that had been presumed to be secret. He also presented in his written report certain private matters concerning several other innocent persons who had been merely associated with Lewinsky. Equally heedless of privacy rights and with amazing disregard for ancient principles about the confidentiality of grand jury proceedings – but eager to scandalize the president for political purposes – an extraordinarily partisan Congress promptly put all the material given to it by Starr on the Internet.

Why was the public not outraged by such a reversal of centuries of Anglo-American law regarding the sanctity of a person's integrity, to say nothing of grand jury testimony? One reason, of course, lay in the enthusiasm with which the media lapped up the opportunity to spread salacious tales. But it is equally important to note the general demise of Americans' *sense of privacy* over the last quarter or more of the twentieth century. As Rosen remarked: "In suits over public disclosure of private facts, courts ask not only whether information is newsworthy" – all of it was, according to court decisions after the 1970s – "but also whether its publication would be 'highly offensive to a reasonable person.'... In an age that is beyond embarrassment, it's rarely clear what a 'reasonable person' would find highly offensive. For every Duchess of York who objects to being captured, by telephoto lens, in a topless romp, there's Jennifer Ringley, a 21-year-old exhibitionist in Washington, DC, who has a Web-camera trained on her bedroom 24 hours a day."

In fact, according to a *San Francisco Chronicle* report of June 1998: "Thousands of people the world over have set up 'Web cams,'... letting anyone on the Internet peer into homes and offices. One woman put herself on the Web in the process of delivering her child." "Bodies aren't as private as they used to be," remarked Linda Williams, author of a scholarly work on pornography. "Because of the Internet, we live our bodies in much more public ways."[15]

In July 1980, *Time* magazine reported: "The American's home may still be his castle, but, given the drift of things, it is easy to imagine that a peering, leering crowd is gathering at the window .... On talk shows like Phil Donahue's, ordinary people regularly recount stories of emotional disturbance, marital discord, incest,... vasectomies ... hysterectomies."[16] That was in 1980. *Time*'s editors had scarcely seen anything yet! They hadn't seen the likes of Maury Povich, Jennie Jones, Ricki Lake, or Rosie O'Donnell, whose midday TV circuses featured poor souls airing family fights and infidelities or revealing "secrets" (usually of a sexual nature) that they had kept from husbands, wives, children, boyfriends, girlfriends, or parents – all of it before live, roaring, participating audiences. Nor were 1980's TV audiences privileged yet to peep in on simulated small-claims court proceedings, where real family and neighborhood spats came to be aired and exposed to the often sarcastic barbs of an impatient, condescending judge. These were the modern equivalents of public hangings, bearbaiting, and cockfights that Americans had long banned as gestures toward a higher level of civil society.

One writer remarked: "In the 1980s, too much of America lost the fear of shame that used to police behavior;... it became fashionable to respect people for putting up with shame provided they were paid well to do so."[17] The writer was referring to the scandals on Wall Street, but the comment applied much more broadly.

The death of shame in America may be epitomized by the publication of a pseudo-novel in 2003 by Stephen Glass, a journalist who was fired by *The New Republic* for inventing numerous stories – including a fraudulent smear of a public figure that claimed the man to be a lecher and wife beater. Plainly

[15] Linda Williams, author of *Hard Core: Power, Pleasure, and the "Frenzy of the Visible"* (University of California Press, 1989), interviewed in the U.C. *Berkeleyan* (30 Sept. 2004), p. 6. Prof. Williams added: "The *New York Times* could not report on the Monica Lewinsky scandal without directly discussing the president's penis. The whole world was talking about the president's penis."

[16] *Time* (14 July 1980), p. 76.

[17] Martin Mayer, *Nightmare on Wall Street: Salomon Brothers and the Corruption of the Marketplace* (Simon & Schuster, 1993).

unembarrassed by his exposure as a serial fraud and liar, Glass found little difficulty getting a publisher *and a movie contract* for his autobiographical "novel,"
The Fabulist, whose main character, "Stephen Glass," is a serial fraud and liar.

By that time, so-called reality programming on television had made public humiliation and embarrassment for money a fashionable phenomenon. Although
it got its name only in 2000, it had its origins in the 1970s. That was when the
Loud family (aptly named) permitted a television crew to enter their home to
record, more or less continuously for many months, everything the entire family
did and said at home, including their arguments and their fights as well as their
moments of intimate discussions, confessions, and desires. In 1983, several of
the family were reinterviewed on TV, some of whom complained about "the horrid psychic damage" they suffered from the TV exposure – which evidently did
not deter them from returning to the medium for another go at "horrid psychic
damage."

Tell-all autobiographies by movie stars, or has-been movie stars, routinely included graphic details about their sexual escapades with other celebrities, often
dozens of them. In 1995, the ex-wife of West Virginia governor Gaston Caper-
ton wrote a novel based on her personal life, detailing her sexual relations with
her husband.[18] In 1997, a best-selling novelist published a memoir relating her
long incestuous affair with her own father.[19] In 1999, a man published a book
that described how his wife had been beaten and raped, speculating on whether
this accounted for her aloofness during his own sexual efforts with her.[20]

As constitutional scholar Robert Post commented: "If we don't sanction people who violate privacy, we can't expect the law to do much of that work for us.
The point is that we should actually care about privacy, and it's not clear that
we do."[21]

*   *   *

Ironically, this sea-change in the culture toward the abandonment of privacy
began shortly after the U.S. Supreme Court had begun to establish a constitutional right to privacy.

There had been, over time, numerous cases that came before the courts in
which judges avowed "the right to privacy" but usually found that right to be
tightly bound by other priorities. In 1952, for example, the Supreme Court declined to overturn a criminal conviction even though the critical evidence had
been illegally obtained and was excludable under federal rules but not under
state rules. Justice Felix Frankfurter, arguing for the Court, affirmed that "[t]he

---

[18] Reviewed in *Time* (31 July 1995), p. 40.
[19] Kathryn Harrison, *The Kiss* (Random House, 1997).
[20] Jamie Kalven, *Working with Available Light: A Family's World after Violence* (Norton, 1999).
[21] Quoted in Rosen, *Unwanted Gaze.*

security of one's privacy against arbitrary intrusion by the police – which is at the core of the Fourth Amendment – is basic to a free society." Yet he declined to "second guess" the state's judgment that excluding such evidence from a trial was not the best way to discipline a rogue police force.[22]

It was not until 1961 that the Court changed course and overturned a state court's criminal conviction by applying the federal standard for admissible evidence.[23] By that time, the civil rights movement – and in particular the conspicuous violation of the rights of minorities by police officers – had sensitized the Court to how fundamental principles of law were at stake regarding the right to privacy ("basic to a free society").

The Court's concerns over the right to privacy continued until 1965 to focus on police truculence and violations of the Fourth Amendment's proscription against the unreasonable search and seizure of private effects. The case that is usually cited as establishing privacy at a higher level among the Constitution's protections is *Griswold v. Conn.* (1965). It was in this case that the Court extended privacy consideration to include choices by private persons that conflicted with a community's moral sensibilities as embodied in law. In *Griswold*, the Court's 7-2 majority ruled that no state could lawfully prevent a married person from buying and using contraceptives; such state action intruded upon private behavior within the scope of personal liberty protected by the First, Fourth, and Fifth Amendments. Although the Constitution does not mention "privacy" specifically, the Court majority found that privacy lay within the "penumbra" of the protections guaranteeing personal liberty. A *New York Times* editorial at the time observed: "The Supreme Court's 7-2 decision invalidating Connecticut's birth-control law is a milestone in the judiciary's march toward enlarged guardianship of the nation's freedoms. It establishes a new 'right to privacy.' "[24]

Griswold was followed by a similar decision in 1972, this time extending to unmarried persons the right to buy and use contraceptives, even though part of the argument in *Griswold* was that the state cannot interfere with privacy sanctified in marriage: "The right of privacy," said Justice William Brennan, "[includes] the decision whether to bear or beget a child." And that right, the Court majority decided, was a personal one independent of marriage.[25] The phrasing Brennan chose, though seemingly innocuous at the time the opinion was issued, was deliberately aimed at the next big issue to come before the Court: the right of women to choose to beget – that is, to produce a child or to have a legal abortion.

[22] *Wolf v. Colorado*, 338 U.S. 25 (1949).
[23] *Mapp v. Ohio* (1961).
[24] *New York Times* (2 June 1965), p. 46, quoted in Stuart A. Scheingold, *The Politics of Rights* (Yale University Press, 1978 [1974]), p. 35.
[25] *Eisenstadt v. Baird* (1972).

Roe v. Wade (1973) picked up on the word "beget." The majority opinion in the case, written by Justice Harry Blackmun and for which he would long be remembered, was a complex and troubling one. Blackmun based the opinion on the newly developing doctrine of the right to privacy, arguing that the right to choose an abortion was a private matter between a woman and her physician. At the same time, Blackmun conceded that the state did have an interest in the well-being of the fetus. In the Court's majority opinion, that interest had to be balanced against the individual woman's right. With respect to the health of the mother, said Blackmun, the balance shifted in favor of the state by the end of the first trimester. Why then? Because, says the *Roe* opinion, at that point the danger of mortality to the woman from abortion becomes greater than the danger of mortality from childbirth. But with respect to the unborn fetus, the state's interest commences only after the second trimester, because that is when the fetus becomes viable. (Blackmun conceded that the 12-week and 24-week periods specified could be rolled back by new medical technology and that in any case were not intended to be fixed or definitive about "viability" or, for that matter, about mortal danger to the mother's health.)

Critics of Blackmun's opinion ranged from antiabortionists, who insisted that life begins with conception (i.e., the moment the sperm enters the egg) and that abortion is therefore murder, to "pro-choice" advocates, who rejected religious doctrine regarding what constitutes "life" and argued that the case for *Roe* would have been much stronger if founded in equal protection rather than privacy doctrine. That is, since women (not men) must undergo all the risks of bearing, delivering, and for the most part caring for the potential person, their right to choose to abort a pregnancy should be protected, within reasonable limits, by their right to equal protection of the law.[26]

The *Roe* decision almost immediately became a focal point for mobilizing the conservative, traditionalist backlash against the liberal progress in the third quarter of the twentieth century, although there was much more to the conservative agenda than opposition to abortion. The "right to life" movement served to rally a broadscale assault on the social revolutions of the Sixties as well as on the growth of federal power regarding taxes, racial relations, social welfare, and the regulation of corporate business. Conservative strategists had already been planning the counterattack by emphasizing the rights of local authorities to enforce or authorize school prayer. Abortion, however, offered a much larger target.

For one thing, it was an issue on which devout Roman Catholics, fundamentalist and evangelical Protestants, Orthodox Jews, and devout Muslims would

---

[26] See especially Edward Lazarus, *Closed Chambers: The Rise, Fall, and Future of the Modern Supreme Court* (Penguin, 1999), pp. 329–425.

likely agree. School prayer, on the other hand, had once alienated many non-Protestants who worried over how school officials in predominantly Protestant America might choose the "wrong" kind of prayers.

For a time, the Court majority held fast against the ideological onslaught that followed and that increasingly contributed to the polarization of American politics and jurisprudence. In *Planned Parenthood of Missouri v. Danforth* (1976), Missouri attorney general John Danforth (later U.S. senator and principal sponsor of Clarence Thomas's controversial nomination for the Supreme Court) tried to force a woman seeking an abortion (1) to get permission from her husband or from the natural father and (2) if a minor, to get permission from a parent. The Court said No: in the first place, a husband or other man cannot veto a potential mother's decision; and second, the argument that a parent had the right to veto a decision made by a physician and minor patient "in order to preserve the integrity of the family" failed on both logical and empirical grounds to satisfy the need to show that an impelling state interest was at stake. Justice Blackmun wrote again for the 7-2 Court; Justices Rehnquist and White dissented, as they had in *Roe*. As yet, conservatism in America had not become dominated by far-right, largely "faith based" ideologues. Three of President Nixon's four Court appointees – Burger, Powell, and Blackmun – were among the majority in *Roe* and in *Danforth*. So were President Eisenhower's appointees, Brennan and Stewart.[27]

But the right-wing coalition that promoted the candidacy of Ronald Reagan for president at the end of the 1970s made repeal of *Roe* its political test, as it would do for subsequent presidential candidates. Thus, the Reagan administration made antiabortion its main requirement for considering court appointments. This was ironic – or a bit of hypocrisy (take your choice) – considering that, as governor of California, Reagan had signed one of the nation's most liberal measures legalizing abortion. That was before abortion had become a wedge issue for insinuating a retroconservative agenda into mainstream politics, an agenda aimed specifically at reversing many of the dramatic social, economic, and political changes in American life of the previous forty years.

When Chief Justice Warren Burger resigned, President Reagan elevated one of the two dissenters in *Roe* (William Rehnquist) to be chief justice, and to replace Burger he appointed Antonin Scalia, a scholar whose conservative religious views often determined his judicial opinions. Subsequent appointments by presidents Ronald Reagan and George Herbert Bush of Sandra Day O'Connor, Anthony Kennedy, Clarence Thomas, and David Souter were supposed to give the

---

[27] Thurgood Marshall and William Douglas, who were the other two of the seven-member majority in *Roe* and *Danforth*, were the only remaining justices on the Court who had been appointed by Democratic presidents.

antiabortionists their victory. Souter, however, proved to be more independent than conservatives expected, and O'Connor drew fine lines between limiting access to abortion and overturning *Roe*. Before the Rehnquist Court ended with the chief justice's death in 2005, the key case was *Planned Parenthood of Southwestern Pennsylvania v. Casey*. In that case, Justices O'Connor, Kennedy, and Souter "defected" to make a majority of five (along with Justice Stevens and *Roe*'s principal author, Blackmun) for upholding *Roe*.[28]

Bit by bit over the course of the twentieth century's last quarter, the Court, Congress, and state legislatures chipped away at the gains made on behalf of women's personal and private choice in the matter of whether to beget or bear a child. It seemed unlikely that the right to choose an abortion would be erased outright in law, but unchecked intimidation by rowdy antiabortionists as well as quasi-legal harassment by zealous and/or politically ambitious district attorneys and attorneys general made access to abortion, especially by the poor, increasingly difficult and even dangerous. Most seriously, as the century came to an end it was evident that the judiciary no longer would serve as a reliable shield against a populist animus that had little regard for personal privacy in general and in particular for the privacy of those Americans whose choices conflicted with other Americans' moral certainties.

Over the course of the third quarter of the twentieth century, then, constitutional law changed in the direction of granting substantial protection to an individual's right to privacy. The changes in law, however, did not meet with overwhelming popular approval and remained politically controversial as the century ended. Meanwhile, public and private agencies as well as government officials and commercial interests increasingly made use of new technology to make uninvited intrusions on Americans' privacy. At the same time, moreover, Americans generally demonstrated a sharply declining interest in personal privacy. Thus, although personal privacy gained some small ground in some features of law during the last third of the twentieth century, the revolutionary change in Americans' regard for privacy consisted in its substantial demise.

---

[28] 112 Sup. Ct. 2791 (1992). Although the majority's opinion did weaken the "right" of a woman to decide on the abortion of a nonviable fetus by upholding Pennsylvania's requirement of a 24-hour waiting period and counseling, the key argument in support of *Roe* emphasized the importance of sticking to precedent especially when the Court faced a highly polarizing issue. "Whatever the premises of the opposition may be," wrote Justice Souter, "only the most convincing justification under accepted standards of precedent could suffice to demonstrate that a later decision overruling the first was anything but a surrender to political pressure, and an unjustified repudiation of the principle on which the Court staked its authority in the first instance." To "overrule under fire," wrote Souter, "would subvert the Court's legitimacy beyond any serious question."

PART THREE

COUNTERREVOLUTION

The impulses behind yesterday's reform may be put in the service of reform today, but they may also be enlisted in the service of reaction.[1]

Richard Hofstadter

Ideology makes it unnecessary for people to confront individual issues on their individual merits. One simply turns to the ideological vending machine, and out comes the prepared formulae. When these beliefs are suffused by apocalyptic fervor, ideas become weapons, and with dreadful results.[2]

Daniel Bell

Traditional ideas are often attractive simply because they are traditional; accepted as eternally true, they remove the need for independent thought and for adjustment to novelty, which is frequently frightening.[3]

William J. Bouwsma

The rapidity of change beginning with the onset of the Second World War evoked both dismay and delight. Certainly most Americans welcomed at least some of the revolutionary changes we have discussed. But for many, the transformation of American society created much anxiety and distress. The entanglement of the United States in foreign alliances and the exposure of the nation to dangers from abroad; the changing culture and structure of business; the breaching of traditional standards of sexual decorum; the challenge to traditional relationships among the races and between men and women, as well as changing attitudes

---

[1] Richard Hofstadter, *The Age of Reform* (Knopf, 1956), p. 21.

[2] Quoted in Mark Gerson, *The Neoconservative Vision: From the Cold War to the Culture Wars* (Madison Books, 1996), p. 94.

[3] William J. Bouwsma, *Venice and the Defense of Republican Liberty: Renaissance Values in the Age of the Counter Revolution* (University of California Press, 1968), p. 4.

regarding relationships between men and men and between women and women –
these and other phenomena of modern America raised questions about policies,
standards, mores, morals, and propriety that probably most people normally
prefer to accept unquestioningly. It was discomfiting to be faced with questions
whose answers had once seemed firm, conclusive, and unequivocal.

As the country entered the final quarter of the century amid a troubled economy and weakened international standing, the tensions evoked by the changes
heightened. And the key agents of change – the liberals who had used the strength
of the Democratic coalition to promote change – became targets for the resentment, disappointment, and frustrations that came to center stage in the seventies.
Even the disgrace of a conservative Republican president failed to revive the by-
then flagging impulse for further gains on behalf of consumer interests, racial and
gender equity, protection for the environment, and the health and welfare of the
country's disadvantaged. The Watergate scandal notwithstanding, a profoundly
regressive antiliberal wave washed over the country for the remainder of the century and on into the new. In fact the scandal, coming at the climax of America's
calamitous engagement in Indochina, seemed only to increase Americans' disenchantment with government generally, a disenchantment already activated by
agitation over some of the effects of the social revolutions and government's role
in promoting them.

All of this is part of the story of the collapse of the liberal Democratic coalition – and its replacement by a radically regressive Republican coalition during
the last quarter of the twentieth century.

14

Liberalism: Ascension and Declension

In an essay written in 1977, the historians Morton Borden and Otis L. Graham, Jr., asked: "What If There Had Been No Watergate?" The scandal that forced the resignation of the president, they pointed out, could have evaporated at a number of junctures except for a series of unlikely developments, not least the almost accidental discovery of the Oval Office tape recordings. Those recordings revealed unequivocally not only that President Richard Nixon had engaged more or less continually throughout his presidency in "dirty tricks," some of them blatantly illegal, against people he labeled "enemies" but also – in the particular case of the break-in at the Democratic National Committee headquarters in the Watergate building complex in Washington, DC – that he had personally directed the attempted cover-up of the burglary.

The investigation that followed uncovered much that was rotten in American politics, from the gross violations of the Corrupt Practices Act (which had outlawed direct campaign contributions by corporations) through abuses and attempted abuses of the various investigating agencies of government: the IRS, the FBI, the CIA, and the military intelligence agencies. It was hard not to descend into woeful cynicism.[1]

If Richard Nixon had not resigned the presidency, he faced almost certain impeachment by the House of Representatives and conviction by the Senate. In July 1974 the House Judiciary Committee, in a bipartisan vote, charged the president with sixteen specific counts of unlawful conduct. They included (1) obstruction of justice, (2) conspiracy, (3) making false statements, (4) illegal wiretapping,

---

[1] Such cynicism gave wings to the probably apocryphal remark attributed to Secretary of State Henry Kissinger (after Vice-President Spiro Agnew had resigned to avoid prosecution for felony corruption) that Nixon had appointed Gerald Ford to replace him in the hope that Congress would never impeach him knowing that the lightly regarded Ford would then succeed to the presidency.

(5) subornation of perjury, (6) violation of civil rights, and (7) illegal use of IRS information, plus eight other particulars. In the end, the committee approved three articles of impeachment: (i) trying to cover up a felony burglary by lying; (ii) interfering with government agencies and obstructing justice by offering and preparing to offer bribes to material witnesses in the felony inquiry; and (iii) repeatedly engaging in conduct that violated the constitutional rights of citizens, that impaired the due and proper administration of justice, and that interfered with the conduct of lawful inquires by Congress and other government agencies. Separately, a grand jury investigation concluded: "There is probable cause to believe that Richard M. Nixon (among others) was a member of a conspiracy to defraud the United States and to obstruct justice." The grand jury asked the special prosecutor to identify the president as an "unindicted co-conspirator" in several and various illegal acts. Only President Ford's blanket pardon of Nixon for all alleged crimes, known and as yet unspecified, saved the man from prosecution for acts that have sent many "ordinary" Americans to jail for many years.

It was reasonable to speculate, then, on how post-Watergate history would have been different if the unlikely had not happened. But after examining the two years following Richard Nixon's resignation, Borden and Graham concluded that the dramatic scandal had made, and would make, little difference. It was, they wrote, an ephemeral "convulsion of the body politic" but little else.[2]

Their essay focused on the growth of presidential power, "the Imperial Presidency" as historian Arthur Schlesinger dubbed it.[3] The authors believed that the growth of presidential power remained undeterred by the ignominious demise of the Nixon presidency. This should not have been surprising. Foreign affairs and national security continued to demand tremendous government resources and attention. Responsibility for dealing with them still lay preeminently with the president, whose power as commander in chief of the armed forces was extended by the unilateral power to suppress information in the name of "national security." The Imperial Presidency would live on. It would, in fact, rise to unprecedented heights with the installation in 2001 of the first administration of G. W. Bush.

But other developments that followed Watergate seem on their face rather less probable, even "illogical." Considering that the Nixon presidency purposefully sought a halt in the progress of Lyndon Johnson's Great Society program, it might have been expected that Nixon's utter disgrace and the defeat of his hand-picked Republican successor in 1976 might have restored force to the reform movement. But that didn't happen; quite the contrary.

---

[2] Morton Borden & Otis L. Graham, Jr., *Speculations on American History* (Heath, 1977), pp. 183–96.
[3] Arthur M. Schlesinger, Jr., *The Imperial Presidency* (Houghton-Mifflin, 1973).

Why did the quarter century following the disgrace of a conservative Republican administration feature a dramatic swing further to the right and climax during the final two decades in a series of ultraconservative Republican triumphs rather than a continuation of the reform movements of the Sixties? What happened to the liberal Democratic coalition, which had propelled the War on Poverty, the Civil Rights Act, Medicare, and Medicaid as well as the environmental, worker, and consumer protection measures that were the gems of liberal reform during the third quarter of the century? Conversely, on what did conservatives – and eventually a radical right wing – build their ascendancy?

*   *   *

When the third quarter of the century began, liberalism was in the ascendant. Lionel Trilling, in his much quoted *The Liberal Imagination* (1950), was moved to remark:

In the United States at this time liberalism is not only the dominant but even the sole intellectual tradition. It is the plain fact that nowadays there are no conservative or reactionary ideas in general circulation. This does not mean, of course, that there is no impulse to conservatism or to reaction .... But the conservative impulse and the reactionary impulse do not, with some isolated and some ecclesiastical exceptions, express themselves in ideas but only in action or in irritable mental gestures which seek to resemble ideas.[4]

Five years later, political scientist S. M. Lipset similarly remarked how there was virtually no intellectual content to antiliberal conservatism in the country besides "laissez-faire," an antigovernment faith in a so-called free market economy.[5] As late as 1962 the sociologist Daniel Bell also noted the dominance of liberal thought: "There seems to be little meaningful polarity today. There is no coherent conservative force .... Nor does a viable left exist in the United States today."[6]

By a "left," Bell and others generally meant advocates of social reform who used Marxist or quasi-Marxist class dynamics to analyze politics and who called for what they regarded as "fundamental changes" in the American political economy. A politics shaped by the left would aim at greater social equality through purposefully redistributive income programs. It would aim at a departure from the capitalist ethic that gave highest priority to economic growth

---

[4] Lionel Trilling, *The Liberal Imagination* (Anchor, 1950), p. 6.
[5] Seymour Martin Lipset, "The Sources of 'The Radical Right'" (1955), in Daniel Bell, ed., *The Radical Right* (Anchor, 1964), p. 360.
[6] Daniel Bell, "The Dispossessed" (1962), in Bell (ibid.), p. 41.

and the accumulation of wealth through the privileging of private self-interested entrepreneurship. It would promote greater state ownership of productive resources, especially enterprises that manage the economy's infrastructure (public utilities, energy, transportation, and similar social overhead agencies). In brief, "the left" in America in the forties and fifties meant some form of democratic socialism, comparable to what developed in many Western European nations including West Germany, Sweden, Britain, and France.

But, as Bell argued, by 1950 there were few in America who still saw any promise of reaching the Good Society in a polity organized along democratic socialist lines. Nearly all of even those intellectuals, labor leaders, and theologians who in the 1930s had shown some measure of enthusiasm for either Fabian or Marxian socialism had abandoned that view – or hope. Fascism and Stalinism had projected portentous images of what a strong, command political economy might produce. For most Americans, including once-radical intellectuals, Hitler and Stalin had made a political economy shaped by minimally controlled private commercial market forces seem a safer, more promising alternative after all. Although many progressive American intellectuals, labor leaders, and the like retained a critical view of corporate domination of American society, by the end of the forties they came to recognize the political impossibility of doing much more than tinkering with a marketplace dominated by megacorporations. They concentrated on using law to shape market outcomes so as to produce a marginally more equitable allocation of social resources and rewards within a liberal capitalist political economy.

In brief, by the 1950s the ideological field was left to liberals who had constructed a widely accepted consensus on the responsibility of government to enhance individual liberty and welfare at home and abroad in the face of attacks from both the right and the left. That consensus included an acceptance of modern capitalism – that is, an acceptance of consigning to market mechanisms the responsibility for allocating most resources and social rewards – although modified to provide public services, including a "safety net" for the disadvantaged, public support for the arts and education, and selective governmental limits on private power. It also included the need for cooperation between the state and private enterprise in order to assure economic growth and control of potentially destructive business cycles. These were things that an uncontrolled market economy could not be expected to provide. Meanwhile, against the absolutism of the Soviet Union and its supporters at home, liberals remained strongly anticommunist.[7]

---

[7] See the discussion of "the ideology of the liberal consensus" in Godfrey Hodgson, *America in Our Time* (Dell, 1976).

But Daniel Bell's appraisal about the end of ideological challenges to liberalism seems to have been badly timed. In the Sixties, both an ideological right and a somewhat confused ideological left surfaced to present major challenges to liberalism. Those on the left attracted the most attention, both in the public arena at the time and in historians' accounts of the Sixties. Yet it was the challenge from the right that proved by far to be the most formidable, effective, and enduring.

An early, sympathetic history of the conservative movement that blossomed in the seventies confirmed the moribund character of conservatism in the immediate postwar decade. "In 1945," wrote George Nash in 1976, "no articulate, coordinated, self-consciously conservative intellectual force existed in the United States. There were," Nash went on, "at most, scattered voices of protest, profoundly pessimistic about the future of their country." But the Sixties would witness "a momentous transformation of the Right" that would move it toward eventual majority status in American government and culture. "Twenty-five years earlier it had been almost an underground phenomenon," Nash observed, but it was clear already in 1972 that the right had gained "a chance to exercise national leadership."[8]

While historians and pundits focused their attention on the radicalism of the left in the Sixties, a conservative wave had already begun swelling in the 1950s and continued to mount until it washed over the country in the eighties. By 1980, with the election of Ronald Reagan to the presidency, a truly deep-seated conservatism had settled in. In fact, except for the media's readiness to accept the terminology preferred by the political managers seeking to reverse the liberal achievements, the so-called Reagan revolution was avowedly reactionary, not conservative at all, and properly should be so described. Its agenda included an almost complete *reversal* of the liberal changes in American society that had begun with the New Deal in the 1930s and had culminated in the Great Society programs of the sixties and early seventies. Although the Republicans would lose the White House in 1976 following designated-President Ford's ill-advised pardon of the deposed Richard Nixon, counterrevolutionary forces had clearly taken control of the country's politics. Democrat Jimmy Carter campaigned for the presidency as a "conservative" and ran his administration (ineptly) on retrenchment principles. Nor did the eight-year Democratic presidency in the nineties do more than hold on to a shrinking defensive perimeter around the liberal gains, with President Bill Clinton fulfilling his campaign promise to "end welfare as we know it" and at one point echoing the conservative mantra that

---

[8] George Nash, *The Conservative Intellectual Movement in America Since 1945* (Harper, 1976), pp. xvi–xvii.

"the age of big government is over." (His successor, George W. Bush, would make a mockery of that prediction – on behalf of a still more retrogressive and increasingly authoritarian political agenda.)

By the late 1970s, the liberal Democratic coalition had been shattered, while some of its remnants conducted a strategic retreat into territory staked out by conservatives. So-called New Democrats found political advantage in joining conservatives in calling for "deregulation" of many industries, in reversing measures designed to assist the poor and reduce poverty, in reducing taxes for the benefit mainly of the top 5 percent of family and individual incomes, and in echoing the disingenuous call for "ending big government." By century's end, the conservative counterrevolution, or reaction, had not entirely succeeded in undoing the liberal achievements of the previous sixty years. But it did compromise many of them, especially in the areas of working conditions, the economic safety net, the environment, civil liberties, and income distribution. In 2000, a freakish presidential election gave new and vigorous impetus to the reactionary trend.

15

The Liberal Democratic Coalition

Modern American liberalism departed in important ways from the minimal-state, market-oriented liberalism that arose in Europe and the United States in the late eighteenth century. From its origins, liberalism placed individual liberty at the center of the purposes of political organization. It tended to measure liberty, moreover, in terms of access to economic opportunity and the expansion of private property rights. It reversed the ancient rule that required individuals to serve the community, the king, or the state, or some transcendent moral order embodied in the king or the state. It substituted "citizen" for "subject," thereby stressing legal equality among members of society rather than hierarchy and subordination. In Europe even after the toppling of the monarchies, a relatively autonomous state remained strong in the hands of a professional bureaucracy or civil service. Liberalism in Europe thus continued to vie with long-standing tory or *noblesse* traditions of government that in many respects subordinated private economic ambition to grander notions of commonweal. In other words, outside the United States, liberalism remained understood as a system of social organization identified with a minimalist state that permitted the maximum pursuit of private personal opportunity and corporate business prosperity in a market economy; whereas, in general, older, traditionalist notions of statecraft vied with liberalism for control of policy.

In the United States, different historical circumstances and traditions called for different strategies. There was little that resembled a professional, independent civil service or bureaucracy in America. Grand notions of commonweal were few and usually were strongly contested. Except in wartime, the business of the private sector trumped most particular purposes of the state. The business of America, as Calvin Coolidge put it, was business.

Indeed, government in the United States historically had served primarily to mediate among Americans' competing business interests. Public policy typically followed the lines of force produced by competition among private economic groups at particular times and on particular issues. The so-called regulatory state that re-emerged in the late nineteenth century had its origins in demands by private business interests seeking help from the state to redress competitive disadvantages in the marketplace. The concentration of power in the private sector, a by-product of the Industrial Revolution, spurred on that development. In brief, the well-celebrated Populist, Progressive, and New Deal reforms developed above all out of tensions within the business community and were not – as some histories have treated them – the result of pressure from social criticism external to marketplace rivalry.

The Great Depression and the Second World War did bring some changes. Among other things, they led Americans to build a significant government bureaucracy that fostered notions of commonweal independent of strictly business concerns. Winning the war, of course, topped priorities for the commonwealth. Typically Americans continued to regard "big government" with suspicion. But while they continued to define liberty almost exclusively in terms of access to private economic opportunity, the concentration of private power during the corporation revolution of the late nineteenth century led many less powerful Americans to see the virtue of an activist state that protected them. Furthermore, by mid-twentieth century – especially during the struggle between organized labor and organized capital – liberals had begun increasingly to extend the definition of liberty to include the communicative freedoms (speech, press, art, assembly). Ultimately they would extend the definition to individual choices of lifestyle.

The Cold War and the civil rights movement combined to move the liberal agenda in that direction. During "hot" wars, Americans have always tolerated considerable governmental controls on personal or civil liberties. The pressure on civil liberties symbolized by McCarthyism and its kin during the seemingly interminable Cold War sensitized the country, and the judicial system, to the importance of the communicative rights for citizens who would call themselves "free." The civil rights movement, meanwhile, sensitized Americans to the evils of adverse discrimination against citizens because of "who they are" – that is, with respect to race, religion, gender, sexual orientation, age, or disability.

American liberalism thus changed emphasis. Liberals came to call upon government to intervene to protect individual liberty and welfare, especially against economic calamity, private business truculence, and social oppression. Liberalism in America thus parted from European liberalism, which remained focused on minimizing the state.

As a political force in the middle third of the twentieth century, American liberals built their strength on four main pillars. They joined with different groups in their commitment to international activism on behalf of liberal objectives abroad as well as to activism at home on behalf of civil rights, on behalf of the needy, and on behalf of moderating undesirable economic outcomes. More than any other single factor, what made their strength effective was their commitment to the Democratic national party. By the mid- to late sixties, each of those pillars began to erode.

The Democratic Party Base

During the thirties, a relatively small number of liberals drawn from organized labor, law, journalism, some sectors of the business community, and a handful of major universities managed to capture key strategic positions within the Democratic Party. The main constituents of the coalition outside the "Solid South" were: (1) urban ethnics (Irish, Italians, Jews, Slavs); (2) blue-collar union members, including many of the same ethnic groups; (3) some internationally oriented businesses that found the Democrats to be more congenial than traditionally isolationist and protectionist Republicans; and (4) a wide variety of intellectuals in and out of academia. Although the intellectuals did not generally share the outlook of racist southerners or urban bosses, they enjoyed political strength from the Southern Democrats who dominated Congress and from big-city political machine bosses. Both the southerners and the city bosses prized the largesse that an activist federal government provided for their constituencies.

Through that coalition, liberal intellectuals enjoyed unusual political power. By the fifties, as one historian noted, "liberal intellectuals [had become] the soul of the party, the guardians of its ideals."[1] Although the alliance with southerners and city bosses placed limits on the liberal agenda throughout the thirties and forties, much of a growing federal bureaucracy meanwhile came to be staffed by liberals. By the fifties, they began a breakout from those limits.

Both the Depression and World War II required the executive branch of the federal government to take a strong leadership role in both domestic and foreign policy making. Both events resulted in a national civil service giving the state capacity to work for purposes of the commonweal as distinct from the purposes of coalitions of particular interest groups. Liberal influence in the federal agencies, even when Republicans controlled the White House as they did in the fifties and early seventies, made it possible during most of the postwar era for liberals to wield unprecedented leverage in the shaping of national policy. In the sixties, presidents Kennedy and Johnson drew heavily on liberal intellectuals from

---

[1] Allen J. Matusow, *The Unraveling of America: A History of Liberalism in the 1960s* (Harper & Row, 1984), p. 16.

major universities, going so far as to bring into the White House such historians as Arthur Schlesinger, Jr., and Eric Goldman as well as political scientist John Roche, a former head of the liberal Americans for Democratic Action.

From its vantage points in the Democratic party, a liberal elite managed to promote like-minded liberals into key places in Congress, among legislative aides, and in the courts at least to the mid-seventies. But eventually a large-scale defection of the southerners from the party over civil rights issues beginning in the late forties would seriously wound the coalition.

More critically, by the late sixties the word "liberal" came to be used as a term of opprobrium not only by conservatives but also by mostly young, self-described radicals. For the impatient young insurgents such as those who triggered the Free Speech movement at the University of California, Berkeley, in 1964, liberals were too compromising, too slow, too committed to incremental rather than radical change, and too feckless on behalf of their own ideals. Convinced that reforms had proven ineffectual in removing the social and economic evils that they saw so clearly, the young radicals demanded an overhaul of "the system," the basic structures of American society. Ridicule and derision were their favorite weapons, directed mostly at liberals. Conservatives, for them, seemed not worth much of their attention. They slipped easily into hyperbole, forgot about modulating their remarks, and went straight to denouncing their targets as "imperialists," "fascists," and "racists."

The battering that the liberals would endure at the hands of the new generation of social activists who were impatient with the slow progress toward their view of a just society would lead many liberal intellectuals to turn their fire to the left. They joined traditionalists in attacking the new radicals. They became exasperated by the ill-mannered, "in your face" scorn directed at them by people who should have joined with them in social criticism. They were put off even more by the ends-focused, means-heedless activism of the New Left (so-called because most of their partisans renounced the old, Marxist left). Liberals had had their fill with the similarly absolutist onslaught of McCarthyism in the forties and fifties, when most of the New Left youth were still in grade school.

Moreover, too much of the behavior of the new radicals reminded liberals of the Stalinists whom liberals had learned to loathe in the thirties. It seemed that anyone who disputed the radicals' demands was a racist or a fascist or both. Crucial numbers of liberal intellectuals began leaving the Democratic Party in the mid-sixties as New Left influence in the party seemed to grow. The desertions accelerated in 1972 with the presidential nomination of Senator George McGovern, whose opposition to the war in Vietnam took on the character of opposing liberal internationalism itself. To counter the McGovern nomination, a group of hard-line Democrats – including John P. Roche, Eugene V. Rostow (an assistant secretary of state under President Johnson), Democratic senator

Henry Jackson's legislative aide Richard Perle, and Georgetown professor Jeane Kirkpatrick – formed a new group they called the Coalition for a Democratic Majority. In 1976 the CDM would merge with the newly revived Committee on the Present Danger, a hard-line group dominated by conservative Republicans. They were led by then-CIA chief George Herbert Walker Bush, who would become vice-president under Ronald Reagan and then president in his own right in 1989.

By the mid-seventies, defection of many leading Democrats sapped the party of some of its brightest and most energetic figures. At the same time, many long-time left-leaning liberals found themselves pondering how they came to stand closer to those who called themselves conservatives while drifting away from erstwhile friends who continued to call themselves liberals.[2] Many leading liberal intellectuals and government workers would find themselves among a growing army of what pundits came to call "neoconservatives." The defections would deal the Democratic party a staggering blow.

Liberal Internationalism

In international affairs, liberals projected a purposeful commitment to American intervention on behalf of liberal objectives. The commitment was decisively anti-isolationist, antifascist, and anticommunist. The "Munich syndrome" informed liberal policy making: Never again appeasement of dictators!

Among the distinguishing features of postwar and Cold War liberal internationalism were, first, the premise that communism's appeal in both industrialized and underdeveloped countries rested primarily on political oppression and economic distress; and second, an insistence that the communist threat to American interests was principally to be found abroad, not in domestic politics.

To fight communism after 1945 conservatives, too, became internationalists. But in contrast to liberals, they argued that communism spread chiefly through the work of single-minded conspirators who were financed and directed mainly by Moscow, helped along by (liberal) dupes and "fellow travelers" who supported communist causes at home and who sought gains internationally and within the United States by means of deception, terror, treason, and sometimes direct military force. Conservatives defined "communist causes" rather broadly. They directed the pejorative at those who sought to enlarge civil rights and protect civil liberties. McCarthyism typified the conservative approach to the "communist menace." Thus William F. Buckley, Jr., founding editor of the leading

---

[2] See e.g. Nathan Glazer, *Remembering the Answers: Essays on the American Student Revolt* (Basic Books, 1970), especially the Introduction and ch. 13.

conservative journal *National Review,* could declare: "McCarthyism is a movement around which men of good will and stern morality can close ranks."[3]

The Republican Eisenhower administration worked strenuously to maintain
the main elements of liberal internationalism, putting down isolationist pressure
within the GOP. But it gravitated increasingly toward subordinating economic
measures to building up military means for containing Soviet power. The return of liberal Democrats to the White House in 1960 saw a renewal of liberal
international activism, with programs such as the Peace Corps, the Alliance for
Progress, and the United States Agency for International Development (USAID).
But the Kennedy and Johnson administrations also bought into the Eisenhower
program of military and paramilitary confrontation – in Cuba, the Congo, and
the Dominican Republic as well as in Southeast Asia. Moreover, USAID proved
minimally successful, largely because it too often served as a cover for CIA paramilitary operations.

Containment was achieved by means of the Truman Doctrine, the Marshall
Plan, and the so-called Point Four program (for technical assistance to developing
countries) – the gems of liberal international achievement. The bold, forceful rejection of North Korea's military invasion of South Korea may count as another.

But the traumatic divisiveness of the Vietnam War would batter the liberal
Democratic coalition. Vietnam would produce, as one close observer remarked,
"a chasm which ... divided American intellectuals more severely even than the
issue of Stalinism and communism in the 1930s and 1940s."[4] A similar chasm
developed among Americans in other sectors of the society. For many in the
1970s, a Vietnam syndrome replaced the Munich syndrome: Never again med-
dle militarily in other nations' "civil wars."

The Regulatory/Welfare State

Liberals joined also in a commitment to a regulatory and welfare state. That
is, they saw the need to use the state to intervene actively (a) to adjust advantages and disadvantages among competitors in the marketplace while promoting
economic growth, and (b) to provide minimal living conditions, a "safety net,"
for less fortunate Americans. The dual objectives aimed at overcoming market failure by stimulating economic growth, providing for sustained consumer
demand, and enhancing profit opportunities *as well as* guaranteeing minimum
resources for people that were poorly served by the market. The commitment involved some redistributive measures and transfer payments. It had two prongs:

---

[3] W. F. Buckley, Jr., & L. Brent Bozell, *McCarthy and His Enemies* (H. Regnery, 1954), p. 335.
[4] Glazer, *Remembering the Answers,* p. 277.

(1) transfer payments to selected business interests in order to sustain the welfare of the industrial and postindustrial economy; and (2) transfer payments on a needs basis to improve the quality of personal life.

Thus, the welfare state's constituency included corporate agriculture as well as children in indigent families; it included the temporarily and chronically unemployed as well as the computer, telecommunications, and pharmaceutical industries that depended on state funding of scientific and technological research;[5] it included timber harvesters and cattle growers as well as the aged and sick; it included exporters and overseas investors as well as small depositors and home owners; it included major defense contractors and airlines as well as rust-belt union members. Most welfare transfer payments went to various sectors of the business community, especially if tax credits and deductions (tax expenditures) are included as payments. But beginning with the New Deal, substantial transfers went for the first time in U.S. history to the poor and disadvantaged as well.

The premise underlying such activism rested on the observation that marketplace outcomes often failed to serve vital public interests, among them stimulating overall economic growth and innovation, moderating boom-and-bust business cycles, maintaining public goods such as roads and parks, and – commensurate with an affluent society – providing humane care for the poor, the unwell, the ineffectual, the disadvantaged, the feeble, and the unlucky.

In developing regulatory agencies and legislation throughout their history, Americans sought to redistribute advantages among entrepreneur, laborer, investor, and consumer competitors for shares in marketplace outcomes. Whatever the rhetoric often expressed by business leaders and their trade journals, the regulatory state had never been "antibusiness" but had in fact mostly been created by rival interests within the business community. The vast majority of measures that went into the making of the regulatory state, from the nineteenth century on, originated in the competition for advantage among diverse business interests – each of which sought to use the state in order to shape or overturn marketplace outcomes. Indeed, by the end of the thirties, some sectors of the business and corporate community had come to acknowledge the necessity for a regulatory state in order to avert the market failures that underlay the Great Depression. Business organizations such as the Committee for Economic Development, an elite corporate umbrella organization, provided much of the policy-making leadership recruited by Keynesian-oriented U.S. administrations throughout the third quarter of the century.

---

[5] Just one example: The pharmaceutical industry accounted for only about 45 percent of all spending for pharmaceutical research in the United States in 2000, while the majority of new drug patents awarded to drug companies had their origin in government-funded research. John McMillan, *Reinventing the Bazaar: A Natural History of Markets* (Norton, 2002), p. 33.

But then, belatedly, in the late sixties liberal activism in domestic policy produced a spate of measures that did come from initiatives outside the business community and that aimed at benefits for nonbusiness sectors of the society. In some cases, those benefits would add costs to doing business in the country.

Many of the measures amounted to the repeal or modification of some of the privileges in law granted to business entrepreneurs during the first 150 years of U.S. history. The privileges were designed to externalize from private firms the social as well as material costs of the commercial, corporation, and industrial revolutions. The privileges, mostly granted over the course of the nineteenth century, included rewriting labor, property, corporation, and liability law so as to reduce entrepreneurial risk. Reducing entrepreneurial risk, it was understood, would facilitate economic and particularly industrial growth. The costs of industrial damage to water, land, labor, timber, and air resources simply were passed on to the society at large. It unburdened the enterprises that produced those costs.

By contrast, liberal activism in the Sixties took on concerns about the environment; employee and consumer health and safety; fraudulent packaging, advertising, labeling, and lending; endangered species; and civil rights. Such concerns were not specifically antibusiness and even enjoyed considerable support from some leaders within the business community. But unquestionably they clashed head-on with businesses' primary concern for profits. As long as the economy remained robust, as it did in the sixties, reformers faced relatively little resistance to measures that served the health of the nation's people and the environment. In the "stagflationary" seventies, however, such measures appeared to clash with the general public's renewed anxiety about economic growth.

The other thrust of the welfare state was directed toward guaranteeing minimum living standards for Americans who were poorly served by the market. It included federal and state redistributive measures, especially on a needs basis, to improve the quality of personal life. Lyndon Johnson's Great Society program marked the high point of such efforts. In an address to the nation in June 1964, the president declared:

We stand at the edge of the greatest era in the life of any nation. For the first time in world history, we have the abundance and the ability to free every man from hopeless want, and to free every person to find fulfillment in the works of his mind or the labor of his hands .... This nation, this people, this generation, has man's first chance to create a Great Society; a society of success without squalor, beauty without barrenness, works of genius without the wretchedness of poverty.[6]

As one historian has described it: "The Great Society ... marked one of the century's most vigorous moments of utilization of the state to shape markets and

---

[6] *New York Times* (26 June 1964).

mitigate their distributional outcomes .... For a remarkable moment, the country's domestic politics focused sympathetically and constructively on the least advantaged."[7]

Looking at the matter from the vantage of a country that historically had depended on continuous economic growth to subdue its ethnic, class, and religious tensions, the Great Society measures may be viewed as an effort to mobilize the underemployed energies and talents of large numbers of Americans as well as to arm them with purchasing power. These would include the poor, whose inadequate skills, training, and/or motivation sapped their productivity, as well as those victims of racial, gender, and ethnic discrimination who were blocked by bigotry or mindless stereotyping from developing the skills, aptitude, and motivation that might have permitted them to contribute more fully to the political economy. Before the Great Society was eclipsed by a politics of greed, the physically and psychologically handicapped came to be included.

It is important to understand that these reforms occurred in the face of adverse political power. That is, here was an example of a state making changes that benefited the weak and relatively powerless, a politically insignificant constituency, while making the rest of the society pay most of the bill. That so much was accomplished says something significant about the willingness of the more affluent majority at the time to pay the price and about the non–zero-sum mentality that underlay that willingness. It also tells much about the high risk that the liberal Democratic leadership undertook – and ultimately would pay for.

Extraordinary economic growth and a flattening of business cycles over the course of sixty years represent some of the gems of the liberal achievement for Americans' economic concerns. Medicare, Medicaid, EPA, OSHA, the Clean Air Act, the Endangered Species Act, and the War on Poverty were among the gems of the liberal Democratic coalition's achievements toward improving Americans' quality of life. The reduction of the incidence of poverty from 20 percent of American households in 1960 to about 11 percent by the mid-seventies was a truly remarkable achievement.

But the economic difficulties of the seventies severely undermined the liberal Democratic coalition. It was a decade of mounting competition from foreign imports, declining business profits, high inflation, and high unemployment. It was an era in which the Baby Boomers were reaching employment age and competing for good-paying jobs and careers in a relatively inelastic job market. It was a time when millions of women and minorities, newly freed from the constraints of traditional roles and adverse discrimination, competed for jobs conventionally

---

7 Ira Katznelson, "Was the Great Society a Lost Opportunity?" in Steve Fraser & Gary Gerstle, eds., *The Rise and Fall of the New Deal Order, 1930–1980* (Princeton University Press, 1989), p. 196. Katznelson's overall argument is that Johnson unfortunately missed an opportunity to overhaul American capitalism altogether.

reserved for white males. In that environment, a great many Americans began to view the liberal achievements as unduly costly – costly to tax payers, to large and small businesses, to opportunities for renewed economic growth, and to wage earners. This view loomed large among voters who could no longer see their opportunities or life chances from a non–zero-sum perspective.

Civil Rights

Civil rights made up the fourth commitment of the liberal Democratic coalition. The Supreme Court decision in *Brown vs. Board of Education,* succeeding decisions ordering the desegregation of all public accommodations and conveniences, and the Civil Rights Acts of 1964 and 1965 were the gems of liberal achievement in this area. For a time, the distinctive feature of the achievement lay in the removal of race as a legitimate legal category, at least for adverse discriminatory purposes.

The successes of the civil rights movement had ramifications beyond easing the oppression of the country's Afro-American and other minority citizens. Insofar as desegregation meant the end of a major American social institution, it led the way in cracking other long-standing social institutions and the attitudes associated with them. That included dramatic changes in "women's place" in American life, and it lifted the burdens of disgrace that had been loaded onto gays and lesbians. It also sensitized Americans to the disadvantages of the physically handicapped, leading to legally mandated accommodations that at long last permitted mobility and independent living.

The nation's official disapproval of racism made possible a trend that encouraged social integration among people of different so-called races. Although still relatively rare, marriage between Afro- and Euro-Americans tripled during the thirty years after 1967, while other "mixed" marriages multiplied even faster. Resistance on all sides persisted, but overt hostility to such liaisons remained largely among Americans generally regarded as beyond the fringe of decent society.

While racism declined, race consciousness would continue to play a strong role in America's social politics. It got a big boost in the eighties from the rise of "multiculturalism." The multiculture phenomenon arose as an expression of resistance to any "standard" definition of what it meant to be "American." It represented a rejection specifically of the white Anglo-Saxon Protestant (WASP) model. It originated in the ethnic and racial pride of minorities whose oppression in American life was beginning to lift. Soon it inspired many other forms of personal identity and alternative lifestyles to demand attention and respect. "Identity politics" became a serious issue. Many Americans made claim to public attention, resources, and sometimes protection on the basis of their group membership.

In general, resistance to racial and ethnic assimilation seemed to be on a gently downward slope. But group identity came to be expressed in a number of ways. For example, gays and lesbians organized to make sexual orientation a legitimate legal category, particularly for purposes of gaining legal recognition of same-sex marriage, partnerships, or what Europeans call "co-habitation." Meanwhile, there arose vigorous opposition to permitting the Census Bureau to add "mixed" to the categories of race, religion, and ethnicity listed in the U.S. Census for fear that reduced numbers for particular groups could reduce their political clout. Racial and religious groups fought against foster care and adoption of children of diverse backgrounds. Sectarian leaders among many minority and religious groups complained that interracial, interethnic, and interreligious matrimony threatened their groups with what they provocatively called "genocide."

But what added most to the re-emergence of race as a social and political factor was the attempt to go beyond eradicating legal barriers to equality to overcome historical or de facto obstacles to equality. First of all, efforts to enforce court orders for the desegregation of schools required federal supervision of admissions practices and of how school-district lines were drawn. A test of compliance required keeping records of students classified by race. When urban housing patterns fell along lines of racial concentration, court mandates required the busing of school children across districts to achieve integration objectives. That usually translated into percentages of "whites" to "blacks" or other minorities. The advent of affirmative action further expanded the effort to go beyond merely de jure desegregation of American society. In 1965, having successfully advanced the Civil Rights Act of 1964 and the Voting Rights Act of 1965, President Lyndon Johnson moved to remedy the deep-seated disadvantages imposed by centuries of racism.

To achieve this, the president ordered that all federal agencies within the jurisdiction of the executive branch of government – together with all private agencies that received contracts or funding from the federal government – undertake "affirmative action" to seek out and recruit members of specific groups of Americans who had suffered from what he called the "scars of centuries" of oppression. The purpose was to require positive steps for bringing "within the loop" millions of Americans who had previously had limited or no access to the familial and other social networks that could inform them of educational and occupational opportunities, thereby permitting them to present themselves as candidates. The policy was, furthermore, an effort to overcome the stereotyping that impeded access to such opportunities.

In its effect, the commitment to civil rights after 1965 took on both regulatory and redistributive features. For one thing, it constricted employers' discretionary power over the makeup of their workforce and similarly intervened at colleges and universities with regard to student admissions and faculty recruitment. In redirecting resources to people identified with underadvantaged groups, it raised administrative costs. Enforcement of affirmative action requirements mandated, among other things, extensive legal and administrative procedures and record keeping. School busing did the same. Beyond these costs, school busing and affirmative action aroused passionate and in some respects polarizing responses among major elements of the liberal Democratic coalition.

Affirmative action in particular touched some raw nerves among many Americans who viewed it as an assault on "merit" as the only legitimate qualification for upward mobility. The liberal Democratic juridical scholar Alexander Bickel put it most emphatically: "In a society in which men and women expect to succeed by hard work," he protested, "it is no trivial moral wrong to proceed systematically to defeat this expectation." It is "morally wrong," he argued, to reject applicants who work over their lifetime to meet "established, realistic and unchanged qualifications" in favor of applicants who meet newer and lesser requirements.[8] Among many liberals, moreover, it seemed to negate a lifetime of work to remove race as a legal category and to treat all Americans equally as citizens. Ethnic groups that were not included in the category of officially designated "minorities" found reason for resentment. They included some groups noteworthy for their contributions to the civil rights movement and who had been a core element in the liberal Democratic coalition.

Along with the Vietnam War, these features of the liberal commitment to civil rights would do the most to break up the coalition.

In short, each of the four commitments that had provided the force behind the liberal Democratic coalition produced progressive achievements that truly were little short of sensational. But each contained elements that would lead to its own breakup. In part, success itself weakened the movement as the original enthusiasm waned over time. More important, however, was that the successes of the coalition produced new losers, too many of them within the coalition itself. For those who remained enthusiastic or who entered the movement late with blossoming enthusiasm, the successes seemed far too little or, indeed, not successes at all but "failures."

---

[8] Quoted in J. Harvie Wilkinson, *From Brown to Bakke* (Oxford University Press, 1979), ch. 10, n. 70.

16

The Failure Syndrome

Rendered fragile by Vietnam, by affirmative action and school busing, by the massive desertion of southern whites from the Democratic Party, and by the drifting away of significant numbers of the liberal intelligentsia, the coalition finally shattered in the 1970s on the shoals of economic recession and a growing demoralization in the American polity. In part, the demoralization had to do with expectations raised too high by the rapidity of positive advances. It arose, too, from the strain of having to cope with the rapidity of the changes. The challenges of the post–World War II revolutions aroused deep resentment in many Americans for whom unquestioning acceptance of received social conventions made life simple and satisfying. Finally, Americans had to cope with the emergence of many serious unintended consequences. The widening of the income gap when great numbers of well-to-do married women entered a relatively inelastic job market was one. The resentment of the unsubsidized working poor over the money and medical benefits granted to the unemployed was another. The unanticipated disaster of the engagement in Vietnam and its domestic effects was, of course, another.

Discontent developed into a general sense that nothing seemed to be working as it should. By the late sixties, Americans began to experience a dramatic swing in mood from the exuberant optimism of the young to the tired pessimism of the jaded. It may best be described as the "failure syndrome."

The word "failure" began to appear in print and in conversation with remarkable frequency. Along with the word "decline," it became a popular way of describing just about everything in America, from the economy and foreign policy to American ideals and the promise of American life. "Failure" seemed to describe the extension of American power abroad and, at home, the regulation of business, labor safety, consumer protection, and the environment. It applied further to civil rights and to the efforts to reduce poverty. The American economy would revive, and the country would soon be asserting its power and authority abroad again (for better and for worse). But the assault on virtually all the liberal commitments as "failures" would be devastating. The attack from the left would be at least as lethal as that from the right.

Let us take this up in more detail, examining the failure syndrome as it applied to liberal internationalism, civil rights, the War on Poverty, and the regulatory state.

Liberal Internationalism

During the first quarter-century after 1940, the American commitment to protecting and advancing liberal institutions abroad enjoyed major successes. First and chief among them was, of course, the defeat of the fascist powers of Germany, Italy, and Japan. Following that triumph, liberal internationalists shaped policies that contributed materially to the reconstruction of European and Japanese governments along democratic lines and to the revival of their industry. In this fashion, liberal internationalism contributed to high levels of economic growth and improved living standards. Success owed in part to the establishment of a liberal international economic regime under U.S. leadership that, by the sixties, led to the quadrupling of international trade and the economic growth that went along with it. American participation in the NATO alliance helped stabilize the European political situation after Soviet influence expanded further west into Hungary and Czechoslovakia in 1947–1948. The defeat by U.S. and United Nations forces of North Korea's attempt to annex South Korea may count as further evidence of the success of liberal activism abroad.

In general, then, Americans, or at least the nation's policy makers, came into the 1960s confident of both the effectiveness and the righteousness of their power. That confidence would be shattered by the horror of the Vietnam War. But even more than the war itself, confidence would be ruined by revelations that U.S. government leaders virtually from the beginning had been misleading the American people, perhaps even themselves, about what was happening there. And because it happened on the liberal Democratic watch, it produced some of the most serious damage to the coalition.

Except for the Civil War, the Vietnam War was the most devastating and tragic calamity in U.S. history to that time. The physical costs were awful: more than 58,000 Americans were killed and more than 120,000 were injured. It was America's longest war, but measured by military casualties only the fourth worst war. The relatively few American casualties, however, arose in part from one of the war's horrific features: the reliance on airborne weapons – including B-52 bombers flying thousands of miles from the Pacific island of Guam and dropping bombs from nearly seven miles up – and heavy artillery fired toward targets as distant as twenty miles away. There could be no expectation of confining the devastation to "military targets." The disregard for massive "collateral damage" seemed epitomized in the spraying of many thousands of acres with sometimes deadly chemical defoliants such as Agent Orange in order to expose targets in jungle areas. Such policies brought to mind the unforgettable comment by one U.S. officer following the destruction of the South Vietnam village of Bien Tre: "It sometimes becomes necessary," he said, "to destroy a village in order to save it." The tactics kept U.S. casualties relatively low while maximizing casualties on the ground, inevitably including thousands of civilians.

Perhaps worst of all were the revelations of incidents such as those at My Lai, where American troops "wasted" civilian men, women, and children – perhaps out of fear that they were concealing armed enemies, perhaps from anger and frustration, perhaps from wanton malice. Lt. William Calley, the only person prosecuted for such crimes, claimed it was "no big deal." When the American right wing lionized Calley and when President Richard Nixon declared Calley "a national hero," they accentuated the growing polarization of American life that proved to be an enduring cost of the war. At one pole were Americans who, in traditionalist fashion, regarded foreigners, and especially foreign enemies, as somewhat less-than-human aliens, "others" who did not merit humane consideration when it might impinge on concerns for "our" security or welfare. Opposing them were Americans who had developed more universalistic sensibilities regarding the application of humane consideration.

My Lai and comparable atrocities were "no big deal" not only because they came to seem all too commonplace to many of the hardened U.S. troops in the line of fire but also because one military tactic, the Operation Phoenix program, was essentially *designed* to "waste" village leaders and other civilians perceived to be pro-communist or communist collaborators. Mao Zedong had urged that revolutionaries should live off the population "like fish in the sea." Live among the masses, exploit them for resources, perhaps recruit them. Operation Phoenix was designed to dry up the sea. It was a technique the British had used with apparent success against communist-led insurgencies in Malaya in the forties and fifties. But General Bruce Palmer, commander of the 9th U.S. Infantry Division in Vietnam in 1968, later complained: "My objection to the [Phoenix] program was the involuntary assignment of U.S. Army officers to the program. I don't believe that people in uniform, who are pledged to abide by the Geneva Conventions, should be put in the position of having to break those laws of warfare."[1]

This is to highlight the outstanding cost of the war for Americans. The conspicuous callous brutality with which the United States came to wage the war confounded the humanitarian ideals for which American liberalism was supposed to

---

[1] From a letter to Douglas Valentine, published in Valentine's *The Phoenix Program* (Morrow, 1990), quoted in the *New York Times Book Review* (21 Oct. 1990), p. 19.

stand. It would divide liberal intellectuals and political leaders, some choosing to stick with their commitment to use American power to resist totalitarianism worldwide and others unable to face responsibility for the mounting devastation. It would leave a lasting demoralizing scar on the country.[2] Of especial importance for politics, it would split the liberal Democratic coalition virtually down the middle.

Many liberals stuck to the original rationale for intervening in Southeast Asia, emphasizing the barbarism of the communist forces and the obligation of a powerful liberal state such as the United States to do something about it. Postwar revelations of massive killings by the North Vietnamese – especially by the Khmer Rouge in Cambodia after the communist takeover of that country – seemed to vindicate the "prowar" loyalists who assailed their one-time liberal friends for their fecklessness in turning against the war.[3]

But the American barbarism stuck in the craw, too. Americans at home had ample opportunity to witness what was happening almost first-hand because of the flood of unfettered, and "unembedded,"[4] news reporters in Vietnam making use of new technology that enabled them to send back film for television broadcasts often within 24 hours of events. The media and Americans generally had not yet acquiesced in the military controls that stifled timely and effective reporting during later military operations in Grenada, Panama, Kuwait, Afghanistan, and Iraq. Many TV broadcasts from the Vietnam battlegrounds had to be prefaced with warnings about scenes of extreme violence and gore.

Some conservatives later blamed "the media" for the U.S. defeat in Vietnam. It is indisputable that press and TV reports of the brutality of the war contributed to the rising tide of opposition in the United States, and it is equally true that Hanoi understood how such opposition would eventually weaken the determination of U.S. political leaders to persevere. President Nixon made several efforts to persuade the country to unite behind his policies because dissidence weakened his negotiating power. That was true as well. But by glowering at his audience as he did in a television address to the nation and declaring, "The communists cannot defeat America; only Americans can do that," Nixon further alienated the war's skeptics.

There were in any case three weaknesses in the effort to blame the media for the outcome of the war. First, it is clear, from what came to be known years later once relations between the United States and Vietnam cooled off and candid exchanges took place, that Hanoi had no intention ever of abandoning its fight to

---

[2] Very possibly, it inured Americans to the still greater callousness with which the second Bush administration waged its "war on terrorism" after September 2001.

[3] See e.g. Norman Podhoretz, *Why We Were in Vietnam* (Simon & Schuster, 1982).

[4] The reference is to the term used by the Pentagon for journalists authorized to travel with military units in the Iraq campaign of 2003.

unite the country under Communist Party rule, no matter what the costs. American policy makers were unprepared to understand Hanoi's willingness to accept horrendous casualties, not only among their military forces but also among innocent civilians. "It took us eight years of bitter fighting to defeat you [French] in Indochina," North Vietnam's leader, Ho Chi Minh, remarked to the French reporter Bernard Fall in 1962. "The Americans are much stronger than the French, although they know us less well. It may perhaps take ten years to do it, but our heroic compatriots in the South will defeat them in the end."[5]

Casualties were of no concern to the Communist leaders. Years after the war ended, the journalist Stanley Karnow interviewed General Giap about the costs of the war to North Vietnam. "How long was he prepared to fight?" Karnow asked. Giap instantly answered, "Another twenty years, even a hundred years, as long as it took to win, regardless of cost." Giap declined to guess about the military casualties, but an aide told Karnow that at least a million died, in a total population of only 17 million. If the same proportion of U.S. troops had been killed, it would have amounted to 15 million Americans. How many civilians died? Giap answered with an uninterested shrug: "We haven't the faintest idea."[6]

In short, a stronger negotiating hand would have failed anyway. Indeed, it is chilling to think of how much more barbaric the war might have become had the media been mute and had the American people more solidly supported the war effort.

Second, the all-too-transparent efforts by the Johnson and Nixon administrations to conceal what was happening contributed to the growing distrust in government and in the war policies. "The seemingly harmless lying of Madison Avenue," wrote Hannah Arendt in 1975, "was permitted to proliferate throughout the ranks of all governmental services .... [T]he phony body counts of the 'search and destroy' missions, the doctored after-damage reports of the air force, the constant [false] progress reports .... These lies concealed no secrets from friend or enemy; nor were they intended to. They were meant to manipulate Congress and to persuade the people of the U.S."[7]

Nixon's attempt to block the publication of the "Pentagon Papers" – a multivolume study of the origins and conduct of the U.S. commitment in Southeast Asia commissioned by Defense Secretary Robert McNamara in 1967 – called attention most famously to government secrecy and dissembling. The president's clumsy efforts to impugn the character of Daniel Ellsberg, the RAND Corporation researcher who leaked the Pentagon Papers to the press, by burglarizing the

[5] Bernard Fall, *Anatomy of a Crisis* (Doubleday, 1969), p. 229.
[6] *New York Times Magazine* (13 Jan. 1979).
[7] Hannah Arendt, "Home to Roost: A Bicentennial Address," *New York Review of Books* (26 June 1975).

office of Ellsberg's psychiatrist were hideous violations of law and moral sense. More than that, they assured that millions of Americans would actually read the Papers and what they revealed about how the public posturing of government spokesmen deviated from what policy makers actually knew. (The U.S. Supreme Court rejected Nixon's censorship effort, and the burglary so incensed the trial court judge that he summarily dismissed the case against Ellsberg for illegally releasing classified documents.)

Over the decades that followed, the conservatives' arguments came to prevail as official government policy for limiting press coverage during times when the president declares the country to be at war, so it may be difficult for the post-2001 public to grasp the issue as it was understood by the courts and by the public in the early 1970s. In any case, it remains troubling that serious people in and out of government should propose that the American people should have had no right to know about how their government was waging a war – specifically, about what were the policy makers' actual understandings of what was happening (as opposed to what they were saying publicly) and about the costs to enemy civilians, to Americans, and most of all to the integrity of American ideals. Looking back ten years after the U.S. pullout from Saigon in 1975, Sidney H. Schanberg, the reporter featured in the film *The Killing Fields* about the massacre of Cambodians by Pol Pot's Khmer Rouge, wrote:

It is true that by and large, the press in Indochina wrote stories critical of the American policy there. But it was not because reporters were unpatriotic. It was, rather, because reporters saw America slipping toward the habits of the totalitarian powers whose activities we deem as less than moral .... The humanitarian tradition in the United States is not a myth .... So when we leave the humanitarian factor out of our foreign policy we debase that tradition.[8]

Concerns about the inappropriateness of U.S. policy in Southeast Asia arose early. In 1966, almost three years after the U.S. took on the greater burden of the fight against the communist insurgency against the South Vietnam government, the reporter Neil Sheehan wrote: "We shall, I am afraid, have to put up with our Vietnamese mandarin allies .... It is unlikely that we shall be able to find any other Vietnamese willing to cooperate with us .... But I simply cannot help worrying that, in the process of waging this war, we are corrupting ourselves. I wonder ... whether the United States or any nation has the right to inflict this suffering and degradation on another people for its own ends."[9]

Therein lay the kernel of "the moral issue" that kept emerging in the Hawk vs. Dove debates for the better part of a decade. There was, at least until 1964,

[8] Sidney H. Schanberg, "Memory Is the Answer," *New York Times* (23 April 1985).
[9] Neil Sheehan, *New York Times Magazine* (9 Oct. 1966).

general agreement among the liberal internationalists about the goodness of American intentions in Southeast Asia. But when the first sizable contingent of U.S. ground troops went into combat in Vietnam, supported by long-range heavy weaponry from air and sea, many Americans began questioning the damage to American principles involved. The journalist James Fallows later put it nicely: "There is a difference between morality of intention and morality of effect .... It was such a calculation – less an examination of the motives than a revulsion at the consequences – that turned mainstream American political opinion against the war by the late 1960s."[10]

Even if one were to justify the intervention solely according to American national interests as defined by "realist" principles, Sheehan's point should have led to a re-examination of the *components* of those interests. Five years later, after studying dozens of journalists' and scholarly researchers' accounts of the war, Sheehan would write: "If you credit as factual only a fraction of the information assembled here about what happened in Vietnam, and if you apply the laws of war to American conduct there, then the leaders of the United States for the past six years at least, including the incumbent President, Richard Milhous Nixon, may well be guilty of war crimes."[11] By that time even Norman Podhoretz, editor of *Commentary,* a fervent supporter of the war and later an angry critic of antiwar liberals, felt impelled to write:

As one who has never believed that anything good would ever come for us or for the world from an unambiguous American defeat, I now find myself ... unhappily moving to the side of those who would prefer just such an American defeat [rather than] a "Vietnamization" of the war which calls for the indefinite and unlimited bombardment by American pilots in American planes ... in that already devastated region.[12]

Insofar as the integrity of the American nation as a model for freedom-loving people and plain human decency should count high among U.S. national interests, the damage done to that feature of national interest by saturation and pattern bombing, by Operation Phoenix, and by murderous search-and-destroy operations that destroyed villages "in order to save them" should have been sufficient to turn policy toward an early withdrawal, probably before the end of

---

[10] James Fallows, "In Defense of an Offensive War," *New York Review of Books* (28 March 1982), p. 7. Fallows's appraisal actually parallels the worried comments made by Defense Secretary McNamara in memoranda he wrote in 1967; see McNamara's memoir, *In Retrospect: The Tragedy and Lessons of Vietnam* (Vintage, 1995), especially ch. 9: "Troubles Deepen."

[11] Neil Sheehan, "Should We Have War Crimes Trials?" *New York Times Book Review* (28 March 1971), p. 1.

[12] Quoted by James Fallows in his review of Podhoretz's *Why We Were in Vietnam,* in *New York Review of Books* (28 March 1982), p. 23.

1965.[13] In testimony before the U.S. Senate Foreign Relations Committee in 1966, the historian and former diplomat and State Department policy expert George Kennan remarked: "The North Vietnamese and the Viet Cong have between them, a great deal of space and manpower to give up .... Any total rooting out of the Viet Cong from the territory of South Vietnam could be achieved, if it could be achieved at all, only at the cost of a degree of damage to civilian life, and civilian suffering generally, for which I should not like to see this country responsible."[14] For the next seven years the attempt was made, with all the devastation and suffering predicted.

About the same time, Secretary of Defense Robert McNamara, who along with the president was directly in charge of shaping U.S. policy in Vietnam, began privately expressing his own distress. His contract with RAND in June 1967 for the study that became the Pentagon Papers arose from his growing unease. In his memoirs, written thirty years later, he reported that his squeamishness about the war began early in 1966. In October of that year he wrote to the president detailing his disagreement with other presidential advisors that the military effort was in any way succeeding. Moreover, he said, the prospects remained, and almost certainly would remain, dim.[15] Later, in 1967, he advised President Johnson: "The picture of the world's greatest superpower killing or seriously injuring one-thousand non-combatants a week, while trying to pound a tiny, backward nation into submission on an issue whose merits are hotly disputed, is not a pretty one."[16] McNamara recommended publicly "acknowledging" that U.S. intervention had "worked"; that China's potential in Southeast Asia had been blunted; and that the United States had sustained credibility as a reliable ally against the spread of communism. Johnson rejected all suggestions for a unilateral withdrawal from the war.

The credibility issue cut two ways. One rationale for persisting in the fight was to reassure allies of American resolve. Yet by 1967, it was becoming plain that many U.S. allies were dismayed by the extravagant military and economic

---

[13] In a passage that he struck from his memoirs, probably because it might have been viewed as a public criticism of his successors' foreign policy, Dwight Eisenhower wrote: "The strongest reason of all for the United States [to stay out of Indochina] is the fact that among all the powerful nations of the world the United States is the only one with a tradition of anti-colonialism .... The standing of the United States as the most powerful of the anti-colonial powers is an asset of incalculable value to the Free World .... The moral position of the United States was more to be guarded than the Tonkin Delta, indeed than of all of Indochina." Quoted in Stephen Ambrose, *Eisenhower: The President* (Simon & Schuster, 1984), p. 177.

[14] *New York Times* (11 Feb. 1966), p. 2.

[15] See especially pp. 262ff in McNamara's memoir, *In Retrospect*.

[16] NcNamara to LBJ, 18 May 1967, in *The Pentagon Papers,* ed. Neil Sheehan et al. (Bantam, 1971), p. 580.

resources that the Americans were expending in Vietnam. Meanwhile, back at home many Americans turned cynical about the loss of credibility of government leaders who frequently garnished the truth and sometimes simply lied in order to cover up what was happening, what they knew, and what they planned to do in Vietnam. That McNamara did not reveal his doubts publicly did not help; he chose loyalty to the president – and eventual appointment as head of the World Bank – instead.

All this took place in the context of dramatic domestic changes that had already compromised the integrity of established authority in both the public and private arenas. The civil rights movement highlighted Americans' hypocrisy regarding social equality. The challenge to sexual conventions and the feminist challenge to ascribed gender roles mocked authoritative wisdom about propriety and decorum. Meanwhile the emerging consumer protection movement revealed epidemic dishonesty in advertising, packaging, food processing, lending, and sales, and the insurgent environmental movement brought to light the poisonous pollution of air, soil, and water by powerful business interests that remained heedless of the injuries they were inflicting on fellow human beings. That such things had been permitted to happen eroded confidence in the authority of government, business, and tradition – at least for educated Americans who were actively concerned about such matters.[17]

On the obverse side, it was not possible to overlook the rising anger among traditionalists throughout the country directed at the federal government over judicial decisions that mandated school busing, that appeared to be "too soft" on crime and criminals, that challenged local customs of piety by banning officially sanctioned prayer in public schools, and that added costs to doing business by requiring record keeping to avoid or defend against suits over racial and gender discrimination. There was a populist rebellion rising from the Main Streets and Elm Streets of the country against the "elite" (often referred to as the Establishment) that many Americans, probably a majority, held responsible for the erosion of a traditionalist social order in which they had felt most comfortable.

In the context of all that was happening, policy shaped by the liberal internationalists toward Vietnam steered the country inexorably toward a big crack-up. Nor could it escape attention that the initiative for the engagement in Indochina came not from a popular clamor for action against "communist aggression" abroad but rather from the executive branch of the government, with little or no

---

[17] It may be of some interest that McNamara acknowledged his own discomfort upon observing that, on his speaking engagements among colleges, "opposition to the administration's Vietnam policy increased with the institution's prestige and [also] the educational attainment of its students." McNamara, *In Retrospect*, p. 253.

input from Congress. This is, of course, almost always true of decisions made on foreign policy matters (cf. the Truman Doctrine, the Berlin Airlift, Korea, Guatemala, and later the Gulf War of 1991 and the invasion of Iraq in 2003). In this case, conservatives later would enjoy referring to the Vietnam disaster as "the liberals' war."[18]

By the end of the sixties, then, liberal efforts to "do good" in the world seemed to young radicals as well as a growing number of liberals to be futile at best, arrogant and imperialistic otherwise, but in any case doomed to failure. These were the ingredients of a renewed preference for an isolationist approach to international affairs. The radicals' favorite historian, William Appleman Williams, put it up front. We must mind our own business, he wrote; "give the other ... peoples of the world a chance to make their own history by acting on our own responsibility to make our own history. If that be isolationism, then the time has come to make the most of it."[19]

Radical activists extended their antiwar agitation to indiscriminate criticism of U.S. containment policies directed at the Soviet Union. They challenged the liberal internationalists' claims to America's moral superiority over the communists, citing examples of U.S. disregard for human rights. The "in your face" militancy of antiwar radicals, typical of the Sixties rebels, succeeded mostly in provoking a powerful anti-antiwar uprising that, by the seventies, attracted many liberal Democrats.

Indeed, it is not possible to conclude an account of why policy makers hung on in Vietnam – long after it was clear that the United States was in a no-win situation there and that the war was having devastating effects on domestic politics as well – without saying something about the role of the antiwar movement; or more particularly about the rancorous anti-antiwar movement that the dissidents managed to activate.

Much, if not most, of the antiwar movement came from the college campuses. The intensity as well as the style of the protesters replicated the attacks on racism and other fixtures of what the mostly young rebels saw as a badly flawed society. Which is to say that the protests were vehement and disrespectful to the point of utter contempt for those who appeared opposed or merely indifferent to their

---

[18] In 2002 a few liberal congressmen resisted the administration's determination to invade Iraq, prompting Robert L. Bartley, editor of the *Wall Street Journal,* to remark in sarcasm: "Younger readers may be puzzled by the spectacle of Al Gore and Teddy Kennedy sounding anti-war rhetoric .... Why? Because Vietnam was a liberal, Democratic and intellectuals war." *Wall Street Journal* (30 Sept. 2002), p. A17.

[19] William Appleman Williams, *Roots of the Modern American Empire* (Random House, 1969), p. xxiv.

causes. Meanwhile, most young college men enjoyed exemption from conscription as long as they remained enrolled. And surely it was no coincidence that the percentage of young men entering and remaining in college during the sixties rose significantly above the ten-year average before and after 1963–1973.

Both the manner and the privilege of many antiwar protesters antagonized millions of Americans who otherwise had little interest in supporting the war except as a patriotic reflex. Too often criticisms came across as scorn for the United States, for its history and its promise. Chants of "Ho, Ho – Ho Chi Minh, The NLF Is Gonna Win" at antiwar protest marches and demonstrations were galling even to the majority of the antiwar protesters who found themselves marching along with them. The assault in 1970 on an antiwar parade in lower Manhattan by unionized construction workers graphically expressed the intensity of the resentment.[20] The workers were not necessarily "pro-war," but they expressed rage over what they viewed as ungrateful, rude, scornful, and anti-American behavior by the radicals. Although in most cases it wasn't anti-American, the radicals' confrontational behavior in opposing the country's policies tainted the antiwar movement. Years later, the military historian Russell Weigley would write:

The working-class soldiers' families back home mainly opposed the antiwar movement, and for that matter so with few exceptions did the soldiers themselves. Opposing the antiwar movement, however, was not the same as supporting the war. The middle-class and upper-class war protesters at home, particularly the college students, fumbled their chance to forge some sort of unity with the soldiers. They did so by speaking and behaving in ways that emphasized the social and economic divisions between them and the fighting men .... On the whole, their attitudes toward the soldiers were arrogant, sanctimonious and insensitive to the moral quandaries of those who had to fight.[21]

When militants abused and burned the flag and carried signs that substituted a "k" for the "c" in "America," clearly suggesting a resemblance to Nazism, public outrage could hardly be contained. In fact, the antiwar militants were probably the first political dissidents in U.S. history to trash reverence for the flag, the symbol of American unity and continuity of the country's traditional dedication to liberty.[22] Americans pledge allegiance not to the nation, the presidency, or

---

[20] There is evidence that the assault was not spontaneous but was organized by local "anti-Red" vigilante groups, probably with police cooperation.

[21] Russell F. Weigley, review of Christian G. Appy, *Working-Class War: American Combat Soldiers and Vietnam* (University of North Carolina Press, 1993), in *New York Times Book Review* (11 April 1993), p. 12. A series of Gallup polls taken in November and December 1969 indicated that, although 78 percent of Americans wanted the Nixon administration to speed up U.S. withdrawal from Vietnam, 77 percent disapproved of the antiwar demonstrations.

[22] For insight into how, even before mid-century, insurgents stressed their own "Americanism," see Gary Gerstle, *Working-Class Americanism: The Politics of Labor in a Textile City, 1914–1960* (Princeton University Press, 2000).

the Constitution, but to the flag. The national anthem is an ode to the flag. For the first time, conservatives would seize virtually exclusive control of "the flag" and indeed of "patriotism."

Aroused and resentful as so much of the public became, it grew more and more difficult for government leaders to change their minds about their commitment to the war. For, if (when) the U.S. pulled out without having defeated the evil communists, then the awful sacrifices suffered in the course of the war by so many hundreds of thousands of families would be seen as without purpose. Worse, it would then appear that the "long-haired antiwar radicals," the privileged "anti-American," "draft-dodging" college kids, had won. What democratically elected American policy maker would wish to be put in that position?

For many of the leaders of the antiwar movement, Vietnam epitomized the failure of liberal internationalism. In their view, a badly conceived and executed intervention proved that international interventions were always a bad idea. A poor memory or a poor knowledge of history may have contributed to that view. For many liberals who joined with the radicals in the antiwar movement by the end of the sixties, something of a Vietnam syndrome replaced the Munich syndrome that had inspired the liberal internationalists at the onset of World War II. Now the knowledge of the less than honorable role that the United States had played in Guatemala, in Iran, in the Congo, in the Dominican Republic, in Chile during the third quarter of the century seemed to grow in importance. Many liberals came to doubt that America could be trusted to use its power in accord with liberal principles.

President Johnson had explained to the American public that the United States did not wish to be in Vietnam but that there was no one else who could help a people victimized by brutal terrorists bent on imposing a totalitarian regime on South Vietnam. The failure of that venture gravely deflated the liberal internationalist spirit. The country would for a time remain immobilized when new causes demanded attention. When genocidal brutality later erupted in Bosnia, Kosovo, Rwanda, and elsewhere, again "there was no one else," but America held back for too long after the massacres began. To those who remained faithful to the liberal vision, inaction was reminiscent of U.S. behavior in the 1930s.

The capture of the Democratic Party in 1972 by antiwar activists with rhetoric that recalled the isolationism of the thirties led to an exodus from the party by many liberal intellectuals and internationalists, including Democrats who had held high positions in the Kennedy and Johnson administrations. Two decades later it would be left to conservative Republican administrations to reassert the country's commitment to international activism. In response to Iraq's across-the-border military invasion and occupation of Kuwait in 1991, President George H. W. Bush rallied a U.S.-led international coalition with UN approval to expel Iraq. Bush's action paralleled President Truman's response to North Korea's invasion of South Korea. This time, it would be mostly Democrats and the left that protested the intervention.

In sum: The American intervention against communist ambitions in Indochina was inspired by the liberal internationalist conviction that a great power such as the United States had an obligation to use its economic and military resources wherever it might reasonably serve to deter brutal, antiliberal aggression. It was the same conviction that underlay the promotion of the United Nations and its various humane and peacekeeping operations; the same conviction that inspired the Marshall Plan, Point-Four, and the Peace Corps; the same conviction that led to the repelling of the North Korean invasion of South Korea; the same conviction that led to NATO's (belated) intervention in the bloody civil wars in Bosnia and Kosovo; the same conviction that charged many liberals with profound guilt over the failure of the great powers to intervene in Rwanda, Sierra Leone, Liberia, and the Congo – where anarchic chaos in the nineties led to massacres and to the deliberate, merciless maiming of many hundreds of thousands of innocent men, women, and children. (In March 1998 President Clinton, in the capital city of Kilgali, formally apologized for "the international community's" lapse of attention to the 1994 massacres in Rwanda.)

Radicals and neoisolationists saw the Vietnam debacle as evidence of the failure (and worse) of liberal internationalism. They saw how power and self-defined good intentions can inspire arrogance and cause misery. "Power," Senate Foreign Relations Committee chairman William Fulbright (D-AR), warned, "tends to confuse itself with virtue and a great nation is peculiarly susceptible to the idea that its power is a sign of God's favor, conferring upon it a responsibility for other nations."[23] For many, the implication was that power conferred no responsibility for other nations.

To modify the cliché, power is indeed susceptible to abuse and corruption. Whereas Munich suggested that power must be used for "good purpose" in international affairs, Vietnam seemed to suggest – especially for those without a sense of history – that U.S. power must never be used internationally except for clear self-interested purposes defined strictly in military and economic terms.

There are no guarantees that those responsible for defining "good purpose" will confine its meaning within the bounds of liberal or humane principles. There is little evidence that the intentions of those who shaped policy toward Laos and Vietnam, from Eisenhower to Nixon, did exceed those limits. But what the Vietnam tragedy suggests is that even when heeding such bounds at the start, political circumstances may drive policy well beyond them. Simply put, political circumstances can impede policy makers from recognizing an imbalance between the

---

[23] From a speech to Congress in April 1966. The statement appears in Senator Fulbright's book, *The Arrogance of Power* (Random House, 1966).

putative gains of "staying the course" and what may well become unacceptable
costs, especially when those costs include lasting damage to liberal humanitarian
values. Such circumstances include the predictable impatience of most Americans with prolonged combat – and when rising casualties make it politically
hazardous for policy makers to acknowledge mistakes.

The seeds of failure in the U.S. engagement in Vietnam were planted in circumstances that had the policy makers politically cornered, a fact that many
of them seem to have recognized early on but could not deal with. The seeds
flourished because of serious misunderstandings of what was happening in Indochina; because of a mistaken exaggeration of Moscow's and Beijing's support
for Hanoi; because of a mistaken appraisal of the effectiveness of heavy military bombardment; because of the self-defeating consequences of filling a small
foreign country with half a million U.S. troops; because of how U.S. endorsement of almost any Saigon government undercut its authority in the eyes of the
Vietnamese peoples, with counterproductive results; and because of how partisan domestic political concerns drove the conduct of the war beyond liberal
boundaries. And yet it must be added that the failure also grew from misjudg-
ing the nature of Hanoi's determination to suffer any and all devastation. That
fact alone put liberal policy in an inescapable corner.

Decades later, in his memoirs, former Secretary of Defense Robert McNamara
put it tersely and to the point: "We were wrong! Terribly, terribly wrong!"[24]

With the election of Richard Nixon to the presidency in 1968, what began as a
liberal internationalist enterprise fell into the hands of conservative internationalists (not yet the neoconservative unilateralists who came to power after 2000).
Nixon and his chief foreign policy advisor, Henry Kissinger, chose to emphasize
military punishment as the main method for getting Hanoi to pull back from its
pressure on the South long enough for the United States to get out "with honor."
In this they had the support of the Joint Chiefs of Staff who – despite contrary
information provided by the CIA – insisted that more firepower would do the
job. Having helped to sabotage ongoing negotiations in Paris in 1968 so as to
prevent his presidential rival, Vice-President Hubert Humphrey, from claiming a
successful peace settlement,[25] Nixon proceeded to intensify the violence against
Hanoi and to spread the war into Cambodia, with awful consequences for that

[24] McNamara, *In Retrospect*.
[25] It seems well established that Kissinger, who was privy to the Paris negotiations in October 1968,
secretly informed Nixon of an impending agreement. It is also reasonably clear that Anna Chen-
nault – widow of a World War II war hero, a member of Nixon's campaign staff with many Asian
connections, and a passionate anticommunist – used her contacts to persuade the Saigon government to reject any agreement reached in Paris. Whether Nixon directly employed her services or
merely encouraged them cannot be confirmed. George C. Herring, *America's Longest War: The
United States and Vietnam, 1950–1975*, 4th ed. (McGraw-Hill, 1996), pp. 263–4; Anthony Sum-
mers, *The Arrogance of Power: The Secret World of Richard Nixon* (Viking, 2000), pp. 297–308;

once-neutral country and its people and to no practical effect in bringing about a "withdrawal with honor." The chaotic evacuation of U.S. embassy personnel from a rooftop in Saigon in 1975 as communist forces swept through the city remains one of the indelible images of the war and of the defeat of American purposes in that devastated country.

In some circles, the Vietnam War came to be referred to as "the liberals' war." In its origin, at least if dating it from the early 1960s, this is not a misnomer. Even if one argues that the original commitment took place during Eisenhower's presidency, it was consistent with the principles of liberal internationalism. Tragically, it may well be that the benign, humanitarian essence of liberal internationalism itself died in Vietnam. As the veteran foreign policy advisor Townsend Hoopes wrote in 1969, the failure of U.S. policy in Vietnam "arrested the growth of an implicit American universalism, born of our extraordinary effort and exhilarating triumph in the great struggle that began in Europe before Pearl Harbor" and took on a self-conscious character after the war "when we first grasped the somber reality ... of the iron challenge of Stalinism."[26]

However it may be called, one lesson of Vietnam may well be: If internationalists in charge of policy plan to throw America's very considerable weight around, they should be careful to recognize how brutalizing innocent people on a large scale – even in an ostensibly "just war" – inevitably contradicts the universalist essence of liberalism and puts the liberal foundations of American society itself in peril.

Civil Rights

As early as 1968, the failure syndrome began to infect the civil rights movement. Although much had been achieved, violence continued to mark the efforts to bring racial equality to realization. And few years in modern U.S. history were more violent than 1968. That April, Martin Luther King, Jr., was assassinated. Massive riots followed in the streets of some 130 American cities, none more fierce than in the nation's capital. In June, Robert F. Kennedy, then the leading candidate for the Democratic presidential nomination, also fell to an assassin's bullet. In July, antiwar and civil rights activists launched huge demonstrations in Chicago, where the Democrats were holding their nominating convention. It culminated in a police riot that sullied everyone's image of America as a civilized

Jussi Hanhiumaki, *The Flawed Architect: Henry Kissinger and American Foreign Policy* (Oxford University Press, 2004), p. 21; and the documentary film entitled *The Trials of Henry Kissinger,* which was based largely on Christopher Hitchens, "The Case against Henry Kissinger: Part One, The Making of a War Criminal," *Harper's* (Feb. 2001), pp. 37–42.

26 Townsend Hoopes, *The Limits of Intervention* (McKay, 1969), p. vi. Hoopes served as a foreign policy consultant in several administrations, most recently as assistant secretary of the Air Force in the Johnson administration.

nation. But most Americans tended to put the blame on the protesters for "start-ing it."

Massive demonstrations on the nation's college campuses continued through-out the year and into the following years. In May 1970, at Kent State University in Ohio, four students were killed and many others wounded when trigger-happy National Guardsmen fired on a peaceful crowd protesting the U.S. invasion of Cambodia. Two others were killed at Jackson State University in Mississippi. Again, most Americans, and certainly most in Ohio and Mississippi, found lit-tle good to say about the students. Most Americans, it seemed, wanted "law and order." In such an environment, the police could do no wrong.

Meanwhile, even before his death, the nonviolent tactics of Martin Luther King, Jr., came increasingly to be challenged by younger, more impatient, and more ambitious civil rights workers. Many, like King, had faced the sometimes murderous assaults by racists in the South, in Chicago, and elsewhere. Unlike King, they were unwilling to remain patient. They bitterly resented the often tardy and ineffectual protection provided by the federal government. King's chal-lengers within the movement went beyond attacking his tactical and philosophi-cal restraint. The "Dream" that King had told America about at the monumental August 1963 rally on the Mall in Washington, DC, had been the full assimilation of Negroes into the American mainstream. The mostly younger activists chal-lenged the character of the mainstream itself as well as the goal of assimilation.

Renouncing the word "Negro" as symbolic of a craven past, young lead-ers of the black civil rights movement declared their pursuit of "Black Power," backing it up with publicity showing angry young men brandishing guns. Black activists, led by Stokely Carmichael, by then had taken over the Student Nonvi-olent Coordinating Committee (SNCC), expelled white members, and pushed the organization into a more belligerent posture. Bobby Seale, Eldridge Cleaver, Huey Newton, and other militants in Oakland, California, organized the Black Panthers, taking the name from the symbol of black voter registration groups in the South. They gained national notoriety, vowing to use violence "in defense" against police and others who threatened them.

For some, these developments signaled the failure of the civil rights move-ment. Christopher Lasch, a professor of history at the University of Rochester and a leading social critic, declared in 1968: "Whatever else 'Black Power' means ... it challenges the belief, until recently widespread, that the United States is making substantial progress toward racial justice .... In the form in which it existed until 1963 or 1964, the civil rights movement is dead .... The appar-ent victories of the civil rights coalition have not brought about any discernible changes in the lives of most Negroes, at least not in the north."[27]

---

[27] Christopher Lasch, *The Agony of the American Left* (Vintage, 1969), pp. 117–18. The chapter from which the quotation is taken originally appeared in the *New York Review of Books* in 1968.

This was a remarkable judgment considering that, at the time it was written, the Civil Rights Act was scarcely four years old, the Voting Rights Act only three, and President Johnson's executive order on affirmative action was still more recent, with enforcement guidelines yet to be defined. Within less than a decade, the lives of millions of Afro-Americans would, in fact, improve remarkably – so much so that, in the mid-seventies, the eminent black sociologist William Julius Wilson would write: "economic class is now a more important factor than race in determining job placement and black life-chances .... [T]alented and educated blacks are experiencing unprecedented job opportunities in the growing government and corporate sectors ... that are at least comparable to those of whites with equivalent qualifications."[28] By then, as high a percentage of black high-school graduates (33 percent) were entering college as their white cohorts.[29] Over the next twenty years, Afro-Americans with middle-class incomes more than doubled.

Lasch might have argued even in 1968 that the advent of "Black Power" may itself be strong evidence that "substantial progress" had already been made. Historically, one sure sign of the progress of any movement has been an increase in militancy and the growing volume of assertions that "no progress" has been made.[30] Before the gains made by the civil rights movement, such assertiveness was invariably met by greater, often malicious, and decisively repressive violence.

By contrast, the desegregation court decisions along with the nonviolent demonstrations of the fifties seemed to have had something of the intended educational effect of softening white resistance. "Now it came to me all of a sudden," Franklin McCain, one of the Negro students in the February 1960 Greensboro sit-in, later said. "Maybe they can't do anything to me. Maybe we can keep it up."[31] McCain and the others had expected to be pulled violently from the lunch counter and beaten and jailed, if not worse. But because of the successes of the movement in the fifties, including especially the Supreme Court decisions declaring desegregation "the law of the land," they felt confident enough to challenge the racial apartheid of their town armed only with what proved to be the valid hope that they could get away with it.

---

[28] Quoted in Bart Landry, *The New Black Middle Class* (University of California Press, 1987), p. 93.

[29] Considering the educational disabilities inflicted on Afro-Americans by a racist educational system in most of the school districts where black children attended school (i.e., the South), such a figure marks astounding progress. See Chapter 10, on the revolution in racial relations, for more figures on the success of the movement.

[30] Alexis de Tocqueville, *On the State of Society in France before the Revolution of 1789,* trans. Henry Reeve (John Murray, 1856), pp. 323–4. See also C. Wright Mills, *The New Men of Power: America's Labor Leaders* (Harcourt Brace, 1948), in which Mills used the increasingly strident expressions of frustration by labor leaders as a test of militancy and growing power.

[31] Clay Carson, *In Struggle: SNCC and the Black Awakening of the 1960s* (Harvard University Press, 1981), p. 9.

The Greensboro demonstrators gained widespread sympathy throughout the country in large measure because it was plain that what they wanted was access to mainstream America. Even the conservative white editor of the Richmond *News Leader,* James Kilpatrick, was forced to observe the contrasting appearances of the Negro students "in coats, white shirts, ties" with their hecklers, "a ragtail rabble, slack-jawed, black-jacketed, grinning fit to kill."[32] The Greensboro students were no "countercultural" protesters. Similar protesters were not always so lucky, as white-supremacist thugs mobilized to brutalize them. But by that time Southern thuggery produced massive sympathy for the civil rights movement nearly everywhere in the country, eventuating in passage of the federal Civil Rights and Voting Rights Acts of 1964 and 1965.

But there was cogency in Lasch's judgment that the civil rights movement was dead if one takes "in the form in which it existed until 1963 or 1964" as the operative clause. By 1968, the civil rights movement had become radicalized. On such short evidence regarding the likelihood of future racial equity, many leaders of the new civil rights movement declared racism in America to be uncorrectable. It was already in 1966 that Stokely Carmichael, the new leader of SNCC, coined the phrase "Black Power," declaring that he was no longer willing to go to jail for acts of civil disobedience. He promised not to be civil anymore.[33]

At that point, the movement hit a minefield. No longer aiming for assimilation in the American mainstream, Carmichael and his allies now urged a restructuring of the nation's main institutions, with violence considered as a possible instrument of that transformation. Separation of the races was one option, at least until liberal capitalism was destroyed. When Eldridge Cleaver insisted that the civil rights movement was only a transitional stage toward "the growth of a broader movement challenging the structure of political and economic power in America,"[34] he touched one of the most sensitive nerves among the nation's rank and file as well as among those of its putative "ruling classes." The radical branch of the movement took on Old Left, Marxist colors, explicitly anticapitalist and antiliberal.

But most troubling, Black Power came to signify a declaration of war on white Americans. "Watch out! I'm gonna get me a gun, honky!" boasted Rap Brown, using the pejorative term for whites that had become popular among

---

[32] Quoted in Carson (ibid.), p. 14.

[33] Carmichael also helped popularize the name "Black Panthers" for the organization that Huey Newton and others founded in Oakland, California. "A man," Carmichael wrote in the Fall 1966 *New York Review of Books,* "needs a black panther on his side when he and his family must endure loss of job, eviction, starvation, and sometimes death, for political activity. He may also need a gun, and SNCC reaffirms the right of black men everywhere to defend themselves if threatened or attacked." Quoted in Hugh Pearson, *Huey Newton and the Price of Black Power in America* (Addison-Wesley, 1994), p. 96.

[34] Eldridge Cleaver, *Soul on Ice* (Dell, 1991 [1968]) p. 110.

some militant blacks.[35] "No matter how endlessly they try to explain it," complained Roy Wilkins, the head of the NAACP, "the term 'black power' means anti-white power .... The quick, uncritical and highly emotional adoption of the slogan [by] some segments of a beleaguered people can mean in the end only black death."[36]

Political scientist James McGregor Burns noted the sad irony in one outcome of Lyndon Johnson's fight for civil rights:

> In sensing black wants, recognizing black needs, arousing black aspirations, legitimating black expectations, meeting black demands, [Lyndon] Johnson had not only helped focus the effort .... He had mobilized in the South and in the ghettos a new breed of militant black who was brassy, noisy, assertive, and moving far beyond the reach of that long presidential arm. Leadership had begat leadership and hardly recognized its offspring.[37]

For many black male activists, Black Power became a kind of proof of manhood.[38] The participants' own accounts of life among the Black Panthers reveal extraordinary adolescent violence and posturing as well as rampant misogyny.[39] Kathleen Cleaver, Eldridge Cleaver's much-abused wife but an enduring apologist, observed in 1971: "As black men move to regain a sense of dignity, to regain a sense of manhood ... and to become ... manly enough to fight against the oppressor, they many times take out their resentment of their position against their own black women."[40] Black Power may have served the morale and the organizational ambitions of Stokely Carmichael, Eldridge Cleaver, and Huey Newton. It may have offered, as Roy Wilkins said, "a solace, a tremendous psychological lift." But the overall flaws of the strategy would become deadly.

King, Wilkins, Bayard Rustin, Philip Randolph, and other veteran leaders of the movement repeatedly warned their younger co-workers that such militancy would not serve the needs of a small minority population. Rustin warned: "SNCC's Black Panther perspective is simultaneously utopian and reactionary – the former for the by now obvious reason that one-tenth of the population cannot accomplish much by itself, the latter because" SNCC's proposal for an independent political party "would remove Negroes from the main area of political struggle" – namely, the Democratic Party. King urged Carmichael to avoid

---

[35] Brown's statement is recorded on a film for television, *From Montgomery to Memphis*, a review of Martin Luther King, Jr.'s, life put together shortly after King's assassination in 1968. In 2002, Brown, who had meanwhile become a Black Muslim minister, was convicted of murdering a white policeman and was sentenced to a life term in prison.

[36] Quoted in Carson, *In Struggle*, p. 219.

[37] James MacGregor Burns, *Leadership* (Harper, 1978), p. 424.

[38] See Pearson, *Price of Black Power*. Pearson, a black writer, deplored the "predominance of posturing over substance" among the Black Power leaders.

[39] See e.g. Elaine Brown, *A Taste of Power: A Black Woman's Story* (Pantheon, 1992), especially pp. 186–90, and Philip S. Foner, ed., *The Black Panthers Speak* (Da Capo, 1995 [1970]).

[40] Kathleen Cleaver quoted in *The Black Scholar* (Dec. 1971).

sloganeering "that would confuse our allies, isolate the Negro community and give many prejudiced whites, who might otherwise be ashamed of their anti-Negro feeling, a ready excuse for self-justification."[41]

Such warnings went unheeded. With King's death in 1968 there was no one to restrain the narrowly focused belligerence that took over. One consequence was a major backlash among American voters, verifying King's predictions. Black Panthers were victimized by far more proactive police violence than they ever inflicted on anyone (except among themselves). The violent and often illegal behavior of racist police validated for thousands of urban blacks, and for sympathetic whites as well, the gun-toting response of the Panthers. But widely publicized photos of Huey Newton proudly posing in a rattan peacock chair while wearing a Che Guevara beret and holding a large rifle suggested something more aggressive and unjustifiable than mere self-defense.

Although not related in fact, the rising rate of violent crime coincided with these displays, leading many Americans to facilely connect "Black Power" – and, by extension, the civil rights movement – with the decreasing safety of city streets. The Panthers and their supporters enjoyed the fear that their posturing infused in white Americans, but they reckoned poorly with the anger it also provoked.

Some of the bravado went to what once might have seemed unimaginable extremes. Imamu Amiri Baraka (né LeRoi Jones), a prolific poet of some intellectual standing, pulled no punches:

> ... you can't steal nothin from a white
> man, he's already stole it he owes you
> anything you want, even his life. All
> the stores will open if you say the magic
> words. The magic words are: Up against
> the wall mother fucker this is a stick
> up!...
>
> smash the windows, daytime, anytime, together,
> let's smash the window, drag the shit from in there.
> No money down. No time to pay.
> Just take what you want....
>
> Let's get together and kill him my
> man, let's get to gather the fruit of the
> sun, let's make a world we want black
> children to grow and learn in do not
> let your children when they grow look
> in your face and curse you by pitying your tomish ways.[42]

---

[41] Both quotations are from Carson, *In Struggle*, pp. 209–10 and 120 (respectively).

[42] Baraka, "Black People" (1967), quoted in Justin Driver's review of Jerry Gafio Watts, *Amiri Baraka: The Politics and Art of a Black Intellectual* (New York University Press, 2001), *The New Republic On Line* (25 April 2002), ⟨www.powells.com/review/2002_04_25.html⟩.

Such blowsy locution served to dismay all but the most cynical of civil rights enthusiasts. Yet possibly nothing injured the civil rights movement more than the widely published photographs of black students at Cornell University in 1969 standing proudly on the steps of the administration building, brandishing assault weapons and wearing ammunition-packed bandoleras in the stereotyped fashion of Mexican outlaws. Their demands? Establishment of a black studies department and (wonder of wonders) segregated dining and housing facilities. Similar campus disruptions (but without the guns) took place on other major college campuses, including Columbia, Harvard, Yale, and the University of California at Berkeley – all featuring similar "nonnegotiable" demands. Such objectives loomed large among locally ambitious student and neighborhood leaders. They had the effects of trivializing legitimate demands for further progress in civil rights and of contributing to a ferocious backlash.

Mindless endorsements of such adolescent posturing by many of those who remained fighters for civil rights turned off many a lamp once held high by middle-class supporters of the cause. Altogether, the demise of the civil rights movement "in the form in which it existed up to 1963 or 1964" did much to sap the strength of the liberal Democratic coalition. The backlash actually did little to undo the gains of the early movement, but it contributed in a major way to the defection of many liberals from the coalition that had achieved so much. This had enormous implications for Democratic Party losses. It also pushed the Democratic Party to the right, thus impeding further progress toward a more liberal society and toward alleviating the poverty that minorities still suffered disproportionately.

Still, as we have already discussed, equally important in provoking that defection – particularly among intellectuals and union members – was the implementation of affirmative action. Ironically, fewer Afro-Americans came to benefit from affirmative action than did other groups. Massive immigration after 1975 turned the policy on its head. Immigrants, who made up only about 4.5 percent of the American population in 1970, were not included in the considerations leading to affirmative action. President Johnson intended his executive order primarily for Negroes, though he did name four other abused minority groups (including Hispanics and Asians). By the eighties, the foreign-born and their offspring approached 15 percent of the population. Following the letter of Executive Order 11246, though not its intent, and without congressional or other public debate, federal agencies accorded the same benefits to "Hispanic" immigrants (in some cases, that included Portuguese) as to natives. Benefits included special subsidies from the federal Small Business Bureau and from housing agencies. Similar benefits were later bestowed on East Asians, Asian Indians, and Pakistanis, although data clearly showed that they had the highest median household income of all immigrant groups and higher than many other Americans. These groups also fared disproportionately well in college admissions, yet affirmative action policy continued to support them. By 1980, 26 million immigrants – including 15 million who had entered the country illegally – were enjoying affirmative action benefits that were denied to native-born white poor.[43]

Mandated intracity busing to achieve racial integration in the public schools upset many of the same constituencies that were troubled by affirmative action. Normally Democratic blue- and white-collar families came to resent having children from mostly low-income Negro families "foisted" upon their children in the schools, especially since the wealthy liberals who pushed racial integration could afford to send their children to expensive private schools. The problem was probably at least as much a matter of social class as one of racial bias. But relatively few white Americans made a distinction between the disorderly lower-class behavior they feared and the race with which they all too readily identified it.

The problem would be compounded by an increasingly aggressive assertion by black chauvinists that proudly claimed precisely such an identity. Historian Hugh Pearson, the son of a middle-class black family, was just one among many who wrote about how he grew up in the sixties and seventies convinced by his peers, as so many black school children were, that doing well in school was "becoming like white people, and not being genuinely black."[44] From the seventies on, many educationally oriented black families pulled their children from the public schools in order to avoid such an environment and the destructive peer pressure it could exert. Just what it meant to be "genuinely black" would continue to roil racial relations for the rest of the century. In response to critics of the often scatological chants of "gangsta rap," many commentators in the 1990s (sympathetic whites as well as blacks) claimed that they were legitimate expressions of "black culture," a claim that members of a growing middle class of Afro-Americans fiercely disputed.

Beginning in the sixties, blue-collar and white-collar voters began drifting out of the liberal Democratic coalition. In 1968 Alabama's champion opponent of desegregation, Governor George Wallace, running for president on an independent ticket, polled 13.3 percent of the national vote and carried five Deep South states. Few of those voters ever returned to the Democratic Party. Wallace, wrote Tom Wicker of the *New York Times,* "is a veritable artist of defiance, a virtuoso of defeat, who has found his greatest strength in picturing himself as

---

[43] Hugh Davis Graham, *Collision Course: The Strange Convergence of Affirmative Action and Immigration Policy in America* (Oxford University Press, 2002).

[44] Pearson, *Price of Black Power,* p. 342. "Most of [Huey] Newton's 'brothers off the block' looked down on anyone serious about graduating from college. They looked down on anyone serious about getting a job. 'A man who lives on his wits, sleeping till ten in the morning, on the hustle in the streets or the poolrooms, he figures a guy working 8 hours a day for $80 per week just isn't smart,' Julius Hobson, a CORE worker, would later observe." Ibid., p. 99.

the little man run down in the schoolhouse door, the 'average American' ignored by the 'pseudo-intellectuals' controlling the major parties."[45]

In 1972, Wallace's popular appeal had spread. By then, the issue had shifted from abolishing de jure school segregation to overcoming de facto segregation by means of busing children across town to achieve racial "balance." Campaigning in the Democratic primaries in Florida specifically against school busing but also against street crime (code for "black violence"), he took 42 percent of the vote in a field of eleven candidates. The results there shook up the liberal camp sufficiently to lead liberal champion Hubert Humphrey to praise President Nixon's call for a halt to court-ordered busing. Wallace went on to outpoll Humphrey in Wisconsin, Pennsylvania, and Indiana. Wallace had not even campaigned in Pennsylvania because he thought he had no chance against the pro-Humphrey union leadership there. In similarly unionized Detroit, he won a 51-percent majority against both Humphrey and the eventual Democratic nominee, George McGovern. At the time he was shot and paralyzed, forcing him out the race, Wallace was ahead of all Democratic candidates for the nomination with 3.4 million votes to Humphrey's 2.6 million and McGovern's 2.2 million.[46]

Wallace supporters typically viewed the gains made by the post-King civil rights movement as shameful capitulations by the government, by universities, and by corporations to the demands of groups that threatened violence and civil disobedience to get what they wanted. They saw themselves as law-abiding, hard-working citizens whose interests government ignored. One historian of the Wallace insurgency summed up the typical supporter's outlook:

Unwilling to give up the belief in the "American Dream," still hoping that hard work and being a good citizen will pay off, he is very angry at student protesters who are disparaging of that dream and those who are getting what they want without going through the "proper channels" – black protesters, "welfare loafers," etc …. [H]e has very little hope, given those particular government priorities which he feels do not include him in their consideration.[47]

Wallace Democrats defected to the Republican Party by the hundreds of thousands. After the early seventies, Democratic Party candidates rarely carried a majority of white voters in any of the southern states.

As King suggested in his warning to Carmichael, much of the force that the civil rights movement had among many whites consisted of a sense of guilt – guilt

---

[45] Tom Wicker, "No, No and Wallace," *New York Times* (25 July 1968).
[46] Michael Barone, *Our Country: The Shaping of America from Roosevelt to Reagan* (Free Press, 1990), pp. 500ff; Jody Carlson, *George C. Wallace and the Politics of Powerlessness: The Wallace Campaigns for the Presidency, 1964–1976* (Transaction, 1981).
[47] Carlson, *George C. Wallace*, pp. 16–18.

about white over black oppression throughout U.S. history. The Afro-American social critic Shelby Steele stated it bluntly: "In the 1960s, particularly the black-is-beautiful late 1960s,... the lines of moral power ... had shifted. White guilt became so palpable you could see it on people .... Suddenly, this huge vulnerability had opened up in whites and, as a black, you had the power to step right into it .... Guilt had changed the nature of the white man's burden from ... the obligations of dominance to the urgencies of repentance."

Few would argue with Steele's observation. But the guilt he described was felt largely by those most well-off in the society and was shared by few among the less well-off, including especially the more recently arrived Euro-Americans. What he went on to say provided an example of exactly what enraged many white Americans who had once given sympathetic support to the civil rights movement: "What exactly is this guilt?" asked Steele. "I think [it] springs from a knowledge of ill-gotten advantage."[48]

That was simply inflammatory. Although those precise words were written in 1990, many black militants and intellectuals had made the sentiment amply plain twenty years earlier. It did not go well with those first-, second-, and third-generation Euro-Americans whose parents as perhaps they themselves had worked eighty-hour weeks as domestics, tailors, and launderers or as owners of small mom-and-pop produce and grocery shops so that their children might be educated and move up the economic ladder. Among all the other privations they and their families had endured, moreover, the Great Depression was still a fresh memory. No "ill-gotten advantages" there.

Guilt had been among the motivations for many people who fought for civil rights, particularly in the Democratic political leadership, but attributing it broadly to white Americans was both mistaken and provoking. Almost certainly most Euro-Americans, including those in the civil rights movement, did not feel guilt. Other ethnic and religious minorities (Jews, Swedes, Finns, Italians, Slavs, Arabs, Armenians, Irish), who were themselves often put upon, shared a sense of abuse and exploitation by the same white Establishment classes that they now saw further "victimizing" them with affirmative action, school busing, forced integration of housing, and the like. Part of the backlash against the coalition arose from a widespread feeling among the working poor, union members, and "unofficial" minorities that an affluent, urban, college-educated elite was making them pay the costs of expiating their own sense of guilt.[49]

---

[48] Shelby Steele, "White Guilt," *American Scholar* (Autumn 1990), pp. 497–506.
[49] For a sharp commentary on the failure of many liberals to respond to the grievances of ethnic workers, see Sean Wilentz's critical review of conservative Dinesh D'Souza's *The End of Racism* (Free Press, 1995): "Color-Blinded," *The New Yorker* (2 Oct. 1995), pp. 91ff.

To put it briefly: The new expectations of what remained possible in the progress toward a just society, borne on the successes of the civil rights movement itself, played an important role in raising assertiveness to self-damaging levels. The liberal Democratic coalition would pay the price for the successes and the expectations that it had raised.

The War on Poverty

Even before Lyndon Johnson's presidency ended, the liberal Democratic coalition was beset on one flank by the rising tide of a new, intellectually respectable conservatism – and more lethally by a strident attack on the left flank by social forces that were actually inspired by its very successes. In few things was the Johnson administration more successful than in the War on Poverty. The successes, however, seemingly called attention to what had yet to be accomplished and thus, for the righteously impatient as well as for the ideologically partisan, they appeared to be failures.[50]

The rapidity with which "success" turned to seeming "failure" says much about the turbulence of the Johnson era. It may say much also about how Johnson's personality and his stubborn pursuit of the war in Vietnam inspired indiscriminate criticism from the left about everything he and his administration attempted. "President Johnson's vision of a Great Society," wrote social policy scholars Sar Levitan and Robert Taggert, contrasted "markedly with the phlegmatic ideology of the preceding decade .... [T]here was a dramatic acceleration of the governmental efforts to insure the well-being of all citizens." Congress moved with remarkable speed to enact a wide range of controversial measures, producing the greatest improvement in social benefits in the country's history. But "[j]ust four years later," Levitan and Taggert remarked, "a very different mood prevailed in the nation – one of fear, distrust, anger, and alienation."

Exploiting the mood, Richard Nixon campaigned in 1968 against the successes of the Great Society. "For the past five years," he declared, "we have been deluged by government programs for the unemployed, programs for cities, programs for the poor, and we have reaped from these programs an ugly harvest of frustration, violence, and failure across the land."[51]

The mood, and the charges of "failure," would prove enduring. As Eli Ginzburg and Robert Solow, two of the country's leading economists, remarked in

---

[50] For a balanced treatment of the successes and failures of the antipoverty program, at least with regard to Afro-Americans, see Nicholas Lemann, *The Promised Land: The Great Black Migration and How It Changed America* (Vintage, 1991), especially pp. 355ff.

[51] Sar Levitan & Robert Taggart, *The Promise of Greatness* (Harvard University Press, 1976), p. 3.

1972: "the belief that many or most of the Great Society programs worked badly or not at all is shared by some people who would still probably describe themselves as liberals or even liberal Democrats."[52] Many historians writing as unreconstructed "Sixties radicals" would help perpetuate the myth for decades.

For example, in his well-researched *History of Liberalism in the 1960s* (written in 1984), Alan Matusow titled one of the chapters, "War on Poverty: The Failure of the Welfare State." In what did the "failure" consist? In the view of this self-described radical historian, poverty is a matter of relative deprivation. Therefore, no victory in the war could be won if it merely raised the poor out of discomfort and need – as he conceded Johnson's programs did – without *reducing* the gap between the rich and the poor. "To attack poverty," Matusow wrote, "the government would have to reduce inequality, to redistribute income, in short, to raise up the poor by casting down the rich." The Johnson programs "did little to diminish inequality and therefore, by definition, failed measurably to reduce poverty."[53] The effect of such sniping was destructive. "Bad talk drives out good," Ginzberg and Solow noted. It was an example of what might be called "Gresham's Law of Political Rhetoric."[54]

One effect of the "bad talk" on the left was to push debate on new social programs beyond realistic bounds and to trigger disarray among the reformers themselves. Efforts to improve the welfare system crashed in a fight between the impatient idealists, some with broad ideological agendas, and the liberal pragmatists. "Most of the interest groups representing welfare clients and potential beneficiaries," Ginzberg and Solow observed, "were so taken up with the shortcomings of the proposed legislation that they were unable to agree among themselves on any compromise that had a reasonable prospect of gaining Congressional approval and Presidential consent." As the leaders of these interest groups saw it, their failure to get what they wanted suggested to them not so much their own organizational and conceptual futility but rather that the political system *qua* system could never achieve what they chose to define as "significant gains." And having lost faith in the system, they drifted off into sulking corners of dissidence, perhaps to lay down self-satisfied judgments about "failure."

Another effect of the bad talk was to provide a huge opening for conservatives and, in fact, to catapult the political agenda far to the right. By the early seventies, most political discussion aimed at reducing not poverty but rather the

---

[52] Eli Ginzberg & Robert M. Solow, *The Great Society: Lessons for the Future* (Basic Books, 1974), p. 5.

[53] Allen J. Matusow, *The Unraveling of America: A History of Liberalism in the 1960s* (Harper & Row, 1984), p. 220.

[54] Ginzberg & Solow, *The Great Society*, pp. 5–6.

costs of antipoverty programs and the damage the programs were allegedly doing to the poor (as well as to the national budget). It had become common "wisdom" that Aid to Families with Dependent Children (AFDC) and other social welfare measures had created a proliferating army of dependency-addicted clients – though nothing was said about the dependency of American farmers and agri-corporations on cash subsidies. Conservatives had long decided that liberalism was a failure. Now they had allies on the left.

The "failure" epithet became fashionable, something of a scapegoat for the domestic and international difficulties troubling the nation at the turn of the decade. The seventies dawned with revelations of the horrendous, cold-blooded murder of hundreds of women, children, and elderly Vietnamese civilians by American troops at My Lai, an atrocity for which only one man, Lt. William Calley, was convicted (and freed after a brief minimum-security prison stay). It began also with the slaying by poorly trained National Guardsmen of four students at Kent State University and two at Jackson State University who had been protesting against the U.S. invasion of Cambodia. It opened with the devaluation of the dollar, a 10-percent tariff on imported goods, and the abandonment of the international gold standard – implicit acknowledgments of the weakening of the U.S. economy and U.S. power. At the outset of the decade, polls indicated that, for the third or fourth year in a row, street violence and rising crime rates topped Americans' political concerns. Amid such turmoil, liberals' intervention on behalf of the poor made easy targets.

In his State of the Union address at the start of 1971, President Nixon – who had praised the convicted Vietnam war criminal Lt. Calley as "a national hero" – attacked the Great Society's antipoverty programs as a "monstrous, consuming outrage." The editors of *Time,* sensing the country's changed mood, commended the speech and declared, with evident satisfaction: "The failure of the United States welfare system is in large measure a defeat for liberalism."[55]

As we have discussed previously, between 1962 and 1973 the percentage of American households enduring poverty declined from about 20 percent to about 11 percent. About half of that improvement owed to continuing economic growth that buoyed up wages and generated job opportunities, but the other half owed to an increase in welfare payments made as part of the War on Poverty. (Since those payments contributed to increased consumer demand, they also must have had some positive effect on economic growth.) One might conclude that such an improvement alone deserved to be regarded as a "success," and in fact there were other improvements. Yet by 1970 the welfare system had come to be nearly

[55] *Time* (8 Feb. 1971).

universally condemned, on the left and on the right, as a failure. That view, which would become a presumption, would skew public policy for the rest of the century.

As late as 1995, while a Democratic president collaborated with avowed reactionaries in moving to destroy "welfare as we know it," public policy professor Susan Meyer and sociologist Christopher Jencks attempted in vain to divert the headlong rush. They pointed out that claims of its failure were virtually pure fiction. "As the White House and Congress struggle over the future shape of American government," they wrote in an extensive *New York Times* op-ed piece, "one of the Republicans' most frequent arguments for cutting social programs is that they don't work. Millions of Americans, including a majority of legislators, seem to believe this claim. Yet almost all the evidence suggests that it is false .... Anyone who bothers to look at the Federal Government's surveys of how Americans have lived over the last generation can see this. But hardly anyone looks."[56]

The antipoverty programs, they noted, did exactly what they were supposed to do: reduce poverty and reduce the misery of those who would remain engulfed in poverty. Similarly, the Medicare and Medicaid programs improved Americans' health greatly. For example, in 1965, before Medicaid arrived, the federal government's annual Health Interview Surveys showed that poor people typically made 20 percent fewer doctor visits than others, though they were more likely to be ill. By 1980, income was no longer a variable in determining the likelihood that someone sick would consult a physician. (Quality might still differ, but not access.) Again: Food Stamps arrived in 1964. At that time, the national Food Consumption Survey found that poor families ate substantially less than others; by 1977, surveys showed that the difference in food consumption between the poor and others had been cut in half while hunger and malnutrition had dwindled, mostly affecting those living in marginal circumstances. Again: Poverty among the elderly and disabled dropped from 19 percent in 1972 to 15 percent in 1982, and to 12 percent in 1992. "Here again," wrote Mayer and Jencks, "Government spending worked."

"Except for SSI," Jencks and Mayer concluded, "major anti-poverty programs have all had one thing in common: they never tried to raise anyone's [cash] income above the poverty line. They were meant to provide benefits that reduce misery – and they have."

It was commonplace to cite increases in the welfare rolls as evidence that the War on Poverty failed. But such claims were based on a curious interpretation of the data. For instance, the number of those benefiting from AFDC grew between 1965 and 1975. Conservatives argued that this proved the *failure* of the program because, they said, the increase showed that the program had created a growing

---

[56] *New York Times* (9 Nov. 1995).

class of dependents. There is little doubt that in some cases the availability of aid provided an incentive for single motherhood or, more likely, helped induce single mothers to keep their unplanned children (a plus for family values?). But there were other reasons for both the increase in single mothers and in the AFDC rolls. The leading reason for the latter was that federal court decisions and changes in state regulations had made it easier for single mothers to get benefits. Even so, at least 20 percent of those who were eligible for cash benefits received none.

In other words, programs to reduce the impact of poverty drew increasing numbers of the already poor into the welfare system. The rolls grew at least partly because more of the poor learned from program workers that they were eligible for aid and also how to gain access to such aid. This seems like strange "proof" of a program's failure. Actually, between 1975 and 1994, the rolls grew only at about the same rate as the general population and, as a proportion of all children, those receiving AFDC remained about the same – even though that two-decade period was marked by high unemployment and declining real earned income for the bottom 50 percent of the working population.

There was some (but not much) merit in the argument that social welfare payments increased the number of Americans addicted to dependency.[57] Surely AFDC payments persuaded some percentage of unwed mothers to keep their children rather than give them out for adoption or to foster homes. But that does not suggest that poor women were opting to have children in order to obtain such payments. In fact, statistics do not show that welfare payments contributed to teenage and unwed motherhood, as was the commonplace claim. Between 1964 and 1975, when such payments were increasing fastest, teenage births fell by 25 percent; whereas, from the late 1980s to 1993, they rose as real AFDC benefits declined. In fact, only slightly more than half of AFDC recipients were families of children and an unwed mother.[58] Meanwhile, births to unwed mothers in several European countries, where changes in welfare could not have been a factor, rose at a steeper rate than in the United States and constituted a higher percentage of all births than in the United States. Obviously, other factors than the availability of funds for infants underlay the changes.[59]

There was, moreover, little evidence that significant numbers of children of welfare parents became welfare parents themselves, as some critics claimed. Those that did, however, tended to become politically conspicuous. Moreover,

---

[57] Charles Murray was the leading publicizer of this view via his book entitled *Losing Ground: American Social Policy, 1950–1980* (Basic Books, 1984). See also James Q. Wilson, *Thinking About Crime* (Basic Books, 1975); George Gilder, *Wealth and Poverty* (Basic Books, 1981).

[58] Mark Abrahamson, *Out-of-Wedlock Births: The United States in Comparative Perspective* (Praeger, 1998), p. 145.

[59] See Lawrence L. Wu & Barbara Wolfe, eds., *Out of Wedlock: Causes and Consequences of Nonmarital Fertility* (Russell Sage, 2001), pp. xxii et seq.

less than a third of families on welfare, including single mothers, remained on welfare longer than three years. That might have suggested a remarkable achievement given that – in the absence of a national child day-care program such as many European governments provided – American mothers must have had exceptional difficulty in caring for their children and earning a living wage at the same time.[60] But that minority of recipients who remained on welfare created a major political problem because of the rich anecdotal material they provided – some of it invented, perhaps most notably by Ronald Reagan in his repeated references to "welfare queens."

Some demographic changes added to the political challenge of reducing poverty. By mid-century it became the fashion, or at least the practice, for retired persons to live apart from their children. This had the effect of keeping transfer payments, such as Supplementary Security Income (SSI), at the maximum while their *reported* income – excluding gifts from their children and Medicare outlays – kept them barely above official poverty levels. Moreover, more college-age Americans were in college, including children of well-to-do families who were living alone and reporting poverty-level incomes, even drawing food stamps to supplement their sustenance.

By nearly every measure, then, the antipoverty program was enormously successful; but for a number of reasons this fact failed to gain widespread recognition. And *that* failure further damaged the liberal Democratic coalition. What was happening?

First, for those on the left, the negative perceptions arose not only from a propensity to view as a failure anything that fell short of their demands or inflated expectations, but also from a shift in the definition of success. Eliminating obstructions to access and providing money to enhance opportunity for the disadvantaged no longer seemed enough; the new test came to be equality of condition. Difficult as it was for most Americans in ordinary times to support the first two goals, the third one – even in the affluent late sixties – was nothing short of a red flag. Americans have usually endorsed the ideal of equality of opportunity, but they have never favored economic equality.

Second, logic and ideal visions ran up against politics as the art of the possible. If reducing unemployment from 7 percent to 4 percent was good, eliminating it altogether had to be better. If the gap between the income of the poor and the near-poor was $12 billion (or less than 1 percent of GNP, as it probably was in 1972), then anything above zero poverty seemed unacceptable. Nor would the idealists accept the political, perhaps sociological realities. For the many Americans who believed that poverty corresponded at least in some measure to

---

[60] An alternative explanation might be that many of the poor subsisted in the "underground" economy. A society that does not provide a substantial safety net for its disadvantaged citizens must expect that economy to be large.

immorality, going that extra one percent would only encourage (further) malin-gering and dependency. The emergence in 1967 of a National Welfare Rights Organization struck such traditionalists as the height of presumption. Although the NWRO for the most part aimed merely to press a dilatory bureaucracy for prompt and honest administration of the antipoverty measures on the books, the idea that welfare recipients had *rights* – rather than enjoyed *favors* from gen-erous Americans – antagonized many voters.

Inevitably the race issue intruded, largely despite the facts. The majority of unwed and never-married mothers were white. Between 1970 and 1985, the un-wed birthrate for white teenagers increased by 90 percent while the rate for black teenagers actually fell slightly in that period. By the 1990s, there were almost 50 percent more white children born of unwed mothers annually than there were black children of unwed mothers. Proportionately, however, the percentage of black children born to single mothers outpaced that of white children by three and even four to one. By the 1980s, between 60 and 70 percent of all black chil-dren were born to single mothers; in some cities, the figures were much higher. That meant that a grossly disproportionate number of Afro-Americans were showing up on the welfare rolls.

Although fewer in number in the nation as a whole, needy blacks were decid-edly more visible than were indigent whites, especially since they were concen-trated in the cities. For many Americans, the problem appeared to be a racial one, coupled with a "cultural" element associated with race. With a powerful nudge from the ghetto riots – beginning most conspicuously with the Watts riot of 1965 and culminating with massive riots in about 130 cities and towns following the 1968 assassination of Martin Luther King, Jr. – old prejudices re-emerged. Combined with the provocative post-King civil rights ethos, the racial element helped make antipoverty programs unpopular.

In addition to all this, the recession of the seventies cut into the real income of most families below the top 30–50 percent of income groups. As we noted ear-lier, an economy of abundance had sweetened popular attitudes and reduced the political risks for the Democrats in adopting antipoverty programs. Then, when the rapid spread of affluence abated and when the populous postwar genera-tion of men and women just coming into the job market struggled for advantage in a more competitive workplace, "Do Your Own Thing," one popular slogan of the Sixties, gave way to "The Me Decade" and "Looking Out for Number One." The last quarter of the twentieth century featured among young middle-class Americans a more self-absorbed, cynical, indeed crabbed mentality and lifestyle, attitudes that were minimally concerned with injustice, averse to per-sonal and community commitments, and focused on career. Not for any joy in constructive labor, but simply to make money: for some, to get rich; for others, merely to hold on to some measure of the lifestyle to which their elders had ascended.

In these circumstances, the near-poor inevitably had their attention drawn to the fact that their net income after taxes barely exceeded – and in some cases fell short of – the income of welfare recipients. Moreover, most welfare recipients also had guaranteed medical care through Medicaid, while most of the working poor had no insurance. The problem would become exacerbated over the course of the century's last quarter not only for the working poor but also for middle-class working families. During the 23-year period 1973–1996, real median family income rose at an annual average of just 0.2 percent, as compared with the 2.7-percent annual average for the third quarter of the century. During these 23 years, real median household income rose by a mere $550, or an average of $24 a year, despite a substantial increase in the number of two-earner households.[61] On these facts alone, there can be little mystery concerning the rise of a politics of resentment among voters who had previously been an important part of the liberal Democratic coalition.

Meanwhile, many of the antipoverty programs were not delivering on their promises or were falling into confusion and corruption. Too much of the administration was delegated to state and local agencies. Arguments for "decentralization" were popular among those on the left throughout the Sixties, partly in line with "power to the people" sloganeering. Such arguments mirrored the conservatives' attack on federal power and their insistence on "states' rights." Decentralization permitted many local officials to turn programs into pork-barrel patronage machines or to stall and to discriminate in the distribution of benefits, often in malignant racial fashion. Record keeping was often poor and accountability channels became tangled, permitting nepotism, embezzlement, and other forms of corruption. And, to be sure, there were those who exploited the programs to double-dip into the welfare pot or to support themselves with welfare payments instead of seeking employment. In short, too often the truly needy went wanting. This provided rich material for conservative nay-sayers.

It did not help that, in proposing the War on Poverty, presidents Kennedy and Johnson had incautiously vowed to *eliminate* poverty. Many critics of Kennedy and Johnson like to emphasize that, in their eagerness to sell the program to taxpayers, they had promised to end the need for antipoverty programs. The Head Start, Job Corps, Upward Bound, and similar programs were designed to help more Americans pull themselves out of poverty – to eliminate poverty altogether and thus the need for cash and in-kind transfer payments.

Such optimism neglected the nature of "hard core" poverty. Much poverty resulted from incapacity of various sorts: age, illness, dementia, neurosis, frailty,

---

[61] Paul Ryscavage, *Income Inequality in America: An Analysis of Trends* (M.E. Sharpe, 1999), pp. 46–7.

and simple ignorance. Some hard-core poverty, moreover, had certain self-sustaining features. When children are seriously neglected and/or abused during the first four or five years of their life, the damage done to mental capacity, energy levels, learning ability, self-discipline, and emotional stability can be irreversible or very nearly so.[62] The spread of heavy drug use among the already poor, the effect of malnutrition on infants, and the rising incidence (especially among the already poor) of unwed and teenage mothers, many of whom were already "damaged" in various ways and who often lacked adequate prenatal care, bequeathed to posterity the certainty of a substantial number of chronically impoverished individuals. Some careful statistical studies show, for example, that "children born outside of marriage are less likely to complete high school than children born within marriage." Teen mothers more likely will have children who will become teen mothers. Unwed mothers most often will have a second child without marrying. Single-parent families make up the largest single component of the poor. These findings hold up regardless of race. They also say much about the makings of hard-core poverty.[63]

Poor education and poor information bred joblessness and poverty, and poverty bred poor education and poor information along with low expectations and embitterment. Liberals and radicals usually argued that poverty was a consequence of social inequality, racism, and exploitation, while conservatives placed the blame on moral weakness, lassitude, and dim wits.[64] The former may have been more sympathetic than the latter, but neither acknowledged the self-sustaining character of much hard-core poverty. In circular circumstances, every cause is an effect and every effect is a cause. With individual determination and outside help, some could work their way out. But at least in the short term there was no ready way for most to break the circle.[65]

The most humane remedy for hard-core poverty would be (1) to reduce the misery of being poor with minimally humane cash and in-kind transfer payments, and (2) to provide, for those who retained some capacity to escape from

---

[62] The likely "irreversibility" of infant and childhood damage caused by neglect remains a controversial question, but there is substantial empirical evidence that supports the theory. See e.g. Rene A. Spitz, *The Role of Ecological Factors in the Emotional Development in Infancy* (University of Chicago Press, 1949), and John Bowlby, *Attachment and Loss,* 3 vols. (Basic Books, 1969, 1973, 1980); see also Wu & Wolfe, *Out of Wedlock,* especially ch. 10.

[63] Wu & Wolfe, *Out of Wedlock,* pp. xviii–xxix and ch. 10.

[64] See William Julius Wilson, *The Truly Disadvantaged: The Inner City, the Underclass, and Public Policy* (University of Chicago Press, 1987), ch. 1, for a discussion of "Cycles of Deprivation"; cf. Oscar Lewis, *Five Families: Mexican Case Studies in the Culture of Poverty* (Basic Books, 1959), and Daniel Patrick Moynihan, ed., *On Understanding Poverty* (Basic Books, 1968).

[65] Dwight Macdonald's renowned *New Yorker* essay, "Our Invisible Poor," made much of the "self-perpetuating milieu" in which too many of the modern poor found themselves. *The New Yorker* (19 Jan. 1963).

the environmental quicksand that was their unlucky birthright, the means and opportunity to do so. That was, of course the purpose of Head Start, Upward Bound, and other elements of the War on Poverty, including affirmative action.

Lost among those who sought to gut the welfare programs were the external costs of *not* providing for the poor: increased emergency-room costs; increased crime; reduced education benefits and hence the loss of potentially constructive energies and talents; and dooming ever more of the poor to an impoverished life. Add to that all the social costs of having a sector of society so alienated as to respond readily to a variety of antisocial temptations and incentives. In the last quarter of the century, the prison population soared to almost 2 million, including almost 2 percent of the adult male population – at an average cost of $40,000 per prisoner per year. That came to about $80 billion per year, or more than government spent on Medicaid ($57 billion) and Head Start ($5 billion) combined in 2000. The poor were no more likely to commit crimes that ruined people's lives than corporate executives who milked or bankrupted major businesses and banks, but there were many more of the poor, their crimes got much more attention, and they lacked the high-priced lawyers who could magically transform their transgressions into mere ethical lapses.

In brief, although the Great Society programs succeeded in reducing poverty by half, in reducing the misery of those who remained poor, and in offering self-help opportunities through Head Start and similar programs, they did increase public expenditures and also provided local bureaucrats with opportunities for self-enrichment. Conservative Republicans understood that federal largesse disbursed by Democratic administrations to friendly local agencies helped sustain the power of the Democratic Party. The antipoverty efforts thus had to be depicted as failures. With many on the left as allies, the conservative backlash took over the field. Cynicism replaced optimism, sapping the strength of the liberal Democratic coalition.

The Regulatory State

Michael Pertschuk, a young congressional aide to a moderately liberal Democratic senator in the sixties and early seventies and chairman of the Federal Trade Commission (FTC) during the Carter presidency, later wrote of how in the Sixties he was so buoyed by the aroused, expansive, generous ethos of the times that he "dismissed as archaic" established political theory's "grim portrait of business's political privilege and disproportionate influence on government decision-making" that, according to the received wisdom, "inexorably [deflected] ... the regulatory impulse." "By 1966," he wrote, "we were confident that such industry domination of congressional decision making was only a rude and un-lamented memory."[66] As a legislative assistant to Warren Magnuson's Senate Commerce Committee, Pertschuk helped write some of the most far-reaching regulatory measures in the country's history and saw them through to passage as well.

As chairman of the FTC a few years later, he would face the fury of the coun-terattack. With the trauma of the war in Vietnam came a growing preference for a less activist state. With the revelations of dissembling (and worse) by the country's leaders over the war, the Watergate felonies, and other matters came a growing distrust of government. With the rising crime rate and the dramatic challenges to conventional decorum in racial relations, gender roles, and sex-ual behavior came a growing assertiveness for a return to "traditional values." Finally, with the decline in the nation's international power and the onset of "stagflation" by the mid-seventies came a growing resistance to the supposed costs of the welfare and regulatory state.

On top of it all, the language of "failure" sapped an activist government of its legitimacy. It became clever to say, as Ronald Reagan often did in the seventies as he worked for the Republican presidential nomination in 1980, "government is the problem, not the solution." For the business world, among academicians, and in the media, "deregulation" became the mantra, a buzzword of the decade. More than that, the corporate community began a vigorous political counter-attack. Corporate leaders for the most part had remained politically acquiescent through the vast social changes of the Sixties. For most business executives, the great conglomerate and multinational reorganization of business amid vigorous economic growth seemingly held their full interest. But the political and eco-nomic traumas of the early seventies, coinciding with a barrage of new federal regulatory legislation, "woke the sleeping giant."[67] Stung by the new govern-mental restraints and requirements amid the economic slump, the megacorpora-tion executives mobilized for political action as they never had in the country's history. Until the seventies, CEOs had shunned direct political involvement, leaving it to trade associations to do the "dirty work" of lobbying the politi-cians, the regulatory agencies, and the media. Neither the top executives nor their favored juniors on their way up the ladder had given much attention to af-fairs in Washington except when government contracts, tariffs, or the like were pending. Direct political involvement was considered to be something less than "respectable" for a business executive; that was what hired lobbyists were for.

[66] Michael Pertschuk, *Revolt against Regulation: The Rise and Pause of the Consumer Movement* (University of California Press, 1982), pp. 8–9.
[67] Ibid., p. 55.

Besides, in the flush times of the fifties and sixties, the costs of new regulations could be readily passed on to consumers.[68]

But in 1972 the one hundred (later several hundred) CEOs of the nation's biggest corporations formed the Business Roundtable, whose explicit purpose was to attack any government intervention in the economy that did not serve their interests. United with several "umbrella" organizations such as the United States Chamber of Commerce and the National Association of Manufacturers, the corporate community rallied for action.

"By 1974," wrote Pertschuk, "the foundations had been laid for a political mobilization effort by business of a scope and breadth for which only the industrial mobilization of World War II provides a sufficiently heroic, if extreme, analogy." Within and across industries, Pertschuk noted, "structures of political coordination and cooperation had proliferated, from the chief executives of the major industrial and financial firms politically united in the Business Roundtable to the 2,700 local congressional action committees of the [U.S.] Chamber of Commerce." Altogether, these organizations made up "a network of close personal friends and supporters of congressmen and other political leaders."[69]

To provide some idea of the sweeping dimensions of the regulatory movement, political scientist David Vogel tabulated federal regulations in several areas for three major periods of twentieth-century reform. He found that, in the area of consumer protection and health, there were 5 new laws in the Progressive Era, 11 during the thirties, and 65 during the sixties and seventies. In the area of job safety, there were 5 in the Progressive Era, 5 during the New Deal, and 21 in the era of the Great Society. In energy and environment, 2 important measures passed in the Progressive Era, 5 during the thirties, and 32 in the sixties and seventies. Not only were there many more regulatory measures coming down from the federal government, but, unlike the early independent regulatory agencies, the new regulations typically aimed at no single industry but rather applied across industrial lines.[70]

In addition to the measures that Vogel tabulated, there were federal mandates regarding civil rights that placed constraints on employers' discretionary power over whom they might employ and promote as well as on property owners' discretion regarding who could lease or buy their property. Meanwhile, the

---

[68] Ibid., pp. 16, 51. On the political aloofness of corporate officers until the seventies, see Edwin Epstein, *The Corporation in American Politics* (Prentice-Hall, 1969).

[69] Pertschuk, *Revolt against Regulation*, pp. 56–7.

[70] David Vogel, "The 'New' Social Regulation in Historical and Comparative Perspective," in Thomas K. McCraw, ed., *Regulation in Perspective* (Harvard University Press, 1981).

independent regulatory commissions, most notably the FTC, became more active in stopping what they found to be dishonest, unfair, and sometimes unsafe business and industrial practices.

There was little doubt that the new social regulations greatly improved the quality of life for Americans. They emancipated the disabled, opened opportunities for minorities and women, reduced work and product hazards, reduced environmental waste and pollution, protected consumers against fraud, misinformation, and harmful products, exposed much financial trickery, and provided the nation's first venture into a health insurance system for some elderly and indigent. By holding private industry accountable for many environmental and health costs, the new regulations restored some of the accountability of employers and manufacturers that nineteenth-century public policy had removed in the nation's rush for industrial growth. They also kept pace with, and helped inspire, similar regulations in other industrial countries.

Congress and the independent regulatory commissions were not the only sources of the new regulatory regime. The courts, of course, were another. Supreme Court decisions on constitutional requirements rewrote the rules regarding not only racial relations but also those governing many other areas of public and private life. They included rules that police must follow when questioning, arresting, and jailing suspects; that states must follow in drawing election district lines and, to some extent, in granting welfare benefits; and that public schools must follow in protecting children from religious proselytizing. Court decisions also held private innkeepers, landlords, and employers liable in civil suits if they or their company were found discriminating against persons because of their race, sex, religion, ethnicity, age, or disability. In each of these areas, the courts imposed national standards where local standards and practices had long prevailed. The courts attempted to do the same with regard to obscenity and pornography and with regard to women's parenthood liberties, including access to contraception and abortion. Many of such decisions were directed at *removing* government control of private behavior yet had the appearance of adding constraints because they required reversal of local law and customs.

When the corporate sleeping giant awoke and moved to shake off the constraints of the new regulations, it found that it had allies from many sectors of the polity – most remarkably, on the left. From that direction came complaints that the regulatory system had failed to protect consumer interests while promoting corporate interests.

There is some irony in the common view that postwar America had become a consumer society. If by the term it is meant that the country's industrial system rested primarily on the production of consumer goods, as opposed to capital goods, then the United States was already a consumer society back in Teddy Roosevelt's time. That was when meatpacking replaced steel as the leading industry, to be by-passed soon after by automobiles. If the term is intended to describe how Americans came to treat shopping as a major form of recreation and not merely an activity to satisfy a subsistence need, then there is some further truth to the notion. But whether the economy was fueled by Americans' avid shopping for consumer goods or by industry's consumption of capital goods, the focus of the economy remained on *production*. The nation's politics clearly expressed that fact.

Until the late sixties, politics still turned on the competition for government favor among rival claims for the rewards of production. For businesses and employers, that meant protective tariffs to ensure profits, tax exemptions, infra-structure development, legal and police restraints on labor unions, and various other subsidies. For labor, it meant support for improving wages, working condi-tions, social insurance, protective tariffs to ensure jobs, and collective bargaining rights. It was not until the late 1960s and early 1970s that politics would begin to reflect Americans' *consumer* interests, as distinct from their producer inter-ests either as profit takers or as wage and salary earners. It was not until then that Americans would begin to gain protection against fraud, misrepresentation, and the adulteration and poisoning of the things they bought, brought into their house, and put into their mouth. It was not until then that consumers gained the right to know what potentially injurious or even fatal ingredients lay hidden in the complex and chemically processed products they used or ate. (Catch-all in-gredients such as "vegetable oils," for example, could include sesame or peanut oil, to which some people are mortally allergic.)[71]

It took a series of scandals to bring consumer interests to the attention of American politics. The work of Ralph Nader early in the sixties in exposing the attempt by General Motors to cover up the flawed design of the company's sub-compact Corvair, which had a lamentable tendency to flip over when making sharp turns, turned a spotlight on corporate arrogance.[72] The scandal became magnified when it was revealed that GM's officers had hired sleuths to dig up dirt on Nader, an effort that failed and boomeranged; GM president (later CEO) James Roche formally apologized in 1966 for the company's disgusting behavior.

The public's indignation did not last. A decade later, as the deregulation movement was underway, it was revealed through a criminal indictment of Ford

---

[71] One could argue that the legislation of the Progressive Era that created the Food & Drug Admin-istration and the meat inspection agency of the U.S. Department of Agriculture were consumer protection acts. But it must not escape notice that both measures were supported and indeed initi-ated by the larger companies seeking protection against the sleazy practices of smaller producers, practices that had inspired bans overseas against American exporters.

[72] Ralph Nader, *Unsafe at Any Speed: The Designed-in Dangers of the American Automobile* (Gross-man, 1965).

Motor Company that company managers had coldly calculated that to recall their popular compact car, the Pinto, because the gasoline tank was dangerously situated, would be more expensive than paying off the few scores of victims and their families when Pintos exploded upon certain kinds of collisions.[73] No outcry. In Illinois the corporation, but no individual executive, was indicted on criminal charges, a first in legal history. It was acquitted. (Criminal guilt must be proved "beyond a reasonable doubt.") What would have happened if Ford had been convicted isn't clear; a corporation cannot be jailed. To have rescinded the corporation's charter or otherwise forced it out of business would have punished only thousands of workers innocent of the crime. No executives were indicted. The Pinto model's creator, Lee Iacocca, had meanwhile moved on to become head of Chrysler, escaping unscathed in reputation and pocketbook.

Before the seventies ended, Congress and the American people made clear their preference for producer interests over consumer interests. The first signal came in 1977 when Congress defeated a measure to hold used-car dealers responsible for revealing to customers what might be wrong with the heaps they were hawking. The nation's representatives followed that up by rejecting proposals to elevate a consumer protection department to cabinet level, alongside the producer-promoting departments of agriculture, labor, and commerce. The Reagan revolution, beginning in the eighties and carrying through strongly past the end of the millennium, restored to its fullest the traditional public policy slant toward producer interests. The newly fashionable supply-side economics called for repeal of consumer protection regulations when cost–benefit analyses determined that regulatory costs to producers exceeded the value (however calculated) of human lives impaired or destroyed by production and distribution processes. Everything, according to "supply siders," had to be determined in terms of supply. Thus, a fair distribution of social rewards and resources for individuals depended on their ability to *supply* talent and energy in the marketplace, not on basic or even subsistence consumer needs.[74] Public policy afforded only the lowest priorities to Americans who could not *produce*. By 2004, a U.S. president would declare his serious interest in replacing all income and corporation taxes with a tax on consumption!

---

[73] Francis T. Cullen, William J. Maakestad, & Gray Cavender, *Corporate Crime under Attack: The Ford Pinto Case and Beyond* (Anderson, 1987); Peter Collier & David Horowitz, *The Fords: An American Epic* (Summit, 1987), pp. 405–6.

[74] See e.g. Haynes Johnson, *Sleepwalking through History: America in the Reagan Years* (Anchor, 1991), especially pp. 105–6. Among its first orders of business after the turn of the millennium, the administration of Bush II opposed requiring auto companies to reveal flaws in their products because, said the administration, it would injure manufacturers. And, incredibly, it refused to *permit* cattle growers to test their animals for mad cow disease because doing so would cast doubt on the safety of eating meat and thus injure agriculture interests.

If America were "a consumer society," precious little of its politics and policy priorities reflected it.

Ironically, at the same time that the consumers' movement was finally getting government to require manufacturers, processors, distributors, creditors, and vendors to meet minimum standards of honesty, safety, and health, leaders of the movement began an assault on some of the independent regulatory commissions. By the end of the sixties, some consumer advocates began charging that the regulatory commissions had become captured by the dominant players in the industries they were supposed to be regulating.

The history of independent regulatory commissions showed indeed that they often had been "captured."[75] It was a common occurrence in the American democratic polity, which lacked a professional policy-making civil service. Commissioners rarely remained on the job for more than three or four years at a time, meanwhile getting cozy with executives of the corporations they oversaw. Perhaps, too, they were always alert to more remunerative employment opportunities in the future with corporations in the same industries they oversaw. The temptations – maybe one can say the incentives – were strong for industry to control the commissions rather than the other way around.[76] (The same dynamic governed the behavior of legislators, especially at the state level where, in many states by the 1990s, term limits abbreviated legislators' political careers.)

The assault was led by Ralph Nader, by all odds the champion of consumer interests ever since his 1965 book, *Unsafe at Any Speed*, indicted the automobile industry for willfully neglecting to correct known unsafe features of their products and causing many hundreds of unnecessary injuries and deaths. Beginning in 1969, Nader began attacking the FTC and the FDA for protecting business interests rather than the interests of consumers. In addition, along with some congressional liberals such as Senator Edward Kennedy, he charged that the Federal Communications Commission (FCC), the Interstate Commerce Commission (ICC), and the Civil Aeronautics Board (CAB) were protecting monopoly or cartel practices that extorted high prices from consumers. The charges were largely accurate with respect to some groups of consumers, though it would be

---

[75] See e.g. Marver H. Bernstein, *Regulating Business by Independent Commission* (Princeton University Press, 1955). Bernstein was a pioneer in recognizing the *cyclical* character of "capture" and "responsiveness" in the regulatory commissions' behavior. Although unhappy with the overall record of the commissions, he noted that they tended to respond to purposeful political leadership and heightened public awareness.

[76] Yet, because the political economy included a multitude of businesses with rival economic interests in policy decisions, there also remained strong personal incentives among regulators to make evenhanded decisions "in the public interest." "With respect to the achievement of fairness and equity in administrative adjudication the record of commissions is good." Bernstein (ibid.), p. 294.

unjust to suggest that the agencies were complicit in extortion. There were, in fact, some benign policy objectives in the oversight of cartel-like practices.

In general, the theory behind regulating the nation's transportation industries – as well as the communications, fuel, and energy transmission industries – was that associated with the notion of a public utility.[77] Public utilities provide the services and energy on which the rest of the society's economic activity depends. Typically they are provided most efficiently – considering their public service purpose – when they have a protected or near-monopoly franchise. Following the theory that underlay state-built and state-maintained roads, postal services, sewerage, water, police, firefighting, street lighting, and military facilities, governments in most other industrial countries typically provided energy (electrical, carbon-based, nuclear), transportation (railroads, airlines), and communications (telephone, broadcast) facilities. The United States almost alone among industrial countries entrusted for-profit private businesses with providing such infrastructure resources.[78] The different policy choice relates to the absence in the United States throughout most of its history of a professional civil service. But it was understood that, given their importance for the health of the rest of the economy, the private franchises required state controls. That is, at least until the 1970s it was understood that a firm providing electrical power had to be, or ought to be, treated differently from a firm making roller skates. Similarly, a democracy might have greater need to prevent monopolistic developments in an industry that provided information (print and broadcast media) than in an industry that produced broiler chickens. That understanding began to wither in the seventies.

But the real difficulty for the consumer movement itself lay in how the charges of complicity in "extortion" contributed to broad unintended consequences. In Michael Pertschuk's words, "Just as Nader's attacks on the unresponsive regulatory bureaucracy had the unintended side effect of feeding public disaffection and distrust of government, so the enthusiastic embrace of deregulation rhetoric by liberals tended to lend legitimacy to the attacks by businessmen and economists ... who pursued the elimination of health, safety, and consumer regulation."[79]

The FCC oversaw the telephone system over which AT&T held a nearly complete monopoly, not only on long-distance service but on residential telephone

---

[77] For a thoughtful commentary see Gerald P. Berk, "Approaches to the History of Regulation," in McCraw, *Regulation in Perspective*, pp. 187–204.

[78] It is interesting to compare the views of Herbert Hoover, expressed when he was Secretary of Commerce in 1922, near the birth of modern broadcasting, with the by-now unquestioned "wisdom" of giving over to "private enterprise" control of the airways. "It is unconceivable," he declared, "that we should allow so great a possibility for service to be drowned in advertising chatter." *Memoirs of Herbert Hoover: The Cabinet and the Presidency, 1920–33* (Macmillan, 1952), p. 140.

[79] Pertschuk, *Revolt against Regulation*, p. 64.

equipment. The ICC fixed both rail and trucking rates, and limited new entries into each industry. The CAB similarly controlled air fares and airline routes, likewise limiting new, competitive entries into the industry and permitting high profits for heavily trafficked routes.

In the case of the telephone industry, technological innovations had negated much of the original rationale for AT&T's monopoly, and it was beyond dispute that for many years AT&T had deliberately blocked innovations while using its monopoly power to keep both telephone equipment and telephone service, especially long-distance service, unduly expensive. In any case, the courts soon ordered the dismemberment of AT&T and – with the aid of computers, fiberglass cable systems, cell phones, and satellite transmitters – the communications industry underwent a vast, competitive reshaping.[80]

But in the other industries, there were sound reasons for the anticompetitive regulations that Nader and other consumer advocates complained of. In the transportation industry, there remained concern that a competitive rush to cut costs would jeopardize both service and safety. That had greater cogency for the rail and trucking industries than for airlines. Although probably more people die each year from trucking and rail accidents than from air crashes, the deaths occur in smaller increments; they rarely top the news and have little or no effect on customer use. In short, trucking companies may well calculate gains in cost cutting that sacrifices safety. Airline companies, on the other hand, have their own vital economic interest in safeguarding against crashes, as does the industry's highly skilled workforce.

But there was another reason for the cartel-type rules governing air traffic: By keeping fares high and profitable for heavily traveled routes (e.g., Washington–Los Angeles, New York–Chicago), the CAB could justify requiring the airlines to service at reasonable rates less trafficked routes (Cleveland–Philadelphia or Missoula–Houston).

In the antigovernment environment of the seventies, leftist liberals as well as right-wing libertarian ideologues saw mostly the negative side of government regulations. Libertarians clung to an almost religious faith in the infallible "efficiency" of the so-called free market. Those on the left emphasized the corruptibility of the regulators: by the seventies, denouncing unresponsive and venal bureaucrats had become commonplace in radical rhetoric. Rather than let "government bureaucrats" decide on how and at what price energy, transportation,

---

[80] Even so, within fifteen years of deregulation of the communications industry, competition no longer seemed to be an unalloyed blessing. The massive consolidations permitted by the free-market ideological environment led to unconstrained monopolistic behavior in many local markets. And the monumental bankruptcies in the industry in 2002 led some analysts to wonder all over again if an infrastructure industry with such enormous overhead in capital equipment – and so essential to the business economy overall – should not be treated as a public utility closely regulated by government.

and communication facilities should be provided, many liberals joined conservatives in looking to "the market."

The champion consumer advocate, Ralph Nader, echoed neoclassical economists in denouncing the ICC. "For generations," he wrote in 1970, "the ICC has operated as a shield, protecting and preserving economic groups from the discipline of the marketplace."[81] The populist Senator Fred Harris (D-OK) declared in 1973: "If we replaced the Interstate Commerce Commission with competition in the transportation industry there would be no worry about truckers and railroads controlling their regulators."[82] By 1975 Nader was calling for the outright abolition of the CAB, a position that even the economist Alfred Kahn – a Nixon appointee and perhaps the country's best-known proponent of airline deregulation – declined to take.[83] "Throughout the land," Nader claimed in a prepared statement at a congressional hearing, "people are repulsed by arrogant and unresponsive bureaucracies serving no useful public purpose, and they are looking to this Congress to get on with the national housecleaning job that is needed."[84]

In the radical environment of the sixties and early seventies, the regulatory commissions seemed to confound "democracy." They became one of the targets of the popular demand for "power to the people." Merely to call attention to the "undemocratic" nature of the independent regulatory commissions provided many radicals with sufficient reason to attack them. Conservatives and affected business interests were quick to pick up the same rhetoric.

There were indeed reasons to distrust the regulatory commissions in an era when a liberal Congress was transforming the political economy with controls that necessarily impinged on businessmen's costs, discretionary power, and proprietary privileges. Bureaucrats do not commonly respond promptly to mandates that they take on new responsibilities. Besides, with the accession to the presidency of Richard Nixon, the Democratic majority in Congress did not believe it could trust newly appointed regulators. For that reason, Congress attempted in some of the new laws to spell out in unprecedented detail exactly what standards the regulators would be required to apply to business practices. Although that made the rules less flexible, it seemed the only way to overcome the perceived tendency of regulators to confound congressional intent.

Yet it was rash to assume that the strong liberal–Democratic slant of Congress in the late sixties and early seventies would last. More rash still was failing

---

[81] Nader's Foreword to Robert C. Fellmeth, *The Interstate Commerce Omission: The Public Interest and the ICC* (Grossman, 1970), p. vii.

[82] Fred Harris, "The Politics of Corporate Power," in Ralph Nader & Mark J. Green, eds., *Corporate Power in America* (Grossman, 1973), p. 39.

[83] Apart from rates and routes, Kahn acknowledged, broad areas of passenger services required attention.

[84] Quoted in Martha Derthick & Paul J. Quirk, *The Politics of Deregulation* (Brookings, 1985), p. 51.

to anticipate that the independent regulatory agencies might someday become a last line of defense for the reforms Congress had initiated.

By the early seventies, the counterrevolution was already in the making. In part, the reaction owed to a change in intellectual *fashion*. It may be that we give too little credit to the role of fashion in policy making. In the 1950s it was fashionable to attribute discontent to inner sources, say, to the "power of negative thinking." By the end of that decade, however, in the wake of McCarthyism, the Montgomery bus boycott, and the confrontation with federal authority at the Little Rock Central High School, among other unpleasant scenes, blaming agitation on mental attitude no longer washed. Many young people, especially on college campuses, could not fail to see that the social evils they were witnessing (and were tolerated by their parents) were no phantoms of their imagination. The radicals' slogan, "the personal is political," expressed the view that discontents were rooted in the System. That was the fashion then. But by the seventies, the winds of fashion had shifted again, opening a second front for deregulation.

The deregulation of the airline, trucking, railroad, and telephone industries that was effected during the Democratic presidency of Jimmy Carter (1977–1981) in some ways poses a historical problem similar to that of the War on Poverty. That is, in neither case was there an obvious constituency. Contrary to expected form, the major players in the industries, both corporate management and the labor unions, opposed deregulation. The public seemed entirely passive if not oblivious. Although conservative organizations supported deregulation as if it were religious doctrine, it was expected that conservatives in Congress would, as usual, respond to the wishes of the major industrial players and oppose it.

As in the poverty case, initiatives for deregulation came from what have to be called *elite* sources. Academia again produced independently initiated research that provided a rationale. "The work of political scientists and historians," noted Martha Derthick and Paul Quirk, specialists in government–business relations, "entered into the critique of regulatory conduct. As the social sciences began to take up the study of regulation, their intellectual products began to invade law-school curricula and publications." This was important because regulators typically were recruited from law schools. Moreover, "people who take their cues from the luminaries of the academic world," including the press, "would have come to think of procompetitive deregulation as a desirable thing."

A generation earlier, the economic and law schools produced studies that took for granted the importance of regulating public utilities in the interest of maintaining services and keeping production costs down. By the end of the sixties, a new fashion had set in. Students of politics always encounter the phenomenon of the half-full glass. One generation will insist it is half-full, the next that it is half-empty. Remarked one economist: "You never have to run the risk of being dead wrong [in] saying regulation has been foolish in a particular sector."[85]

"Apart from the properties of the fashionable idea itself and the properties of its sponsors," wrote Derthick and Quirk, "the creation of ... policy fashion is to be understood also by reference to the nature of the community." Washington, they observed, was "highly susceptible to fashions." Washingtonians were intensely competitive and status conscious. "The notion of deregulation itself," they concluded, "as prescription turned symbol turned fashion, had an influence on events that was to some degree independent of the resources [i.e. evidence] deployed by particular advocates."[86]

By the seventies, in any case, a mostly young cohort of economists and political scientists had emerged determined to challenge the wisdom of their elders about the need for regulating business, particularly infrastructure businesses. This was mostly an independent intellectual development, not a venal one. But those who argued that regulations "distorted the market" and thus led to "economic inefficiency" could depend on financial and media attention. In particular, a growing number of scholars began producing studies indicating that regulations governing the transportation and telephone industries, among others, had stunted development and raised consumer costs.[87] As the economy deteriorated, their findings gained more attention, especially as they coincided with the criticisms coming from conservative business groups. As Michael Pertschuk remarked, using the supply-and-demand model cherished by free marketeers: "where a healthy demand from business for ideologically compatible economics exists, market incentives help to stimulate a supply."[88]

But of course the deregulation mania that swept the country for the last quarter of the twentieth century owed also to concrete economic interests and their political expression. Criticism from the business sector may be easily understandable. The new regulations were costly; and the costs came to be applied precisely at the moment when the United States was losing its unchallenged economic supremacy and when foreign competition cut into American production. Moreover, the costs of compliance with OSHA, EPA, and civil rights guidelines fell disproportionately on smaller businesses, thereby alienating one of the liberal Democratic coalition's most important constituencies.

---

[85] Derthick & Quirk, *Politics of Deregulation*, p. 54.

[86] Ibid., pp. 55, 57.

[87] See e.g. Chris Argyris et al., *Regulating Business: The Search for an Optimum* (Institute for Contemporary Studies, 1978); Alfred E. Kahn, *The Economics of Regulation: Principles and Institutions* (MIT Press, 1989); Barry M. Mitnick, *The Political Economy of Regulation: Creating, Designing, and Removing Regulatory Forms* (Columbia University Press, 1980); James Q. Wilson, ed., *The Politics of Regulation* (Basic Books, 1980).

[88] Pertschuk, *Revolt against Regulation*, p. 65.

Meanwhile, product safety requirements seemed to be drifting toward "no risk" levels. There was a tendency in the recent evolution of tort law to restore ancient notions of "strict liability" – that is, to override the need to prove negligence in claiming recompense for injury. That principle had cogency in a pre-industrial era when most business and employment relationships took place in a face-to-face environment. But when the Industrial Revolution inspired the production of goods and services on a mass scale for mass markets served by numerous intermediaries, traditional principles of liability would have impeded economic development. By the end of the nineteenth century, tort law had followed these economic imperatives and greatly reduced employer and producer liability. By the middle of the twentieth century, however, consumer, labor, environmental, and humanitarian interests became persuasive in arguing that reducing entrepreneurial risk had gone much too far. Hence the movement in the sixties and early seventies to restore accountability to perpetrators of personal and environmental damage.

With the onset of stagflation in the mid-seventies, the focus shifted once again to the harmful effects of laying a heavy burden of liability on employers and producers. Anecdotal examples of both the inequitable and economic burdens of the new liability rules gained insistent attention. For example, if eight people were injured by an alleged malfunction of a machine or a dire reaction to a medication, even though thousands had been sold and used safely over many years, a liability suit could drive the manufacturer out of business. There seemed little consideration for the risks associated with (a) rising costs of products, (b) diminished availability of products, including especially some pharmaceuticals and medical devices, or (c) increased exposure of companies to ruinous litigation. Similar points could be made regarding controlling and cleaning up toxic wastes, which affected the bigger corporations as well. Reasonable people could differ on what levels of pollution or hazard were *tolerable* in relationship to the costs of proposed remedies – including lost employment opportunities. Slowed economic growth also had implications for the life chances of the poor. Finally, some scholars began noting that the concept of risk itself often seemed capricious, that it was something of "a social construct" insofar as people often took for granted certain serious risks while focusing on lesser ones.[89] By the seventies, in the political and social environment already described, such considerations began to outweigh earlier indignation over the arrogant negligence of manufacturers (e.g., General Motors and Ford).

---

[89] See e.g. Mary Douglas & Aaron Wildavsky, *Risk and Culture: An Essay on the Selection of Technological and Environmental Dangers* (University of California Press, 1983); also, John D. Graham & Jonathan Baert Wiener, eds., *Risk versus Risk: Tradeoffs in Protecting Health and the Environment* (Harvard University Press, 1995).

Meanwhile, the oil embargo orchestrated in 1973 by the Organization of Petroleum Exporting Countries (OPEC) triggered a quadrupling of fuel prices within a year and created energy shortages throughout the world. The prices and particularly the shortages hit Americans where their heart lay: in their devotion to their cars. Long lines of irate American drivers waiting at gas stations to fill their tanks before supplies ran out seemed to signify graphically the end of affluence and a return to an economy of scarcity. By 1973, the United States depended on imports for almost 40 percent of its petroleum needs. Gone were the days when, as in 1967, America could use its oil surplus to fill shortages in Europe when OPEC attempted a similar embargo.

The oil and natural gas interests were among the first out of the gate in the seventies in the race to the regulatory bottom. If it doesn't already, political theory ought to postulate that those who most proclaim the virtues of the "free market" and who rail against "big government" most likely speak for industries with the greatest dependency on government subsidies and privileges (e.g. agribusiness) or whose industries are among the least competitive (e.g., the oil and natural gas industry). Indeed, the oil and gas industry must set the model. For there are few industries in which monopoly power is exercised more transparently than the energy industry yet few that pay more for ads touting the free market. John Blair, who studied the oil industry for almost forty years in and out of government, put a complicated subject into a nutshell: In domestic oil, he wrote, monopoly practices stemmed "from an amalgam of a moderately high level of concentration, an extraordinary maze of interlocking corporate relationships, an extreme degree of vertical integration, and governmental intervention to limit supply." To top it off, in foreign oil OPEC supplemented domestic corporate concentration.[90]

Inevitably, the oil companies claimed that the inflated prices and fuel shortages after 1973 resulted not from their own monopolistic practices or OPEC but rather from regulations that made it "too costly" for the companies to explore and to produce oil domestically. They demanded an end to government controls. Regulation of the industry for half a century was designed to keep fuel costs down so as to protect the nation's commercial, transportation, manufacturing, farming, and consumer interests. But in the discussion that took place in the seventies, the nation was asked to treat the oil industry as any other for-profit enterprise, such as selling deodorant or toothpaste.

None of the experts seemingly felt impelled to explain how deregulating the domestic fuel industry could possibly enable market forces to govern when the industry was itself so highly concentrated and so long as the OPEC cartel overrode the international market by rigging production. And this was even before deregulation mania permitted the mergers of Chevron with Gulf, Texaco, and

---

[90] John M. Blair, *The Control of Oil* (Pantheon, 1976), p. ix.

Unocal, Exxon with Mobil, Phillips with Conoco, and British Petroleum with Arco, Amoco, and Sohio.

Banks and other financial institutions quickly followed the deregulation trend. There were some good reasons to readjust government supervision of the financial services industry, especially as relatively unregulated brokerage houses and insurance companies began engaging in services conventionally provided by banks. But so spirited was the rush to pull government out of its supervisory role that by the end of seventies the Federal Reserve Board, the Comptroller of the Currency, the Treasury Department, and the Securities Exchange Commission – all the major governing agencies – simply looked the other way while banks engaged in giant mergers across state lines, in clear contravention of federal law and well before Congress got around to considering what laws to repeal or amend and how much to deregulate.[91] Competition for money in a deregulated environment, moreover, led to legislation in 1982 that permitted savings and loan associations to diversify their loan portfolios and to invest more heavily in more risky commercial ventures. One consequence of this deregulation was the massive failure of the savings and loan industry at the end of the 1980s.[92]

To sum it up: A number of partially independent developments boosted the impact of the new political strategy to dismantle the country's regulatory systems. First, the slowness of many American industries to respond to new market developments and opportunities squeezed profits; examples include electronics, fuel-saving automobiles, and low-cost steel production. Whether or not American business leaders looked to adjust their operations internally, their most public response was to blame "big government" for saddling them with regulations. Second, the new regulations were marginally costly, and the costs came to be applied precisely at the moment when the United States was losing its economic supremacy and when foreign competition was cutting into American

---

[91] Sanford Weill – CEO of Citicorp, fashioner of multiple mergers of financial megacorporations such as the brokerage house Shearson, Hamill, Travelers Insurance, and others – bragged about how his bold, extralegal absorption of commercial, mortgage, insurance, and investment banking companies trashed the Glass–Steagle Act of 1933. After the stock market collapse of 2000 and after the collapse of Enron, WorldCom, and other giant corporations revealed massive fraud at the highest corporate levels, the spotlight moved to the workings of the financial services industry. With many suits and government investigations still pending, Weill's Citicorp paid over $42 billion in settlements to clients who had become victims of the massive conflicts of interest within the company that cost them billions of dollars in losses; Glass–Steagle had been designed to preclude just such conflicts of interest. Citicorp's doings were only the tip of the iceberg.

[92] Just for a start, readers should consult Davita Silfen Glasberg & Dan Skidmore, *Corporate Welfare Policy and the Welfare State: Bank Deregulation and the Savings and Loan Bailout* (de Gruyter, 1997). Deregulation did not "cause" the collapse, but it did create an environment of "anything goes." In other words, it created an environment that permitted business practices to descend to the least prudent and the least scrupulous.

markets at home and abroad. Third, that the costs of compliance with regulatory guidelines fell disproportionately on smaller businesses produced allies for big business among some of the liberal Democratic coalition's most important constituencies. Finally, the assault from the left on the regulatory agencies gave unanticipated impetus and legitimacy to the deregulation mania.

17

The Rise of the New Left and the Birth of Neoconservatism

As we have noted, the influence of liberal leaders in government and within the Democratic Party beginning in the 1930s gave liberal reform nearly unprecedented leverage. That influence was crucial in producing an effective War on Poverty that had no political constituency or grassroots movement to initiate or support it. It was equally vital in the fight for civil rights, where a "silent majority" of Americans and political obstructionism by a coalition of conservative Republicans and Southern Democrats would have doomed measures such as the Civil Rights Act of 1964, the Voting Rights Act of 1965, and the Open Housing Act of 1968. Liberal leadership helped to develop a foreign policy that placed significant emphasis on economic assistance to old industrial and newly developing countries on the theory that economic development served most effectively in combating the expansion of Soviet communism – apart from its importance for the American economy and humane ideals. Liberals in the judiciary system helped to enlarge the liberty of ethnic and racial minorities, of women, of gays and lesbians, and of political dissidents, meanwhile offering protection to persons accused of crimes from high-handed police behavior and similarly protecting personal choices in family planning and sexual behavior.

Yet by the seventies, leading liberals began leaving the Democratic Party in serious numbers. James Burnham, erstwhile radical socialist *cum* conservative, remarked on what appeared to be "a collapse of the morale of the governing elite."[1] One important reason for the collapse was the rising influence of the New Left, sometimes referred to as the Movement.

The Movement consisted of mostly young, white American activists, mostly associated with universities, who were motivated by ideals that most of them

---

[1] Quoted in George Nash, *The Conservative Intellectual Movement in America Since 1945* (Harper, 1976), p. 295.

had absorbed in their liberal middle-class homes but who rejected their parents' cautious, incrementalist approach to reform. To espouse ideals without vigorously and purposefully pursuing their fulfillment, they insisted, was *hypocrisy*. With that as a weapon, self-righteousness came easily.

They were the postwar children of affluence for whom tradition and history had no relevance. They grew up in the chill of the Cold War and in the shadow of the Bomb, both of which seemed to them mere signs of a madness fostered by an economic system that featured the mindless pursuit of individual self-interest and relentless material gain. They rejected their parents' up-tight social attitudes, their pursuit of stability, their quest for Success. They lived, as many of them complained, on virtually a different planet from their parents, who seemed gratefully at peace with the world once they had got past the Depression and the war and had managed to stay clear of Joe McCarthy and his imitators. Neither McCarthyism nor Stalinism had much meaning for those born after World War II. Neither did Guernica, Munich, Nazism, Stalinism, or the Holocaust. Their facile dismissal of the fear engendered by McCarthyism made it easy for them to scorn liberal anticommunism. Nor did Marxism offer much that they found useful – hence the *New* Left, equally scornful (or almost equally scornful) of liberalism and of Old Left ideologies.

They grew up with the comfort of penicillin and, soon enough, the Pill. Neither old taboos nor the authority that purported to enforce them had much relevance for them. They expressed their disregard and disrespect with their language, their music, their clothes, their hair. A commercial system that created the category of Youth, for fashion, music, and attitude, furthered their sense of separation and uniqueness. So too did the early stirrings of the sexual revolution, which made personal commitment as trivial as other elements of the conventions they rejected. They believed they had larger commitments to tend to.

They were rebels, but not like the "Beats" of the fifties who turned their discontents inward or into flight or to aimless destructive gestures. They shared the alienation from American middle-class culture of many of that period's literary characters – Jack Kerouac's Sal Paradise, J. D. Salinger's Holden Caulfield, Wallace Stegner's Rodman.[2] But they were rebels *with* a cause. The source of their discontents, they determined, lay not within themselves but in the evils and idiocies of the society that produced them. To respect authority, therefore, was to be complicit with injustice. To flee or to feel guilt was not for them, either. Their ready access to college and university, which the prosperity of the System they deplored had afforded them, armed them with the power of skeptical

---

[2] Jack Kerouac, *On the Road* (Viking, 1957); J. D. Salinger, *Catcher in the Rye* (Little, Brown, 1951); Wallace Stegner, *Angle of Repose* (Fawcett, 1971).

reasoning and sharp argument.[3] They learned how to probe beyond mere incidences or symptoms of injustice to the root cause. They claimed to have found it in the System, which they decided had to be dismantled.

Although those attracted to radical action were never more than a small minority of all students, there were many more millions of college students in the Sixties than ever; more than twice as many by 1970 (7.5 million) as in 1960 (3.6 million).[4] Even only 5 percent of, say, 7.5 million amounts to 375,000 active minds and bodies capable of disturbing complacency, capturing attention, and goading consciences. At various peaks of agitation during the Sixties, the rebels could count on three and four times that number concentrated on campuses and in cities in support of dissident action.

As the decade of the fifties ended, there was as yet little sign of a radical insurgency. Even the civil rights movement remained within the bounds of the System. The nonviolent demonstrations by King's Southern Christian Leadership Conference aimed primarily at persuading white America to accept black America into the System. The NAACP, with Thurgood Marshall as its chief counsel, had made major advances through the legal system that paved the way for King's bus boycott in Montgomery in 1955 and the federal–state confrontation over integrating the Little Rock high school in 1957.

But there was already toward the end of Dwight Eisenhower's presidency a growing impatience among the socially conscious with that president's obtuse attitude toward civil rights as well as with his administration's seemingly complacent response to all kinds of international and domestic problems. Eisenhower's studied identification with "middle America," his publicly imperturbable golf and bridge playing, his postured piety, and his championing of the commonplace and the conventional amid the fast-changing conditions of the postwar world had the effect of accelerating the growing disaffection among so many bright, young, and skeptical Americans from what they were told were the society's core values. They had their own ideas about core values, which seemed to be in sharp contrast with those represented by Americans who "liked Ike" – along with John Wayne, Lawrence Welk, pickup trucks, and Velveeta faux cheese.

The "direct action" of the black students at the Greensboro lunch counter in February 1960, and the rash of similar sit-ins that followed in the South, inspired among the young a broader, more daring approach to change than Martin Luther King or Thurgood Marshall so far had employed.[5] That April, university

---

[3] Wrote Todd Gitlin, an early leader of the Students for a Democratic Society: "Without thinking about it, we all took the fat of the land for granted." *The Sixties: Years of Hope, Days of Rage* (Bantam, 1987), p. 104.

[4] Figures retrieved from ⟨www.census.gov/population/socdemo/school/tabA-1.xls⟩.

[5] Some historians separate the black civil rights movement from the Movement. For purposes of brevity here I treat them as part of the same phenomenon, although acknowledging that most of

students, mostly from black colleges in the South, met in Raleigh. The outcome of the conference was the organization of the Student Nonviolent Coordinating Committee (SNCC). Its members would dedicate themselves to direct confrontation of racism in the South and elsewhere.

That June, with some funding from the United Auto Workers, a number of Northern students, mostly from Michigan, gathered in Manhattan for the first convention of the Students for a Democratic Society (SDS), a renamed and revitalized version of the moribund Student League for Industrial Democracy. Their president-elect, Al Haber, declared: "We have taken the initiative from the adult spokesmen and leadership .... Pessimism and cynicism have given way to direct action."[6] That was premature, as the tiny turnout for the meeting – only 29 members from nine colleges – might have suggested.

A more full-blown convention in Michigan in 1962 would produce "The Port Huron Statement," outlining the SDS purpose. Written mostly by a young Tom Hayden, the manifesto began: "We are people of this generation, bred in at least modest comfort, housed now in universities, looking uncomfortably to the world we inherit." "Many of us," it went on, "began maturing in complacency." But awareness of racism and the glowering presence of the Bomb in the context of the Cold War called attention to "complicated and disturbing paradoxes in our surrounding America." What about "equality" in America? What about "democracy" in America? What about America's protestations of its peaceful intentions?[7]

No concise 500-word Declaration of Independence or Gettysburg Address, this; it was more like a substantial "White Paper." It catalogued what was wrong and what had to be done to make things right. It expressed the sense of *urgency* felt by "people of this generation" and their exasperation over how most Americans wallowed in *apathy* – born, they thought, of powerlessness and fear. The Port Huron Statement complained about manipulation by the media, about the educational system, and about bureaucracy, politics, and big business. It foreshadowed later, more radical assaults on American imperialism and colonialism and on the emptiness or irrelevance of a university experience. It warned of the decline of organized labor in the face of automation and of the growing meaninglessness of work. Most specifically (and perhaps imprudently), it called on liberals to oust the Southern Democrats from the party so as to get past the

the black participants were hardly the "postwar children of affluence" who generally characterized the New Left.

[6] Quoted in Kirkpatrick Sale, *SDS* (Vintage, 1973), p. 27.

[7] Among the many fine accounts of the Movement, in addition to those already mentioned, see especially James Miller, *"Democracy Is in the Streets": From Port Huron to the Siege of Chicago* (Simon & Schuster, 1987), and Terry H. Anderson, *The Movement and the Sixties: Protest in America from Greensboro to Wounded Knee* (Oxford University Press, 1995).

congressional stalemate on civil rights and to extend Social Security coverage, medical insurance, and antipoverty measures.

The statement was, on the whole, a moderate and sensible call to action. Few liberals at the time could have found much in it that was objectionable. In fact, many of the demands would soon become realized during the Johnson administration (with the consequence of turning many Southern Democrats into Republicans and of thrusting most other Southern Democrats from office). Over time, however, the sense of urgency and exasperation would grow faster than what would be achieved.

The SDS and SNCC were not the whole of the Movement. There were other civil rights organizations, other activist student groups, independent antiwar campaigns, women's rights organizations, and so on. But in many ways, SDS and SNCC made up much of what most people understood to be the New Left. Both would become more militant, and violent, as the Sixties progressed. Just how violent would reach tragic dimensions, as when, on 3 March 1970 in Greenwich Village, a group of "Weathermen" – a splinter of SDS dedicated to violent revolution – accidentally blew up three of their own members and a building that they had turned into a bomb factory. (At least three others managed to stumble out of the wreckage and disappear.) It marked the beginning of the end for SDS and for most of the persuasive force of the New Left.

In the meantime, most of the violence would come from another direction. White and black Freedom Riders, determined to implement the Supreme Court's ruling against segregated transportation facilities, rode buses into southern cities – and were set upon by fire bombs and club-wielding thugs. Local police and FBI agents deliberately stood by and watched the one-sided melees. Many Negro churches were bombed, including one in Birmingham where four little girls were killed. No one was prosecuted, though the perpetrators bragged to friends of their "wonderful" deed on behalf of southern traditional values. Civil rights workers were beaten, lynched, and assassinated. The names Medgar Evers, Viola Liuzzo, James Chaney, Michael Schwerner, and Andrew Goodman would stand out among the many activists, white and black, who were murdered by the crazed and cynical defenders of the country's racial traditions.

Such outrages encouraged the radical rhetoric of Black Panthers and SDS Weathermen. For the great majority of Americans (who, as always, watched from the sidelines), only the radical responses evoked outrage.

Meanwhile – in the fall of 1964, using the tactics of civil disobedience that had been employed in Greensboro and other places where local law violated what the Supreme Court had determined to be constitutional rights – nearly a thousand university students and street people in Berkeley, California, joined in a frontal assault on campus authority. What began in the summer as a dispute over the placement of a table in the center of campus for the collection of political campaign funds (for the presidential candidacy of right-wing Republican Barry

Goldwater) escalated by the fall into a massive sit-in inside the main administration building. The event climaxed with the use of scores of police from nearby Oakland to free the building of the occupiers. Thus was the Free Speech Movement (FSM) born, an event that resonated with young college people across the country and, indeed, in many parts of the world.

The protesters made the case that they were fighting for free speech – that is, the right to carry on political discourse publicly on the campus of a public university. On that issue, they had considerable faculty support (although no one had disputed students' right to engage publicly in political discourse a few yards away on city property). Officials strove to defend a long-standing policy designed to keep the university free of political (and religious) controversy in earlier decades, when right-wing and conservative politicos had a proclivity for interfering with academic affairs. It was a weak line to maintain against students who paid little attention to history, especially at a time when racism, poverty, and the escalating U.S. military involvement in Indochina had become hot political issues of direct concern to educated young Americans. Frail as their rationale was, but fearful of right-wing concerns about a "radicalized" Berkeley campus (McCarthyism still loomed prominently in their minds), university officials insisted on enforcing the ban on political activity. Student defiance then turned the issue into the integrity of administrative authority. On this issue, many faculty supported the administration. Yet by pressing charges against a few leaders of the defiant students, the administration triggered the massive sit-in. The administration still had substantial support from the faculty, many of whom believed that the protesters were abusing the tactic of civil disobedience by employing it against a university where law and rules permitted continued discourse and peaceful reform. But when the governor, at the request of the Berkeley chancellor (but over the objections of university president Clark Kerr), called in the police to forcibly remove the protesters from Sproul Hall, most of the faculty deserted the administration. Somehow, the act seemed to the mass of faculty to violate some unspecified tradition of a university as a sanctuary from outside coercive authority.

Curiously, much of the faculty reaction stemmed from a still-active paternalistic sense that they owed protection to students, *their* students, from the brutality that inevitably followed upon a massive police invasion (especially police from the nearby city of Oakland, which for years had purposefully recruited southern rednecks). This was remarkably ironic, because part of the student rebels' demand was that they be treated as mature adults and that the university discard its traditional *in loco parentis* role.[8]

---

[8] See Robert Cohen & Reginald E. Zelnik, eds., *The Free Speech Movement: Reflections on Berkeley in the 1960s* (University of California Press, 2002). For a similar anthology, somewhat less one-sided and compiled soon after the events, see S. M. Lipset & Sheldon Wolin, eds., *The Berkeley Student Revolt* (Anchor, 1965), which includes a reprint of an article by this author, "The

The pattern of student protest (sometimes outright provocation) followed by administrative overreaction would be repeated on dozens of other campuses around the country, and on some campuses overseas. The confrontations would climax in 1968 and 1969 in places like Harvard, Yale, Columbia, and Chicago, as well as in London and Paris. The year 1968 witnessed the Tet offensive in South Vietnam, President Johnson's decision not to run for re-election, the assassinations of Martin Luther King, Jr., and Robert F. Kennedy, massive urban riots across the country following King's murder, and the police riots against antiwar protesters outside the Democratic national convention in Chicago. Liberals on and off university campuses began to find themselves wishing a plague on everyone's house. They had come to seem "irrelevant," as so many student radicals had insisted liberalism to be from the beginning.

"How does a radical," pondered sociologist Nathan Glazer, "a mild radical, it is true, but still one who felt closer to radical than to liberal writers and politicians in the late 1950s, end up a conservative, a mild conservative, but still closer to those who call themselves conservative than to those who call themselves liberal in early 1970?" Partly, Glazer answered his own question, because radicalism changed its character and partly because the conservative elements of his own mid-century radicalism came to claim a more central part of his thinking. Mid-century radicalism, he recalled, "had a good deal in common with conservatism – the skepticism at government intervention in various areas, the willingness to let people decide for themselves how to spend their money, the disbelief that the theoretical and political structures reared by liberals to control policy in the foreign and domestic realms really had solid bases or would work, the allergy to Communist repression, the bias toward the small."

But Glazer noted further that he also came to appreciate more the complexity of governing and how much of what was valuable about modern American society "was owed to its political and organizational structures" – not least, the politically free environment of universities. And so when the turmoil erupted on the Berkeley campus, where he was then teaching, he was less willing than many of his colleagues to endorse the scornful assault by the students on administrative authority in the name of freedom to promote political causes. "I did not share some of my colleagues' views of administrators; I believed they were doing necessary and difficult things in reconciling [the campus's] complex interests, and I appreciated whatever measure of freedom I possess because they were doing these things." Although he found himself agreeing in some measure with the FSM leaders on the wrong-headedness of the war in Vietnam and about the destructive character of bureaucracy, why, he asked, did they have to turn from reasoned discourse to occupying buildings, blockading troop trains, "and finally

Student Rebellion at Berkeley: An Interpretation," that was originally published in the *Massachusetts Review* (Winter/Spring 1965).

proceeding through the whole sequence of escalations with which we are by now [1970] all too familiar."[9]

Without the campus agitation in the Sixties, humane and progressive reform would have lacked much of its necessary political energy. The force behind the War on Poverty, civil rights measures, and eventually legislation protecting consumers, the workplace, and the environment did have sources elsewhere in American society, and especially from leadership in the top agencies of government. But agitation by student organizations gave important impetus to such causes. And yet it was indeed the radicals' rejection of reasoned discourse, their insistence on "nonnegotiable demands," their scornful and contemptuous attitude toward liberals, and the ultimate turn to violence by some of them that alienated so many who had been in the forefront of the agitation for humane progressive change in American society up through the fifties. Among Americans generally, student activism especially after 1965 tended to evoke mostly negative responses. Ronald Reagan would win the governorship of California in 1966 largely on the strength of his attacks on the "student riots" on the Berkeley campus.[10]

Then, in the seventies and especially after the end of military conscription in 1973, college student radicalism all but disappeared except on a single narrow and highly provocative issue: racial and lifestyle *diversity*. Almost nothing except affirmative action and agitation for gay, lesbian, and bisexual rights could get students out into the university plazas for large-scale protests such as had characterized campus life in the Sixties.[11] Nothing else attracted significant attention. Gross cutbacks in social services; renewal of destructive abuse of public lands and water by corporations, whose lobbying and campaign finance practices shaded up to and sometimes slipped over the line to outright bribery of public officials; federal revenue policies that blatantly redistributed Americans' tax burden downward and away from the rich; even cuts in funds for student scholarships – none of these and other retrogressive developments evoked a noteworthy response on the nation's campuses. Nor did the Iran–Contra scandal of the late eighties arouse many students, despite the fact that it involved clear White House mendacity and abuses of power and even though it presented the country with a constitutional crisis whose magnitude was no less serious than that of the Watergate scandal. On these and other issues critical to national and international progress, there was hardly a peep of complaint from the campuses. But nonnegotiable demands

---

[9] Nathan Glazer, *Remembering the Answers: Essays on the American Student Revolt* (Basic Books, 1970), pp. 3, 7, 8, 9. For the negative effect of some of the antiwar agitation, see the previous chapter in this book.

[10] Matthew Dallek, *The Right Moment: Ronald Reagan's First Victory and the Decisive Turning Point in American Politics* (Oxford University Press, 2004).

[11] Campus demands for universities to divest holdings in far-away South Africa in protest against apartheid were among a few exceptions.

for the appointment of more women and "persons of color" to law schools and colleges, and for the establishment of autonomous departments of Black, Hispanic, Asian, Native American, Gay, Lesbian, and Bisexual Studies, periodically occupied the attention of the country's leading universities.

If conservatives and reactionaries had written the script themselves, these developments could hardly have suited them better. However worthy in itself, "diversity" became a diversion, a major detour from more critical issues of national and international concern. Justin Dart, one of the right wing's most important financial supporters in the seventies and eighties, made it clear: "All I gave a damn about," he remarked, "was that [Reagan] was philosophically oriented in the right direction .... Look ... abortion, NAACP, equal rights, and all those [things]. Those are all, forgive me, trivial issues."[12] What was important to people like Dart were deregulation, privatization, union busting, and tax cuts yielding an upward redistribution of income. With a little help from their putative enemies on the campuses, they got what they wanted.

For all its excesses and counterproductive behavior, the New Left did activate thousands of relatively moderate young people on campuses to support humane reforms. The Movement figured substantially in the successful promotion in the Sixties of historic progressive measures. Counterproductive excesses did not disappear altogether; they reappeared from time to time, but nearly exclusively in the demands for "diversity." Meanwhile, the absence of relevant activism on the nation's campuses targeting the erosion of the progressive legislation of the sixties and early seventies or the corruption of election processes by massive corporate money must count among the reasons for the decline of the liberal Democratic coalition and the ascendancy of the post-Watergate reaction.

Over the years, many disaffected liberals came to be identified as "neoconservatives." That was a term used to describe a wide variety of those who were turned off not only by the derisive and absolutist manner of the young radicals but also by the perceived feckless acquiescence of their former liberal associates in the countercultural and neoisolationist drift of the Democratic Party. Like Nathan Glazer, they bitterly resented being labeled "racist" for expressing doubts about affirmative action, being labeled "reactionaries" for expressing concerns about expanding aid to growing numbers of unwed mothers, being called "imperialists" for supporting containment policies,[13] and having their anticommunism and their doubts about Alger Hiss's protestations of innocence attacked as "McCarthyism."

---

[12] Quoted by Haynes Johnson, *Sleepwalking through History: America in the Reagan Years* (Anchor, 1991), p. 74.

[13] Unlike most "neocons," Glazer opposed the war in Vietnam, although he remained strongly anti-Soviet.

Unlike Glazer and small numbers of other critics of the New Left, most neo-conservatives joined in the wholesale rightward shift of the American political agenda during the final quarter of the century. Many moved virtually without reserve in support of conservative goals of reducing taxes for upper-income classes, paring social welfare outlays, stepping up "the war on drugs" and on street crime, and deregulating industry, finance, and commerce. Most of them also fell in line against abortion and for school prayer, rather than challenge their new allies in the Republican Party. Most important, neoconservatives became the strongest proponents of an aggressive, unilateralist foreign policy directed at "international communism" and – after the collapse of the Soviet Union in 1992 – against anti-Israel Islamic regimes. They would be among the leaders in supporting a postmillennial "war on terrorism" that featured the novel presidential doctrine of "preemptive war" as well as the erosion of civil liberties and regard for law in the treatment of citizens and others suspected of connections to international terror groups.

In some respects, the more militant neoconservatives mirrored the young activists against whom they so largely reacted. No less idealistic – which is to say, convinced of the rightness of the causes they promoted – while affecting a hardened "realism," they urged aggressive pursuit of the Cold War abroad and "law and order" at home in the name of protecting individual liberty. They insisted on a hard line: against street crime, even at the risk of eroding civil liberties; against the Soviet Union and its allies abroad, even at the risk of elevating military priorities and sullying America's image as a humane rather than an imperialistic power; against the racial discrimination that they saw implicit in affirmative action and school busing, even at the risk of weakening their support for social equality; and against the growing scope of social services that they denounced as "entitlements" – especially increased welfare benefits for the poor, which they believed undermined personal responsibility and individual liberty.

Their views solidified and became less restrained as they defended their political shift against attacks by their old liberal friends.[14] There are none so passionate as a convert; none so defensive as an apostate! By the mid-seventies, many of them threw caution to the wind in urging aggressive, often military responses to perceived threats from abroad. They intensified their justifications for the U.S. intervention in Vietnam, while some of them did not hesitate to denounce their antiwar friends as "anti-American leftists" whom they charged with underestimating the global threat of communism. Nor, in the name of "realism," were some beyond urging, as early as 1973, preparations to invade Saudi Arabia and Kuwait in order to overcome Arab control of oil supplies – urgings that the conservative Nixon administration successfully resisted. They joined California

---

[14] See e.g. Norman Podhoretz, *Breaking Ranks* (Harper, 1979).

governor Ronald Reagan and other right-wing Republicans in denouncing President Nixon's efforts to advance détente with the Soviet Union and to normalize relations with mainland China. By 1980, calling themselves "Democrats for Reagan," most of them abandoned the Democratic Party. When President Reagan, no "soft-core liberal" by any measure, later negotiated a nuclear arms reduction agreement after his 1987 meeting with Soviet premier Mikhail Gorbachev in Iceland, one-time Democratic advisor Richard Perle and erstwhile liberal journalist Norman Podhoretz (among other neocons) attacked Reagan for abandoning a hard line against the Soviet Union.

In the meantime, a powerful movement among long-standing conservatives (unkindly dubbed "paleoconservatives") was on the rise. What some in the fifties had begun calling the New Conservatism targeted the overall liberal conception of the Good Society, effectively exploiting the internal lines of schism within the liberal Democratic coalition. It would gain a penetrating beachhead during the presidency of Ronald Reagan, and it would overrun much of the nation during the polarizing presidency of George W. Bush after the turn of the millennium.

18

Right-Wing Ascendancy

As historian George Nash described the "Right-wing renascence," there were three branches. The first consisted of what he called "the 'classical liberals' or 'libertarians'," such as Friedrich Hayek, Ludwig von Mises, Joseph Schumpeter, all strong "antistatists." Many of these people had fled to the United States after having suffered from the European authoritarian revolutions carried out in the name of fascism and communism. They had a number of American-born disciples or counterparts, including Henry Hazlitt, Milton Friedman, and Murray Rothbard. Their conservatism was nearly all about laissez-faire: a free-market economy and a noninterventionist state.

A second strain, wrote Nash, consisted of "a militant, evangelistic anti-Communism, shaped decisively by a number of influential ex-radicals of the 1930s, including Whittaker Chambers, James Burnham, Frank Meyer, Elizabeth Bentley, and many more." For those people who believed they had seen the Devil and had fled to sound the alarm, liberalism was just an early stage of communism.

A third component consisted of a resurgent "traditionalism [that] urged a return to traditional religion and ethical absolutes and a rejection of the 'relativism' which had allegedly corroded Western values and produced an intolerable vacuum that was filled by demonic ideologies." Leaders in this group ranged in style and intellectual substance from Leo Strauss, Russell Kirk, Peter Viereck, and William F. Buckley, Jr., to Billy Graham, Pat Robertson, and Jerry Falwell.

The first two branches of the New Conservatism that Nash described expressed primarily resentment toward the evolution of American liberalism away from its classical antistatist phase. "Classical" or nineteenth-century liberalism had focused almost entirely on (a) the centrality of private property for a free society and (b) a market economy as the only legitimate allocator of social resources and rewards. For the eighteenth and early nineteenth centuries, that was perhaps a natural focus considering that liberals regarded the repression of individual liberty by the absolutist, monarchial state and its mercantilist, state-regulated political economy as the main problem for the then-emerging concerns with personal liberty. Enlargement of the immunities ("rights") of private property served the dual purpose of providing a multitude of centers of power to counterbalance the state's power and of freeing up the energies of private persons to maximize their own life chances or opportunities – and, not coincidentally, the wealth of the nation as well.

But in the late nineteenth century, as the industrial and corporation revolutions created great concentrations of *private* power, the concern of American liberals to protect individual rights turned them back to the state to counterbalance the new sources of power and to protect the interests of smaller or at least less successful competitors in the marketplace. Hence the rise, or more accurately the re-emergence, of the regulatory state. In other words, American liberals turned to the state in order to constrain private-sector power, to moderate the calamitous oscillations of the business cycle, and, later, to promote and protect civil liberties, civil rights, Americans' long-term interest in a healthy environment, and a modest redistribution of social, political, and economic advantages. By mid-twentieth century in the United States, an important element in conservatism emerged as a reaction to liberalism's modern interventionist stage.

For many European-born intellectuals, especially economists like Hayek, von Mises, and Gottfried Haberler, the state still seemed to be liberty's main enemy. Thus the modern liberal agenda seemed to them indistinguishable from the authoritarian and totalitarian regimes they had fled. Hence Hayek's facile claim that a state given limited regulatory and redistributive powers inexorably trod "The Road to Serfdom." The same myopia afflicted many Americans whose acquaintance with notions of an activist government came almost entirely from their wretched experiences with Marxism or the Communist Party. For them, there could be no stopping point between a liberal democratic regime and communism.

Frank Meyer put it all together, enumerating what he called certain "undeniable truths." First, he claimed, "contemporary Liberalism is in agreement with Communism on the most essential point – the necessity and desirability of socialism." Second, he argued, liberalism "regards all inherited value – theological, philosophical, political – as without intrinsic virtue or authority." Therefore, "no irreconcilable differences exist between it and Communism – only differences as to method and means." "Liberals," he concluded, "are unfit for the leadership of a free society, and intrinsically incapable of offering serious opposition to the Communist offensive."[1]

---

[1] Quoted in George Nash, *The Conservative Intellectual Movement in America Since 1945* (Harper, 1976), p. 150. As late as 1987, Pat Buchanan – a leading spokesman for a part of the conservative

The third branch of the New Conservatism was and would remain largely authoritarian in its objectives. Its most serious intellectual heritage owed much to central European émigrés such as Thomas Molnar, Leo Strauss, and Eric Voegelin, who had fled the Nazis and the Communists. The focus of their critique of modern times lay on the erosion of belief in the eternal truths of Natural Law. For Voegelin, modern liberalism was a direct descendant of ancient heresies, notably Gnosticism, which (at the risk of oversimplification) postulates salvation through knowledge, particularly knowledge of the mysteries of the universe that arises more or less intuitively from divinely or transcendentally inspired self-knowledge. In the place of eternal truths, they argued, grew a self-determined relativistic view of truth that paved the way to nihilism and to totalitarianism. Liberalism's skeptical regard for universal truths underlay the disease from which modern civilization suffered. The rush to statism, they argued, resulted from a desperate need for community in an otherwise atomistic, chaotic world.

But in their view, perhaps liberalism's greatest sin was placing individual freedom at the center of the state's purpose. The purpose of social organization, Strauss insisted, was not freedom but virtue; freedom had value only as it led the way to a virtuous society. In this respect, the corruption of modern life had its origins in the eighteenth-century Enlightenment, when the American and French revolutions overturned the traditional relationship of individuals to the authority of church and state while elevating "the rights of man." Strauss never suggested how to overcome people's tendency to prefer only their own theologian or metaphysician for defining virtue. Yet he and, more importantly, his students and followers (he taught philosophy for two decades at the University of Chicago) did insist that the only legitimate political policy, foreign and domestic alike, was one that provided for personal and national security, "not humanitarian benevolence."[2]

The mass of ordinary Americans that the conservative movement sought to mobilize had little interest in, and little ability to understand, the disputations of the Strausses (or Straussians, as they refer to themselves). What they readily understood was what Modernism had done to their universe. The complexities of the modern world, from international politics to science, medicine, and technology, were beyond their ken; nor did it appear that they cared much to reach into them. What seemed clearest was that they resented any need to digress from their daily, mostly prosperous lives to grapple with complexities. They welcomed a

movement and its presidential candidate in 2000 – was still writing things like: "The liberal wing of the Democratic Party has made itself the ally of ... communism." Quoted in *Newsweek* (13 July 1987).

[2] See e.g. Thomas G. West, "Leo Strauss and U.S. Foreign Policy," ⟨http://www.claremont.org/writings/crb/summer2004/west.html⟩. West condemned the policies of neoconservatives such as William Kristol and Robert Kagan as anti-Straussian because of their vision of proactively promoting American institutions abroad in the form of a "benign imperialism."

philosophy that spoke to their conventional commitments and beliefs. The Cold War, the war against a palpable evil empire, permitted them to focus on simple understandings of virtue and vice. It was Us versus Them. Anticommunism became a source of communitarian strength. It was the symbolic target that held all the various conservatives together.

For many millions of Americans, what distinguished a "true" anticommunist was a publicly avowed belief in God. It was not enough for Americans to pledge allegiance to "one nation, indivisible, with liberty and justice for all," because – as the Reverend George M. Docherty explained to his Presbyterian congregation one Sunday in 1954 with President Eisenhower in the audience – "little Muscovites [could] repeat a similar pledge to their hammer-and-sickle flag." It was necessary therefore to distinguish the American pledge from the Bolshevik pledge. More than that, to make the pledge without "under God," the patriotic reverend insisted, was to omit what he called "a definitive factor in the American way of life." As for Americans who claimed the freedom to reject a belief in God, Docherty proclaimed, "an atheistic American is a contradiction in terms." The message touched President Eisenhower. Later that day he told Americans in a radio message (much quoted and derided afterward) that "our government makes no sense unless it is founded in a deeply felt religious faith, and I don't care what it is." And so, with encouragement from their wildly eclectic president, Americans dictated by congressional statute that "under God" be inserted into the 62-year-old Pledge of Allegiance.[3] Congress also mandated that "In God We Trust" be engraved on the country's paper money, perhaps signifying the union between capitalism and old-time religion.

The heavyweight philosophical works of Voegelin and Strauss were echoed among less metaphysical versions in the multitude of conservative journals that bloomed in the fifties, such as *The Intercollegiate Review, Modern Age, The American Spectator,* and *The National Review.*[4] They were aided by dozens of so-called think tanks that sprang up during and after the fifties, such as Paul Weyrich's Free Congress Foundation, The Liberty Fund, The John M. Olin Foundation, The Heritage Foundation, The American Enterprise Institution, The Cato Institute, The Freedoms Foundation at Valley Forge, The Council for InterAmerican Security, The Hoover Institute, and dozens of other foundations and institutes, many of them financed by genetic billionaires. In the journals and among the think tanks, one could sometimes find fierce disagreements among conservatives with different agendas, but they were united in their condemnation

[3] Paul Carter, *Another Part of the Fifties* (Columbia University Press, 1983), pp. 114ff.
[4] See Nash, *Conservative Intellectual Movement,* pp. 50ff, and Sara Diamond, *Roads to Dominion: Right Wing Movements and Political Power in the United States* (Guilford, 1995), pp. 31ff.

of liberalism. All the same, the fusion of the various strands – the libertarian with the authoritarian, the self-defined traditionalist alongside universalist Natural Law – suggests an example of the human being's uncanny ability to hold mutually contradictory ideas in mind at the same time.

The intellectual developments gave to conservatism the respectability that Lionel Trilling had found lacking in his 1950 essay. Roman Catholics made up much of its leadership.[5] Among them were, preeminently, William F. Buckley, Jr., whose *National Review* (founded in 1955) became the most widely read conservative journal in the country. Paul Gottfried, William Simon, Michael Novak, Pat Buchanan, William Bennett, Buckley's brother-in-law Brent Bozell, and Frank Meyer (the latter two converts to Catholicism) were among many others. Their religious commitment fueled both their anticommunism and their view that the Good (American) Society should be specifically a Christian one.

"We of the Christian West," declared Bozell, "owe our identity to the central fact of history – the entry of God onto the human stage." It is our task, Bozell insisted, to defend "a Christian civilization." The enemy, of course, was communism; but it was also liberalism, which, Bozell stated baldly, "comes down to a revolt against God."[6] When Hungarians rose up against their Communist rulers in 1956 at the same time that the British and French invaded Egypt over the nationalization of the Suez Canal, President Eisenhower joined with the Soviet premier, Nikita Khrushchev, in demanding that Britain and France withdraw. William Buckley exploded in a *National Review* editorial: "Over the humiliated forms of our two oldest and closest allies [Britain and France], we clasp the hands of the murderers of the Christian heroes of Hungary, as we run in shameless – and vain – pursuit of the 'good will' of Asia and Africa's teeming pagan multitudes."[7] "To liberals," the New Conservatives' sympathetic historian commented, "such judgments no doubt smacked of arrogance and chauvinism; to conservatives the failure to make such judgments showed how diseased liberalism was."[8]

But the intellectuals were not the main source of conservatives' *political* strength. Acting within the Republican Party, the mobilization of the country's major corporation leaders against the welfare state and the regulatory state provided solid support, however much conservatives, or at least many of the intellectual kind, expressed criticism of "materialism" and other features of modern society. Along with the enormous financial power of corporate America, it was pietist or "faith based" traditionalism (of a somewhat radical sort) that became

[5] See especially Patrick Allitt, *Catholic Intellectuals and Conservative Politics in America, 1950–1985* (Cornell University Press, 1993).
[6] Quoted in Nash, *Conservative Intellectual Movement*, pp. 271, 312.
[7] *National Review* (6 Dec. 1956), quoted in Nash (ibid.), p. 263.
[8] Nash (ibid.), p. 271.

the grassroots political force of the American conservative movement that roared out of the seventies.

Not much of it was of a highly refined intellectual nature. The pietist force had been building since the late 1940s, when well-placed and well-heeled business conservatives found political capital in the evangelical Christian preachers. Although the preachers could and did raise millions of dollars on their own account, from the start they also enjoyed ample financial support from mega-corporations and genetic billionaires with antitax and deregulation agendas.

"The fifties," writes one historian of the rise of the so-called Christian Right, "were an extraordinarily successful decade for conservative white Protestant Christians in America. Not for more than a century had they felt so closely in tune with and wielded as much influence over the national ethos and culture .... Their chief spokesman and symbol, Billy Graham, not only was the nation's best-known preacher and one of its most admired men but had the ear of the world's most powerful leader, the president of the United States."[9] What made him especially attractive to conservative politicians and millionaires was his coupling of Christian piety with an unqualified endorsement of free enterprise. William Randolph Hearst ordered the editors of his newspaper and magazine empire to "puff" him, while Texas billionaire oilman Seth Richardson, "though not famous for his piety, took a special liking to him and began to introduce him to other rich and powerful men." In his widely popular radio program, "Hour of Decision," Graham drilled in the message of communism's Satanic purposes, the need to restore "old-fashioned values," and "the God-blessed superiority of the free enterprise system."[10]

As he built his massive following, Graham backed away from traditional hellfire preaching. There was a lot of self-fulfillment and catharsis, as well as warnings about how modern life endangered the spiritual life, but little religious content in his sermons. It was left to individuals to determine what it was about modern life that distressed them. It is not hard to grasp what it was in the South, the most fertile field for the evangelicals, that disturbed a great many white Americans.

Even so, Graham did not become the most powerful of the evangelicals leading American politics far to the right during the last quarter of the twentieth century. That role rested on the new fundamentalist, Pentecostal, and "charismatic" Christians – self-promoting splinters of Protestantism outside the mainstream of American ministries.

---

[9] William Martin, *With God on Our Side: The Rise of the Religious Right in America* (Broadway, 1996), p. 47.
[10] Ibid., pp. 29–31.

In the age of deregulation, government control of broadcasting as a public resource withered. Tax-free religious ownership of television stations and networks proliferated. During the Nixon administration, the FCC rescinded its long-standing ban on stations selling airtime to religious programs, rescinding also the requirement that TV stations donate a certain amount of airtime for such programs. Free to sell their airtime, local stations saw a lucrative windfall opportunity. Evangelical preachers saw an investment opportunity in taking up the offers, financing their purchases with unabashed solicitations from enthralled viewers. Unwilling to solicit money with televised appeals, mainline Protestant, Catholic, and Jewish groups soon were driven nearly entirely off the air, yielding to evangelicals with few scruples about commercializing religion.

Starting with 25 television ministries in the late seventies, the Christian evangelicals ran more than 330 of them by the mid-eighties. Meanwhile, they expanded the definition of the gospel. They preached insistently on social issues as an integral part of their religious mission, from which followed their political campaigns against abortion, contraception, and homosexuality and in support of prayer in public schools. But their claim to political relevance extended far beyond personal morality to issues concerning economic and foreign policy. The message had little to do with traditional religious concerns and much to do with playing on the anxieties of Americans who had become discomfited by what the revolutionary changes of the times had done to their once-comfortable assumptions. Evangelical claims that questions of faith, morality, and even private conduct belong in the political arena paralleled the Sixties radicals' insistence that "the personal is political." To enhance their power, they became embedded in the Republican Party, not unlike the way liberals had become a guiding force in the Democratic Party forty years earlier.

Pat Robertson, among the most successful of TV evangelists, regularly put conservative Republicans on his shows, always supporting cuts in social welfare and of corporation taxes and always on the side of military dictatorship in places like Guatemala and Chile, regularly raising money for the "Contras" who were fighting to overthrow the legitimately elected government of Nicaragua after Congress banned funding. Robertson parlayed a single TV station in the seventies into over 200 stations by 1980, using solicited donations of a minimum $10 per month from his viewers plus some questionable profits from stock deals made with tax-deductible money.

In 1980, the evangelicals completed their political mobilization and had gained a center seat among the policy makers of the Republican Party. That particular year, they exploited the issue of prayer in public schools, and most particularly President Carter's support for an IRS ruling that denied tax exemption to racially segregated religious schools. Right-wing conservatives portrayed the ruling as an attack on religion. According to Paul Weyrich, who helped lead the campaign, "what galvanized the Christian community was not abortion, school prayer, or the ERA ... [but rather] Jimmy Carter's intervention against the Christian schools, trying to deny them tax-exempt status on the basis of so-called de facto segregation."[11]

Ronald Reagan campaigned to "bring God back into our schools." Carter, a Southern Baptist from Georgia and a self-declared "born-again Christian," had taken an estimated 50 percent of the evangelical vote in 1976; he took only 20 percent in 1980 against the evangelicals' candidate, Ronald Reagan. They campaigned aggressively for Reagan, issuing "moral report cards" to parishioners as they exited churches, detailing how candidates stood and voted on every issue. Everything, from supporting tax cuts and the death penalty to opposing gun controls and welfare programs, became a moral issue. They distributed advertisements (paid with tax-free dollars) filled with scary warnings that imitated the hyperbolic style of Red China's denunciations of the "running dogs of American capitalist imperialism." "Danger!" one of them read. "Christian Americans are under siege. School children are being threatened and adults jailed for the peaceful practice of God-given rights!"[12]

The nearly invariable linking by the media preachers of evangelical Christianity with antigovernment business conservatism would be puzzling without understanding that the underlying animus of the Christian Right was its rejection of "Modernism." Modernism meant a readiness to substitute science for faith and rational skepticism for belief, but it also meant a readiness to substitute a focus on social justice for a focus on individual responsibility. Most of all, Modernism meant seeking happiness in material well-being – in overcoming want and oppression – rather than in spiritual solace.[13] The core of the message always was to seek contentment in the union of one's self with God. Social reformers, they insisted, diverted attention from that truth. It is easy to see how closely Modernism resembled liberalism and how, like communism, it represented in the eyes of the Christian conservatives a threat to Christian civilization.

---

[11] Martin, *God on Our Side,* p. 173.

[12] Diamond, *Roads to Dominion,* p. 77.

[13] None of this evidently applied to the preachers themselves. The most prominent among them – Oral Roberts, Pat Robertson, Jimmy Swaggart, Jim Bakker, and Jerry Falwell – used the millions of dollars that flooded to them from TV followers to buy themselves several million-dollar homes, finance lavish entertainment and travel, and gain access to custom-designed jet planes and yachts. Bakker would eventually go to jail for defrauding investors in one of his resort schemes, Swaggart was exposed soliciting prostitution, and Oral Roberts's empire went bankrupt (defaulting on a $25 million debt); Pat Robertson managed to sidestep several government inquiries into shady financial deals. But "televangelism" remained widely popular.

From the beginning, the Christian Right joined in pious denunciations of liberal political programs, from labor legislation and antitrust to a progressive income tax, environmental protection, and even civil rights. It could be overly cynical to observe that evangelical preachers might anticipate that financial benefits would flow from their antiliberal campaigns. Indeed, it would be unfair to make venality the source of, say, a Billy Graham crusade. But no one could deny that the money that facilitated the evangelicals' access to a massive public played a major role in promoting the conservative political agenda. What small percentage of a billionaire's wealth, for example, could make a best-seller out of a preacher's sermons? Or buy access to the steps of the Capitol for well-publicized mass prayer sessions? Or lobby for television licenses for full-time religious programming? But in fact the relationship was symbiotic rather than solely venal. The evangelicals could and did raise their own millions, and their mailing lists and direct exhortations from the pulpit or revival arenas proved to be as much an invaluable resource for conservative politicians as conservative millionaires and media moguls could be for them.

In fact, millions of Americans, bewildered and seemingly threatened by the fast-changing contours of American society (and of the world), proved responsive to self-declared messengers from God who offered comfort and comradeship. The burdens of international involvement, racial insurgency, the rise of sexual candor and experimentation, the secularist character of the campaigns for religious toleration, and the youth rebellion that rejected long-standing norms of decorum – these and other challenges to the traditional social and political order threw into question a great many "givens" in American life. Such features of Modernism had the greatest impact on those who had fallen largely out of touch with the pace of changes taking place in the big metropolises and university environs.

That the most fertile soil sowed by the evangelicals was in the South gave special force to the conservative cause. There, in the region that for more than sixty years had provided solid, unwavering support for the Democratic Party, conservatives could reap the harvest for the Republican Party of white southerners' resistance to civil rights while emphasizing "traditional values." ("I think we just delivered the South to the Republican Party for a long time to come," President Lyndon Johnson remarked to his aide, Bill Moyers, on signing the Civil Rights Act in 1964.)[14]

---

[14] Robert Dallek, *Flawed Giant: Lyndon Johnson and His Times, 1961–1971* (Oxford University Press, 1998), p. 120. Racial bigotry had kept the South "solidly" Democratic because – for eighty years after the Civil War – the party there (with the national party's complicity) was deeply committed to segregation. That ended after World War II.

Meanwhile, bucking his church's official stand against racism, the devoutly Catholic and stoutly conservative William Buckley offered readers of his *National Review* a slightly more intellectualized rationale for opposing civil rights. In 1957, the year of the Southern Manifesto proclaiming defiance of the Supreme Court's *Brown v. Board of Education* decision and the year President Eisenhower had to send a thousand troops into Little Rock to enforce a court order requiring racial integration of the city's Central High School, Buckley wrote:

> The central question that emerges ... is whether the White community in the South is entitled to take such measures as are necessary to prevail, politically and culturally, in areas in which it does not predominate numerically. The sobering answer is Yes ... because for the time being, it is the advanced race .... The claims of civilization supercede those of universal suffrage.[15]

Hence by the 1960s – amid all the clamor from and about the New Left, the counterculture insurgency, and the racial, sexual, and gender revolutions – a largely absolutist conservatism was already beginning to blossom, rooted by no means exclusively but most powerfully in religious faith. Fusion of religious commitment with laissez-faire capitalism tended to conflict with both Protestant and Catholic teachings regarding *social* responsibility, but other agendas prevailed. The religious–laissez-faire connection depended on notions of *personal* responsibility, hence the opposition to social welfare programs for the poor and to the regulatory state (*caveat emptor*). In this the evangelicals joined forces with libertarians, who sought a shrinking government on principle, and with business people, who sought a highly selective withdrawal of government from its regulatory responsibilities. The arguments presented usually seemed more a reassertion of classical liberalism, a "retro" laissez-faire posture, than of classical conservatism of the Tory democrat or *noblesse* sort.

Moral certainty among the religio-traditionalists did inspire demands for an interventionist state to enforce traditional standards of personal decorum. That placed them in conflict with the libertarians. What sustained the coalition of conservative libertarians, conservative business interests, and conservative religio-traditionalists was their anticommunism. Buckley's colleague and Catholic convert Frank Meyer remarked that, without anticommunism, the antigovernment libertarian message was undifferentiable from anarchism.[16]

By the nineties – after the Cold War ended with the Soviet Union's collapse in 1992 but before a radical-right federal administration declared a "war on terrorism" following the September 11, 2001 ("9/11") massacres in New York City and

---

[15] "Why the South Must Prevail," *National Review* (24 Aug. 1957), pp. 148–9, quoted in Diamond, *Roads to Dominion,* p. 35.
[16] Nash, *Conservative Intellectual Movement,* p. 316.

Washington, DC – the underlying cultural divisions in the nation had bobbed to the top.[17] "Anticommunism," always as much a surrogate among conservatives for antiliberalism as it was opposition to authoritarian socialism, metamorphosed into resistance to "multiculturalism." That usually translated into opposition to civil rights and lifestyle diversity, with a good deal of antiscience and anti-intellectualism thrown in. Business groups with a stake in the use of fossil fuels dismissed decades of scientific studies that demonstrated how pollution contributed to global warming, going so far at times as to deny clear evidence that the atmosphere was indeed growing warmer. Antiabortionist officials in some states and small-town communities persisted in promoting the claim that abortion contributes to breast cancer – in the face of scientific studies showing no connection whatever. Creationists re-emerged from the 1920s to challenge common sense as well as scientific demonstrations of the evolution of species over billions of years. By the 1980s, the term "secular rationalism" came to be used to describe what conservatives were fighting against.

Politically, then, the mid-century antistatist conservative impulse in America, linked up as it was with the television-generated popularity of evangelicalism, came to bloom in the last quarter of the century. Financed in large part by corporate interests and billionaire ideologues united against unfriendly government intervention in the economy, the right-wing coalition formed an immensely powerful political force. With the turn of the millennium and the rise to power of an extreme right-wing national administration, the cultural divide would evolve into the most polarized political environment since the Civil War. The political basis for that development was laid with the election to the presidency of Ronald Reagan.

---

[17] "When the Soviet Union peacefully collapsed of its own colossal ineptitude ... the right wing was left without an external enemy against whom to mobilize. So it turned to a domestic substitute by demonizing the latte-drinking, Volvo-driving, school-busing, fetus-killing, tree-hugging, gun-fearing, morally relativist and secularly humanist so-called liberal elitists, whose elders had been 'soft on communism' while they themselves coddle criminals, women, and same sexers, eat brie, drink chardonnay, support Darwin, and oppose capital punishment in defiance of the 'moral values' of ordinary, god-fearing, flag-waving, assault-gun-carrying Americans." Jason Epstein, "What's the Matter with Kansas?" *New York Review of Books* (6 Oct. 2004).

19

The Reagan Revolution

In the days leading up to Ronald Reagan's first inauguration as president in January 1981, hundreds of private and corporate jet planes descended on Washington from all over the country. Waiting their turn to land, they circled the capital like condors eager to get on with the business of feeding on the carcass of the liberal Democratic coalition. The coalition was indeed dead. What life had remained in it by the mid-seventies ended during the disastrous Democratic administration of Jimmy Carter. Meanwhile, what life had remained for moderate Republicans in their own party also had died with the 1976 defeat of the Gerald Ford–Robert Dole ticket. The nomination of Ronald Reagan for president in 1980 represented the full-blown capture of Abraham Lincoln's party by what used to be called "the extreme right wing." His election confirmed the ascendancy of conservatism in America. Joy in the event among members of the right-wing coalition seemed unbounded.

In the midst of an economy that featured double-digit inflation combined with nearly double-digit unemployment, Ronald Reagan put on a spectacle of imperial wealth unparalleled in the history of presidential inaugurations. So many of the rich and powerful from American business arrived by private jets to celebrate his victory that Washington National Airport (renamed "Ronald Reagan Washington National Airport" in 1998) could not accommodate all of them. Many of those symbols of corporate and personal wealth had to take off again after delivering their owners to the ground. The cost of renting limousines, another symbol of wealth and privilege, soared to $2,000 per day – when eager takers could find any not already leased.

The Reagan inaugural was the costliest in the country's history. There were dozens of pre-inaugural and post-inauguration parties, with the guests bedecked with diamonds and sporting minks, sables, and silks. The new First Lady's gown was reported to have cost $25,000, paid for by private donors.[1] Although Reagan claimed that private donations, not the taxpayers, covered the costs for all the festivities, an independent report by the U.S. General Accounting Office thirty months later showed that government agencies – most notably the Defense Department, "without proper legal authority" – had covered much of the $16.3 million event. (One might have questioned whether it was ethically better to accept private donations for a public function from individuals and corporations with stakes in government policy making or rather to spend taxpayer money for such purposes; but no one raised the question, then or since.) As the veteran Washington correspondent Haynes Johnson noted, many wits remarked at the time how the Reagan inauguration "represented a marriage of the New Right with the New Rich."[2]

The presidency of Ronald Reagan marked the decisive point of the conservative ascendancy in American politics. It halted and partly reversed half a century of movement of the country toward liberal priorities. It provided evidence of the triumph in politics of image over substance and of money over principle. It expressed the country's craving for reasons to feel optimistic amid deepening cynicism and a burgeoning belief that "greed is good."[3] More and more college students, a near majority of whom apparently voted for Reagan, showed a fulsome disdain for public service and an enthusiasm to go to work on Wall Street. Voting patterns indicated that America's young had translated their Sixties' "do your own thing" motto into "looking out for number one." "The Me Decade," as some pundits had already labeled the 1970s, would stretch on into the new millennium.

Whether an admirer or a critic, no one could deny that the Reagan presidency rivaled those of Lyndon Johnson and Franklin Roosevelt in its impact on

---

[1] Throughout her eight years in the White House, Nancy Reagan received gowns worth tens of thousands of dollars as gifts from various designers, gifts that she failed to report or to return as federal law requires of government officials and their families. To accommodate her lavish wardrobe, she converted the entire bedroom of President Carter's daughter into a walk-in closet. *Time* (24 Oct. 1988), pp. 29–30.

[2] Haynes Johnson, *Sleepwalking through History: America in the Reagan Years* (Anchor, 1991), pp. 19–22.

[3] In Oliver Stone's 1987 film *Wall Street*, protagonist Gordon Gekko utters the statement: "Greed is good." It was apparently inspired by a similar speech of Ivan Boesky – billionaire arbitrageur and later convict – in his 1986 commencement address for the School of Business Management at Berkeley. "Greed is all right, by the way," Boesky is reported to have said. "I want you to know that. I think greed is healthy." But the idea had long before already been advanced by Ayn Rand in her best-selling novels *Atlas Shrugged* (1957) and *The Fountainhead* (1952). Some conservatives (notably Alan Greenspan, appointed by President Reagan to chair the Federal Reserve Board) were among Rand's avid followers. Rand's novels enjoyed a massive reprinting beginning in the 1980s.

American government and American society. The impact, however, tended, and was intended, to reverse the trends set in motion by FDR and LBJ over the previous half-century. The Reagan administration launched an economic policy designed to redistribute income and wealth – upward. It declaimed against high taxes and forced through what was then the largest reduction of corporate and personal income taxes in history. Yet by raising Social Security and other taxes and by forcing state and local governments to raise user fees for public services and amenities, it accomplished (intentionally) not a reduction but a redistribution of the total tax burden – downward. In the name of "the free market" it deliberately sought to reduce government oversight of corporate business behavior, both by repealing regulatory measures and by starving the regulatory agencies it could not get Congress to abolish. It turned a blind eye to monopolistic practices, dimming a century of federal antitrust scrutiny.[4]

The Reagan administration railed against "big government," but it incurred the largest peacetime national debt in U.S. history while doubling expenditures to build up an already cost-overrun military. It slashed eligibility for welfare payments and outlays for school lunches and low-income housing. It warred against the protection of the environment and against the preservation of national wilderness areas. It subjected consumer and labor safety measures to cost–benefit analyses that weighed the alleged costs in business profits against an arbitrarily calculated dollar value of human life. It dealt a crippling blow to organized labor, already staggering from the long-term decimation of jobs in the heavily unionized manufacturing sector, when Reagan abruptly fired 12,000 striking air-traffic controllers and forbade their rehiring after the strike was broken. Corporate leaders took gleeful note.

Reagan promised to "get government off the backs of the American people," but his administration sought to lay the heavy hand of government on Americans' private lives. It used federal power to interfere with Americans' private sexual practices and preferences. It proposed to overrule individuals' private decisions to use contraceptives in planning parenthood. It sought to use government power to force American schoolchildren to participate, however passively, in religious ceremony and prayer. It eased proscriptions against domestic surveillance and spying on dissident groups by government agencies. It extended its ideological reach abroad by cutting off funds for United Nations agencies that ran educational programs about the use of contraceptives both to reduce unwanted pregnancies among the poor and to fight the new scourge of AIDS.

Perhaps most troubling of all, in foreign affairs the Reagan administration raised the magnitude of uncontrolled presidential power to a level only Richard Nixon could have contemplated when Nixon declared, "If the President orders

---

[4] See Chapter 9.

it, it is legal." Among other things, Reagan defied Congress' explicit prohibition against attempting to overthrow the legitimate government of Nicaragua, and he and his officials lied to Congress about financing the effort. Reagan and his right-wing supporters had denounced the Carter administration's withdrawal of U.S. support for the brutal dictatorship of Anastasio Somoza, the last of a family of thugs that had terrorized the country for forty years. The Somoza government fell in 1979 to a leftist group of insurgents calling themselves "Sandinistas," named after the leader of a similar insurgency in the 1920s. As soon as he took office, Reagan declared the Sandinistas a "communist threat" and authorized the organization of "Contra-Revolutionaries." But, given evidence of the terrorist tactics that the Contras employed, Congress in 1982, and again in 1984, forbade any further aid. That didn't stop Reagan. The Contras may have been terrorists, but they were *our* terrorists. Using a "money laundering" technique usually associated with international drug traffickers, Reagan reimbursed client countries (e.g., Israel, Panama, Taiwan) to move money and resources to Nicaragua's Contras. Bypassing Congress, he solicited funds from foreign governments (e.g., from the obscenely rich Sultan of Brunei) to help the Contras. After 1985, Reagan used Israel and other countries to serve as conduits for the administration's project to sell weapons to Iran in an effort to free American hostages held by terrorists – an act forbidden not only by the law but also by Reagan's own public declamations against negotiating with terrorists. Then, officials in Reagan's National Security Council funneled some of the money earned in those covert transactions to the Contras.

Richard Nixon had been forced from the presidency because of an implicitly authorized "petty burglary" and his own explicit efforts to cover up that felony, a serious matter of obstructing justice. Ronald Reagan authorized a deliberate violation of law and public policy, and several high officials in his government – including his secretary of defense, his top national security advisor, and almost certainly Vice-President Bush – lied under oath about it. Historians may argue about which affront to American constitutional government ranked as the more serious. Several of Nixon's aides went to jail (although the chief culprit enjoyed a full pardon by his successor, Gerald Ford). Except for Elliott Abrams, a second-tier official in Reagan's State Department, none of the major culprits paid a similar penalty. Before they could be indicted, most received presidential pardons by the similarly tainted George H. W. Bush when he became president in 1989; many, including Elliott Abrams, would become important figures in the postmillennial administration of George W. Bush.[5]

So much for reducing the dangers of "big government."

---

[5] Among those pardoned were Secretary of Defense Caspar Weinberger and National Security Council head John Poindexter. For an account of the appointment to high office of the Iran–Contra

Ronald Reagan the person embodied similar contradictions. In campaigning for the presidency he adopted the conservative mantra about "family values," but he was himself the only divorcee ever to win the presidency. Nor did he enjoy cordial relationships with his children, also unique among twentieth-century American presidents; and for more than two years, intimates reported, he showed no interest in his first-born grandchild. As governor of California he signed the country's most liberal measure legalizing abortion,[6] but as president he became the champion of some of the nation's most militant antiabortionists.

His greatest strength as a politician lay in his ability to communicate sincerity and honesty. He presented himself as someone with a straight-shooting, down-to-earth, "Joe Six-pack" sensibility. Yet his remarkable inability to detach fact and truth from fiction and myth became legendary. He claimed publicly that in World War II he participated in the military liberation of a Nazi concentration camp when in fact he never left Hollywood where the military assigned him to make propaganda films. On several occasions he spoke of participating in events that happened only in movies, not all of them his own. He made up provocative anecdotes to illustrate his opposition to social welfare and repeated them even after it became known that they were fictitious. After taking criticism for laying a wreath at a German cemetery containing the remains of notorious Nazi SS officers, an act he defended as "morally right," he told a false story about a young Jewish woman who had encouraged him to do it.[7] To justify his opposition to environmental regulations, he proposed the absurdity that trees contributed more to pollution than did automobiles. He once told an acquaintance who had ruefully confessed that he had unwittingly repeated a claim that proved to be untrue: "That's OK. You believed it because you wanted to believe it. There's nothing wrong with that. I do it all the time."[8]

The practice had an enduring impact on American politics. Wrote Washington columnist David Broder: "He was able to persuade himself – and therefore, other people – of things that were palpably not true." Some, like the concentration camp tale, were disturbing but harmless. Others bore seriously on public policy matters. "In the Iran–contra affair," Broder recalled in 2004, "Reagan clearly believed, against all evidence, that he had not authorized trading arms for hostages."[9] But even before the shameless lying and lawbreaking in that affair

---

malfeasers by the second President Bush, see "Elliott Abrams. It's Back!" *The Nation* (2 July 2001). For Abrams's angry and self-justifying account of being abandoned by Reagan, see Elliott Abrams, *Undue Process* (Maxwell Macmillan, 1993).

[6] Lou Cannon, *Governor Reagan: His Rise to Power* (Public Affairs, 2003), pp. 210–12.

[7] *New York Times* (9 May 1985).

[8] David Broder, "The Great Persuader," *Washington Post National Weekly Edition* (14–20 June 2004), p. 4.

[9] Ibid.

for which Reagan and the top members of his administration bore responsibility (but paid no penalty), Broder had expressed his exasperation with the president's obliviousness to facts. "More and more, it is evident," Broder wrote in 1984, "that the political calculus that operates in Reagan's mind is that the voters are unable to link cause and effect, or make any connection between general policy and specific effect. He is betting, in short, that most people's minds are like his own, heavily responsive to symbol and almost immune to logic."[10]

Reagan may have remained oblivious to his gaffes rather than willfully deceptive. Historians will argue about that. But it is evident that thereafter many of his political followers would use the technique more deliberately to distract voters from the consequences of policy mistakes or from calculated policies that had little popular appeal on their own. The disjunction between what the man publicly said, and repeated, and what the facts clearly demanded was often so great as to challenge disbelief. Reagan was an intuitive practitioner of what Robert Bartley, editorial page editor of the *Wall Street Journal*, gleefully called "the power of the outrageous."[11] The political effectiveness of the practice would not be lost on his successors. By the mid-nineties it would produce a woeful degradation of American politics that surpassed even the shameful partisanship of the McCarthy period while foreshadowing further development of the technique during the postmillenial administration of George W. Bush.

"But Reagan was disarming," Broder added in his column after Reagan's death. His charm seems to have muted most contemporary criticism.[12] In a less amiable man, or with a less able PR corps ("spin doctors") working for him, such behavior would have led to withering criticism. In his case, the public – perhaps led by the press – most often found it simply amusing.[13] Hence his reputation as "the Teflon president."

Curiously, Reagan's personal popularity – he won election in 1980 and reelection in 1984 by substantial majorities – was not matched by public approval of his policies. Contemporary polls repeatedly showed that most Americans supported environmental, Social Security, consumer protection, and tax policies

---

[10] Broder, "The Wreckage of Reagan Policies," reprinted from the *Washington Post* in the *San Francisco Chronicle* (13 Feb. 1984).

[11] Johnson, *Sleepwalking through History*, p. 103.

[12] Broder, "The Great Persuader."

[13] Compare the savaging of Democratic presidential candidate Al Gore in 2000, when it was alleged that he had laid claim to having invented the Internet – a deliberate distortion of what he had actually said. Gore's big mistake was publicly apologizing for having permitted misinterpretation of his words. Political "realists" never apologize, never retract, never admit changing course. Reagan never did. For a revealing account of the media's kid-glove treatment of Reagan, see Mark Hertsgaard, *On Bended Knee: The Press and the Reagan Presidency* (Farrar, Straus & Giroux, 1988).

sharply at odds with those Reagan pushed through a Congress that was intimidated by a president of such evident popularity. And nothing enhanced his
popularity more than when he fell victim to an attempted assassination only
nine months into his presidency. Although gravely wounded, his cheery quip to
his wife, Nancy, "Honey, I forgot to duck" – a well-known line he took from
Jack Dempsey on losing his heavyweight title bout with Gene Tunney in 1926 –
typified Reagan's confident optimism and endeared him enduringly to the public. The assassin – a sick young man infatuated from afar with movie star Jodie
Foster, whom he had hoped to impress – was in no way politically motivated, but
he set in motion a powerful political reaction that made opposition to Reagan
almost an unpatriotic act.

Not even his closest aides and allies would deny that, as president, Reagan
was aloof, scandalously uninformed, often given to irrelevant anecdotes and
analogies, and uninterested in details or in the management of government and
policy.[14] Although Reagan kept journals that suggest he was well informed on
policy issues years before he began his presidency, as president he often showed
little grasp of detail in discussions with aides. Martin Anderson, a strong supporter of Reagan's policies, complained: "He made no demands and gave almost
no instructions .... Essentially he just responded to whatever was brought to his
attention and yes, no, or I'll think about it. At times he would change the subject,
maybe tell a story."[15] David Stockman, Reagan's first director of the Office of
Management and Budget, wrote and spoke candidly of how the president would
grow glassy-eyed and gaze into the distance whenever he tried to get him to grapple with the soaring deficits that Reagan's tax cuts and military increases were
causing.[16] Stockman, a true believer in free markets, despaired that Reagan refused to confront the ballooning business and agriculture subsidies that his own
Republicans pushed through Congress, measures that Reagan readily signed.[17]

Reagan, however, enjoyed lavish praise for what some saw as the clarity of
his "moral vision," his decisiveness, and the consistency with which he iterated

---

[14] Lou Cannon, *President Reagan: The Role of a Lifetime* (Simon & Schuster, 1991), has the most
    detailed analysis of President Reagan's inability to focus on the complexities of almost any is-
    sue. He had a fixed, general idea as to where he wanted things to go but left it to others to work
    out the details. He often told anecdotes that supposedly expressed his take on problems but, to
    the dismay of his closest aides, often had little relevance. Cannon, a journalist, covered Reagan
    during most of his California governorship as well as his presidency. How early in his adminis-
    trations Reagan began to show the effects of his coming dementia will probably be debated by
    historians for generations.

[15] Martin Anderson, *Revolution: The Reagan Legacy* (Hoover Institution, 1988; updated and re-
    printed 1996), pp. 289–90.

[16] William Greider, "The Education of David Stockman," *Atlantic* (Dec. 1981).

[17] David A. Stockman, *The Triumph of Politics: Why the Reagan Revolution Failed* (Harper & Row,
    1986).

the main themes of his ideology – namely, anticommunism and reducing the government. Decisiveness, of course, comes easiest to those who are ideologically inflexible. And seemingly unwavering resoluteness, whatever its wisdom, played well with voters. It recalled Nixon's advice to Kennedy after the Bay of Pigs fiasco that voters are not interested in leaders intent on the "statesmanlike" thing but want leaders who act boldly.[18] Unlike the pragmatic Nixon, however, on domestic issues Reagan followed an ideological script. Reagan never publicly deviated from the positions he had adopted in the fifties, when he began working in public relations and advertising for General Electric. And he never failed to express his views with a twinkling smile – except to strike a scolding pose when criticizing opponents for "obstructing" the progress of his agenda. These were well-trained gestures cultivated during his acting career. They persuaded voters who revered him, or who remained innocent of the techniques of political chicanery. But they seemed transparent to others. They troubled Reagan's own hand-picked biographer, Edmund Morris, who wrote: "Children respond to sincerity rather than to smoothness, and, having watched [several] Presidents address young audiences, I can report that Reagan was distinctly the least successful. He talked ... to the whole room rather than its individual parts with a delivery precisely directed to the farthest television camera, and with benign indifference to whether any child understood him, as long as the applause was general."[19]

But Reagan seemed altogether a refreshing change from the excruciating seriousness, indecisiveness, and ineffectuality of his predecessor, Jimmy Carter. President Carter was an easy act to follow. A sincere and genuinely religious man, Carter campaigned as a "New Democrat" and Washington "outsider." He was determined to reduce government spending, aid the deregulation movement, and attack "bureaucracy." His administration oversaw the selective deregulation of the telecommunications, transportation, and financial services industries. Symbolically, he walked to his inaugural, carried some of his own luggage into the White House, dimmed the lights of government agencies, held back on federal pay increases, and in other ways emphasized frugality. He reportedly sometimes even charged reporters for the breakfasts they ate at morning press conferences in the White House. He succeeded in demoralizing federal workers and alienating the press. Young, public-spirited professionals left or stayed away from

---

[18] "The average voter," Nixon explained to Kennedy, "is not interested in the technicalities of treaty obligations .... He favors the candidate who wants to do something ... dramatic and forceful – and not the one who takes the 'statesmanlike' and the 'legalistic' view." Richard M. Nixon, *Six Crises,* quoted in Edwin C. Hoyt, *Law and Force in American Foreign Policy* (University Press of America, 1985), pp. 123, 251.

[19] Edmund Morris, "The Unknowable: Ronald Reagan's Amazing Mysterious Life," *The New Yorker* (28 June 2004), pp. 40–51.

public service. The press repaid his breakfast "favors" by savaging him at every opportunity.

And Carter offered up numerous opportunities. A thoughtful and intelligent man, he incurred biting ridicule for his difficulty in making important decisions about both appointments and policy. His efforts to make support for Human Rights an international priority earned him mostly scorn from foreign policy "realists," especially among the neocons who by then were nestling deep into the Republican Party. Eventually, though not during his or his successor's presidencies, those efforts gained respect; especially by the nineties amid international urgings for UN intervention in countries where "ethnic cleansing" and other forms of intranational barbarisms were going on. His negotiation of a new treaty with Panama that relinquished control of the Canal, a measure long in the making, predictably drew a blizzard of flag-wrapped stones from Reaganites. ("It's ours! We paid for it! And we're going to keep it!" Reagan had declaimed earlier.) Given the ascendancy of the right wing in the Republican Party following President Ford's defeat in 1976, it was Carter's further misfortune to take the flak for presiding over the completion of President Nixon's initiatives regarding an arms reduction agreement with the Soviet Union (SALT-II) and formal recognition of the government of Red China, both furiously opposed by the New Conservative forces within the GOP. Carter's one great accomplishment – brokering the "Camp David Accord" that formally ended hostilities between Egypt and Israel – gained for him little of the acclaim that it deserved.

Most helpful to Reagan, however, was the Iranian Revolution in 1979, at the outset of which the revolutionaries took the entire staff of the U.S. embassy in Teheran captive. The staff members remained hostages for more than a year, while the revolutionaries maliciously held onto them until minutes after Reagan was sworn into the presidency so as to deny Carter any "credit" for the return. In the meantime, almost daily and very publicly, Carter anguished over the hostage situation. He compounded his political difficulties by agreeing to a ludicrous rescue attempt that ended in spectacular failure and loss of American life in the Iranian desert, hundreds of miles from the uncertain location(s) of the hostages.

In the comparable hostage situation during his presidency, Reagan and his handlers kept all notice of the crisis at the lowest key, and off the front pages. Reagan's negotiations for the hostages' release were kept secret – especially because some of the deals contradicted his repeated bravado posturing and, moreover, involved violation of U.S. law. All of this awaited the outing of the Iran–Contra scandal during the final years of Reagan's presidency. Then it was revealed that the president had been carrying on a covert foreign policy outside the law and concealed from Congress and the American people.[20]

---

[20] Although much became entirely clear about the scandalous abuse of presidential authority in the case, President Reagan could not be questioned closely because his tendency to confuse fact

In the meantime, however, Reagan kept his aggressive foreign and domestic policies on the front pages. He slashed corporate and personal income taxes on the supply-side theory that the increased spending of the rich would improve investment, provide jobs, and "trickle down" to benefit the less advantaged. He drove the nation deep into debt in order to finance the tax cuts along with a radical increase in military expenditures. Not incidentally (we have David Stockman's word for it), he used the soaring deficit to persuade Americans that the country could not *afford* social services or effective monitoring of consumer, employee, and environmental protection (a practice later dubbed "starving the beast").

Meanwhile, the Reagan revolution *did not* shrink the federal government. Primarily because of increased military outlays but also because of continued subsidies to important Republican Party constituencies in business and agriculture, total federal spending as a percentage of a rising gross national product (GNP) actually stayed the same (22 percent) in the 1980s. At the same time, less of federal outlays went to public goods and services. Measured against the nation's GNP, one index of a country's ability to bear debt, the U.S. national debt soared from about 34 percent in 1980 to nearly 54 percent in 1987 and rising. Net interest paid on the debt rose from 9 percent of all federal outlays in 1980 to more than 15 percent by 1990.[21] America became increasingly dependent on Japanese and European investors to purchase the government's IOUs.

Repudiating the détente strategy of the Nixon administration for reducing international tensions, Reagan declared the Soviet Union "an evil empire" and vowed to roll back world communism (a variation on the abortive "liberation" theme of the early Eisenhower years). When 241 U.S. peacekeeping servicemen stationed in Lebanon (to protect its pro-American regime) were killed in a suicide car-bombing, Reagan abruptly pulled out all the marines; meanwhile, a fortuitously pre-planned invasion of the tiny island of Grenada to overthrow a supposed communist government there successfully diverted attention from the humiliation in Lebanon.[22] Reagan disowned the Anti-Ballistic Missile Treaty negotiated with Moscow by Nixon and bought into the promise of an effective anti-ballistic missile (ABM) weapon. The administration advertised the new program as the Strategic Defense Initiative (SDI), but it was better known as "Star Wars," a name associated with science fiction. Somewhat disingenuously, Reagan insisted that launching SDI did not technically violate the ABM treaty; formal repudiation of the treaty awaited the administration of Reagan's successor, George H. W. Bush.

---

with what he imagined meant that his denials of knowledge about the deals could not be reliably tested.

[21] U.S. Census Bureau, *Statistical Abstract*: 1991, pp. 316–17; 1992, p. 315; 1995, pp. 337–8.

[22] Reagan's press aide, Michael Deaver, later volunteered in an interview that "this country was so hungry for a victory, I don't care what the size [of the country] was, we were going to beat the shit out of it," and it "would be a good story." Hertsgaard, *On Bended Knee*, p. 211.

Reagan's cheery disposition helped to mute outrage at the transgressions committed during his reign. In no previous administration, including the notorious presidencies of Ulysses S. Grant and Warren G. Harding, had so many top officials been indicted or jailed and so many other transgressors spared prosecution by a Justice Department eager to protect friends. In a two-page compendium headed "Scandals, Etc., From A to Z," the conservative *National Journal* as early as 1984 listed forty "improprieties" committed by Reagan appointees. As one front-page *Wall Street Journal* article noted, people screened for appointments in the Reagan administration found that "there was strong emphasis on ideological loyalty to Mr. Reagan's conservative philosophies, with less concern about background or ethical standards." Reagan appointed to his transition team in 1980–1981 the vice-president of the Teamsters Union, who was then under investigation for corruption but also a friend of Reagan's legal advisor (and later attorney general) Ed Meese. Reagan appointed a man to the National Security Council (NSC) even though the Securities and Exchange Commission had recently forced him to pay $427,000 in fines for insider trading, and NSC head Richard Allen was forced to resign after it was revealed he had accepted money from the Japanese government. Reagan's Director of the Environmental Protection Agency was forced to resign after being cited for contempt of Congress for refusing to divulge incriminating documents. The assistant administrator of the EPA was convicted of lying to Congress about her business contacts with corporations that were subject to toxic-waste oversight by her agency.[23]

These and dozens of other cases occurred long before the scandals of Reagan's second administration and the Iran–Contra superscandal. Much more was to come. Most of those officials found to have committed "improprieties," some of them felonious, were forced to resign. But Reagan's second-term attorney general, Ed Meese, stayed on despite revelations that he had neglected to report an interest-free loan of $15,000 to his wife from a political contributor who subsequently enjoyed a government appointment. Several other contributors gained places in the federal government through Meese's kindliness. Although investigators confirmed Meese's "improprieties," he escaped prosecution because it was decided they were not serious enough. Lyn Nofziger, another close Reagan aide, was found guilty of violating federal law that prohibited lobbying within a year of leaving a high government position, but a friendly judge set aside the conviction on the grounds that in his view the law was "silly." Independent Counsel Whitney North Seymour, Jr., charged that Reagan's former deputy chief of staff Michael Deaver not only violated the 1978 Ethics in Government Act but also had perjured himself three times before a grand jury investigating conflicts of interest. He, too, eluded jail. Reagan's Justice Department declined to prosecute

---

[23] See e.g. *Wall Street Journal* (6 April 1984), p. A1, and *The New Republic* (20 April 1987), pp. 17–20.

a top Agriculture Department official, Everett Rank, Jr., who directed a 1983 subsidy program that produced $1.2 million for a farm in which he was a partner and that enriched him by about $300,000 while holding his government job. Reagan's CIA chief, William Casey, refused for almost four years to divest or put into a blind trust his corporate interests worth several million dollars. It eluded most of the media – but few Americans who were paying attention – that Casey's position afforded him unique access to the government's most secret economic data, giving him a valuable advantage in managing his investments.[24]

In all, an estimated 190 Reagan administration officials were indicted or convicted of illegal activities.[25] As in the case of the hostage crises of his administration, Reagan chose to say nothing about the scandals, neither in criticism nor in extenuation of his appointees, thereby effectively keeping his distance from what was going on and also shortening the news life of the stories. Whether this was political strategy or an example of the man's inability to confront difficult and unpleasant matters remains unclear. That it may well have been at least partly the latter is suggested by the fact that, after the assassination attempt in 1981, Reagan never again personally visited with Jim Brady, his press secretary who suffered permanent brain damage from a stray shot fired by the would-be assassin.[26] Nor would he ever join with Brady and his wife in their subsequent campaign for gun control legislation (although *after* he left the Presidency, he declared his support for banning private sale or ownership of assault weapons). Reagan's detachment from the management of his presidency, his clear aversion to unpleasant news or tasks, and indeed his cool aloofness in personal relationships with everyone besides his wife became legendary, remarked by journalists, political allies, and White House aides alike. Martin Anderson, a chief economic advisor ("manager" might be a more appropriate word), candidly wrote that Reagan was "basically uncaring about the human feelings of those around him, 'a warmly ruthless man.'"[27]

When Reagan died in June 2004, many obituaries credited him with "winning the Cold War" and making the world safe for free markets.[28] He would be, as a *New York Times* editorial put it, "forever linked with the triumph over

[24] *The New Republic* (20 April 1987), p. 17; William Safire, "Spousal Arousal," *New York Times* (24 Sept. 1984), p. 21; *San Francisco Chronicle* (8 Oct. 1983), p. 7; ibid. (6 June 1985), p. 5.

[25] William E. Pemberton, *Exit with Honor: The Life and Presidency of Ronald Reagan* (M.E. Sharpe, 1998), p. 146.

[26] Reagan kept his promise to keep Brady on the payroll as his official press secretary throughout both terms and seemed genuinely pleased to learn reports of his progress, but he never invited him to the Oval Office or visited with him elsewhere. Mollie Dickenson, *Thumbs Up: The Life and Courageous Comeback of White House Press Secretary Jim Brady* (Morrow, 1987); *Washington Post* (7 Dec. 1987), p. 36; Morris, "The Unknowable."

[27] See e.g. Pemberton, *Exit with Honor*, pp. 110–12.

[28] See e.g. the cover story in *The Economist* (10 June 2004) and similar stories in *Time, Newsweek,* the *Wall Street Journal,* and the *Washington Post* (and elsewhere).

Communism abroad and the restoration of faith in free markets at home."[29] Historians will argue these matters probably for the next few generations. Some will claim that his military buildup and his bold (if futile) SDI program shook the Russians' confidence that they could sustain the arms race and that this helped destroy the Soviet Union. On the other hand, at least by contrast with the hard-line rigidity of his Defense Department advisors Caspar Weinberger, Richard Perle, and Paul Wolfowitz – some of whom would become major foreign policy makers in the administration of George W. Bush – Reagan showed a willingness to negotiate, exercising a measure of flexibility that enabled him to accept a mu-tual arms reduction agreement with Premier Gorbachev after their meeting in Iceland in 1987.

Probably more important in the Soviet Union's downfall, however, was the covert military aid that the United States provided to the Islamic *mujahidin* fighters against the Soviet occupation of Afghanistan beginning in 1979 during the Carter administration and continuing through the eighties. This had two consequences, one favorable for American interests but the other decidedly un-favorable. It turned Afghanistan into Moscow's Vietnam, throwing the Soviet Union into both economic and military distress. Unfortunately, many of the U.S.-armed anti-Soviet fighters eventually joined Islamic extremists led by the Taliban, a radical sect with a medieval restorationist program. The Taliban be-came a base and an inspiration for the anti-U.S. terrorism that emerged in the nineties and rose to horrifying levels after the turn of the millennium.

Many will point out that the Soviet Union was on the brink of collapse be-fore Reagan's SDI and that the Soviet premier, Mikhail Gorbachev, deserves the major credit for ending the Cold War three years after Reagan left office. By ini-tiating *glasnost* (open dialog) and *perestroika* (restructuring) at home and by declining to use military force to prevent either the defection of Poland from Communist party rule or the secession of several Soviet republics, Gorbachev began a series of events that snowballed into his own political demise and that of the Soviet Union as well. On the other hand, with the Soviet Union already badly weakened by corruption and by the strains of its war in Afghanistan, Reagan's hard-line policy during his first term may have helped Gorbachev to persuade his military to accept the concessions that produced the conclusive thaw in the Cold War.[30]

---

[29] *New York Times* (7 June 2004), p. A28.

[30] Career diplomat and scholar Jack Matlock, Reagan's ambassador to Moscow in the late eight-ies, has written the most comprehensive account of the post-1987 thaw: *Reagan and Gorbachev: How the Cold War Ended* (Random House, 2004). For cogent but differing views, see John Lewis Gaddis, "The Cold War, the Long Peace, and the Future," *Diplomatic History* (Summer 1992), and Daniel Deudney & G. John Ikenberry, "Who Won the Cold War?" *Foreign Policy* (vol. 87, 1992).

There is no doubt that, with the collapse of the Soviet Union, market economics enjoyed a fast-growing popularity around the world. Reagan and the concurrent policies of the British prime minister, Margaret Thatcher, gave an enormous boost to the dismantling of government controls and ownership of economic agencies. With the leaders of the two countries most identified with liberal capitalism actively reducing the state's role in managing the economy, "privatization" and "deregulation" became the bywords of reformers intent upon stimulating economic growth throughout the world. The power of the United States to promote such policies cannot be overestimated. America provides a major market for the products of industrial and industrializing countries throughout the world. The United States also has much to say about the distribution of loans from the IMF and World Bank, among many other resources, a power that affected advanced industrial countries such as Germany and Italy as well as developing ones.

Nonetheless, faith in the efficacy and justice of an economic regime that depended mainly on market mechanisms for distributing societies' resources and rewards had its severe limits. In many less developed countries, austere financial programs and privatization of public utilities often led to massive distress, popular protests, and political instability. They also contributed to an anti-American animus abroad. The fact is, no other advanced industrial nation pursued a purely market-driven political economy as single-mindedly as did the United States.[31] Other advanced industrial nations that in some respects anticipated or followed the American example in reducing government activism rejected the American lead with regard to health care, social welfare, pensions, and servicing the national debt. Other industrial nations, such as France, Germany, and even Britain, held steady or increased social services and reduced defense expenditures while they cut back on some business regulations and privatized some previously state-owned industries. With the exception of Social Security, Americans saw the nation's work and income security programs, as well as state support for many social services, sharply cut while defense outlays soared along with interest payments on the national debt.[32]

The enduring impact of "Reaganomics" internationally, for better and for worse, remains undeniable. Many of the developing countries worked to separate the state from the running of major industries. In those countries that suffered from massive bureaucratic corruption, withdrawal of the state from the

---

[31] By the end of the nineties and in the early twenty-first century, many democratically organized countries began repudiating the American "free market" doctrine. For example, the election of left-oriented governments in Brazil, Venezuela, Argentina, and Uruguay owed greatly to an anti-U.S. animus in those developing nations.

[32] See e.g. Bruce Schulman, "The Reagan Revolution in International Perspective: Conservative Assaults on the Welfare State across the Industrialized World in the 1980s," in Richard S. Conley, ed., *Reassessing the Reagan Presidency* (University Press of America, 2003), especially pp. 98–9.

economy often had some positive effects. But many of the advanced industrial countries without such problems moved in the same direction. As noted earlier, America's callous labor policies gave a competitive advantage to U.S. industry and put pressure on European and Japanese governments to pull back from their more socially responsive policies.

In these developments, Reagan's (and Margaret Thatcher's) influence was apparent. But as two *Wall Street Journal* analysts commented shortly after Reagan's death in June 2004: "On other economic fronts, it's less clear that the Reagan legacy is surviving as robustly. At home – amid corporate scandals and seemingly laggard regulatory attempts to rein them in – there's now a tense debate over whether reliance on market forces has gone too far."[33] Private-sector corruption and incompetence, particularly at the executive levels of megacorporations, rarely gets the attention of minimal-state economic and political theorists. The collapse of the savings and loan industry in the eighties followed by the criminal behavior revealed in the Enron, WorldCom, and other giant scandals at the end of the century illustrate some consequences of such neglect.

Apart from support among the antistatist conservatives of the economic, religious, and libertarian sorts, Reagan's political strength as president rested mainly on the way in which he restored a sense of pride and optimism for a nation humbled by the multiple calamities of the seventies: the defeat in Vietnam; the forced devaluation of the dollar; Watergate; stagflation; the Iranian hostage crisis; and the inability to respond effectively to the oil crises of 1973 and 1979. The Reagan campaign slogan of "morning in America" accurately expressed the feeling he brought to the majority of Americans, at least at the outset of his administration. It was clear, too, that whatever the majority of Americans thought of his policies (as opposed to his personality and image), Reagan and conservative allies exploited his popularity to radically change the American political agenda. They moved it dramatically to the right so that, as some pundits put it, the right became the center and the extreme right became the right. That moved what used to be called "the lunatic fringe" into position as "the extreme right." Meanwhile, the left sank beneath the political horizon altogether.

*   *   *

The momentum of the Reagan revolution carried through the presidencies of George Herbert Walker Bush (the man who had once called Reagan's economic policies "voodoo economics" but copied them anyway) and William Jefferson

---

[33] David Wessel & Gerald F. Seib, "How Reagan Recast Debate on Markets, Taxes – And Deficits," *Wall Street Journal* (7 June 2004), pp. A1, A8.

Clinton. As the Reagan program progressed, it accentuated the cultural divide in America. By the time Clinton won the presidency in 1992,[34] the country was well on its way toward bitter polarization.

Bill Clinton, born in rural Arkansas of a widowed mother (his father died shortly before he was born), graduated from Georgetown University, won a prestigious Rhodes scholarship to Oxford, and earned a law degree at Yale. He was the first of the Baby Boom generation to hold the presidency. He bore several of the characteristics of that generation. He was extraordinarily intelligent, attentive, and informed, and also remarkably self-indulgent. His politics were both cautious and single-mindedly ambitious. Mindful of the conservative, anxious, and self-concerned sentiments of his generation, Clinton joined with the group that called themselves New Democrats in the hope of forging a new electoral majority. They aimed to move the party away from "old liberalism" and further to "the center," which meant joining those who tended to view government as a source rather than as a remedy for economic injustice. They yielded to Republicans' identification of "liberalism" with "the left," with all the quasi–un-American weight that the term had come to bear in the minds of the discontented voters of the Reagan era.

The first Democrat to serve two full terms since Franklin Roosevelt began his fourth term nearly half a century before, Clinton managed to hold the line (temporarily) against a wholesale repeal of a half-century of advances in protecting the environment, labor benefits, consumer interests, social emancipation, and civil liberties. He did so despite the fact that his personal foibles – unaccountably stupid dalliances with various women, coupled with a habitual lack of candor about them – left him vulnerable to the nastiest partisan and personal attacks on a sitting president since the beginning of the twentieth century. He survived in part because much of the public came to see the attacks as unseemly and overreaching. House Republicans, apparently giddy with having won control of both houses of Congress for the first time in forty years, sought to oust the president for his sexual indiscretions by means of a uniquely partisan vote for impeachment against nearly unanimous Democratic and some Republican opposition. (The Senate quite properly refused to convict.)[35]

---

[34] Clinton won only 43 percent of the popular vote, to Bush's 37 percent, with most of the rest going to the eccentric billionaire Ross Perot, who ran on and financed his own ticket.

[35] The only other president to be impeached – Abraham Lincoln's successor, Andrew Johnson – was the victim of highly charged post–Civil War disagreements primarily over policy. He, too, was acquitted by the Senate that was able to distinguish disagreements over presidential prerogatives and policy from impeachable acts. (Nixon resigned rather than face certain impeachment.) Few things illustrate better the degradation of fin de siècle American politics than the right-wing's campaign to destroy a president on the basis of catching him in embarrassingly disreputable but entirely legal private behavior and then trapping him into committing perjury.

But Clinton survived in large measure also by moving into conservative territory on issues such as balancing the budget, reducing the mountainous national debt that Reagan had compiled, and building an unprecedented budget surplus – meanwhile cutting welfare support for millions of indigent Americans. Preempting Republican claims to be "tough on crime," he helped push through an anti-crime bill that included a federal "three strikes" measure mandating life imprisonment for persons convicted of three felonies (no matter whether an early guilty plea was part of a settlement that spared the accused unaffordable litigation nor how long it was between convictions). Clinton supported increased outlays for new federal prisons and for cities to hire thousands of additional police. More important, he endorsed legislation to extend unmonitored FBI surveillance of Americans suspected of criminal activity, despite the FBI's rancid history of abusing such power against legitimate political protest groups (exposed in the widely publicized Senate hearings of 1975 by the so-called Church Committee, chaired by Senator Frank Church of Idaho).

Clinton held office long enough to appoint many federal judges, including two justices to the U.S. Supreme Court. But, typically, they were centrist individuals, not of the mettle of those who had starred in the Warren Court era. Even so, Republicans managed to stall and prevent many of his most important appointments by filibuster and, after gaining control of the Senate, by simply refusing to hold confirmation hearings or report out to the full Senate. In a few cases, he was forced to withdraw nominations in the face of certain rejection by partisans in the Senate. His most important domestic achievements of a liberal nature concerned environmental matters, although as exercises of executive power they could be (and would be) reversed by a later conservative administration. On the whole, the Clinton administration partially stalled the American rush to the right but did little more than that.

Clinton began his administration with a couple of sharp gestures toward the political left. First, he ordered the military to revoke its ban on homosexuals. Second, he appointed his wife – the exceptionally able Hillary Rodham Clinton, an attorney – to head a task force charged with drafting a universal health-care plan. Both actions backfired. Heeding the still-powerful provincial hostility to homosexuals, congressional Democrats and Republicans joined the military brass to gang up on him. The president was forced into a humiliating compromise ("don't ask, don't tell") that left gays essentially in the same position as before the revocation order.

Meanwhile, the First Lady took heavy fire from all sides. The American Medical Association, the insurance industry, the U.S. Chamber of Commerce, and the Business Roundtable joined small-business groups in opposition to any plan that required employer contributions. But other factors counted as well. Many women joined the opposition, not very subtly expressing their resentment of

Hillary Clinton's eminence, achieved, as they were prompted to argue, merely on the coattails of her husband. In any case, Republicans would not abide any health-care plan sponsored by a Democratic administration. This guaranteed that the flak would fly. In the end, the unceasing potshots at the task force's proposals so crippled the effort that the Democratic congressional leadership could not even bring it to a vote. The subsequent Republican sweep of the 1994 congressional elections seemingly rewarded the opposition.

Thereafter, Clinton retreated into safe, conservative territory. In domestic policy matters, his administration had just the two landmark achievements, both typically conservative objectives: balancing the budget, and (in Clinton's campaign rhetoric) "ending welfare as we know it." Some economists attribute the economic boom of the nineties to Clinton's fiscal conservatism. That conclusion will continue to occupy differing economists and historians, but they must note that although median family income showed significant improvement after 1993, recovering the ground lost in the previous decades, the gains owed much to an increase in two-earner families and the figures did not include single-person households.[36] Meanwhile, the welfare reform measure of 1995 (euphemistically called "The Personal Responsibility and Work Opportunity Reconciliation Act") placed strict limits on the duration of welfare eligibility. It forced recipients – a high percentage of whom were single mothers – to hunt for jobs. It was hailed for many years as a great success, as it surely was in driving people off the welfare rolls. Anecdotal reports indicated that many former welfare recipients welcomed their change of status to job holders; for them it was revitalizing to take responsibility for their own welfare. But without adequate financing of child day care and without raising significantly the minimum wage prevailing in the majority of jobs that former welfare mothers (and otherwise encumbered individuals) might hold, it created widespread distress. When the stock-market balloon burst at the end of the century and job opportunities shrank, those forced off welfare faced still greater troubles. Once off welfare, moreover, in most cases Americans lost their eligibility for Medicaid within 10–15 months of the measure's passage. Although the percentage of all Americans without any kind of medical insurance remained about the same from about the mid-eighties to the end of the century, the actual number of Americans without insurance increased from 31.0 million in 1987 to 39.8 million in 2000. (The figures continued to rise sharply: by 2004, the number of Americans without insurance had risen to 45.8 million.)[37]

---

[36] See the discussion of poverty in Chapter 16.

[37] Health insurance data retrieved from Historical Health Insurance Table HI-4, ⟨http://www.census.gov/hhes/www/hlthins/historic/hihistt4.html⟩. There were few careful studies of the overall impact of the welfare reform legislation, although there appeared to be something of a consensus that it was "hugely successful." Christopher Jencks, an expert on welfare and income

Since these consequences were predictable, the philosophy behind "welfare reform" appears to have been, "better that some worthy but unlucky Americans suffer unjustly than that some idle, unworthy Americans continue to live off public revenues." A more generous society might have reversed that scenario.

In foreign policy matters, Clinton's major success came with forcing through Congress the North American Free Trade Agreement (NAFTA), which provided for opening up U.S. markets to Canada and Mexico in exchange for their freeing of their markets for U.S. producers. But NAFTA divided Democrats. Old-line liberal internationalist Democrats supported the principle of free trade while labor Democrats feared a union-busting migration of jobs to Mexico, where labor costs were low and environmental regulations few and badly enforced.

Otherwise, Clinton had some near misses on major achievements. He got Israeli Prime Minister Yitzak Rabin and Palestinian leader Yasser Arafat to shake hands and agree to a semi-autonomous Palestinian authority in Gaza and the West Bank, but this proved to have more symbolic than lasting significance. Toward the end of his administration, he made some progress in heading off a North Korean nuclear weapons program, but this was summarily undermined by his successor, who harbored a visceral distrust of everything proposed by the Clinton administration. When eighteen U.S. troops were killed in a futile humanitarian intervention in anarchic Somalia, Clinton promptly ended that venture. That incident deterred other humane efforts. The evident unwillingness to put American troops in danger contributed to United Nations Secretary-General Kofi Annan's decision to withhold UN intervention against the unspeakable massacres in the tiny African country of Rwanda, despite clear warnings of their imminence, although the inaction of the French and Belgian governments (which had troops in the area) deserves the greater blame.[38] Given the European indifference and the partisan political risks at home, Clinton also delayed intervening in the mutually inflicted barbarism among Croats, Serbs, Bosnians, and Kosovars in the disintegrated Yugoslavia until after thousands had been killed. Once the United States did enter, the major violence quickly ended.

Clinton responded with restraint to lethal bombings of U.S. embassies in Africa, of the U.S. destroyer *Cole* in a Yemeni port, and of the World Trade

---

issues, offers a judicious appraisal of the positive and negative effects of Clinton's welfare reform in "What Happened to Welfare," *New York Review* (15 Dec. 2005), pp. 76ff. For different, somewhat anecdotal accounts, see David K. Shipler, *The Working Poor: Invisible in America* (Knopf, 2004), and Barbara Ehrenreich, *Nickeled and Dimed: On (Not) Getting By in America* (Holt, 2001). To his credit, Clinton tried to persuade an increasingly conservative Congress to develop a more comprehensive child-care program and pushed for increases in the minimum wage.

[38] The best brief account appears in Samantha Power, "A Hero of Our Time," *New York Review of Books* (18 Nov. 2004), an essay prepared as a foreword to *Shake Hands with the Devil: The Failure of Humanity in Rwanda* – a forthcoming memoir by Romeo Dallaire, the commander of the 2,500-man UN mission in Rwanda at the time.

Center in New York City in 1993, all perpetrated by Islamic extremists. The names of Al Qaeda and Osama bin Laden were not yet widely known outside U.S. intelligence agencies. It may never be clearly known how much this restraint owed to (1) a dearth of reliable intelligence, (2) a concern that a massive attack on known locations of Al Qaeda leaders and training areas would cause unacceptably high civilian casualties, or (3) the diversion of Clinton's attention by the extraordinarily partisan personal attacks on him throughout his administrations. As it was, when Clinton ordered the bombing of Al Qaeda camps in Afghanistan and Sudan, Republicans pounced on him for trying to divert attention from their campaign to highlight his sexual follies.

The fact is, throughout nearly his entire presidency, Clinton faced a continual barrage of largely mendacious accusations regarding his personal life and various minor or invented other transgressions. There can be little question that it had an evil effect on his ability to govern. Even before he took office in January 1993, partisans were busy concocting stories about him and his wife that they fed to a press eager for salacious tales. Some of the stories, particularly about Clinton's philandering, had elements of truth, however trivial and governmentally irrelevant they were. His lack of candor about his sexual dalliances served to whet the appetite of media pundits for relentlessly pursuing the stories. In addition, while Bill Clinton was governor of Arkansas, he and his wife engaged in some questionable business deals that suggested conflicts of interest and about which they seemed less than forthcoming. The press, which somehow had missed the 1980's story of the savings-and-loan looting by many corporate executives – costing the government half a trillion dollars for insured and some wealthy uninsured depositors – tirelessly pursued a story of how a $1,000 investment by Hillary Clinton when she was the Arkansas governor's wife had netted her $100,000 in a short time. Such deals, suggestive of insider trading, were common enough for many prominent Americans, including Dwight Eisenhower before he became president. The small amount of money involved was not small enough to deter anti-Clinton partisans in Congress and in the media from making a long-running front-page story of it.[39]

But that degradation of American politics seems pale compared to the long-running, well-financed attempt to pin a murder on the president and his wife. When Vincent Foster, a close friend of the Clintons and one of their political consultants, committed suicide – tormented as he was by the unceasing nastiness of Clinton's political enemies – billionaire Richard Scaife along with others commandeered various friendly media to propagate charges, which circulated

---

[39] Compare the press coverage – or, rather, lack of coverage – regarding George W. Bush's $600,000 investment (mostly borrowed money) in the Texas Rangers baseball team that was quickly turned into a $15 million profit.

for nearly eight years, that the Clintons had murdered Foster to keep him quiet about the couple's Arkansas business deals. The stories persisted long after the charges had been proven plainly false. An early investigation by Independent Counsel Robert Fiske, Jr. (a Republican and former federal prosecutor) came up with no incriminating evidence against the Clintons in their business deals, and he also confirmed Foster's suicide. But that did not end matters.

Republicans then induced a panel of three conservative judges to appoint a *new* independent counsel – Kenneth Starr, a Republican insider and reactionary ideologue – to renew investigations of the president's life before and after his election to the White House. Conservative partisans took advantage of Bill Clinton's reputation as a sometime adulterer by recruiting an Arkansas floozy to charge that as governor he had made improper advances to her.[40] Well financed, the relentless publicity, which the scandal-mongering media lapped up, took on historic dimensions that included the unprecedented expenditure of more than $40 million of public money by two independent counsels over the course of the two Clinton administrations. Eight years of meanly motivated investigations costing months of the president's attention finally proved that neither of the Clintons had done anything illegal in business matters. But they did entrap Bill Clinton into falsely denying under oath that he had engaged in some hanky-panky with a young, sexually liberated White House intern named Monica Lewinsky.

Some Americans considered Clinton's perjury regarding his sexual play with a consenting adult to be a momentous matter.[41] Clearly, many thought it serious enough to pass the Constitutional test for impeachment. Most of the same people saw nothing nearly so serious in President Reagan's willful violation of federal law by secretly funneling millions of dollars to Central American "Contras" for the purpose of overthrowing the democratically elected government of Nicaragua while selling arms to Iran, nor in his vice-president's almost certainly false claim under oath that he was "out of the loop" in White House discussions about the Iran–Contra deals. What is worth noting is how that stark divide in ethical sensibilities reflected the cultural divide that was widening across the country. For provincial America, lying about a private sexual matter was momentous whereas the mendacious usurpation of power at the presidential level received a pass. The clash of provincial versus metropolitan America was reflected even in Kenneth Starr's lengthy report to Congress, replete as it was with

---

[40] There remain doubts as to the validity of the charges, but there are no doubts as to the active recruitment.

[41] I call it "sexual play" because there was never any question of Clinton having had an *affair* involving sexual intercourse with the woman. By contrast, several of his most vociferous Republican accusers *had* engated in such affairs. Most notably, Republican Speaker Newt Gingrich was involved in an adulterous affair even while he was busy assailing the president's behavior (see Chapter 12).

unnecessarily graphic sexual details. Starr clearly aimed at galvanizing village Americans' outrage, while to metropolitan Americans it exposed the man's niggling prurience. Starr's performance also exemplified the fanatic's insensitivity to the collateral damage done to innocent bystanders whom he bullied into collaborating with his determination to *get* something on his enemy, the president.[42]

The partisan harassment of President Clinton throughout his two administrations succeeded in diverting attention from the Reagan revolution agenda of diminishing a half-century of gains for civil liberties and for an equitable distribution of income and social benefits, for protection for the environment, and for employee safety, consumer interests, and health care for the needy. It succeeded also in dampening renewal of enthusiasm for public-spirited participation in government. Most important, it almost certainly had the effect of diverting the Clinton administration's full attention from multiple barbaric civil conflicts abroad – in the Congo, Kosovo, and Ethiopa – along with the growing threat of anti-U.S. terrorist attacks.

For this we have the word of, among others, the country's most experienced antiterrorist government official. Richard A. Clarke, chief advisor on terrorism to four presidents beginning with President Reagan, wrote (after resigning from the administration of Clinton's successor): "Bill Clinton ... identified terrorism as the major post–Cold War threat, ... acted to improve our counterterrorism capabilities, and ... (little known to the public) quelled anti-American terrorism by Iraq and Iran and defeated an Al Qaeda attempt to dominate Bosnia .... [But] weakened by continued political attack, [he] could not get the CIA, the Pentagon, and the FBI to act sufficiently to deal with the threat."[43]

Although Clinton would win re-election easily in 1996 and though Democrats recovered some lost ground in the congressional elections of 1998, the Republican Party, by then dominated by right-wing ideologues and corporate employees, retained firm control of Congress. The Reagan revolution had solidified its hold on the country's political agenda.

---

[42] See Chapter 13. One victim, Susan McDougal, refused to collaborate and spent a year in prison for contempt of court. According to her account, she refused to tell untruthful tales about the Clintons that Starr and his aides were pressuring her to tell.

[43] Richard A. Clarke, *Against All Enemies: Inside America's War on Terror* (Free Press, 2004), p. xxiv. See also James M. Lindsay, "The New Apathy," *Foreign Affairs* (Sept./Oct. 2000).

20

Summary

The reversal by the mid-1970s of the public ethos that supported the agenda of the Liberal Democratic Coalition had many causes. For every change, there are winners and losers. In the heyday of rising affluence, few perceived themselves as losers, even as various oppressed and disadvantaged groups began gaining larger shares of the country's resources and product. But by the seventies, competition for jobs as well as for domestic and international market shares became intense. In the job market, Baby Boomers, women, and minorities began competing with white males for prime positions in the professions, in business management, and in the shrinking sector of high-wage manufacturing. Meanwhile, international competition from the revived and fast-growing industrial centers of Europe and Asia cut into the viability of core domestic industries, leading to massive layoffs of once-prospering wage earners. At the same time, the American economy became more heavily dependent on imported oil than at any time in its history. The oil crisis of 1973, followed by another in 1979, signified for many a return to an economy of scarcity, a mindset seemingly confirmed by the decade's "stagflation," which featured double-digit inflation and more than 8-percent unemployment. A zero-sum mentality cultivated a retrogressive political environment. All this occurred as the radical nature of the revolutionary changes in American life began to dismay the still traditionalist core of the American polity.

Many of the liberal achievements had begun to agitate sectors of American voters that either had previously shown little concern with the changes or had become sensitized to how the changes had cost them. At the same time, the success of many features of the liberal thrusts embodied in Lyndon Johnson's Great Society led to a thinning of the ranks of reform enthusiasts. Some dropped away with a sense of "mission accomplished." Others drifted away troubled by some of the unintended consequences of the reforms they had championed. For many liberal intellectuals, affirmative action seemed to restore legal status to race, once thought to have been overturned in the 1954 *Brown v. Board of Education* decision, with effects that some called "reverse discrimination." This and court-mandated school busing to achieve "racial balance" in public schools antagonized millions of ethnic Americans who usually had voted Democratic but felt excluded from the benefits of such measures, having become sensitized to their own historic mistreatment at the hands of a "white Anglo-Saxon Protestant establishment." The perceived threat of affirmative action to the principle of seniority among unionized workers further undercut the coalition, even as the shrinking of the economy' heavy-industry sector hit union membership the hardest. Many industrial workers also joined business corporations in blaming the costs of the new social and environmental regulations for the exporting of jobs to lower-cost developing countries in Asia and Latin America. ("If you're hungry and out of work," jibed a union bumper sticker in Michigan, "eat an environmentalist.")[1] Finally, of course, the Democratic Party's responsibility for most of the advances in civil rights cost it the support of the once solidly Democratic South.

Liberal internationalists had entered the sixties confident that an activist United States could do great good things for resisting the spread of totalitarian communism and cultivating liberal democratic institutions abroad. That confidence foundered on the disasters in Southeast Asia. The Vietnam War split the liberal Democratic coalition down the middle and led to the departure from the party of some of its most effective intellectual leadership. On one side, many liberals lost faith in the ability of the United States to do great good things abroad. For them, the lesson of Vietnam required a cautious approach to the uses of power in acknowledgment of the unpredictable and often terrible costs of foreign interventions no matter the benevolent intentions.

Other liberals emerged from the Vietnam era more resolved than ever to use U.S. power abroad. They determined to reckon "more realistically" with the nature of foreign threats to American interests; to respond to those threats without squeamish fretting over the collateral damage that even the benevolent uses of power inevitably cause; and, in sum, to be bold and unapologetic about using in its own interests the superpower that the nation had acquired over the course of its history. Celebration over the collapse of the Soviet Union in the nineties, which "Reagan Democrats" joined with Republicans in attributing to the hardline application of their realism, reinforced their convictions. It was left to such neoconservatives, now embedded in the Republican Party, to carry forward the liberal internationalist ambition to use American power in defense of what they viewed as liberal principles, as when Iraq suddenly invaded and occupied Kuwait

---

[1] Michael Schaller & George Rising, *The Republican Ascendancy: American Politics 1968–2001* (Harlan Davidson, 2001), p. 69.

in 1991. To many this seemed like a replay of North Korea's across-the-border invasion of the South, except that in this case Americans' interest in safeguarding access to Middle Eastern oil accentuated the impulse to punish military aggression on principle.

It was Reagan's successor, George H. W. Bush, who fashioned an international coalition backed by the United Nations, launched the Gulf War, and drove the Iraqis back behind their original borders. There, to the distress of some neocons, they stopped. They left Saddam Hussein in power in Baghdad but imposed economic sanctions on exports and imports and also required Saddam to submit to UN inspections aimed at preventing any future development of nuclear, biological, or chemical weapons. Many on the liberal left could now be found in criticism of foreign intervention.

Meanwhile, from the fifties on, a New Conservatism, explicitly antiliberal both in philosophy and in political agenda, began its surge toward ascendancy. It gained political energy from a TV-generated revival of evangelical religious enthusiasm but it also absorbed many of the country's disaffected intellectuals. By the end of the seventies, those intellectuals came to deplore "statism" while emphasizing the primary need for a strong military response to international perils. They lamented the effect of the revolutionary changes in American life on long-standing behavioral conventions. They recoiled against the more militant, "nonnegotiable" demands coming from the left, from some minority groups, and from some self-designated spokesmen for welfare recipients. They became skeptical of environmental and safety rules that seemed aimed at unreasonable, zero-risk levels. They came to join with those who argued for the greater "efficiency" of a market-driven allocation of society's resources and rewards over an allocation modified by government interventions. In sum, they came to stand on common ground with the New Conservatives. The Reagan revolution signified their ascendancy. Their more complete triumph awaited the advent of the new millennium and the outcome of the century's most bizarre presidential election.

The triumph of the New Conservatives would not have been possible without the active support of most of the business community. The successes of liberal internationalism in the post–World War II era had been equally dependent on support from the business community. As American business looked abroad to exploit new investment opportunities and markets after the war, their interests diverged from the conservative, mostly Republican preference for a protectionist and isolationist foreign policy. But by the seventies, the Republican Party had abandoned protectionism, an issue by then mostly raised by labor unions in response to cheap goods produced abroad by multinational corporations. Meanwhile, pressed by international competition and by the costs of increasingly restrictive regulations, American business leaders mobilized to resist and undo many of the measures designed by the liberal Democratic coalition. They targeted those measures intended to reduce the injurious effects of industrially contaminated air, water, food, and earth. They resisted, often successfully, efforts to remedy the injuries to consumers and employees as the consequence of industrial and medical negligence. They put a brake on reforms designed to widen health-care insurance coverage, especially any that might require employer contributions. They became an important part of the conservative Republican coalition.

In that role, business leaders brought their financial resources, including influential positions in the media, to the new socially conservative leadership of the Republican Party, thereby giving political support to traditionalist social objectives and village morality. This added force to the New Conservative coalition's opposition to women's family planning choices, to domestic partner benefits, and to federal gun controls while backing the right of public school districts to pressure children to engage in prayer during school hours. They joined in opposing measures to reduce the effects of adverse discrimination based on race, religion, ethnicity, gender, age, sexual orientation, or disability. They joined in opposition to measures aimed at alleviating the effects of poverty.

Especially in its weakened state, the liberal Democratic coalition could not withstand the political counterattack. In some respects, it was weakest in the undeniable fact that most of its achievements depended not on "the power of the people" but on top-down leadership. When "the people" mobilized against them, led by candidates like Ronald Reagan who affected a populist posture, the liberal coalition had no effective political answer. In the process, they lost control of the strategic sites of government – most importantly, the presidency and the courts – from which they had launched their progressive actions.

In the climax of *Network,* Paddy Chayevsky's 1976 film, the lead character (played by Peter Finch), outraged by the corruption of radio and TV journalism, "loses it" and shouts hysterically that it is time for people to wake up and to put their head out the window and shout as loudly as they could: "I'm mad as hell and I'm not going to take it anymore." The film's message was intended to call attention to the domination of news media, and indeed of American society, by corporate avarice. But at the very time that the film was winning Academy Awards, "the people" were directing anger not at corporate power but at the reform movements that had sought to contain that power and to substitute a more generous spirit for Americans' overarching acquisitive quest.

PART FOUR

EPILOGUE

21

"The New American Century"

People don't want to go to war .... But, after all, it's the leaders of the country who determine the policy and it's always a simple matter to drag the people along whether it's a democracy or a fascist dictatorship or a parliament or a communist dictatorship .... Voice or no voice, the people can always be brought to the bidding of the leaders. That is easy. All you have to do is tell them they are being attacked and denounce the pacifists for lack of patriotism and exposing the country to great danger. It works the same way in any country.[1]
                                                                    Hermann Göring

Allow the President to invade a neighboring nation, whenever *he* shall deem it necessary to repel an invasion ... and you allow him to make war at pleasure .... [This would place] our President where kings have always stood.[2]
                                                                    Abraham Lincoln

The sixty years of U.S. history treated in this book began with Henry Luce's hopeful reference to the twentieth century as "The American Century." Writing in 1941, before America's entry into the Second World War but after Hitler's conquest of nearly all of continental Europe west of the Soviet Union, Luce made a plea for the United States to take on the leadership role that its industrial and cultural strengths made more or less obligatory. He noted especially the force of America's prestige and the spread abroad of many of America's cultural and scientific achievements as evidence of the readiness of much of the world to follow the United States. In a world beset by the expanding power of totalitarian regimes in Europe and Asia, Luce's call for American leadership contained

---

[1] Quoted in Jason Epstein, "What's the Matter with Kansas?" *New York Review of Books* (5 Oct. 2004).

[2] Quoted in David Herbert Donald, *Lincoln* (Simon & Schuster, 1995), p. 126; emphasis in the original.

the main elements of liberal internationalism. In the aftermath of the war, the United States did indeed take on the responsibilities demanded of it by its unique power and by the principles of liberal internationalism. By that time, Americans' business interests had begun to dovetail with the wisdom of the policy. (Things happen when wisdom and economic interest come together.) America's postwar activism produced great positive effects for most of the people in Western Europe and parts of Asia, and for Americans as well.

For liberals, the strengthening of a sense of the universality of humankind was one of the great achievements of the postwar era. It was a sense that had its modern origins in the eighteenth-century Enlightenment, a sense that transcended tribe, race, ethnicity, religious faith, and nationhood. It was implicit, if not much featured, in the establishment of the United Nations and its many agencies of collective transnational assistance – political, financial, scientific, military, and humane.

Such a sensibility grew only slowly around the world. It was tragically confounded in too many places: Cambodia, Yugoslavia, Rwanda, East Timor among them. Unspeakable massacres, inspired by little more than primitive passions rooted in differences in class, religion, and tribe, more than matched the Holocaust in the sheer physical barbarism of the rampages if not in total number of the dead and mutilated. "Us vs. Them" retained its vicious power. But it was a power that seemed to be on the defensive – perhaps thus its extreme expression – in the face of the communications and transportation revolutions that almost literally shrank the planet. The spirit of universalism conveyed across the globe by computers and commerce threatened the coziness, the close comforts of "belonging," the exhilarating exclusiveness of tribalism.

The universalist sensibility grew slowly in the United States, too. But there, much progress was made during the course of the movements for civil rights, women's rights, and gay and lesbian rights. It grew with the nearly unprecedented sympathetic attention to the miseries of the poor. It grew with the laws requiring accommodations for physically handicapped people, so many of whom before the Sixties led lives of shut-ins, ignored as "others" by all except their immediate families. It grew with the lowering of national and ethnic barriers to hopeful immigrants, barriers that until the Sixties had greatly limited especially Asians and Southern and Eastern Europeans from joining others who had fled from hardship and oppression in their choice of America as a land for settlement and the rewards of hard work. It grew with the broadly felt need for armed intervention by international peacekeepers to end lethal strife within and between nations. In growing, this sensibility began to challenge the 300-year-old principle of "national sovereignty" in the name of universalist human empathy.

These were historic achievements. They raised the level of civilized behavior to heights never approached before. For this, American liberal leadership deserved much of the credit. But for many Americans, it also had the effect of upsetting the comforting certainties of tradition. By the end of the century, their reaction had become passionate. Once more, as in the Sixties, the personal became political, this time in rejection of many of the dramatic changes that had transformed the country during the third quarter of the century.

Things began to turn sour by the mid-1960s. Ever since the Korean War, liberal internationalism had been yielding ground to a simple anticommunism as the principal guide for foreign policy.[3] This had a corroding effect. The U.S. support for brutal dictatorships, in Latin America and elsewhere, whose only "virtues" were that they were anticommunist sullied the liberal cause. Most Americans knew little of that. But the disastrous American intervention in Indochina brought the world's and Americans' attention to the potential evils of wrongful use of power.

As we have seen, liberal internationalists split on whether the Indochina intervention exemplified one of those evils. Some remained adamant in their justification of the Vietnam War,[4] as did much of provincial America. Nevertheless, the Vietnam calamity inevitably led to some re-examination of the liberal criteria for legitimate intervention abroad. It also forced re-examination of some previous foreign interventions, such as in Guatemala and Iran, about which most of the details had remained hidden in inaccessible government files. The Freedom of Information Act of 1966, broadened in 1974 and inspired by the evident secretive conduct of the Johnson and Nixon administrations, quickened discovery of some behavior by U.S. policy makers that was difficult or impossible to justify on liberal principles. Many Americans and people abroad began to see the United States as something of an international bully.

After the turn of the millennium, the foreign policy of George W. Bush would seem to validate the concerns of post-Vietnam liberals and their more radical critics who viewed with anxiety the extension of American power abroad "for good purposes." The antiwar critics of the Sixties (joined by many others) would come to view the invasion of Iraq in 2003 as an example of what perils may develop both at home and abroad from a felt obligation by presidents to deploy American power overseas in purportedly good causes. Some might argue that the bold action of President Truman in responding promptly to the invasion of South Korea in 1950 in advance of a congressional mandate set a bad precedent for the unauthorized use of presidential power. But the belligerent unilaterism of the Bush foreign policy departed significantly from the liberal internationalist approach. Among other things, Truman was responding to an across-the-border

---

[3] See Chapter 7 as well as Richard M. Abrams, "Anticommunism and Liberal Internationalism: A Review Essay," *Reviews in American History* (Sept. 1982).

[4] See e.g. Norman Podhoretz, *Why We Were in Vietnam* (Simon & Schuster, 1982).

military invasion and, moreover, the United States had official UN endorsement. George W. Bush's father, the first President Bush, had done the same in throwing back Iraq's invasion of Kuwait in 1991. But Bush the son claimed the unilateral power to launch a "preemptive war," despite UN resistance and worldwide protests.

Already by the seventies, as we have seen, many Americans at home had begun to express profound disappointment over the damage done to the image of America as a paragon and agent of a new, humane, freedom-cherishing world regime. America had enjoyed that image throughout most of the Western world at the beginning of the twentieth century and – after some tarnishing in the twenties and thirties, as Henry Luce remarked – had been renewed by its successes in and after the Second World War. But the Vietnam disaster badly damaged America's image.

By the end of the twentieth century, in fact, America had lost much of its claim to world leadership in anything besides military power. Things would get worse during the second Bush presidency. Within the first few years of the new millennium, by nearly all accounts U.S. prestige abroad dropped to an all-time low.

Among all the advanced industrial countries, the United States had become unique in many unenviable ways: It was unique in its homicide rate, and in the private ownership of guns; unique in applying the death penalty for hundreds of criminal offenders; unique in a "three strikes" law that prescribed life imprisonment for Americans with three relatively minor criminal law violations; unique in the high percentage of its male population held in prison. The United States was also unique in failing to make available any kind of medical insurance for more than 40 million of its citizens and in forcing most Americans to shop among profit-seeking insurance companies for varying levels of medical care. Meanwhile, the nation's child immunization rates were lower and its infant mortality rate higher than in other advanced countries; and, on average, life expectancy in the United States was lower. The nation's job holders were permitted the least paid leisure and recreational time and had the least protection against peremptory dismissal, partly because law gave little advantage to union organization. The country was also conspicuous for the gaping and growing distance between the salaries and bonuses of senior corporate executives and the salaries and wages of their employees, as well as for the epidemic of criminal dishonesty that roiled its business and financial systems. On a per capita basis, Americans paid the lowest taxes of any advanced country in the world, which helped to explain why their public social services remained among the poorest, perhaps most notably in its major cities' inadequate public transit systems and its woeful intercity passenger rail services. At the same time, by the 1980s the United States had become the world's leading debtor nation, beholden especially to German, Japanese, and (by 2002) Chinese buyers of U.S. Treasury bonds. In short, Americans could no longer be confident that their country, the land that they loved, could boast of the highest standard of living and culture in the world.

In the eyes of much of the world, the country's foreign policy in the new millennium also fell short of admirable. It was conspicuous among only a handful of nations in its rejection of the Kyoto Protocol to slow global warming by reducing atmospheric pollution. It was among only a few in its rejection of the jurisdiction of the International Criminal Court. It was virtually unique in withdrawing financial support for international population control agencies. Its sabre-rattling approach to foreign affairs did not inspire warm friendship among nations.

Meanwhile, the cultural divide in America produced a rancorous politics that further damaged the country's prestige. Differences over policies turned into uncompromising moral conflicts, especially as part of the New Conservative insurgency targeted "moral relativism" and "secular rationalism" as twin evils sapping the essence of *America* and all the virtue implied by that word. Small margins of political advantage no longer inspired efforts to find a unifying consensus or middle ground. An "in your face" ethos of winner-take-all came to prevail. The impeachment of President Bill Clinton exemplified the new political environment, offering to the world the spectacle of a small majority of passionate partisans in the lower house of Congress pouring unstinting resources and energy into nothing more noble than humiliating the president of the United States. The rancor would grow more poisonous after the turn of the century.

＊　　＊　　＊

As the twentieth century neared its end, and as many Americans congratulated themselves for victory in the Cold War and the final triumph over Soviet communism, a group of politically influential scholars and journalists formed "The Project for the *New* American Century." The Project was chaired by conservative journalist William Kristol, son of the leading neoconservative intellectual Irving Kristol and editor of the right-wing *Weekly Standard*. On its board of directors sat several conservative scholars and political individuals who had served in the Reagan administration. They included some who in the seventies had joined the Coalition for a Democratic Majority and then made their way into the Committee for the Present Danger and the Republican Party. They included others who had waited for years as outsiders on the fringes of right-wing politics. Several would become influential members of George W. Bush's administration.

In its "Statement of Principles," which had elements of a liberal internationalist outlook, the Project argued that the peace of Europe, Asia, and the Middle East depended on Americans taking on their responsibility to lead. "The history of the past," it observed, "should have taught us to embrace the cause of American leadership." But the authors of the Statement emphasized only America's military advantages, making no mention of America's cultural or political attributes. "As the 20th Century draws to a close," they noted, "the United States stands as the world's preeminent power." They went on to ask with a distinctly unilateralist overtone: "Does the United States have the resolve to shape a new century favorable to American principles and interests?"[5]

In 2000, the Project produced a position paper entitled "Rebuilding America's Defenses: Strategy, Forces, and Resources." It called for the United States to pursue "global leadership" by bolstering its military preeminence. "This report proceeds," it began, "from the belief that America should seek to preserve and extend its position of global leadership by maintaining the preeminence of U.S. military force." With the collapse of the Soviet Union, the U.S. stood without any great-power rival. "The challenge for the coming century," it concluded, "is to preserve and enhance this 'American peace'."

The picture projected in the position paper was one of the United States directing other nations that were expected to follow in its wake toward goals set by American leaders. There was little in it to suggest, as in the past, an America joining vigorously with a coalition of other nations that moved along toward mutually defined goals – for example, the organization of the United Nations; rehabilitation of Western Europe's and Japan's economies; containment of Soviet communism; numerous mutually beneficial commercial, humanitarian, and peacekeeping enterprises; and serving as models for the world of the advantages in human terms of both democratic political institutions and price-and-market systems. To the contrary, the paper stressed "American political leadership *rather* than that of the UN" [emphasis added].

Most significantly, the plan cited the need for a major U.S. military presence in the Middle East and specifically with regard to Iraq, which had been flouting UN sanctions following its defeat in the Gulf War. "While the unresolved conflict with Iraq provides the immediate justification," the paper declared, "the need for a substantial American force presence in the Gulf transcends the issue of the regime of Saddam Hussein."[6] By one means or another, the authors of "Rebuilding America's Defenses" demanded a strong U.S. military presence in the region of the Persian Gulf, with Iraq very much a center of attention.

When George W. Bush came into the presidency in January 2001, he indicated that he would reject the liberal internationalists' concern for "doing good" abroad. Implying criticism of President Clinton's interventions in Somalia and Bosnia (one a failure, the other a success), Bush said he would not engage in "nation building." His agenda stressed carrying forward the Reagan revolution, that is, lowering taxes and dismantling many of the nation's regulations that

---

[5] Statement retrieved from ⟨www.newamericancentury.org/RebuildingAmericasDefenses.pdf⟩.
[6] Ibid.

governed labor and environmental conditions, as well as championing the social causes of the so-called Christian Right. Then came September 11.

September 11, 2001, "changed everything." At least that was what American government leaders claimed. It was the immediate "official" response to the most murderous single attack in history on Americans on their home soil by foreign enemies. It was reiterated endlessly by the media, which thrives on drama. It was a prophecy they did their best to fulfill.

It was not the first terrorist attack against Americans at home and abroad, but it was horrendously more destructive. There were nearly 3,000 killed by the suicide plane crashes that collapsed both of the gigantic twin towers of the World Trade Center in New York City, from a third plane that crashed into the Pentagon building across the Potomac River from the Capitol, and from a fourth hijacked airliner that passengers, informed by private cell phones of the other hijackings, forced to crash in a Pennsylvania field. The fourth plane was evidently headed for the White House. The fatalities approximated those from the Japanese attack on Pearl Harbor on December 7, 1941.

The President of the United States declared war. (The Constitution had placed that power with Congress, but it had been a dead letter ever since the Korean War.)[7] "9/11" had the effect that the attempted assassination of President Reagan had had, also early in his presidency. It aroused broad support for a president who had ascended to office under questionable circumstances and despite having lost the nation's popular vote by half a million. The tidal surge of support for George W. Bush had an ironic character given the new president's evident neglect of warnings by members of the previous administration of a likely terrorist attack months before September 11.[8]

All the evidence indicated that Al Qaeda, inspired by a wealthy Saudi radical named Osama bin Laden, had carried out the airborne attacks on the United States. It appeared clear also that Afghanistan's retro-radical Taliban government was hosting bin Laden. When the Taliban rulers refused U.S. demands that they surrender bin Laden, the United States launched a military invasion of Afghanistan. Bin Laden and the Taliban leaders escaped, but the Taliban regime was ousted. Its followers thereafter proceeded to wage a continuous and

[7] Except that in the case of the Korean War, which President Truman called "a police action," the U.S. acted as a partner in a coalition duly authorized by the Security Council of the United Nations. But thereafter, U.S. military operations in places like Vietnam, Grenada, and Panama were unilateral undertakings on the president's initiative.

[8] Richard Clarke later wrote: "George W. Bush, who failed to act prior to September 11 on the threat from Al Qaeda, despite repeated warnings ... then harvested a political windfall for taking obvious yet insufficient steps after the attacks; and [then] launched an unnecessary and costly war in Iraq that strengthened the fundamentalist, radical Islamic terrorist movement worldwide." Richard A. Clarke, *Against All Enemies: Inside America's War on Terror* (Free Press, 2004), p. xxiv.

gradually escalating guerrilla war against U.S. occupying forces, against the new U.S.-created Afghan government, and against all Muslims and "infidels" who cooperated with the United States and its allies.[9]

Most of the world sympathized with the Americans' initial military response to the bombings in New York City and the Pentagon. Most of the world does not easily accept the targeting of civilians in any cause. Most Americans and most of the United Nations supported the U.S. occupation of Afghanistan and its pursuit of bin Laden and his Taliban protectors. Even Pakistan, a strongly Muslim state with large numbers of Taliban sympathizers, became an American ally in the campaign against Islamic terrorists. The United States was poised once more to resume its role as a respected world leader.

The Bush administration quickly squandered that opportunity. Hundreds of Afghans and Muslims of other nationalities encountered on the battlefields were rounded up by U.S. military forces and their Afghan warlord allies. Other suspects were taken by U.S. agents in other countries, far from the Afghan battlefields. The U.S. president declared the captives to be "illegal enemy combatants," which enabled him to deny the relevance of the century-old Geneva Conventions governing treatment of war prisoners. Most captives were shipped off to Guantanamo, a U.S. naval base secured on the island of Cuba after the Spanish-American War in 1898 by a leasing arrangement with the newly independent Cuba. There prisoners were held totally incommunicado and were interrogated in a variety of brutal ways that the Red Cross, after being permitted to investigate, declared to be akin to torture. Among the captives were many innocents who happened to be in the way of the U.S. military sweep. Since "illegal enemy combatants" were entitled to no judicial or even administrative proceedings, no one knew how many innocents were among them – although years later, when a trickle of prisoners was set free, the numbers seemed not small.

In violation of international law, other captives were taken secretly to foreign countries to be interrogated. "Rendition" was the legal term. It was reasonable to surmise that the captives would be subjected to unsavory coercive techniques including outright torture. In late 2005, revelations that the Bush administration had used secret prisons in Europe for some of those captives created an uproar in Western European countries. The tumult underlined Europeans' sharp disagreement with the U.S. government's view of permissible abuse of prisoners. It was generally understood that captives held secretly outside the United States

---

[9] It is worth noting that the radical Islamic war on the United States, and on "Western values" generally, paralleled in many respects the American right-wing, traditionalist assault on "liberalism" and Modernism. Both the radical Islamists and the Christian Right lamented what the decades (in the case of the Islamists, centuries) of social, technological, and scientific revolutions had done to their view of the Good Society, grounded as they saw it in age-old traditions.

would be subjected to improper treatment. American officials refused to confirm or deny the existence of such prisons but condemned the leaking of the information.

In the face of international protests as well as protests by American human-rights advocates, the American government strove to justify brutal techniques by U.S. interrogators. While denying that the United States employed "torture," White House lawyers proceeded to redefine the term. By long-standing international agreement, torture was deemed impermissible among civilized nations, but the new definitions coming out of the White House, the Justice Department, and the Defense Department seemed like attempts to finesse that long-standing consensus.[10] Objectors to the surprisingly grandiose claims of presidential power faced charges of "undermining the war on terrorism" and "thinking in a pre-9/11 mindset."[11] However manipulated, the words that administration officials used to describe permissible techniques of questioning could not fail to permit, possibly to encourage, barbaric abuse of prisoners by military and CIA interrogators.

"9/11 changed everything" – including, many critics protested, the reversing of a century of progress in humanitarian sensibilities and respect for law. Defenders of the U.S. government's policies claimed that civil libertarian principles had to yield when terrorism held Americans' security at bay. Critics argued that principles are most valuable precisely during crises in order to restrain naked power and to provide a guide for legal, humane, and judicious behavior under stressful conditions. Administration officials argued that the extralegal techniques used to gather information were appropriate in the novel environment of a war against terrorism and claimed that the techniques had successfully prevented any repetition of terrorist attacks on U.S. soil (at least as of the end of 2005).

The Bush administration acted with "resolve" to go full speed ahead and damn the torpedoes of domestic and international disapproval. Most of the policy makers had come into the administration with an unconcealed scorn for the

---

[10] When Republican Senator John McCain, himself a survivor of torture as a military prisoner during the Vietnam War, introduced legislation to outlaw the use of torture by U.S. interrogators, the Bush administration vigorously opposed it. When the Republican-dominated Congress passed the law anyway, Bush signed the measure but vowed that he would interpret it "in a manner consistent with [what he determined was] the constitutional authority of the president to supervise the unitary executive branch and as commander in chief and consistent with [his view of] the constitutional limitations on judicial power." *New York Times* (16 Jan. 2006). In other words, President Bush announced that he would ignore the law.

[11] U.S. officials permitted the International Red Cross to inspect prison facilities in Iraq and Guantanamo, but only on condition that it transmit its findings exclusively to U.S. government officials. A leaked report in 2004 accused U.S. captors of treating prisoners in Guantanamo in ways that were "tantamount to torture," including sexual abuse. The chair of the U.S. Joint Chiefs of Staff, General Richard B. Myers, dismissed the report: "Let's not forget the kind of people we have down there. These are the people that don't know any moral values." *New York Times* (1 Dec. 2004), p. A23.

United Nations as well as for several traditional U.S. allies (e.g. France).[12] Their animus was played out in America's disregard for international opinion in devising the government's rationale for invading and occupying Iraq.

Among the leading foreign policy makers in the Bush administration, including especially Vice-President (and former Defense Secretary) Dick Cheney, were several of those who had criticized the president's father for allowing Saddam Hussein to retain power after his defeat in the Gulf War. They did not accept as sufficient the arguments by the first Bush administration – including those put forward at the time by General Colin Powell, later the younger Bush's much underconsulted Secretary of State – that to pursue the Iraqi army into Baghdad and overthrow Saddam would expose U.S. military forces to a cross-fire of militant tribal, religious, and political forces whose rivalries could tear the region apart, inspire prolonged guerrilla warfare, and inflict unacceptable casualties on both innocent Iraqi citizens and U.S. armed forces.

The determination of the hawks grew as, over the nineties, a feckless UN gradually relaxed its post–Gulf War sanctions and, most egregiously, permitted Saddam to expel the weapons inspectors. It was one of the reasons – but probably not the most important reason – that the authors and signers of the Project for a New American Century had suggested invading Iraq, long before 9/11. Having gained key offices in the government after the election of 2000, many of those signatories began planning an attack. "From the very beginning," Bush's first Secretary of the Treasury, Paul O'Neill, is quoted as saying in his authorized biography, "there was a conviction that Saddam Hussein was a bad person and that he needed to go." O'Neill's perplexity over the administration's priorities was echoed by others privy to White House deliberations.[13]

With the war on terror as its justification, the Pentagon began amassing an invasion force in the Persian Gulf. The UN agreed to support the American effort to force Saddam Hussein to readmit weapons inspectors and to rid his country of any "weapons of mass destruction" (WMDs). The buildup worked. The inspectors went back in. For this, the second Bush administration deserved full credit.

But after searching diligently for several months, the inspectors found no WMDs nor any evidence suggesting that Saddam's regime had recently been developing them. They continued to search. Separate CIA investigations (it was later revealed) also concluded that there was no solid evidence that Saddam still possessed WMDs or was working to produce them. Defense Secretary Donald

---

[12] Following his re-election, in 2005 Bush appointed John Bolton – a man who had long and loudly opposed American collaboration with the United Nations – to head the U.S. delegation to the UN, thereby seemingly confirming his government's contempt for the world's most important international organization.

[13] Ron Suskind, *The Price of Loyalty: George Bush, the White House, and the Education of Paul O'Neill* (Simon & Schuster, 2004).

Rumsfeld remained unconvinced, so he set up his own intelligence agency within the Defense Department that he hoped and expected would produce the "evidence" he and other militants in the administration needed to justify an invasion of Iraq.

Publicly the administration pressed for an invasion because there was evidence that Saddam had some links with Al Qaeda (and by inference with the 9/11 attack) and that he possessed WMDs that could imperil U.S. national security. But the evidence that U.S. officials presented struck many, in Europe and at home, as highly questionable. At least in retrospect, it appears that administration officials purposefully misled the public about the alleged WMD threat. Privately, policy makers such as Deputy Secretary of Defense Paul Wolfowitz focused more particularly on the need to gain control of Iraq's oil.[14] "In the new administration's discussions of terrorism," wrote Richard Clarke, who had been rebuffed in his attempts early in 2001 to get the White House to take Al Qaeda seriously, "Paul Wolfowitz had urged a focus in Iraqi-sponsored terrorism against the U.S., even though there was no such thing. In 2001, more and more talk was of Iraq, of CENTCOM[15] being asked to plan to invade. It disturbed me greatly."[16] The dissembling would intensify after 9/11 and would continue long after all available evidence indicated that Iraq not only had nothing to do with the 9/11 attack but also had had no more connection with terrorists connected with Al Qaeda and bin Laden than U.S. allies Saudi Arabia and Pakistan, to say nothing of Iran, Sudan, and Syria. None of the perpetrators of the 9/11 massacres was an Iraqi, whereas all but three of the nineteen were Saudis. Administration officials skillfully employed the "power of the outrageous" that had emerged as a political tactic during the Reagan era.[17]

A majority of the members of the UN's Security Council, including Russia, China, Germany and France, refused to sanction a military invasion of Iraq, pointing out that UN inspectors were still on the job. American officials criticized their long-time allies, Germany and France, as "Old Europe" and cited the support of England, Italy, and Poland. Finally, in March 2003, expressing impatience with the failure of the inspectors to find what the president claimed *he*

---

[14] After U.S. forces occupied Iraq and found no WMDs, Wolfowitz – one of the authors of the position paper, "Rebuilding America's Defenses" – said that Iraq's oil was sufficient reason for the invasion.

[15] United States Central Command.

[16] Clarke, *Against All Enemies*, p. 264. Clarke found that no facts could dissuade GWB & Co. from their "idee fixe, a rigid belief ... a decision already made and one that no fact or event could derail." Ibid., p. 265.

[17] As late as the presidential campaign of 2004, long after the administration's claims had been proven false about Iraq's connection to Al Qaeda and its possession of WMDs, Vice-President Dick Cheney (among others) repeatedly defended the invasion by making precisely those connections. The tactic worked. Polls indicated that at least half of Americans continued to believe it.

knew was there in Iraq, the United States ordered UN inspectors out of Iraq in preparation for an American invasion.

Bush proclaimed the right of the United States to launch a "preemptive war." "Preemptive war" is a generally accepted right in international law – except that it was understood to mean the right to strike first when facing an imminent attack, and that seemed entirely unlikely in the case of Iraq. As a U.S. invasion approached, many millions of people throughout the world and in the United States marched in the streets to protest. In London alone, a spectacular and unprecedented demonstration by more than a million protesters filled the streets, denouncing their government's intention to join the United States in its belligerence. But President Bush was "resolved," never mind the historic worldwide demonstrations and similarly massive demonstrations in the streets of American cities. He said he would not let "focus groups" determine policy for him.

Never mind, too, all the cautions that had restrained the first Bush administration from occupying Iraq. Never mind all the unheeded warnings that had proved telling during the Vietnam era. Was it not appropriate to recall the warning in 1956 of Louis Halle, President Eisenhower's Assistant Secretary of State: "When a nation intervenes in a foreign country, it not only tends to turn the people of that country against it, but it also discredits the regime that accepts its support."[18] Might they not have heeded Dwight Eisenhower's own meditation, originally included in his memoirs: "The strongest reason of all for the United States [to stay out of Indochina] is the fact that among all the powerful nations of the world the United States is the only one with a tradition of anti-colonialism .... The standing of the United States as the most powerful of the anti-colonial powers is an asset of incalculable value to the Free World .... The moral position of the United States was more to be guarded than the Tonkin Delta, indeed than of all of Indochina."[19] Perhaps they might have recalled Charles DeGaulle's advice to President Kennedy to avoid "an endless entanglement" that putting troops into Indochina would produce. "The more you become involved out there against Communism," he warned, "the more the Communists will appear as the champions of national independence, and the more support they will receive, if only from despair."[20] Substitute "terrorists" and "radical Islamists worldwide" for "Communists."

Not that there were no warnings of the same nature immediately before the invasion. Jordan's chief of state, Abdallah II, and President Hosni Mubarak of

---

[18] Quoted in George McT. Kahin & John W. Lewis, *The United States in Vietnam,* rev. ed. (Dell, 1969), p. 38.

[19] Quoted in Stephen Ambrose, *Eisenhower: The President* (Simon & Schuster, 1984), vol. 2, p. 177.

[20] Charles de Gaulle, *Memoirs of Hope: Renewal, 1958–1962* (Weidenfeld & Nicolson, 1971), p. 256, quoted in Edwin Hoyt, *Law and Force in American Foreign Policy* (University Press of America, 1985), pp. 112–13.

Egypt both opposed the invasion on the grounds that it would destabilize the area and enflame Muslims everywhere against the United States. Brent Scowcroft, the first President Bush's director of the National Security Council, tried repeatedly to warn off the son's "resolve" to invade Iraq. In August 2002, as it became evident that no finding by the inspectors in Iraq about the absence of WMDs would deter the administration's determination to go to war, Scowcroft publicly worried: "I think we could have an explosion in the Middle East. It could turn the whole region into a cauldron and destroy the war on Terror."[21] Later the same month, he went further. "Any campaign against Iraq," he warned, "is certain to divert us for some indefinite period from our war on terrorism. Worse, there is a virtual consensus in the world against an attack on Iraq at this time .... Ignoring that clear sentiment would result in a serious degradation in international cooperation with us against terrorism. And make no mistake, we simply cannot win that war without enthusiastic international cooperation."[22]

The rest is well known. Predicting that U.S. troops would be welcomed as liberators by Iraqis tossing flower petals (CIA chief Allen Dulles had made a similar prediction in 1961 about Cubans before the Bay of Pigs disaster), GWB ordered the invasion. Incomparable military technology swiftly put to rout the feeble resistance mustered by the Iraqi military (defenseless without any WMDs or other modern weapons), while U.S. casualties numbered in only two digits. Iraqi civilian casualties from the awesome preliminary barrage of U.S. fire power were not reported. The president of the United States put on a triumphal show, flying onto an aircraft carrier off the Pacific coast dressed in an Air Force combat costume to proclaim "victory" under a banner that read "Mission Accomplished." The theatrics went over well in the American media. On the other hand, most of the world seems to have viewed it as the crowing of a large bully who has just beat up a small boy.

It soon became clear that the predictable and predicted troubles for the United States in Iraq had only begun. To start with, altogether too many Iraqis greeted U.S. troops with rocket-launched grenades and suicide bombings rather than with rose petals. By the end of 2005, American military fatalities exceeded 2,200 and were climbing at an accelerated rate, with over 12,000 wounded. Typically, government officials declined to estimate Iraqi and other casualties, but independent agencies estimated about 100,000.[23] Arab media featured such "collateral damage" for an increasingly agitated Muslim public around the world, generating volunteers to fight the Americans. Meanwhile, hard-searching U.S. troops and investigators found neither WMDs nor operable equipment that could

---

[21] *Times of London* (5 Aug. 2002), ⟨http://www.commondreams.org/headlines02/0805-02.htm⟩.

[22] Quoted in *Forum for International Policy* (15 Aug. 2002), ⟨http://ffip.com/opedso81502.htm⟩.

[23] Late in 2005, President Bush publicly conceded "about 30,000."

produce any. (At the same time, U.S. occupying authorities – while protecting oil facilities – neglected to prevent the looting of warehouses filled with "conventional" weapons, many of which almost certainly came to be used against U.S. troops by Iraqi insurgents.) The reports by UN inspectors and prewar claims by Iraqi officials of the WMDs' nonexistence proved to be accurate. The "intelligence" that U.S. leaders claimed to have turned out to be based on unreliable informants and in some cases forged documents.

The president and his militant aides acknowledged no mistakes, even as they offered alternative justifications for the invasion (e.g., Saddam Hussein was a very bad man and Americans would promote democracy in the region). Before the end of 2003, so low had the international prestige of the United States fallen that members of the administration of Canadian prime minister Jean Cretien, who had expressed support for George W. Bush for president in 2000, found it possible publicly to call the American president "a moron" and "a failed statesman."[24] Earlier the same year, the U.S. president was heckled while addressing the Australian parliament; the following day, members of the parliament gave a standing ovation to China's president Hu Jintao.[25]

Still worse was to come. Early in 2004, photographic evidence emerged on news networks and on the Internet, and rebroadcast around the world, of unspeakably brutal mistreatment and humiliation of Iraqi and other Arab prisoners perpetrated by U.S. military officials at what was once Saddam's notorious prison in Baghdad, Abu Ghraib. Reports of similar abuses at other prison facilities began coming in during the next two years. By early 2005, the U.S. military confirmed the murder of at least 26 Iraqi and Afghan prisoners by American authorities in detention centers other than Abu Ghraib. Most of the American press gave the stories back-page coverage, while the Arab media gave them featured attention. Considering that the administration had claimed to be bringing democracy to Iraq, and by its example to the Middle East, this was a devastating blow to America's influence around the globe. But there seemed to be little appreciation of the damage among U.S. government leaders, nor apparently among most American voters.

The president said that the abuse of the prisoners at Abu Ghraib "disgusted" him, but he declined to accept any responsibility for it. Nor did he respond to subsequent revelations of similar abuses at other detention camps, including Guantanamo. In fact, no one in the administration accepted responsibility. Defense Secretary Donald Rumsfeld, the leading hawk and the official formally in

---

[24] Associated Press article (12 Dec. 2003), ⟨http://www.cnn.com/2003/ALLPOLITICS/12/12/us.canada.ap/⟩.

[25] Noted in a story about China's growing international trade agreements, *Wall Street Journal* (3 Oct. 2005), pp. A1, A14.

charge of the operations in Iraq, attributed the atrocities merely to some rogue behavior by low-ranking members of the armed forces. How many Americans accepted that interpretation remains uncertain. Although some conservative journals such as *The Economist,* a British publication that supported the invasion, demanded that Rumsfeld resign as at least a token of American remorse, he remained firmly in charge of the Defense Department and the increasingly problematic conduct of the occupation. He remained there, too, after Bush's 2004 re-election, although other top cabinet members (e.g., Secretary of State Powell, Attorney General Ashcroft) left or were forced out.

No concessions, no compromises, no apologies, admit no mistakes. Politically, it seems to have worked well. As Richard Nixon once told Jack Kennedy, voters don't much care about law and the statesmanlike thing; they admire leaders who act boldly. The message was well taken in later Republican administrations. When a member of the Joint Chiefs of Staff proposed admitting a mistake as the best way to deal with a damaging news story, President Reagan's Defense Secretary Caspar Weinberger angrily responded, "Do not do that .... Never, never, never, never, never admit you made a mistake."[26]

✻ ✻ ✻

On November 3, 2004, American voters ratified the bold activeness of the Bush administration by re-electing the president with a plurality of about 3 million more than Senator John Kerry's 56 million votes. Most of the rest of the world looked on with amazement. Historian, classicist, and social commentator Garry Wills headlined an op-ed piece the day after the election: "The Day the Enlightenment Died."[27] By that time, U.S. prestige had already fallen to an abysmal low. Shortly after President Bush's re-election, a leader of a peacekeeping effort in central Africa who called for international intervention specifically ruled out any U.S. participation as certain to "exacerbate the conflict."[28] Later, while Britain, Germany, and France negotiated an agreement with Iran designed to contain its development of nuclear weapons, the United States looked on in carping criticism. In December 2004 more than a hundred nations attempted to shape guidelines for reducing global pollution in a meeting in Buenos Aires, where, it was widely reported, the United States took on the role of obstructionist. The country, meanwhile, had fallen to forty-third among 120 countries working individually and cooperatively to reduce global pollution. At a G-8 meeting in Scotland in July 2005 (coinciding with multiple terrorist bombings

---

[26] Quoted in William E. Pemberton, *Exit with Honor: The Life and Presidency of Ronald Reagan* (M.E. Sharpe, 1998), p. 119.

[27] *New York Times* (3 Nov. 2004).

[28] Samantha Power, "A Hero of Our Time," *New York Review of Books* (18 Nov. 2004), p. 11.

in London), President Bush stood conspicuously alone in his resistance to the setting of limits on atmospheric pollution by the industrial nations. After four years of stalling and hurling epithets at North Korean leaders, the Bush administration was finally persuaded in 2005 by the Chinese government to restart face-to-face negotiations, which had shown some promise during the Clinton administration, in an effort to halt North Korea's nuclear weapons program. In December 2005 Orban Pamuk, a Turkish dissident on trial in Turkey for daring to challenge that authoritarian government's limits on a free press, wrote in sorrow: "These days the lies about the war in Iraq and the reports of secret C.I.A. prisons have so damaged the West's credibility in Turkey and in other nations that it is more and more difficult for people like me to make the case for true Western democracy in my part of the world."[29]

And so it went. To such depths had U.S. leadership fallen.

Was this to be "The New American century"? As Yogi Berra, the New York Yankees' Hall of Fame catcher and faux savant, is supposed to have said: "The future ain't what it used to be."

---

[29] Orban Pamuk, *The New Yorker* (19 Dec. 2005), p. 34.

Index